PASCAL
FOR
ENGINEERS AND SCIENTISTS
WITH
TURBO PASCAL

**University of
Hertfordshire**

Prentice-Hall International, Inc.

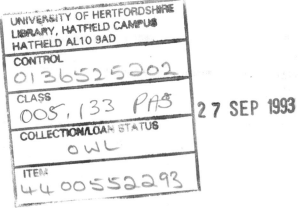
This edition may be sold only in those countries to which
it is consigned by Prentice-Hall International. It is not to
be re-exported and it is not for sale in the U.S.A., Mexico,
or Canada.

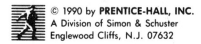
© 1990 by **PRENTICE-HALL, INC.**
A Division of Simon & Schuster
Englewood Cliffs, N.J. 07632

The author and publisher of this book have used their best efforts in preparing this book. These efforts
include the development, research, and testing of the theories and programs to determine their
effectiveness. The author and publisher make no warranty of any kind, expressed or implied, with
regard to these programs or the documentation contained in this book. The author and publisher shall
not be liable in any event for incidental or consequential damages in connection with, or arising out of,
the furnishing, performance, or use of these programs.

Printed in the United States of America

10 9 8 7 6 5 4 3 2

ISBN 0-13-652520-2

Prentice-Hall International (UK) Limited, *London*
Prentice-Hall of Australia Pty. Limited, *Sydney*
Prentice-Hall Canada Inc., *Toronto*
Prentice-Hall Hispanoamericana, S.A., *Mexico*
Prentice-Hall of India Private Limited, *New Delhi*
Prentice-Hall of Japan, Inc., *Tokyo*
Simon & Schuster Asia Pte. Ltd., *Singapore*
Editora Prentice-Hall do Brasil, Ltda., *Rio de Janeiro*
Prentice-Hall, Inc., *Englewood Cliffs, New Jersey*

CONTENTS

PREFACE

Pascal for Engineers and Scientists with Turbo Pascal is designed to teach students how to write programs in Pascal, especially Turbo Pascal. Since its introduction in 1984 by Borland International, Turbo Pascal has become the most widely-used implementation of Pascal on personal computers. Moreover, the Pascal language itself is being used almost universally as the introductory language for teaching computer programming, both at the university and the secondary school levels. In fact, it is the standard language for the Advanced Placement Test in Computer Science.

WHY TURBO PASCAL?

Turbo Pascal is unique because it is both an ideal teaching language and a powerful language for writing programs to solve practical problems. It provides all the features of structure and type declaration that make Pascal a good teaching language. At the same time, it contains several well-designed extensions, such as a standard string type, functions that directly access the operating system, pre-compiled program units, and object-oriented programming capabilities. These extensions make Turbo Pascal the language selected by many engineers and scientists for writing programs to solve practical problems.

If students are introduced to computer programming on personal computers, there seems to be no better language choice than Turbo Pascal. The latest version provides a modern and convenient programming environment. It also includes an easy-to-use source code debugger, and no student should be required learn computer programming without the availability of this important, time-saving software tool.

THE IMPORTANCE OF LEARNING TO WRITE PROGRAMS

This is not a book on computer literacy, but rather a book on computer programing. Even though the subject matter is programming, most of the students who use this textbook will not work as professional programmers. Almost all of them will, however, use personal computers in their professional lives. Much of the time they will run application programs, but from time to time they will need to write their own programs. Turbo Pascal is an excellent language choice for writing programs to solve technical problems. Many students will continue to write Turbo Pascal programs throughout their undergraduate and graduate years, as well as in their later professional lives.

The textbook shows students how to write practical programs in Pascal. It includes information on the language extensions available in Turbo Pascal. While the book covers most features of Pascal syntax, it is not meant to replace the language reference manuals. We have tried, however, to include enough information in the book and its appendices so that the *Turbo Pascal Owner's Handbook* will seldom need to be consulted.

SPECIAL FEATURES OF THE BOOK

The book is written for students in engineering and science and as often as possible, draws its examples and problems from the worlds of technology and science. Part I of the book presents Pascal language topics in an order that encourages students to write modular programs. They are introduced to text files in the first part of the course so realistic programs can be written using files for input and output. Part II discusses several practical applications of computer programming, with emphasis again on topics that may be of special interest to engineers and scientists.

The material is suitable for a one-semester or two-quarter course in a secondary school, college, or university curriculum. By omitting several chapters (for example, the chapters on numerical methods and on special features), the book would be a suitable text for a one-quarter course. Students are expected to have completed high school algebra, and for the chapter on numerical methods, they should have had an introduction to calculus.

Several areas have been given special emphasis:

- The early use of text files for the storage of information.
- An emphasis on modular program development and top-down program design using functions and procedures.

- The importance of good program design using a short main program consisting of calls to functions and procedures.
- An introduction to program testing, an often-overlooked subject in introductory textbooks. Specific ways to test an example program are shown and discussed.
- An early discussion of source program debugging techniques with a special emphasis on the Turbo Pascal debugger.
- Special sections, called Turbo Pascal Notes, placed throughout the text to explain the unique features of Turbo Pascal.
- Extensive use of example programs to show how Pascal statements are used and to help explain how they work.
- Several chapters on practical applications of computer programming in technical and scientific fields.
- A chapter showing how Turbo Pascal can access the operating system and perform many tasks that would normally require assembly language programming.

A textbook is written to teach, to explain those small but difficult points that may not be understood by a student even after attending lectures. Every effort has been made to write clear and complete explanations. After years of experience teaching college students, the author has found certain ideas that students sometimes have difficulty understanding. These ideas are explained in detail, often with diagrams and tables.

Some point requiring special attention and explanation are the following:

- The difference between a variable name and a variable value.
- Just how do variables store information in computer memory.
- The difference between a number and a string of digits.
- The use of indexed variables, especially for students with a limited mathematical background.
- The concept of program files and data files, how they are similar and how they differ.
- What happens when a disk file is over-written or erased.
- The concept and scope of local and global variables.
- The different methods for passing information to and from functions and procedures.
- The difference between pointers to dynamic variables and the dynamic variables themselves.
- Exactly how does recursion work, as illustrated by the example of the quicksort algorithm.

Programming cannot be learned just by reading but requires active practice with a computer. The book assumes that each student will have access to a personal computer, preferably an IBM PC-compatible computer, and will write programs.

Material is presented in such a way that students can start writing programs during their first week of class. A list of important points, a dozen or more self-test questions, and several practice problems are included at the end of each chapter.

Test data for these problems, as well as all example programs in the book, are available on a floppy disk for IBM PC-compatible computers. This disk is packaged with the instructor's Solutions Manual and may be freely copied by any student using this book in a course. You can also obtain the disk directly from the publisher. Information on how to use the example program disk is contained in a disk text file named README and in Appendix J of the book.

OBJECT-ORIENTED PROGRAMMING

As this book was going to press, Borland International released Version 5.5 of Turbo Pascal with additional capabilities and new reserved words to implement object-oriented programming. These are important extensions to Turbo Pascal, primarily because object-oriented programming appears to be a significant new technique for designing and writing computer programs to solve complicated problems.

It is not clear at this time whether object-oriented programming should be included in the first computer programming course. Many colleagues in computer science believe it should be introduced in a later course. As object-oriented programming becomes more widely practiced, however, it may well become part of a student's first introduction to computer programming.

Due to time and schedule considerations, we were not able to include a discussion of object-oriented programming in this edition of the book. We plan to include one or more chapters on obect-oriented programming in future editions. There is, however, an excellent introductory discussion, with example programs, of object-oriented programming in the *Turbo Pascal Object-Oriented Programming Guide* that is enclosed with each copy of the latest Turbo Pascal software. If you are interested in learning more about the subject, we recommend this manual.

ACKNOWLEDGMENTS

Many people contributed to the development of this book. It was used in introductory programming classes, in a steadily improving and expanding form, for several years before publication. The students in these classes made many contributions through their questions and comments, and I greatly appreciate the feedback they provided. My graduate teaching assistants also helped find and correct errors in both text and programs and my thanks goes to them. Professor James Cohoon, of the Department of Computer Science at the University of Virginia, used a draft of the book in a course one semester. His comments, especially on sorting algorithms, have been most helpful.

Critical reviewers are an important asset when writing a new textbook. I was fortunate to have the help of three experienced teachers who helped me turn the first draft into a much better book. My thanks to the following reviewers:

Michael Gonzales, Gwynedd Mercy College, Gwynedd Valley, Pennsylvania; Keith B. Olson, Montana College of Mineral Science and Technology, Butte, Montana; and Barbara S. Harris, DeVry Institute of Technology, Chicago.

Writing a book in one's spare time means that not enough time is left for other things. My special thanks to my wife Edie for her support and understanding during all those weekends and vacations when I spent so many hours in front of a computer screen and keyboard.

1

GETTING STARTED

1.1 INTRODUCTION

In this chapter we define a number of computer terms that will be used throughout the book. We discuss the MS-DOS operating system that is used on many personal computers, and introduce several operating system commands. Finally, we examine a specific implementation of Pascal, the Turbo Pascal system, describing its commands and built-in editor.

1.2 COMPUTERS AND COMPUTER TERMINOLOGY

It is customary for first-course computer language books to include a chapter that describes computers and their capabilities. Today, however, most students entering a college or university are familiar with computers. In fact, a majority of first-year engineering and science students have used a computer for some application, probably for developing computer programs.

We will assume, therefore, that you are aware of the existence of computers and are somewhat familiar with the roles they play in our modern life. Banks could not operate without computers, many airplanes and automobiles could not run without computers, and much of the national telephone system depends on computers.

The situation is even more clearly defined in technology and science, where computers have become one of the primary tools for engineers and scientists. We used to say jokingly, fifty years ago, that you could always tell an engineer by

1

his slide rule. Twenty years ago, slide rules gave way to calculators, and now the essential tool for an engineer is his or her computer.

Early computers were large, stand-alone machines that the ordinary engineer or scientist was not allowed to operate. Instead, a computer user prepared a program on punched cards, submitted these cards to the computer operator, and some time later (often days later) received the results.

The next advance in computer technology was time sharing, which allowed many users at terminals to access a central computer simultaneously. This mode of operation was a tremendous improvement, until the number of terminal users became so large that the computer slowed down and response time became excessively long. Another problem occurred when the central computer stopped working (it happened quite often), and all of the terminal users were without service.

A recent advance in computer technology is the development of the personal computer. At first, personal computers were very limited in their capabilities, but the latest machines in this category can handle most computing needs of engineers and scientists. The modern engineer's slide rule is the personal computer.

An increasingly large number of personal computers are connected to computer networks or can access other computers through the telephone system. This flexibility allows one to use the personal computer for most computing tasks, only accessing another, remote computer when the special capabilities of that machine are required.

Computers, and their attached peripheral devices, are called *hardware*. Computer hardware can perform useful functions only when it is given explicit instructions by a computer program, called *software*. In this book, we learn how to design and write computer programs.

Hardware Definitions

We use the term *computer system* to denote a computer and its associated peripheral equipment, as well as the programs required to make the computer operate. We shall start by defining some of the hardware items in a typical computer system, as shown in Figure 1.1.

Computer.   This term refers to the central processing unit (CPU) that performs actions based on software instructions, and its associated electronics. The term is often used, however, to refer to the complete computer system. Most IBM PC-compatible computers use the Intel 8088, 8086, 80286, or 80386 CPU.

Numeric Coprocessor.   This is an electronic device that performs arithmetic operations (multiplication, division, and so forth) in hardware rather than in software. Programs with many arithmetic operations run much faster when a numeric coprocessor is present. The 8087, 80287, and 80387 are numeric coprocessors for the 8088 (or 8086), 80286, and 80386 CPUs.

Memory.   Memory is an array of electronic devices or chips, within the computer, where information is stored in electronic form. **You must remember that when you turn off your computer system, all information stored in memory is lost.** Memory is sometimes called RAM, short for Random Access Memory.

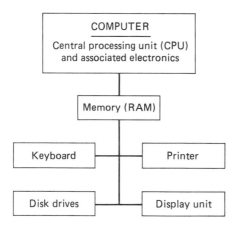

Figure 1.1   Diagram of a computer system.

Bit.   The bit, or binary digit, is the smallest unit of memory. A bit can store only one of two values, usually denoted by 0 and 1.

Byte.   A byte is a common unit for specifying memory size, consisting of eight bits.

Memory Location.   This is the address of a place in memory where a particular item of information is stored. We discuss how an address is specified in Chapter 16.

Keyboard.   The typewriterlike device with keys that you press to enter characters into the computer system is the keyboard. When you press most keys, a character also appears on the display unit screen.

Display Unit.   The display unit is the televisionlike device with a screen on which characters are displayed. These characters may be sent to the screen from the keyboard or from the computer.

Disk Drive.   This device is similar to a phonograph record player. It has magnetic disks on which information is recorded and stored in a relatively permanent form. The disk may be fixed in place and called a *hard* or *fixed disk*, or it may be removable and be called a *floppy disk*. Information stored on a disk is not lost when you turn off your computer system. If a disk is physically damaged, however, its stored information may be destroyed.

Memory is much faster than a disk (about one hundred times faster), which means that it takes longer to write information on a disk than into memory, and reading from a disk is also slower. A fixed disk is an order of magnitude faster than a floppy disk.

Printer.   This is a mechanical or laser-driven device, connected to your computer directly or through a computer network, that prints characters on paper as they are received from the computer.

These items are the most common units that make up the hardware of a computer system. Other peripheral devices, such as plotters or magnetic tape drives, may be added to meet special needs.

Software Definitions

Software is an important part of any computer system. We now define several software terms.

Program.   The program is a sequence of instructions to the computer, telling it how to accomplish a specific task. For example, the task might be to sort a list of names and print out the sorted list on a printer. The individual instructions are called *program statements*. In our example, one program statement might be used to print a single name. The program itself may be stored in memory or in a file (see next definition) on a computer disk.

File.   A file is a collection of characters or other information, usually stored on a computer disk. Each file is identified by name, and a directory of all files is maintained on the disk. A file may contain any collection of characters, such as a computer program or a letter to a friend; it is then called a *text file*. The contents of text files can be displayed on the screen. On the other hand, a file may contain noncharacter information and it is then called a *binary file*. Binary files cannot be displayed on the screen.

Operating System.   This is a special program that controls the operation of the computer. A major task of the operating system is to maintain the disk organization and supervise the reading and writing of disk files.

Program Statements.   These statements are instructions in a computer program that cause the computer to carry out a particular action. For example, the statement

```
Writeln ('Hello!');
```

tells the computer to display the phrase "Hello!" on the display unit screen. The phrase is not displayed until the statement is executed (see the following definitions).

Compilation.   This is the process of translating a computer program from its original or *source program* form into *machine language* instructions, creating an *object program* that is understood by the computer. If machine language instructions are written on a file, the file is a binary file. Compilation is done by a special program called a *compiler*.

Execution.   The process of carrying out machine language instructions contained in an object program is the execution of that program. The computer carries out specific actions in compliance with program statements.

Commands.   These are direct instructions given by the user to the computer. Whereas a statement is an instruction that is part of a computer program, a command is an instruction that is given directly to the computer (or more accurately, to a software system, such as the MS-DOS operating system or the Turbo Pascal language system) by the user.

Turbo Pascal Note

For example, in Version 3 of Turbo Pascal, the command

```
Run
```

tells the computer to compile and then execute the computer program in memory. In Versions 4 and 5, the Alt R key (press the Alt and R keys simultaneously) performs the same function.

1.3 THE MS-DOS (PC-DOS) OPERATING SYSTEM

We assume in this section that you are writing, compiling, and executing your programs on an IBM PC-compatible computer. The operating system is assumed to be MS-DOS (or PC-DOS; they are essentially the same). You need to learn how to access an application program (such as Turbo Pascal) from the operating system, and how to use MS-DOS commands to maintain file directories.

Disk drives in an MS-DOS system are designated by letters. On most computers, drives A and B are floppy disk drives, while drive C is a fixed disk drive.

File Directories

Each disk, either floppy or fixed, contains at least one file directory. This directory is called the *root* directory and is denoted by the backslash character (\). Additional directories can be created, under the root directory, so that different kinds of files can be stored in different directories. Figure 1.2 shows the directory structure of a disk with several directories. Most floppy disks have only a root directory, while fixed disks usually have many directories.

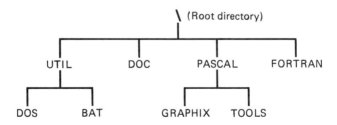

Figure 1.2   Structure of file directories on a disk.

File and Path Names

Finally, each file itself is identified by a *file name*. This name can be up to eight characters long, and may be followed by a period and a three-character *extension*. The period and extension are optional. File name and extension characters can be either letters or digits. Some other characters are allowed (see your MS-DOS manual), but you will be safe if you use only letters and digits. **Note carefully that a blank space is not a valid file name character.**

The extension usually describes the type of file: PAS for a Pascal source file, EXE or COM for an executable binary file, TXT for a text file, and so forth. These extension names are recommended but not required.

The complete identifier for a file, called its *path name*, consists of the disk letter, the various directory names (separated by backslash characters), the file name, and an optional extension. Here are some examples.

A:\FIRST.PAS	Pascal program in the root directory of the disk in drive A
A:FIRST.PAS	same as above; the backslash is not required here, but recommended
C:\PASCAL\FIRST.PAS	Pascal program in directory PASCAL of disk C, probably a fixed disk
C:\UTIL\DOS\TYP.COM	executable command file in directory DOS under directory UTIL of disk C
B:\BOOK\CH12	unspecified file in directory BOOK of the disk in drive B

You start up your computer by turning it on and, if you have only floppy disk drives, inserting an operating system disk in drive A. The operating system will proceed to load itself, a process called *booting*. A fixed disk system will normally boot itself up as soon as the computer is turned on.

The computer may or may not ask you for the current date and time, depending on whether it has its own clock. If it does ask, be sure to give the date in MM-DD-YY format, and the time in HH:MM format. **The colon separator between hours and minutes is required.**

Whenever you type information using the keyboard, you signify that you have finished typing by pressing the Enter key. This key is also called the return key or carriage return, and is sometimes denoted by a broken arrow (←) on the key. Pressing the Enter key tells the computer to do whatever it is programmed to do next. In a few instances, such as when you give commands to Turbo Pascal, the computer takes action as soon as a letter key is pressed and does not wait for you to press the Enter key. **If in doubt and nothing is happening, press the Enter key.**

If everything has worked correctly, you will know that the computer is ready for further instructions when the prompt

A>

is displayed on the screen. If you booted up from a fixed disk, the prompt is C>.

The standard MS-DOS prompt is often modified to show the name of the current directory. If this change has been made to your operating system, you may see a prompt like

```
A:\->
```

indicating that the current directory is the root directory, designated by a single backslash.

The A> prompt tells you that the A drive is the current disk drive. At this point, you can enter any one of several MS-DOS commands.

MS-DOS Commands

We do not list all possible commands at this time but discuss four of the most useful commands. You should consult your MS-DOS manual for further information.

DIR.   This command lists the contents of the current file Directory. If the A drive is the current drive, the command

```
DIR
```

lists all files on the disk in drive A. The command

```
DIR  C:\DOS
```

lists all files in directory DOS on the disk (usually a fixed disk) in drive C. The command (DIR) is separated from the path name (C:\DOS) by at least one space. We use two spaces in our examples so that the separation between command and parameters is easier to see, but in practice, one space is sufficient.

COPY.   This command copies a file from one disk or directory to another disk or directory. The command

```
COPY  B:\BOOK\CH12.TXT  A:\
```

copies the file CH12.TXT in directory BOOK on the disk in drive B into the root directory of the disk in drive A. Spaces are used again to separate the command name and the two path names. Note that when we copy a file, we do not erase the original version; so we end up with two files having the same contents.

DEL.   This command deletes a file from the disk. Assuming that drive A is the current drive and the root directory is the current directory, the command

```
DEL  FIRST.PAS
```

deletes the file FIRST.PAS in the root directory of the disk in drive A. It is better practice to use the command

```
DEL  A:\FIRST.PAS
```

where the disk and directory are stated explicitly.

TYPE.   This command lists the contents of a file on the display unit screen. The command

```
TYPE  B:\BOOK\CH12.TXT
```

displays the contents of the specified file.

Protecting Your Programs

Here is a word of advice about how to recover when you delete a program file by mistake. Nothing seems more devastating than to mistakenly delete a file, probably late at night, after you have spent hours creating it. If this happens to you, immediately remove the disk if it is a floppy disk, or turn off the computer if it is a fixed disk machine. Do not write anything else on that particular disk.

At the first opportunity, consult a computer expert. Deleting a file in MS-DOS does not physically erase the file, but rather removes its name from the file directory. **It is usually possible to recover a deleted file, provided nothing else has been written on the disk.**

While we are giving advice, we remind you **always to make at least one back-up copy of every important file**. Sometimes you lose a file due to a momentary power failure. More often, a bad area develops on a disk and information written on that area cannot be read. Remember it is not a question of whether or not you will be unable to read an important program; it is just a question of when that event will happen. Develop the habit of always making back-up copies, on separate disks, of any file that you change.

1.4 HOW TO USE TURBO PASCAL

Turbo Pascal Note

Section 1.4 refers exclusively to Turbo Pascal, Versions 3, 4, and 5. See the Turbo Pascal reference manuals for further information.

Turbo Pascal is more than just a Pascal language compiler; it is a complete software development system that runs under MS-DOS (and other microcomputer operating systems). The relationship between the operating system (MS-DOS) and the language system (Turbo Pascal) is shown in Figure 1.3. There are two main parts to the Turbo Pascal system, the editor and the compiler.

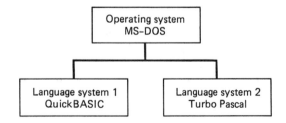

Figure 1.3 Relation between operating and language systems.

The usual way to enter the Turbo Pascal system is by typing the command

```
A>TURBO
```

in reply to the MS-DOS prompt. Note that MS-DOS displays A>, while you type
TURBO (or Turbo or turbo; case of the characters is ignored) and press the Enter
key. If you are using Version 3, the system asks if you want to include error
messages, and you should reply Y for yes.

We recommend that you start Turbo Pascal from the disk drive and directory
where your programs are stored. For example, if your program disk is in drive B,
make this drive your *current disk drive* by typing B: in response to the A> prompt,
as shown.

```
A>B:
```

Furthermore, if your programs are stored in directory CH02, enter the command

```
B>CD CH02
```

to change to that directory and make it your *current directory*. Then type the
command

```
B>A:TURBO
```

to start Turbo Pascal from the disk in drive A. If the MS-DOS prompt has been
modified (as described in a previous section) you might see a different prompt than
the one shown, but you still enter the same command:

```
B:\CH02->A:TURBO
```

Borland International recently released Version 4 of Turbo Pascal, followed a
few months later by Version 5. Many people are still using Version 3, however, so
we list first a set of commands for that version. We then discuss briefly the different
user interfaces of Versions 4 and 5.

If you have a choice, select Version 5 for writing and running your programs.
It is a complete and powerful language system, with a better user interface than the
older Version 3. In addition, it is an improvement over Version 4 because it contains
an excellent set of commands for finding program errors. These commands, called
debugging commands, make Version 5 an especially good choice for beginning
programmers.

Turbo Pascal, Version 3

When the Turbo Pascal system is loaded into the computer, a command menu is
presented. At this point, we discuss only a few of the many Turbo Pascal commands.
These commands can be entered only from Turbo Pascal, not directly from MS-
DOS. Just the first letter of a command is required, either uppercase or lowercase.

The *work file* is used to identify and hold programs while they are being
developed. The Turbo Pascal prompt is like the MS-DOS prompt, an angle bracket
(>) but no disk drive letter is displayed. To name a work file, reply

```
>W
```

and you will be asked for the work file name. Our example shows both the prompt
(>) and the command (W). You type only the command.

The work file can be an existing file you wish to modify or run, or a new file you wish to create. An existing file is brought into, or a new file is created in, an area of memory called the *work space*. Only one file can be in the work space at a time. If you are writing a new file, your program statements will be written in the work space.

To edit the file in the work space (the work file), enter the Edit command

>E

The editor is invoked and you can proceed with editing. After you have finished editing, hold down the control key (usually marked Ctrl), and press the keys K and D, one after the other, to quit the editor. We denote this action by the symbol

^KD

where the caret (^) signifies holding down the control key. Note that the command to quit the editor may have been changed in your installation of Turbo Pascal; the F10 function key is often designated for this purpose.

A program in the work space can be compiled and executed by entering the Run command

>R

If the program compiles successfully, the expected results are displayed on the screen. If not, an appropriate error message is displayed, and the editor is reloaded with the cursor pointing to the position where the error occurred.

After writing a new program or modifying an existing one, be sure to save your work on disk by using the Save command

>S

Any program in the work space that has not been saved is lost when you leave the Turbo Pascal system or specify a new work file. Turbo Pascal usually gives you warning that you have not saved a file that has been modified, but you should get in the habit of saving your work frequently. **Note that it is not possible to change the name of a file with the Save command.**

To place a different file in the work space, again use the work file command

>W

You are asked to specify a file name, which may be the name of an existing file or a new file. This file then becomes your new work file and can be edited by invoking the Edit command.

When you are finished, use the Quit command

>Q

to exit the Turbo Pascal system. You will return to the MS-DOS operating system.

The Turbo Pascal Editor

Let us look at the editor a little more closely. It is a full-screen editor, meaning that you can move the cursor anywhere on the screen and change a program statement or comment. Most of the keys on an IBM PC-compatible numeric keypad work as indicated on the keys. Figure 1.4 shows the action of several editing keys. Once again, the individual key assignments may have been changed in your installation of Turbo Pascal. Remember that a caret (^) means to hold down the control (Ctrl) key while pressing the specified key or keys.

`Arrow Keys`	move the cursor, as shown by the arrows
`PgUp,PgDn`	moves the cursor up or down one page Note: a page is usually 24 lines
`Home,End`	moves cursor to left or right end of line
`^Home,^End`	moves cursor to top or bottom of screen
`^PgUp,^PgDn`	moves cursor to top or bottom of program
`Ins`	switches between insert and over-write modes for entering characters
`Del`	deletes character under the cursor
`^N`	inserts new line at cursor position
`^Y`	deletes line containing the cursor
`^QY`	deletes from cursor to end of line
`^T`	deletes word to right of cursor, also deletes line break at end of line and joins two lines together
`^KD`	quit the editor
`^KB`	marks beginning of a block of statements
`^KK`	marks end of a block of statements
`^KH`	hides or removes marking from a block
`^KY`	deletes a marked block
`^KV`	moves marked block to cursor position
`^KC`	copies marked block to cursor position
`^KP`	prints a marked block
`^KW`	writes marked block to a disk file
`^KR`	reads a disk file into the current program

Figure 1.4 Selected Turbo Pascal editing keys.

If the cursor does not move when the arrow keys are pressed, try pressing the NumLock key once. NumLock works as a toggle key, switching the keypad between numeric mode and cursor control mode. You should be in cursor control mode.

Turbo Pascal allows all of the editor keys to be customized, using a utility program named TINST.COM (TINST.EXE in Versions 4 and 5). If the key assignments in your copy of Turbo Pascal are not standard, you should be provided with information about the changes. Alternatively, you can run the TINST program (type TINST in response to the MS-DOS prompt) and customize your own editor keyboard.

Turbo Pascal, Version 4

Version 4 of Turbo Pascal presents a user interface that is more window oriented than Version 3. The term *window* refers to areas of the screen, consisting of rectangles enclosed by lines. These windows may remain in place as long as you are using Turbo Pascal, or "pop up" for some particular purpose and then disappear when no longer needed.

The display unit screen is normally divided into two windows. The upper, and larger, window holds a program that is being written or edited. This program is called the *current program*. The lower window displays output produced when the program runs.

Pop-up windows are used to hold command menus, user prompts, and reports to the user. The Version 4 commands are similar to those for Version 3. Note also that essentially the same editor is used in both versions.

The main menu of Turbo Pascal offers five choices:

```
        File    Edit    Run    Compile    Options
```

At this time, we discuss only the first three choices.

The `File` command produces another window and command menu that allows you to load and save program files, to exit temporarily to the MS-DOS operating system, and to quit Turbo Pascal. If one of the names in the main menu is highlighted (or displayed in a different color), you are in the main menu. If not, you are probably in the editor, and you must press the F10 key to move to the main menu.

To select the `File` command menu from the main menu, move the highlight block on the top screen line over the word File (if it is not already there) and press the Enter key. You move the highlight block with the left-arrow and right-arrow keys on the numeric keypad.

Within the `File` menu, use the up-arrow and down-arrow keys to select a specific command. Figure 1.5 shows the choices.

Load *Open*	read a program file from the disk
Pick	select one of the eight most recently used files
New	erase screen to type in a new program
Save	save the current program on disk
Write to *Save as*	same as Save, except you can change the program file name before saving
Directory	display a specified directory; press Enter key to display the current directory
Change dir	specify another directory as the current directory
OS shell	go to the MS-DOS system; use the command EXIT to return to Turbo Pascal
Quit	leave Turbo Pascal and return to MS-DOS

Figure 1.5 Menu of File commands.

The Esc key returns you from the `File` menu to the main menu. Note also that several of these commands can be invoked by pressing a function key, as shown on the bottom line of the screen. In particular, the F3 key loads a program file from disk, while the F2 key saves the current program file.

The `Edit` command allows you to edit a program file. You select this command by again moving the highlight block on the top screen line (the main menu). You can always get back to the main menu from a command menu by pressing the Esc key one or more times. A shortcut to invoke the editor is to press Alt-E (this means holding down the Alt key and pressing the E key). As mentioned previously, the Version 4 editor is very similar to the Version 3 editor.

While in the editor, you can run the current program by pressing Alt-R. The F10 key returns you from the editor to the main menu. Alt-X causes an immediate exit from Turbo Pascal and returns you to MS-DOS.

The `Run` command executes the current program. While developing a program, you will probably find it more convenient to use the Alt-R command from the editor.

Turbo Pascal, Version 5

The main addition to Version 5 is its set of debugging commands. The lower window on the screen is used for displaying debugging information or program output. In order to see a full screen of program output, you must press Alt-F5 (hold down the Alt key and press the F5 key).

The main menu now offers a choice of seven commands:

| File | Edit | Run | Compile | Options | Debug | Break/watch |

As before, we discuss only the first three choices. Debugging is discussed later in Chapters 4 and 6.

The `File` menu is exactly the same as in Version 4. The `Edit` command and the editor are also essentially the same. The `Run` command (or Alt-R), however, now displays a command menu rather than running the current program. You can run a program, however, by pressing Alt-R and then Enter.

Within the `Run` menu, the first command actually runs the program. This command can also be invoked from the editor by pressing Ctrl-F9 (hold down the Ctrl key and press the F9 key). The last command in the `Run` menu displays program output and can be invoked by pressing Alt-F5. It is usually not possible to see the program itself and all program output at the same time.

It is possible, however, to divide the screen into two windows by pressing the F5 or Zoom key. This key is a toggle key; if pressed once the screen is divided into an edit window and another window; if pressed again, the entire screen is used for editing. The F6 or Switch key is also a toggle key; it moves the cursor between the edit window and the other window.

The upper window is always the edit window, while the lower window starts out as a watch window for program debugging. The use of the lower window can be changed, however, by pressing Alt-F6 while the cursor is in that window. This key toggles the lower window between a watch window and an output window. In the latter status, the lower window displays program output.

Reference Manuals

The preceding description gives only a glimpse of the many features of Turbo Pascal. If you are writing programs in Turbo Pascal, you should own or have access to a copy of the Turbo Pascal Reference Manual (Version 3) or the Turbo Pascal Owner's Handbook (Version 4 or 5). There is also an Update manual for Version 5. Plan to spend some time studying the appropriate reference manual as you read through the chapters of this book.

Online Help System

You should also become familiar with the excellent online help system in Turbo Pascal, Versions 4 and 5. Pressing the F1 key at any time displays a pop-up window of helpful information. Pressing the Esc key returns you to your current task.

Sometimes the F1 key displays a secondary menu of help items, and you must move the highlight block and press Enter to select your choice. When writing a program, place the cursor anywhere over a reserved word and press Ctrl-F1 for specific information on that word.

Experiment yourself with the online help system and use it frequently. You will find that its use greatly reduces your need to look up items in the owner's handbook.

File Names in Turbo Pascal

When using Turbo Pascal, a file in the current directory can be specified by using only its file name. A file in another directory must be specified by its path name.

If you do not specify an extension for a file name, Turbo Pascal will automatically add the extension PAS. **If you do not want any extension, put a trailing period after the file name.**

If you look at your file directory, you will notice that back-up files, having the extension BAK, have been created for each existing program file that was edited. The back-up version is the last version of that program file prior to editing. This back-up feature can be disabled in Versions 4 and 5, but we recommend that you continue to use it as another way to prevent program loss.

Example Programs in Turbo Pascal

When showing concrete examples of Pascal use, it is desirable to use some specific version of Pascal. We assume that most readers of this book are using Turbo Pascal; so we have written all example programs (except for two programs in Section 3.6) in that implementation of the language.

As indicated in this chapter, there are three versions of Turbo Pascal in wide use as this book goes to press. Most example programs will run under any version. Where that is not the case, we have placed a comment in the program comment section. In Chapter 16, where the differences between the three versions become more significant, we have written two different versions for several programs, one for Version 3 and the other for Version 4 or 5.

Listing Programs and Output on a Printer

When discussing the editor, we said that the Pascal program being written is displayed on the screen. We pointed out that the current program (the work file) can be saved on a disk file. When explaining the Run command, we noted that whatever output is produced by the program is displayed on the screen.

If a printer is available, however, it is often desirable to have a printed listing of a program. Moreover, in a class environment, the instructor usually requires students to hand in a printed copy of program output.

The MS-DOS COPY command can be used to print a file as well as copy a file. Having saved your program on disk, leave the Turbo Pascal system and when you see the MS-DOS prompt, enter a command such as

```
COPY  B:HW02.PAS  PRN
```

This command copies the file HW02.PAS from the disk in drive B to an attached printer. **Before executing this command, you must make certain that the printer is turned on and attached to your computer.** If either of these conditions is not satisfied, your computer may stop completely and have to be restarted.

The procedure for obtaining a printed copy of program output is slightly more complicated and is discussed in Appendix F. Be sure to check with your class instructor because it is possible that your particular computer facility, especially if it is part of a computer network, uses a different method for printing program output.

IMPORTANT POINTS

- You must remember that when you turn off your computer system, all information stored in memory is lost.
- A blank space is not a valid file name character.
- When entering a new time in MS-DOS, the colon separator between hours and minutes is required.
- If you have typed in a command or instruction and nothing is happening, press the Enter key.
- It is usually possible to recover a deleted file, provided nothing else has been written on the disk.
- Always make at least one back-up copy of an important file you want to keep.
- We recommend that you start Turbo Pascal from the disk drive and directory where your programs are stored.
- Any program in the work space that has not been saved is lost when you leave the Turbo Pascal system or specify a new work file.
- It is not possible to change the name of a file before saving it in Version 3.
- The Write To command in Versions 4 and 5 allows you to save the current file using a new name.
- If you do not want any extension with a file name in Turbo Pascal, put a trailing period after the file name.
- Before copying a disk file to a printer, you must make certain that the printer is turned on and attached to your computer.

SELF-STUDY QUESTIONS

1. What is the definition of
   (a) computer hardware;
   (b) computer software.

2. If the electrical power goes off for one second, is information lost that is stored
   (a) in memory;
   (b) on a disk?

3. Can a floppy disk be used for storing
   (a) a computer program;
   (b) a letter to a friend?

4. Can the contents of the following files be displayed on the screen in a form that can be read:
   (a) a source program file;
   (b) an object program file;
   (c) a document file?

5. What is the definition of
   (a) a Pascal statement;
   (b) an editor command;
   (c) an operating system command?

6. In MS-DOS, what is
   (a) the root directory of a disk, and
   (b) how is it designated?

7. What is the maximum number of characters (excluding the optional extension) that can be used in an MS-DOS file name?

8. Which of the following characters can be used in an MS-DOS file name:
   (a) the letter A;
   (b) a space;
   (c) the letter a;
   (d) the digit 0?

9. What is the difference between an MS-DOS file name and an MS-DOS path name?

10. When entering the system time, what character is used to separate the hour digits and the minute digits?

11. If you have just typed in the letters of an MS-DOS command such as DIR, what key do you press to tell the computer that you have finished entering the command?

12. Describe the action taken by the command

```
COPY  B:\PASCAL\MYPROG.PAS   A:\PROG\DEMO.PAS
```

13. Describe the action taken by the command

```
DEL  B:\PROG\CH09\EX0901.PAS
```

14. If you accidentally delete a file on a floppy disk,
   (a) is it possible to recover that file;
   (b) what precautions, if any, should you take to make the recovery easier?

15. **(a)** When should you make a back-up copy of a disk file?
   (b) Should the back-up copy be on a separate disk?

16. **(a)** What is the meaning of the E command in Turbo Pascal, Version 3?
   (b) How does it differ from the W command?

17. If you have just written and executed a program in Turbo Pascal and quit Turbo Pascal without saving the program, is there any way to go back and recover the program?

18. **(a)** If you are writing a Turbo Pascal program and the power goes off for one second, what happens to your program?
   (b) What procedure(s) should you follow to minimize any loss of information from power failures?

19. If you have just written a program in Turbo Pascal and saved it using the name MYPROG
   (a) will the file name be given an extension by the system, and if so,
   (b) what is the extension?

20. In the Turbo Pascal editor, which key
   (a) moves the cursor to the beginning of the current line;
   (b) deletes the character under the cursor;
   (c) deletes the line containing the cursor?

21. **(a)** Which command in Turbo Pascal, Version 4 or 5, executes the current program?
   (b) Which command exits the Turbo Pascal system?

2

WRITING SIMPLE PROGRAMS

2.1 INTRODUCTION

In this chapter we present the general structure of a simple Pascal program, and introduce several basic Pascal statements. Identifiers and named variables are discussed, and we show how to assign a value to a variable.

The concept of declaring and using different variable types is examined. We present four simple variable types: integer, real, character (char), and boolean.

2.2 PROGRAM ORGANIZATION

Every Pascal program should start with a PROGRAM statement and must end with an END statement followed by a period. Here is the general structure of a Pascal program:

```
PROGRAM MyFirstTry (Input, Output);
(* Declaration Block *)

BEGIN
  { Main Program }
END.
```

Reserved Words

Certain words in Pascal are called *reserved words*, also called *keywords*. In our program listings, we use the convention of displaying most Pascal reserved words in lowercase letters. We make an exception, however, for the reserved word PROGRAM in the program heading statement and the reserved words BEGIN and END serving as brackets that enclose the main program. These particular reserved words are displayed, as shown, in uppercase letters. Reserved words are listed in Appendix A.

Identifiers

An *identifier* is a word used to identify some particular item in the program. Thus, the name MyFirstTry in the PROGRAM statement is a user-declared identifier that identifies this particular program. We follow the convention of capitalizing the first letter of all identifiers, both those defined by the user and standard Pascal identifiers. Reserved words may not be used as identifiers.

Legal Pascal identifiers vary from one implementation of the language to another, but you will be safe if you use only letter and digit characters, always starting with a letter. An identifier may contain any number of characters, but in most implementations, only a certain number of characters (such as the first eight characters) are unique. Check your language reference manual to find out how many characters are recognized by your compiler.

Turbo Pascal Note

In Turbo Pascal, identifiers may contain up to 63 unique characters. The underscore (_) character is allowed in addition to letters and digits. The first character of an identifier should be a letter, although the underscore character can be used.

Turbo Pascal does not differentiate between lowercase and uppercase letters. The identifier myfirsttry means the same as the identifier MyFirstTry, although the latter is clearly easier to read.

Here are some valid identifiers

```
MyFirstTry
X
MILES_PER_HOUR
```

and some invalid (illegal) identifiers

```
3rdProblem     (starts with a digit)

Second Try     (contains a space)
```

The PROGRAM Statement

The PROGRAM statement not only specifies the name of the program, but also specifies any files that are used by the program. You will remember from Chapter 1 that files are defined as collections of characters or other information, often stored on a magnetic disk. A file is identified by a *file variable name*, and information can be written on the file or read from the file.

We extend the concept of files to include physical devices from which information can be read or on which information can be written. As contrasted to disk files, these physical device files usually are able only to read information or write information, but not both. The keyboard is considered the standard input file for Pascal and is given the special name Input. The display unit screen is considered the standard output file and is given the name Output.

The PROGRAM statement usually contains the standard file variable names, Input and Output, as parameters. It may also contain other file variable names. The syntax of the PROGRAM statement is as follows:

PROGRAM ProgramName (Input, Output, FileVarName, ...);

The symbol ProgramName represents any identifier or sequence of characters that identifies the program. In practice, the two identifiers, Input and Output, are often included as program heading parameters, because most programs have both keyboard input and screen output. Even if a program requires no input or produces no output, it does no harm to include these two parameters.

The symbol FileVarName represents one of a series of optional file identifiers that may be included as parameters. These parameters identify other files from which information may be read or on which information may be written.

Note that a trailing semicolon is required to separate this PROGRAM statement from the next following statement in the program.

Turbo Pascal Note

We include a PROGRAM statement in all of our example programs, even though this statement is not required in Turbo Pascal. The statement is required in most other versions of Pascal, and we believe a beginning programmer should become familiar with its syntax and use. For the same reason, we include the predefined identifiers, Input and Output, in the PROGRAM statement.

Because the statement is optional, the information it contains about file names is ignored by the Turbo Pascal compiler. This means that another method must be used to identify external files names, and so **we do not include these names in PROGRAM statements**. We will explain, in Chapter 3, how external files are handled in Turbo Pascal.

Comment Brackets

The second program line consists of words enclosed in special brackets. Each bracket is a pair of characters, a parenthesis and an asterisk. This line is a comment and is ignored when the program is compiled and executed (see definitions in Chapter 1). In this instance, it serves to remind us that a *declaration block* must follow the PROGRAM statement. We will examine the declaration block in detail in later sections. The two-character brackets that surround a comment may be replaced by braces or curly brackets (the characters { and }), and we shall use these symbols in most of our programs.

The third program line is a blank line. Blank lines are allowed anywhere in a Pascal program and serve to make the program more readable.

Compound Statements: Begin and End Brackets

The fourth program line is the word BEGIN. The word BEGIN always occurs with the word END as part of a pair. This pair of words forms a set of brackets that is used to enclose one or more program statements to form a block of statements, called a *compound statement*. The begin and end brackets are used here to enclose the main Pascal program. Because BEGIN is considered a bracket rather than a statement, no semicolon is needed to separate it from the following statement.

The Final Period

The fifth line is another comment, representing the one or more Pascal statements that make up the main Pascal program. We enclose this comment in braces, rather than the two-character brackets used previously. The sixth line is the END part of the begin-end bracket pair. This END bracket is followed by a period to signify the end of the Pascal program. **One, and only one, END bracket with a following period is allowed, and is required, in a Pascal program**.

2.3 A SIMPLE PROGRAM

The Writeln Statement

Before discussing the organization of a Pascal program in more detail, we write a simple example program. This example uses the Pascal statement Writeln (write a line) to display characters on the screen. A list of items, separated by commas, follows Writeln and is enclosed in parentheses. The first item in the list is the file variable name Output, which signifies that the remaining items in the list are to be written on the display unit screen. The second item in the list consists of the characters to be displayed enclosed in single (not double) quotation marks. Identifier names, like Output, are not enclosed in quotation marks.

```
PROGRAM EX0201 (Input, Output);
(* Example program 2-1.*)

{ Display a string of characters on the screen. A }
{ declaration block is not needed in this program.}

BEGIN
  Writeln (Output, 'Welcome to Engineering!')
END.
```

String Constants

When this program is compiled (translated to machine language) and executed, the phrase "Welcome to Engineering!" (without the quotation marks) is displayed on the screen. A declaration block is not needed, as we explain in the next section. The `Writeln` statement is indented to show that it is contained within the begin-end brackets and is, thus, a main program statement. The sequence of characters within single quotation marks is called a *string constant*. The action of the `Writeln` statement is to display the string constant on the screen and then move the cursor to the beginning of the next line.

Single Quotation Marks

Here is a practical hint about producing the single quotation marks used in `Writeln` statements to enclose string constants. **Both these marks must be the acute accent (ʼ),** usually found on the same key as the double quotation mark ("). You will get an error if you use the grave accent ('), which may look exactly the same, as in this book and on some display screens. So be careful which key you press!

Numeric Constants

Another variation of the program displays a number, also called a *numeric constant*.

```
PROGRAM EX0202 (Input, Output);
{ Display a number on the screen.}

BEGIN
  Writeln (999)
END.
```

If no file variable name appears in the `Writeln` statement, as in this example, the standard output file, representing the display unit screen, is assumed. Note that numbers or numeric constants are not enclosed in quotation marks. This program displays

    999

on the screen. Decimal numbers behave somewhat differently, as we will discuss in Chapter 3.

2.4 VARIABLE DECLARATIONS

A variable name in a computer program identifies a memory location where information is stored. Variable names, like program names, are Pascal identifiers and usually consist of a sequence of letters. Certain names (like `BEGIN`, `END`, and `PROGRAM`) are reserved by Pascal and may not be used as identifiers. They are listed in Appendix A. Certain other names are used by Pascal for predeclared identifiers (like `Writeln`) and should not be chosen for user-declared identifiers. These names are listed in Appendices D and E.

A Variable as a Mailbox

You might imagine a variable name as the label of a mailbox where information is stored. Only one item of information can be stored in a mailbox at any time. There are different types of mailboxes: one type for storing whole numbers or integers, another for storing decimal numbers, another for storing single characters, and so forth. These mailboxes are actually, of course, memory locations, and when a new variable is declared, a section of memory is reserved to hold the value stored in that variable.

A unique property of variable mailboxes is that they can hold only one value at a time. If a variable mailbox contains a value, and another value is assigned to the variable (placed in the mailbox), the original value is overwritten and destroyed, and cannot be recovered.

One of the features of Pascal is that the name of each variable must be declared before any information can be stored in it. Moreover, the *declaration* statement must identify the type of information that will be stored in the variable itself. Variable declarations are gathered together in a declaration block that is headed by the identifier `var`. This identifier can be used only once in the block.

The statement

```
var
    Number: integer;
```

declares and designates a variable named `Number` for the storage of whole numbers or integers (numbers without a decimal or fractional part). The identifier `integer` is a standard Pascal `type`. Note that a colon is required to separate the variable name from the type name. Once again, a semicolon is needed to separate this declaration statement from the following statement in the program.

The Assignment Statement

Once a variable name has been declared, that variable can be used in other statements. In particular, information can be assigned to or stored in the variable using an *assignment* statement. For example, the value 15 can be assigned to `Number` using the statement

```
Number:= 15;
```

The pair of characters (`:=`) is used to indicate an assignment operation, and is called the *assignment operator*. Note that **the value on the right side of the assignment operator is assigned to the variable on the left side.** Using our previous analogy, we can say that the value 15 has been stored in the mailbox labeled `Number`. Assignment is always from right to left, so that the reverse statement

```
15:= Number   { not a valid statement }
```

is not a valid assignment statement because 15 is not a valid variable name.

Another example program combines these ideas to display a whole number or integer on the screen. Only the standard file identifier `Output` is included in the `PROGRAM` statement, because input from the keyboard is not required.

```
PROGRAM EX0203 (Output);
{
    Declare a variable, assign a value to it,
    and display that value on the screen.
}
```

```
var
  Number: integer;

BEGIN
  Number: = 15;
  Writeln (Output, Number)
END.
```

This program produces the display

```
15
```

Note the new format of using braces on separate lines to enclose opening comments. We will use this format in most of our example programs for enclosing multiline comments, because we think it is easier to read.

A comment cannot be enclosed in a mixed pair of brackets; so the comment

```
(* NOT a legal comment }
```

is not allowed. A program block containing comments enclosed in braces cannot itself be enclosed in braces but can be enclosed in two-character brackets. For example, the following structure is allowed

```
(*
Speed: = 100;    { initial speed of vehicle        }
Distance: = 275 { braking distance at this speed }
*)
```

where the (* and *) brackets are used to *comment out* a block of program statements with individual comments. This technique is often used when trying to find errors in a program.

There are several points about Pascal syntax that we should examine further. Any text that begins with the character { and ends with the character } is considered a single comment, no matter how many lines it may occupy. The same point applies to the declaration statement, which could just as well be written

```
var Number: integer;
```

or even as

```
var
  Number
    :
      integer;
```

A single statement can extend over one or more lines, and extra spaces in a statement are disregarded.

Several statements can be placed on the same line, as long as they are separated from each other by semicolons. The main program block in Program EX0203 could be written as

```
BEGIN Number: = 15; Writeln (Output, Number) END.
```

although this format is not recommended because it is more difficult to read.

Use of Semicolons

The proper use of semicolons is always a problem for beginning programmers. It is helpful to remember two rules:

1. Semicolons do not end lines; they separate statements.

2. The words BEGIN and END are not statements; they should be thought of as brackets.

    The declaration block can be, and usually is, used to declare more than one variable. These declarations can be separate or combined together. For example, if two variables named Number and Value are to be declared as integers, you can use the syntax

```
var
   Number, Value: integer;
```

or the syntax

```
var
   Number: integer;
   Value: integer;
```

Here is another example program that displays two numbers:

```
PROGRAM EX0204 (Output);
{
   Assign values to two variables
   and display them on the screen.
}
var
   Alpha, Beta: integer;

BEGIN
   Alpha: = 123;
   Beta: = 7;
   Writeln (Alpha);
   Writeln (Beta);
END.
```

This program produces the screen display

```
123
7
```

Semicolon at End of Last Statement

Note that a semicolon is placed at the end of the second Writeln statement. This separator is not needed because no statement follows the Writeln statement, only the bracket END. The semicolon is allowed, however, and represents an empty or null statement preceding the END bracket.

    This style of writing a program is commonly used. If another statement is added to the program, the extra semicolon will be needed to separate it from the preceding statement. Many programmers think it is better practice to include the extra semicolon when the program is first written, rather than risk the possibility of forgetting to insert it later if another statement is added; thus creating an error.

Find out for yourself what happens if you put a semicolon (and create a null statement) after a BEGIN bracket.

2.5 SIMPLE VARIABLE TYPES

We have already introduced variables of type integer. The three other simple variable types in Pascal are real for decimal numbers, char for characters, and boolean for the logical values of true and false. These four types, integer, real, char, and boolean, are often called *simple types*.

The Integer Types

Integer variables are used to store whole numbers whose magnitude is less than some implementation-dependent size. A predefined system constant named MaxInt exists in every Pascal implementation. **Integer values must be less than or equal to MaxInt and greater than or equal to − MaxInt.** (See the specific range for Turbo Pascal in Figure 2.1.) The reason for this limitation is that only a small amount of memory space (usually two bytes in microcomputers) is reserved for the storage of an integer value.

Turbo Pascal Note

In Turbo Pascal on an IBM-compatible computer, the value of MaxInt is 32,767, and the range of an integer value is from − 32768 to 32767. Turbo Pascal, Version 3, also supports a subset of the integer type named byte. The range of values of type byte is from 0 to 255.

Versions 4 and 5 of Turbo Pascal support a total of six integer types, as shown in Figure 2.1.

TYPE	RANGE			SIZE
byte	0	to	255	1 byte
shortint	−128	to	127	1 byte
integer	−32768	to	32767	2 bytes
word	0	to	65536	2 bytes
longint	−2147483648	to	2147483647	4 bytes
comp	−9.2E+18	to	9.2E+18 (approx.)	8 bytes

Figure 2.1   Integer types in Turbo Pascal, Versions 4 and 5.

Note that the comp type is available only if the computer contains a numerical coprocessor (8087 or equivalent).

Some example integer values are

    77   −2   0   1   19227   −3688

When these numbers appear in a Pascal program, they are called *integer constants*.

The set of integer values is a countable set, extending from approximately −MaxInt to MaxInt. Variables whose values are countable are called *ordinal variables*. Character and boolean variables share this property, and, thus, all three types, integer (and its variations), char, and boolean, are ordinal types.

The Real Types

Real variables are used to store numbers with a decimal or fractional part, or whole numbers larger in magnitude than MaxInt (or the largest integer type provided in a particular implementation). The real type is not an ordinal type, and **real values stored in a computer are only approximations of the actual numeric values**, retaining a precision determined by the particular computer and its configuration.

Turbo Pascal Note

Real numbers in Turbo Pascal on IBM PC-compatible computers have 11 to 12 significant digits and range in size from approximately 2.9E-39 to 1.7E+38. If a numeric coprocessor (8087 or equivalent) is installed in the computer and Version 3 is being used, the number of significant digits is increased to 15 or 16, and the range in size is increased to approximately 4.2E−307 to 1.7E+308.

Versions 4 and 5 of Turbo Pascal support the same real type by default, whether or not a numerical coprocessor is present. If a numerical coprocessor is present, these versions support three additional real types, as shown in Figure 2.2.

TYPE	APPROX. RANGE	DECIMAL DIGITS	SIZE
	With or without a numerical coprocessor		
real	2.9E−39 to 1.7E+38	11 to 12	6 bytes
	Only with a numerical coprocessor		
single	1.5E−45 to 3.4E+38	7 to 8	4 bytes
double	5.0E−324 to 1.7E+308	15 to 16	8 bytes
extended	1.9E−4951 to 1.1E+4932	19 to 20	10 bytes

Figure 2.2 Real types in Turbo Pascal, Version 4 and 5.

Note that both positive and negative values are permitted in any specified range.

Real values require more storage space in memory, usually three times as much space as integer values. Real numbers can be written in *decimal form*, which we use first, or in *exponential form*, which we will introduce next. Some example real values or constants are

   3.5   −17.202   917262.0   0.0095

Real numbers must always contain a decimal point and may not contain a comma. At least one digit must be placed before and after the decimal point, so that 0.0095 is required rather than .0095. None of the following numbers are allowed as either real or integer constants:

   .0095   13.   14,200   −.01

Type Errors in Assignments

Note that the number 9 represents an integer constant, while the number 9.0 represents a real constant. The difference is important in certain expressions and in the amount of storage space required for the numbers. **Only an integer constant can be assigned to an integer variable**, but either a real constant or an integer constant can be assigned to a real variable. In the latter case, the integer value is converted to a real value during the assignment process. The following example program illustrates these assignments.

```
PROGRAM EX0205;
{
    Examples of legal and illegal assignments.
    ***********************************
    ** THIS PROGRAM WILL NOT COMPILE **
    ***********************************
}
var
  A: integer;
  X: real;

BEGIN
  A:=2;     { legal, 2 is an integer constant         }
  X:=2.0;   { legal, 2.0 is a real constant           }
  A:=2.0;   { illegal, cannot assign real to integer  }
  X:=2;     { legal, 2 is converted and stored as real }
END.
```

The Exponential Form

The other form for displaying real numbers is the exponential form. This form is especially useful for very large or very small numbers. For example, the number

    1475000000000

can be written as

    1.475E+12

This form is shorthand notation for 1.475 multiplied by 10 raised to the twelfth power (or 1.475 multiplied by a number consisting of a one followed by 12 zeroes). The plus sign is optional; the number can also be written as

    1.475E12

Small numbers can be represented in a similar fashion; the number

    0.0000228

can be written as

    2.28E-5

which is 2.28 divided by 10 raised to the fifth power.

We have discussed several restrictions on the form of real and integer constants, especially real constants. Some Pascal compilers allow more flexibility, and the real number forms that we say are not allowed can be used. You should encounter no problem with any compiler, however, if you comply with the restrictions we have described.

The Char Type

Character variables, denoted by the type char, are used to store single characters. Most implementations of Pascal use a set of characters called the *ASCII* set, where ASCII stands for the American Standard Committee (or Code) for Information Interchange. There are 128 characters in the ASCII set, including all the digits, the uppercase and lowercase letters of the alphabet, and most common punctuation marks, as shown in Appendix B.

Turbo Pascal Note

An extended ASCII set of characters is supported by Turbo Pascal. This set includes 256 characters, consisting of the standard 128 characters plus an additional 128 characters. On an IBM PC-compatible, these additional characters are special characters, foreign letters, and graphical characters, as shown in the MS-DOS or PC-DOS Reference Manual.

It is important to remember that **a character variable can hold only a single character**. If you try to assign more than one character to such a variable, you will get an error message. Later we will introduce the string type that can hold many characters.

Here is a variation of an earlier example program, showing how two character variables are declared and how character values are assigned. Note that character values must be enclosed in single quotation marks.

```
PROGRAM EX0206 (Output);
{
   Assign values to two variables
   and display them on the screen.
}

var
   Alpha, Beta: char;

BEGIN
   Alpha: = 'a';
   Beta: = '?';
   Writeln (Alpha);
   Writeln (Beta);
END.
```

This program displays the characters

```
a
?
```

Each character is displayed on a separate line. The same variable names are used as in Program EX0204, but in this case the variables are declared as character variables.

Note particularly that, whereas the variable Beta produces the same screen display in each program, in the first case (EX0204) this display represents a number (7), while in the second case (EX0206), it represents a digit character (7). **These two values may look the same, but they are not equal and are stored in completely different ways in memory.**

The Boolean Type

The fourth type of simple variable is the boolean type (named after the English mathematician George Boole). A boolean or logical variable can have only one of two possible values, true or false. Boolean variables are used primarily in Pascal statements that make decisions. We mention them here for completeness, but we will not show you an example until we use branching and looping decision statements in Chapter 7.

Turbo Pascal Note

Another type of variable, the string type, is available in Turbo Pascal. Variables of this type may contain up to 255 characters. They are particularly useful in programs that work with text and for holding such information as file names. We discuss string variables in detail in Chapter 5.

2.6 A SIMPLE LOOP: THE FOR STATEMENT

Let us suppose that we want to display a horizontal row of ten asterisks on the screen. We know how to write a program to perform this relatively simple task.

```
PROGRAM EX0207 (Output);
{
  Display a horizontal row of ten
  asterisks on the screen.
}

BEGIN
  Writeln ('**********');
END.
```

This program produces the display

```
**********
```

Repetition without Looping

Now suppose we want to write a program that displays a vertical column of ten asterisks. Again, we know how to write such a program, but it looks a bit cumbersome.

```
PROGRAM EX0208 (Output);
{
   Display a vertical column of
   ten asterisks on the screen.
}

BEGIN
   Writeln ('*');
   Writeln ('*');
   Writeln ('*');
   Writeln ('*');
   Writeln ('*');
   Writeln ('*');
   Writeln ('*');
   Writeln ('*');
   Writeln ('*');
   Writeln ('*');
END.
```

This program produces the display

```
*
*
*
*
*
*
*
*
*
*
```

Our program becomes even more cumbersome if we wish to display a vertical line of fifty asterisks. This last example illustrates a class of program where we need the capability to create a *loop*; that is, repeat a statement many times.

Pascal provides a for statement that allows another statement to be repeated a specified number of times. The syntax is

```
for control variable:=initial to final do
   simple or compound statement;
```

where the control variable is of any ordinal type, usually integer, and initial and final are values of the control variable. The statement following do may be either a simple or compound statement.

The Control Variable

The control variable is assigned the initial value and the statement is executed. The control variable is then incremented to the next ordinal value (if an integer, it is incremented by one), and the statement is executed again. The loop stops after the control variable is assigned the final value and the statement executed the last time. Here is another version of Program EX0208 that produces the same output.

```
PROGRAM EX0209 (Output);
{
   Display a vertical column of
   ten asterisks on the screen.
}
var
   Count: integer;

BEGIN
   for Count:= 1 to 10 do
     Writeln ('*');
END.
```

The variable Count starts out with the value of 1. After the first asterisk is displayed, the value of Count is incremented by one to a new value of 2 and another asterisk is displayed. This process continues until ten asterisks have been displayed. The for statement now notes that the next index of Count(11) exceeds the final value of 10. The loop stops at this point and program control moves on to the next statement, which in this case is the END statement.

Several points about the for statement should be noted. **After the for loop has executed, the value of the control variable is undefined.** In the previous example, you should not assume that Count has a value of either 10 or 11 after leaving the loop, but rather assume it is undefined.

If the initial value of the control variable is equal to the final value, the statement is executed only one time. If the initial value is greater than the final value, the statement is never executed.

Finally, be aware that errors can result if the value of the control variable is changed anywhere within the for loop. **The value of the control variable is controlled by the for loop and must not be modified by the program inside the body of the loop.**

We now consider a program that displays a square (or more accurately, a rectangle) of asterisks. Based on the last example, it is a straightforward task to write the program.

```
PROGRAM EX0210 (Output);
{
   Display a figure of ten by ten
   asterisks on the screen.
}
var
   Count: integer;

BEGIN
   for Count:= 1 to 10 do
     Writeln ('**********');
END.
```

This rectangular display is produced on the screen

```
**********
**********
**********
**********
**********
**********
**********
**********
**********
**********
```

The statement controlled by a for statement can be any simple or compound statement, including another for statement. We can write a more general program to accomplish the same task by using a for statement to produce each row of asterisks.

```
PROGRAM EX0211 (Output);
{
   Display a figure of ten by ten
   asterisks on the screen.
}
var
   Row, Column: integer;

BEGIN
   for Row:= 1 to 10 do
   begin  { start of compound statement }
   for Column:= 1 to 10 do
      Write ('*');  { put one asterisk in the row }
   Writeln;         { after the loop, start new row }
   end;    { end of compound statement }
END.
```

Note that the statement controlled by the first for statement is a compound statement (enclosed in begin and end brackets) and contains the second for statement.

The Write Statement

While Row has a value of 1, Column is assigned the values from 1 to 10, writing the first row with a Write statement. This statement is very similar to the Writeln statement, but after the parameter value has been displayed (in this example, the asterisk), the cursor does not move to the beginning of the next line.

After a complete row of asterisks is displayed, a Writeln statement (with no parameter) positions the location of new output at the beginning of the next row, and variable Row is assigned the value of 2. Variable Column again goes through its range of values, displaying the second row. The process continues until all ten rows have been displayed.

The Downto Word

A variation of the for statement decrements, rather than increments, the control variable. The syntax is

```
for control variable:=initial downto final do
   simple or compound statement;
```

In this case, the initial value of the control variable must be greater than or equal to the final value. Each time the statement is executed, the value of the control variable is decreased by one (or by one ordinal value).

Here is an example program that uses both variations of the for loop. Note the use of Writeln statements, without parameters, to create blank lines in the output display. First we show a general outline of the program.

Display first triangle pointing down
Display two blank lines
Display second triangle pointing up

Look carefully at the statements that display the first triangle. The for loops with control variable J use variables for the initial and final values. The first J loop creates an increasing left margin for each new line of stars. The second J loop displays a decreasing number of stars in each new line. Here is a specific outline for displaying the first triangle.

Initial left margin is one space
First row of stars contains 11 stars
For each row of stars, row 2 through row 6
   Increase margin by 1 space for each new row
   Decrease number of stars in each new row by 2

We now list the program itself.

```
PROGRAM EX0212 (Output);
{
   Use TO and DOWNTO in FOR loops
   to create triangular figures.
}
var
   I, J: integer;

BEGIN
   { Display triangle pointing down.}
   for I:=1 to 6 do  { six lines of stars }
     begin
     for J:=1 to I do
       Write (' '); { create an increasing left margin   }
     for J:=I to (12 - I) do
       Write ('*'); { rows of stars of decreasing length }
     Writeln;        { start a new row of stars           }
     end;
```

```
{ Display two blank lines.}
Writeln; Writeln;

{ Display triangle pointing up.}
for I: = 6 downto 1 do   { six lines of stars }
  begin
  for J: = 1 to I do
    Write (' ');   { create a decreasing left margin    }
  for J: = I to (12 - I) do
    Write ('*');   { rows of stars of increasing length }
  Writeln;         { start a new row of stars           }
  end;
END.
```

This program produces the following display

```
**********
 ********
  *******
   *****
    ***
     *


     *
    ***
   *****
  *******
 ********
**********
```

The first figure is produced when the value of I varies from 1 to 6, while the second figure is produced when I varies from 6 down to 1. A compound statement (enclosed in begin and end brackets) is executed within the I loop. One J loop in this statement produces one or more spaces. Another J loop produces eleven or less asterisks.

In the first figure, the initial value of I is one, and the compound statement displays one space followed by eleven asterisks. Each succeeding line displays one more space and two less asterisks. In the second figure, the initial value of I is six, and the compound statement displays six spaces followed by one asterisk.

IMPORTANT POINTS

- In some Pascal systems, such as Turbo Pascal, external file names need not be listed as parameters in the PROGRAM statement. In fact, the PROGRAM statement itself is optional in Turbo Pascal.

- One, and only one, END bracket with a following period is required in a Pascal program.

- If no file variable name appears in a `Writeln` statement, the standard output file is assumed.
- All single quotation marks must be the acute accent (`'`).
- A variable name identifies a memory location where information is stored.
- The value on the right side of the assignment operator is assigned to the variable on the left side.
- A comment cannot be enclosed in a mixed pair of brackets.
- A single statement can extend over more than one line.
- Several statements can be placed on the same line.
- Semicolons do not end lines; they separate statements.
- The words `BEGIN` and `END` are not statements; they should be thought of as brackets.
- Integer values must be less than or equal to `MaxInt` and greater than or equal to `-MaxInt`.
- Real values stored in a computer are only approximations of the actual numeric values.
- Real numbers must always contain a decimal point and may not contain a comma. At least one digit must be placed before and after the decimal point.
- Only an integer constant can be assigned to an integer variable.
- A character variable can hold only a single character.
- A character variable and an integer variable may each contain the same digit, but the two values are not equal and are stored in completely different ways in memory.
- After a `for` loop has executed, the value of the control variable is undefined.
- If the initial value of the control variable in a normal `for` statement (used in a `for-to` loop) is equal to the final value, the statement is executed only one time. If the initial value is greater than the final value, the statement is never executed.
- The value of the control variable is controlled by the `for` loop and must not be modified by the program inside the body of the loop.

SELF-STUDY QUESTIONS

Answer these questions as they apply to your particular implementation of Pascal.
1. Is the `PROGRAM` statement required in every Pascal program? Explain your answer.
2. (a) What is a Pascal identifier?
   (b) How many unique characters are allowed in a Pascal identifier?
3. What is the default name for
   (a) the standard input file or device;
   (b) the standard output file or device?
4. Braces, { and } , are used to enclose comments in Pascal. What other characters can be used instead of braces?

5. What words or symbols are used to enclose one or more simple Pascal statements to form a compound statement?

6. What is the purpose of the Pascal statement `Writeln`?

7. Write a statement that displays the string constant

```
This is a test of Pascal.
```

on the display unit screen.

8. Answer true or false for each part. The two quotation marks used in Pascal to enclose a string constant are
   (a) both the acute accent,
   (b) both the grave accent, or
   (c) one of each kind.

9. What is one purpose of the declaration block in a Pascal program?

10. Should a numeric constant, assigned to a numeric variable, be enclosed in quotation marks?

11. What is meant by the `type` of a variable?

12. (a) How are variables declared in a Pascal program?
    (b) Which variables, if any, can be used without a prior declaration?

13. If a new value is assigned to a variable that already has a value, what happens to the original value?

14. What symbol is used as the assignment operator in Pascal?

15. Is there any limit to the number of blank lines allowed in a Pascal program?

16. Answer true or false for each part. A Pascal statement
    (a) must be written on a single line;
    (b) can be split between two lines;
    (c) can be split between more than two lines.

17. Is the comment line

```
{ Program to sort a file.*)
```

allowed in Pascal? Explain your answer.

18. How many Pascal statements can be placed on the same line?

19. What is the purpose of the semicolon in Pascal?

20. Is it ever illegal to place a period after the `END` bracket? Explain your answer.

21. What are the four simple variable types introduced in this chapter?

22. What system identifier, if any, specifies the largest integer value allowed in an implementation of Pascal?

23. What system identifier, if any, specifies the largest real value allowed in an implementation of Pascal?

24. What is meant by an ordinal variable?

25. Answer true or false for each part. Real number constants in standard Pascal must contain at least
    (a) one decimal point;
    (b) one comma;
    (c) one digit before the decimal point?

26. How many characters can be stored in a character variable?

27. If the variable `Number` is declared of type integer, is the statement

```
10 := Number;
```

a legal statement? Explain your answer.

28. (a) Can a real value be assigned to an integer variable?
(b) Can an integer value be assigned to a real variable?

29. How many characters are in
(a) the standard ASCII set;
(b) the extended ASCII set of an IBM PC-compatible computer?

30. We say that the number 7 and the character 7 are not the same in Pascal. Explain what is meant by that statement.

31. If `Flag` is a variable of type boolean, what values can it have?

32. How many times will a `for-to` loop be executed if the initial value of the control variable is greater than the final value?

PRACTICE PROGRAMS

In each of the following assignments, write a Pascal program that produces the specified results.

1. Display these lines on the display unit screen in the format shown, with each line centered over the one below it.

```
        Final Report
   Project ADM - 3177 (v.2)
 Lake Monray Research Project
```

2. Display your full name, local address, and telephone number on the screen, placing each item on a separate line.

3. Assign three numeric values, representing water pressure readings in pounds per square inch, to three named variables of type real. Display these values on the screen, one above the other, on separate lines. Without reassigning values to the variables, display the values again in reverse order.

Test your program using the values 78.65, 50.51, and 48.25.

4. Assign three character values representing water quality to three named variables of type char. The letter E stands for excellent quality, G stands for good, and P stands for poor.

Display these values on the screen, one above the other, on separate lines. Without reassigning values to the variables, display the values again in reverse order.

Test your program using the values P, G, and E.

5. Use nested `for` loops to create the following display, which represents the location of piles to support a building.

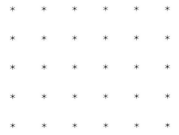

6. Use nested `for` loops to create the following display, again representing pile locations for a structure of a different shape.

```
*       *       *       *       *

*       *       *       *

*       *       *

*       *

*
```

7. At times it is useful to be able to create a vertical list of numbers, such as item numbers for the outline of an engineering report. Use a loop to display the digits from 1 through 5 inclusive, arranged in a vertical column, with a period after each digit and four blank lines between digits.

8. Another common format needed in engineering report tables is a horizontal list of column headings. Use a loop to display the digits from 1 through 9 inclusive, arranged in a horizontal row with four spaces between adjacent digits.

3

Input and Output Procedures

3.1 INTRODUCTION

Methods for entering information from the keyboard and displaying information on the screen are discussed. Techniques for controlling the display format are examined.

We extend our concept of input and output to include files stored on disk. We show how to access disk files from Turbo Pascal programs. Procedures for writing information on a file and reading information from a file are presented.

3.2 HOW TO USE THE KEYBOARD AND THE SCREEN

We have already used the `Writeln` statement in example programs. `Writeln` is actually not a statement but a standard Pascal procedure for producing output. We define procedures in Chapter 5.

The `Readln` Statement

A companion statement or procedure, used to enter information into a program, is the standard Pascal procedure named `Readln`. When this procedure is used with a single variable, as in the following example program, the program pauses until the user enters the desired information from the keyboard and presses the Enter key. This last action signifies that the entry process is complete, and the program continues.

```
PROGRAM EXO301 (Input, Output);
{
  Enter an integer value from the keyboard
  and display it on the screen.
}
var
  Number: integer;

BEGIN
  Writeln (Output, 'Enter integer on the next line:');
  Readln (Input, Number);
  Writeln (Output, 'You entered the integer ', Number);
END.
```

We have included the standard input and output identifiers in both the Writeln and Readln statements. Remember that the standard input file identifier represents the keyboard. These identifiers are usually omitted when input is from the keyboard and output is to the display unit screen. We include them here to remind you that the Writeln statement can be used to write information to, and the Readln statement can be used to read information from, any appropriate file or device.

Here is how the screen looks when the program is run. Underlined characters are those entered by the user, not displayed by the program. This underlining is not entered by the user and does not show on the screen, of course, when the program is actually run. The broken arrow symbol (←⎯) serves as a reminder that the Enter key must be pressed after the number is entered.

```
Enter integer on the next line:
213←⎯
You entered the integer 213
```

Other than the first line written by the program, there is no prompt or other indication that the program is waiting for a number to be entered. If a decimal number or a nonnumeric value is entered, an error message is displayed and the program stops.

Note that the second Writeln statement has three parameters: the standard output identifier, a string constant, and the integer variable. When output is displayed on the screen, the spacing between the end of the string constant and the number value varies with different Pascal implementations. This spacing can be controlled, and we will show how to do so in a later section.

Syntax for Writeln and Readln

The general syntax for Writeln and Readln is

```
Writeln (FileVarName, Item1, Item2, Item3, ...);
Readln (FileVarName, Item1, Item2, Item3, ...);
```

In our examples, **the Readln procedure usually has only a single item parameter**, while the Writeln procedure frequently has two or more item parameters. It is also common to use Writeln without any parameters, in which case it produces a blank line.

If standard input (the keyboard) and standard output (the display unit screen) are being used, the FileVarName identifier is usually omitted.

Dividing a String Constant

The last statement of Program EX0301 can also be written as

```
Writeln (Output, 'You have entered the integer ',
         Number);
```

but *not* as

```
(**************************************)
(** THIS STATEMENT IS NOT CORRECT **)
(**************************************)
Writeln (Output, 'You have entered
         the integer ', Number);
```

A string constant cannot be divided between two or more lines but must always be written on a single line. However, a string constant can always be split into two or more separate string constants, and thus, the previous statement can be written as

```
Writeln (Output, 'You have entered ',
         'the integer ', Number);
```

Input Prompts

We have already introduced the Write statement in Chapter 2. **This statement is useful for writing prompts when input is expected.** Here is the previous example, rewritten with a prompt and with a blank line between the prompt line and the next display line.

```
PROGRAM EX0302 (Input, Output);
{
  Enter an integer value from the keyboard
  and display it on the screen.
}
var
  Number: integer;

BEGIN
  Write ('Enter an integer value: ');
  Readln (Number);
  Writeln;
  Writeln ('You entered the integer ', Number);
END.
```

This program produces the following display, with entered characters underlined and the broken arrow symbol (←┘) showing that the Enter key must be pressed. Remember that you do not enter the underlining itself.

```
Enter an integer value: 45←┘

You entered the integer 45
```

The `Write` statement is also useful for displaying or printing long string constants. For example, a `Writeln` statement containing a string constant of seventy-seven characters presents a problem because it is too long to display in a program listing. The string itself, however, can be displayed or printed on a single line.

To solve this problem, divide the string constant into two or more parts. One solution that we have already shown is to use a single `Writeln` statement, with each part consisting of a string constant and written on a separate line.

```
Writeln ('This is a long string constant that ',
         'contains approximately seventy-seven ',
         'characters.');
```

Another solution is to use separate `Write` statements to display all except the last part, and then a `Writeln` statement to display the last part. All statements are on separate lines.

```
Write ('This is a long string constant that ');
Write ('contains approximately seventy-seven ');
Writeln ('characters.');
```

The Read Statement

The `Read` statement is an alternative to the `Readln` statement. We will not discuss it now because its behavior varies considerably among different implementations of Pascal. In most cases, we find the `Readln` statement preferable when entering information from the keyboard. The `Read` statement is useful when reading information from files, as discussed in Chapters 10 and 11.

Use of Single Parameter with Readln

If you are entering character values, **we recommend that you use only one parameter with each `Readln` statement**. This means, for example, that if you want to enter three characters, you should use three `Readln` statements. Here is an example:

```
PROGRAM EX0303 (Input, Output);
{
  Enter and display three characters.
}
var
  Alpha, Beta, Gamma: char;
```

```
BEGIN
  Writeln ('Enter three letters of the alphabet.');
  Write ('First letter: '); Readln (Alpha);
  Write ('Second letter: '); Readln (Beta);
  Write ('Third letter: '); Readln (Gamma);
  Writeln;
  Writeln ('The three letters are ', Alpha,
           Beta, Gamma);
END.
```

This program produces the following display; the characters on a shaded background are values entered from the keyboard. Remember that this shading does not appear on the screen. The Enter key must be pressed after each entry.

```
Enter three letters of the alphabet.
First letter: A←
Second letter: B←
Third letter: C←

The three letters are ABC
```

Problems can arise if you use a single Readln statement like

```
Readln (Alpha, Beta, Gamma);
```

in place of the three, separate Readln statements. In this case, you cannot prompt for each character. Moreover, the program executes properly only if exactly three characters are entered. If only two characters are entered, say A and B, the program displays

```
AB→
```

where the right arrow is displayed by Turbo Pascal for a carriage return. When you press the Enter key, it generates a carriage return character that is assigned to the variable Gamma. If you type in four characters, only the first three characters are displayed. We believe it is preferable to use only a single character variable with Readln statements, and thus avoid the possibility of odd behavior when improper data is entered.

3.3 CONTROLLING OUTPUT FORMAT

Display of Integer Numbers

Having mentioned previously that there was a way to control the format of displayed variables, we now discuss how integers and real numbers can be formatted. Here is the syntax of a Writeln statement used with an integer variable.

```
Writeln (IntegerVariable: FieldWidth);
```

The identifier FieldWidth is an integer constant, variable, or expression denoting the width in characters of the field in which the value of IntegerVariable is displayed. **If the specified field width is less than the length of the integer to be displayed, the field will be expanded to the same size as the integer.** If the specified field is greater than the length of the integer, the integer will be displayed right-justified in the field. Here is an example.

```
PROGRAM EXO304 (Output);
{
  Display an integer in several
  fields of different widths.
}
var
  TestNum: integer;

BEGIN
  TestNum:=737;
  Writeln ('***', TestNum:1, '***');
  Writeln ('***', TestNum:3, '***');
  Writeln ('***', TestNum:6, '***');
END.
```

This program produces the following display; asterisks show the resulting field widths.

```
***737***
***737***
***   737***
```

In the first line, the field width is specified as one character, but is expanded to three characters to accommodate the assigned integer (737). In the second line, the field width is specified as three characters and is a perfect match with the integer. In the third line, the field width is specified as six characters, and the integer is right-justified in that field.

Display of Real Numbers

A Writeln statement used with a real number has the following syntax:

```
Writeln (RealVariable:FieldWidth:DecimalWidth);
```

The identifier FieldWidth behaves as before. The identifier DecimalWidth, which can be an integer constant, variable, or expression, specifies the number of decimal digits that are displayed. Some compilers allow a minimum value of zero for the number of decimal digits, while others limit the minimum value to one. Here is an example program.

```
PROGRAM EXO305 (Output);
{
  Display real numbers using both
  field width and decimal width.
}
```

```
var
  A, B, C: real;
  Field: integer;

BEGIN
  A:= 17.936;
  B:= 1.2E+3;  { 1200 or 1.2 times 10 cubed }
  C:= 0.0012;
  Writeln ('***', A:1:0, '***');
  Writeln ('***', A:1:2, '***');
  Writeln;
  Writeln ('***', B:6:0, '***');
  Writeln ('***', B:6:1, '***');
  Writeln;
  Field:= 6;
  Writeln ('***', C:Field:2, '***');
  Writeln ('***', C:Field:4, '***');
  Writeln ('***', C:Field, '***');
END.
```

This program produces the display

```
***18***
***17.94***

***  1200***
***1200.0***

***   0.00***
***0.0012***
*** 1.2E-03***
```

Note that **a Writeln statement with a decimal field specification rounds
the last decimal digit**. If the decimal field specification is omitted, the number is
displayed in exponential notation, as shown. The usual field specification converts a
number entered in exponential notation to the standard decimal format. Experiment
with this or a similar program until you feel confident in your ability to control the
format of displayed numbers.

Turbo Pascal Note

Turbo Pascal does permit the number of decimal digits to be zero; so it is possible
to display a real number without a decimal point or decimal fraction. If you have
a situation using Version 3 where you need to use and display large integers (larger than MaxInt), you should use real numbers instead and display them with a
decimal width of zero. Remember that real values have a total of only 11 (16 with a
numeric coprocessor) significant digits and are only approximations to the actual
values.

In Versions 4 and 5, variables of type `longint` can hold values up to a magnitude of about 2,000,000,000, whereas variables of type `comp` can hold integer values up to about 9.2E + 18.

3.4 USING TEXT FILES IN PASCAL

We have discussed how to read information from the keyboard and write information on the screen; it is a simple extension of these techniques to read information from disk files and write information on disk files. The major complexity is that different implementations of Pascal use different statements for accessing text files on disk.

To use a disk file in a Pascal program, we need to accomplish three tasks:

1. Associate the disk directory file name (in MS-DOS, the MS-DOS file name) with the Pascal file variable name,
2. Open an existing file or create a new file, and
3. Close the file when we are finished using it.

We discuss first how these tasks are accomplished in Turbo Pascal.

Turbo Pascal Note

The `Assign` Statement

The first task is accomplished with the `Assign` statement. As is the case with the `Writeln` statement, `Assign` is actually a standard procedure. The syntax is

```
Assign (FileVarName, file name string);
```

where the identifier `FileVarName` is often called a file variable. This identifier is a Pascal variable, declared in a declaration block, that is used by the Pascal program to identify the file. One of the predefined file types in Pascal is the type `text`, and we will limit our present discussion to files of this type, commonly called *text files*. **All information stored in a text file is written on the file as ASCII characters**. This set of characters was discussed when we introduced the `char` type in Section 2.5.

The second parameter in the `Assign` statement, the file name string, is a string constant or string variable containing the MS-DOS name of a disk file.

MS-DOS File Names

We discussed MS-DOS file names in Chapter 1, and you will remember that file names can be only eight characters long, with an optional period and an extension consisting of three characters or less. Note that the extension is often used to indicate the kind of contents in a file, although a particular extension is not required for a specific file.

We recommend that you use only letter or digit characters in file names and extensions, although certain other characters are allowed in MS-DOS. The first character must be a letter. **Spaces or blank characters are not allowed.** Here are some examples of valid file names.

```
ABET.DOC            document file.
SKIN04.DAT          data file.
REPLY.PAS           Pascal program file.
```

Here are some examples of invalid file names.

```
HW 1.PAS            a space is not allowed.

SENSATIONAL.DOC     the file name has over eight
                    characters.

SUMMARY.TEXT        the extension has over three
                    characters.
```

MS-DOS Directories and Path Names

A disk may be organized with more than one file directory under the single root directory, with each directory containing several files. In this case, you must specify the directory name as well as the file name when referring to a file. In general, you access a file by specifying its path name. This path name is a combination of the disk drive letter, the directory name or names, the file name, and the extension. For example, the file named RESULTS.DAT, located in directory CH02 on the disk in drive B, is designated by the path name

```
B:\CH02\RESULTS.DAT
```

The first backslash character (\ ) after the disk drive name (B:) represents the root directory, the main directory on every disk. The second backslash separates the directory name (CH02) from the file name (RESULTS.DAT).

If a disk has only one directory, it is not necessary to specify a directory name, and the backslash after the disk drive name may be omitted. If the disk in our previous example contained only the root directory, a proper path name for file RESULTS.DAT would be

```
B:RESULTS.DAT
```

We recommend that you review our discussion of path names in Chapter 1, Section 1.3. More information about file names and disk directories can be found in your operating system (MS-DOS) manual.

Turbo Pascal Note

Using the `Assign` statement, if we wish to assign the file variable identifier FV to a text file named OUTLINE.TXT on the disk in drive B, the proper statement is

```
Assign (FV, 'B:OUTLINE.TXT');
```

If we wish to assign the file variable OutFile to a text file named RESULTS.DAT, located in directory CH02 on the disk in drive C, the proper statement is

```
Assign (OutFile, 'C:\CH02\RESULTS.DAT');
```

The Reset Statement

Our second task is to open the file for use in the program. If we wish to open an existing text file for reading, we use the statement

```
Reset (FileVarName);
```

Imagine that there is a *file pointer* in every file that points to or indicates the next item of information to be read from the file, or where the next item will be written on the file. This file pointer moves ahead one position whenever an item is read or written. The Reset statement positions that file pointer at the beginning of the file.

If we plan to open the existing file in our previous example (whose MS-DOS file name is OUTLINE.TXT), we enter the statement

```
Reset (FV);
```

The Rewrite Statement

On the other hand, if the text file does not exist and we wish to create and open it, we use the statement

```
Rewrite (FileVarName);
```

If a text file with the same name already exists, it is deleted, erasing any information it contains, and a new file is opened. The file pointer is positioned at the beginning of the empty file.

If we plan to write information on the file in our previous example, the proper opening statement is

```
Rewrite (FV);
```

The Close Statement

The final task is to close a file after we are finished using it. The syntax of the Close statement is

```
Close (FileVarName);
```

and the proper closing statement for our example is

```
Close (FV);
```

You should develop the habit to **always close a file when you are through writing on it.** Information written on a file may actually be residing in a section of memory called a *file buffer*, and may not yet have been transferred to the disk. This file buffer is not necessarily emptied when the program ends. We recommend that you always include a `Close` statement in your program to empty the file buffer and by doing so, ensure that all information has been properly written on the disk.

3.5 WRITING AND READING TEXT FILES

Turbo Pascal Note

All programs in this section are written for Turbo Pascal. They will not run in most other implementations of Pascal, but equivalent methods of writing and reading text files are usually available.

Writing on a File

Here is a program similar to the first program we wrote, but modified to write on a disk file named `TEST.TXT` that is located in the root directory of the disk in the current disk drive. The *current disk drive* is usually the drive from which you started Turbo Pascal, unless you have explicitly changed disk drives. If you want to write the file someplace else, change the path name in the `Assign` statement.

In this case, the string of characters we write on the file is the title of an engineering report.

```
PROGRAM EX0306 (Output);
{
  Open a text file in Turbo Pascal and
  write a string of characters on the file.
}
var
  FileVar: text;

BEGIN
  Assign (FileVar, 'TEST.TXT');
  Rewrite (FileVar);
  Writeln (FileVar, 'Gas Production - 1989');
  Close (FileVar);
  Writeln ('String has been written on file TEST.TXT.');
END.
```

The only screen output produced by this program is the information message to the user,

```
String has been written on file TEST.TXT.
```

The first `Writeln` statement specifies that information will be written on the file identified by file variable `FileVar`. Note that we include a subsequent `Writeln` statement to notify the user that the file has been written and closed. This statement gives the user added assurance that the program has run as planned.

Another example program asks the user to enter a number, in this case the value of an angle, and then writes that number on the file `TEST.TXT`.

```
PROGRAM EX0307 (Input, Output);
{
  Ask user to enter a number and then
  write that number on the file TEST.TXT.
}
var
  FileVar: text;
  Angle: real;

BEGIN
  Write ('Enter angle in radians: ');
  Readln (Angle);
  Assign (FileVar, 'TEST.TXT');
  Rewrite (FileVar);
  Writeln (FileVar, Angle:1:3);
  Close (FileVar);
  Writeln ('Value of angle has been written',
           ' on file TEST.TXT.');
END.
```

The field width and decimal width values that we have used previously for formatting numbers on the screen can also be used to control the format of numbers written on a text file. In this case, we specify three decimal digits in a field wide enough to contain the entered number.

This program produces the following screen display. We no longer show the broken arrow symbol after an entered value, but remember that the Enter key must be pressed after each entry from the keyboard.

```
Enter angle in radians: 1.335
Value of angle has been written on file TEST.TXT.
```

Note what happens if we first run Program EX0306 and then run Program EX0307. The Rewrite statement in the latter program deletes and then recreates file TEST.TXT, effectively erasing that file. The number we enter from the keyboard (in our example, 1.335) is then written on the file.

Reading from a File

Finally, we write a program to read the value of the angle from the file TEST.TXT and display it on the screen. We use the Reset statement to open the file for reading.

```
PROGRAM EX0308 (Output);
{
  Read a single number from the file TEST.TXT
  and display it on the screen.
}
var
  FileVar: text;
  Number: real;
```

```
BEGIN
  Assign (FileVar, 'TEST.TXT');
  Reset (FileVar);
  Readln (FileVar, Number);
  Writeln ('The angle read from file TEST.TXT is ',
          Number:1:3, ' radians.');
END.
```

The `Readln` statement specifies that information will be read from the file identified by the file variable name `FileVar`. Note that we do not close the file in this example program because we have written no information on the file. Some programmers, however, prefer to close all files after use, especially if many files are used in a program. This procedure avoids the problem caused by MS-DOS, which allows only a limited number of files (usually 3 to 15) to be open at any one time.

The final `Writeln` statement adds an appropriate label to the displayed number. This program produces the display:

```
The angle read from file TEST.TXT is 1.335 radians.
```

As an experiment, go back and modify Program EX0307 by deleting the `Close` statement. Run the program again, and then run Program EX0308. Did you read the same numeric value that you wrote on the file? If not, the lack of a `Close` statement in Program EX0307 resulted in the number you entered being lost in the file buffer and never actually written on the file.

Format for Storing Data in Text Files

Text files can be used to store data or numeric information rather than documents like letters or term papers. We have shown in our example programs that a number can be written on, and subsequently read from, a text file.

Our usual practice is to write numbers on a text file using a separate line for each value. We achieve this file format by using only the `Writeln` statement (not the `Write` statement) to write on a text file, and then only with a single parameter.

The resulting file has individual lines separated from one another by an end-of-line marker, usually a pair of nonprinting characters, the carriage return and the line feed. For example, if the file contained a sequence of numbers representing measured velocities, each number would be on a line by itself.

While this practice may waste some space in the file because of the large number of end-of-line markers written on the file, it results in a uniform file format that is easy to read. The text files for use with our example programs are all written in this manner.

Here is an example program that uses a `for` loop to write numeric values on a file. These values represent a weekly record of the number of x-ray machines produced for each of the five working days of the week. The working days Monday through Friday are numbered one through five. Note that the file name is coded to indicate the year, while the extension is coded to indicate the week of the year. Remember when writing text files to use a `Writeln` statement with a single variable.

```
PROGRAM EX0309 (Input, Output);
{
   Ask a user to enter the production total for each
   working day of the week and write these totals on a
   file named XRAY88.17. This file stores data for the
   seventeenth week of 1988.
}
var
   FileVar: text;
   Day, Number: integer;

BEGIN
   Assign (FileVar, 'XRAY88.17');
   Rewrite (FileVar);
   Writeln ('PRODUCTION OF X-RAY MACHINES');
   Writeln;
   for Day:= 1 to 5 do
     begin
     Write ('Day ', Day:1, ' production? ');
     Readln (Number);
     Writeln (FileVar, Number);
     end;
   Close (FileVar);
   Writeln;
   Writeln ('This data has been written',
            ' on file XRAY88.17.');
END.
```

Note that the Write statement shows each specific number being requested. This program produces the following output.

```
PRODUCTION OF X-RAY MACHINES

Day 1 production? 38
Day 2 production? 42
Day 3 production? 41
Day 4 production? 46
Day 5 production? 39

This data has been written on file XRAY88.17.
```

If a text file has been written with a single value per line, it should be read with a Readln statement containing only a single variable. As each line of the file is read, the value stored in that line is assigned to the variable.

If a user knows exactly how many values have been written on a file, a for loop can be used to read the file. That is a safe assumption in this example where five values are always written, using the value zero if the day is a holiday.

In general, this is not the case and the number of values is unknown. A better method for reading values from a file is to use a while loop and the end-of-file function, both introduced in Chapter 7.

Here is an example program that reads and displays the text file created in Program EX0309.

```
PROGRAM EX0310 (Output);
{
  Read a text file named XRAY88.17 that
  contains the number of x-ray machines
  produced on each day of the week and
  display these values on the screen.
}
var
  FileVar: text;
  Day, Number: integer;

BEGIN
  Assign (FileVar, 'XRAY88.17');
  Reset (FileVar);
  Writeln ('WEEKLY PRODUCTION RECORD');
  Writeln;
  for Day:=1 to 5 do
    begin
    Readln (FileVar, Number);
    Writeln (Number:1, ' machines produced on day ',
            Day:1);
    end;
END.
```

The following display is produced.

```
WEEKLY PRODUCTION RECORD

38 machines produced on day 1
42 machines produced on day 2
41 machines produced on day 3
46 machines produced on day 4
39 machines produced on day 5
```

After we introduce string variables in Chapter 8, we can use text files for storing and retrieving nonnumeric data. We still continue to use only a single variable in the Writeln and Readln statements that access the file.

Turbo Pascal Note

The Append and Flush Text File Statements

Two other text file statements are available in Turbo Pascal. The statement

```
Append (FileVarName);
```

can be used in place of `Rewrite` to open an existing file for writing. `Append` will not create a new file; it must already exist. New information is written at the end of existing information in the file.

The statement

```
Flush (FileVarName);
```

can be used to empty the file buffer for file `FileVarName` and write its contents on the disk without closing the file. In fact, the file must be open when the `Flush` statement is used.

3.6 DIFFERENCES IN STANDARD PASCAL TEXT FILES

Standard Pascal does require the `PROGRAM` statement, and if external files are used, their names must be included in the `PROGRAM` statement's parameter list. The file name, as it appears in the parameter list, is both the external name of the file and the file variable name. There is no distinction between these two names.

There are two problems with this method of designating files. One problem is that external file names must be specified when the program is written. It is not possible to write a program that allows a file name to be entered by the user and then assigned to a file variable.

Another problem is that a conflict may exist between the characters allowed or required in an external file name (for instance, a disk directory file name) and the characters allowed in a Pascal file variable name. In standard Pascal, an identifier can contain only letters and digits, while in MS-DOS, a full file name (path name) may contain a colon, period, and one or more backslashes.

These problems come from the original design of Pascal as a teaching language, rather than as a language for writing practical programs. Most implementations of Pascal provide an acceptable solution to the problems, as we have seen in the `Assign` statement of Turbo Pascal.

In standard Pascal, if the external file name meets the requirements of a legal Pascal identifier, it can be included in the parameter list of the `PROGRAM` statement. This file name must be declared to be of type `text`. The `Assign` statement is neither allowed or needed. All the other file statements that we have introduced, `Rewrite`, `Reset`, and `Close`, work as previously explained. Here are two example programs, similar to Programs EX0307 and EX0308, rewritten for standard Pascal.

Turbo Pascal Note

The next two programs will not run properly in Turbo Pascal.

```
PROGRAM EX0311 (Input, Output, Message);
{
   Ask user to enter a number and write it
   to an external file named Message.
   This program will not run in Turbo Pascal, but
   should run in most implementations of standard
   Pascal.
}
```

```
var
  Message: text;
  Number: real;

BEGIN
  Write ('Enter a number: ');
  Readln (Number);
  Rewrite (Message);
  Writeln (Message, Number);
  Close (Message);
  Writeln ('Number has been written on file Message.');
END.

PROGRAM EX0312 (Output, Message);
{
  Read a single number from an external file
  named Message, and then display it on the screen.
  This program will not run in Turbo Pascal, but
  should run in most implementations of standard
  Pascal.
}
var
  Message: text;
  Number: real;

BEGIN
  Reset (Message);
  Readln (Message, Number);
  Writeln ('Number read from file Message is ',
           Number:1:1);
END.
```

IMPORTANT POINTS

- Writeln and Readln are strictly not statements, but rather standard Pascal procedures. It is common practice, however, to call them statements.
- The Readln statement should have only a single parameter, and read only a single item.
- A string constant cannot be divided between two or more lines, but must always be written on a single line. However, a string constant can always be split into two or more separate string constants.
- The Write statement is useful for writing prompts when input is expected.
- If the specified field width is less than the length of an integer, the field will be expanded to the same size as the integer
- The Writeln statement with a decimal field specification rounds the last decimal digit.

- All information stored in a text file is written on the file as ASCII characters.
- Spaces or blank characters are not allowed in file names.
- Always close a file when you are through writing on it.
- Use a separate line for each number when writing numeric values on a text file.

SELF-STUDY QUESTIONS

1. What statement is used to enter information into a computer program from the keyboard?
2. Can a `Writeln` statement have more than one parameter representing an item to be displayed?
3. What is the difference, if any, between the `Write` and `Writeln` statements?
4. How do you produce a blank line in a Pascal program?
5. If you need to enter two characters into variables of type char, is it better to use one or two `Readln` statements? Explain your answer.
6. If the integer variable `Number` has a value of 1895, what is displayed when you execute the statement

   ```
   Writeln ('The value is ', Number:1);
   ```

7. If the integer variable `Number` has a value of 1895, what is displayed when you execute the statement

   ```
   Writeln ('The value is ', Number:7);
   ```

8. If the real variable `Reply` has a value of 1895.0, write a Pascal statement that displays this value as a whole number, without a decimal point.
9. What statement is used in Turbo Pascal to associate the Pascal file variable name with the MS-DOS path name or file name?
10. What statement is used to
    (a) open a text file for reading;
    (b) open a text file for writing?
11. What is the end-of-line marker (two characters) that is placed at the end of every line of a text file?
12. Is it necessary to execute a `Close` statement after you have finished
    (a) writing information on a file;
    (b) reading information from a file.

PRACTICE PROGRAMS

1. Ask a user to enter the nine-digit serial number of his or her engineering workstation from the keyboard. Assign the entered number to a variable and then display it again on the screen for verification. Consider whether the numeric variable should be of type real or type integer. Display the serial number in decimal (not exponential) format, but without a decimal point.

   Test your program using the serial number 812350555.

2. Prompt a user to enter a voltmeter reading in the format DDD.DDD, where each D represents a digit. For example, the user might enter the voltmeter reading 112.835. Then display a blank line, followed by the line

    `Voltage is 112.835 volts.`

    There should be a single space between the word `is` and the first digit of the numeric value. There should also be a single space between the last digit and the word `volts`.
    Test your program using the value 107.315.

3. The engineering officer on a single-screw vessel maintains a record of daily engine hours. If the vessel is tied up or anchored, the number of hours may be small or even zero. Each week, the seven values for that week are entered into a separate file.
    The name of the file is `HRSyyyy.ww`, where yyyy is the year designation and ww is the week number for that year. For example, file `HRS1992.38` contains engine hour information for the thirty-eighth week of 1992.
    Your program should open a file for the second week of 1987, ask a user to enter engine hours for that week, and write the values on the file. Prompt the user for each day of the week, designating Monday as day 1.
    Test your program using the values 24.0, 23.5, 24.0, 24.0, 13.2, 1.5, and 1.7.

4. Read seven engine-hour values from a text file named `HRS1987.02` (like the file that was written in Practice Program 3). Display these numbers on the screen, one above the other, in a format that has one decimal digit after the decimal point. Identify each engine-hour value with its day number in an appropriate label, and place an appropriate heading at the top of your display.

5. Use MS-DOS commands to create a subdirectory on your program disk named `SSWILSON.87` and to copy the file `HRS1987.02` to that subdirectory. Modify the program in Practice Program 4 so that it reads this subdirectory file.
    Test your modified program to be sure that it works properly.

6. An engineer has performed ten measurements and calculations of the permeability of a magnetic material identified as X107 and written these numeric values on a file named `MAGNET.DAT`. The numbers are all greater than 100 and less than 1,000 and have a single digit after the decimal point. Read these values from the file and display them on the screen in a single horizontal row, with two spaces between adjoining numbers. Display the title PERMEABILITY OF X107, centered above the row of numeric values and followed by a blank line.

4

PROGRAMS THAT CALCULATE

4.1 INTRODUCTION

Simple arithmetic operations, using both integers and real numbers, are discussed. We show examples of simple engineering calculations.

   We examine ways to find program errors and discuss how the `Writeln` statement is used to probe the inner workings of a program. We introduce the integrated debugger of Turbo Pascal. We also discuss several programming techniques that help produce error-free programs.

4.2 ARITHMETIC OPERATIONS

The operations of addition, subtraction, multiplication, and division are defined for both integers and real numbers. **There is no operator defined in Pascal for exponentiation or raising to a power.** However, an expression for calculating the value of a number raised to a power is given in Chapter 5, Section 5.2.

Addition, Subtraction, and Multiplication

The usual symbols of plus (+) and minus (−) are used for addition and subtraction. The asterisk (*) is used as the symbol for multiplication. Arithmetic expressions may contain both numeric constants and numeric variables.

Real and Integer Expressions

Care must be used to distinguish between variables and constants of type real and those of type integer. In general, these two types should not be mixed in an arithmetic expression, but there are certain exceptions.

For example, an expression containing any combination of variables and constants, both real and integer, can be assigned to a real variable. The integer values are converted to real values during the assignment process. On the other hand, only if all the variables and constants in an expression are integers can the result be assigned to an integer variable.

Here is an example program that contains both legal and illegal assignments; therefore, it will not compile.

```
PROGRAM EX00401;
{
   Examples of legal and illegal assignments.
   ***********************************
   ** THIS PROGRAM WILL NOT COMPILE **
   ***********************************
}
var
   A, C: integer;
   X, Z: real;

BEGIN
   A := 1;
   X := 1.0;

   {Assignments to an integer variable C }
   C := A + 2;    {legal, all integers in expression }
   C := A + 2.0;  {illegal, 2.0 is a real constant    }
   C := X + 2;    {illegal, X is a real variable       }

   {Assignments to a real variable Z }
   Z := X + 2.0;  {legal, expression is all real       }
   Z := A + 2.0;  {legal, expression converted to real }
   Z := X + 2;    {legal, expression converted to real }
   Z := A + 2;    {legal, expression converted to real }
END.
```

Real and Integer Division

There are two division operators. The slash (/) is used as the operator symbol for real number division, while the operator div is used for integer division.

The Div Operator.   Only integer constants or variables can be used with the div operator. It returns the quotient without the remainder; that is, the number of integer times that the divisor goes into the dividend. Some examples may help explain how it behaves.

```
7 div 2 is 3
14 div 5 is 2
```

The following example, which looks reasonable, is not allowed.

```
7 div 2.0 {produces an error }
```

The divisor (2.0) is a real value and cannot be used with the div operator.

The Mod Operator.   A companion operator, the mod operator, returns the remainder without the quotient. Here are some examples.

```
7 mod 2 is 1
14 mod 5 is 4
```

Real Number Division.   **In real number division, the dividend and divisor may be either integers or real numbers, but the result of the operation is always a real value.**   For example,

```
14.4 / 2.0 is 7.2
4 / 2 is 2.0
```

Here is an example program, using arithmetic operators, that requests a temperature in degrees Fahrenheit and displays the corresponding temperature in degrees Celsius.

```
PROGRAM EX0402 (Input, Output);
{
  The user enters a temperature in degrees Fahrenheit
  and the equivalent temperature in degrees Celsius is
  displayed.
}
var
  TempCelsius, TempFahrenheit: real;

BEGIN
  Write ('Temperature in degrees Fahrenheit? ');
  Readln (TempFahrenheit);
  TempCelsius:=(5 * (TempFahrenheit - 32.0)) / 9;
  Writeln ('Converted to degrees Celsius is ',
            TempCelsius:4:1);
END.
```

User interaction might look like the following.

```
Temperature in degrees Fahrenheit? 98.6

Converted to degrees Celsius is 37.0
```

Precedence of Arithmetic Operators

It is not always clear how to interpret an algebraic expression. For example, the expression

$$2 + 3 \text{ div } 1 + 4$$

might be interpreted as (2 + 3) div (1 + 4), or alternately, as 2 + (3 div 1) + 4. The first interpretation has a value of 1, while the second has a value of 9. We must understand how the Pascal compiler evaluates arithmetic expressions.

The answer is that multiplication and division (including the mod operation) have equal and highest precedence, while subtraction and addition have equal and lowest precedence. The precedence of arithmetic operators is shown in Figure 4.1.

> First: *   /   div   mod
> Second: +   −

Figure 4.1   Precedence of arithmetic operators.

Operators with the same precedence are evaluated from left to right. Thus 2 + 3 div 1 + 4 is equivalent to 2 + 3 + 4, or 9, because the division is evaluated first. We should note that real division has the same precedence as integer division.

Note that parentheses remove ambiguity because expressions in parentheses are evaluated first, starting with the innermost level of parentheses. The expression (2 + 3) div (1 + 4) is equivalent to 5 div 5 or 1. If you are writing a complicated expression, we urge you to use lots of parentheses.

Here is an example program that demonstrates the point.

```
PROGRAM EX0403 (Output);
{
  Show how parentheses change the
  value of an arithmetic expression.
}
var
  A, B, C: integer;

BEGIN
  A:=30; B:=7;
  Writeln ('A equals 30, B equals 7');
  C:=A - 14 div B + 3;
  Writeln ('A - 14 div B + 3 is ', C:2);
  C:=(A - 14) div (B + 3);
  Writeln ('(A - 14) div (B + 3) is ', C:2);
  C:=A - (14 div B) + 3;
  Writeln ('A - (14 div B) + 3 is ', C:2);
  C:=A - (14 div (B + 3));
  Writeln ('A - (14 div (B + 3)) is ', C:2);
END.
```

The results displayed are

```
A equals 30, B equals 7
A - 14 div B + 3 is 31
(A - 14) div (B + 3) is  1
A - (14 div B) + 3 is 31
A - (14 div (B + 3)) is 29
```

You can see that placing parentheses at different locations produces different results.

Compiler Directives

Most implementations of Pascal allow special directives, called compiler directives, to be given to the compiler. These directives are often included in the Pascal program, using a distinctive notation to separate compiler directives from program statements or comments.

Turbo Pascal Note

Turbo Pascal allows instructions to the compiler to be included in a Pascal source program. The directive consists of a dollar sign ($), an uppercase letter, and usually a plus ($+$) or minus ($-$) sign, all enclosed within braces. A plus sign turns on the directive, while a minus sign turns it off. In some directives, the plus or minus sign is replaced by one or more parameters.

The N Compiler Directive.   Versions 4 and 5 of Turbo Pascal have a compiler directive that tells the compiler to produce a program requiring, or not requiring, a computer with a numeric coprocessor. The directive {$ N+} generates program code for real number arithmetic in hardware (using a numeric coprocessor), while the directive {$ N-} generates code for real number arithmetic in software. The default state (no N compiler directive) is different for Versions 4 and 5; see your reference manual.

Version 3 has different versions of the Turbo Pascal system for computers with and without a numeric coprocessor.

4.3 FINDING AND CORRECTING ERRORS

A large portion of the time spent developing a computer program is devoted to finding and eliminating errors. We discuss several techniques for helping a programmer find errors. In addition to learning how to find errors, it is important to learn how to write programs that contain few errors. We present a recommended procedure for writing computer programs that are likely to run correctly the first time they are executed.

Playing Computer

Our goal is to write programs that contain no errors. It is probably an impossible goal to attain, but we need to learn how to reduce the number of errors to a minimum. At the same time, we must develop skills that help us find errors and then remove them from our programs. This process is called *debugging*.

One of the best methods for finding errors is to read through a computer program pretending that you are the computer. You make all the calculations and decisions that would normally be made by the computer. Many simple errors will be revealed.

This method is easy to understand and to apply, but it can be tedious. You will find it most useful for examining small sections of a program. You will make better progress if you write down intermediate results on paper in a systematic format. If complicated arithmetic calculations are involved, the process can be accelerated by using a hand calculator.

In spite of the limitations, we recommend that you try this method first. It is a natural way to find errors if a program is not working properly.

Temporary `Writeln` Statements

Beginning programmers often say "I know that the value of variable X at this point in the program is 15.2, but when I make a calculation using X and print the results, they are wrong." Our response is "How do you know that the value of X is 15.2?"

One way to answer the question is to put a temporary `Writeln` statement into your program and see what the value of X actually is at the point of calculation. It is surprising how often it will be different from what you thought it should be.

It is not unusual to insert half a dozen temporary `Writeln` statements in a program before finding an error. Sometimes it is helpful to include a label in the `Writeln` statement to help identify its location. For example,

```
Writeln ('In report section: X =', X:1:1);
```

identifies the variable being displayed and the program section where it has this value. A single `Writeln` statement can also be used to print out the values of several different variables; for example,

```
Writeln ('After search: I,  Sum = ', I:1,
         '  ', Sum:1:2);
```

You must, of course, remember to delete the temporary `Writeln` statements after you have found the error. In many cases, these two techniques, playing computer and inserting temporary `Writeln` statements, are sufficient to identify programming errors.

We recommend a systematic approach to debugging programs. First, read through your program carefully and see if you can spot an obvious error. Another person will often find errors in your program that you have not noticed. As you read your program, you will automatically start to play computer and ask yourself what the values of different variables should be.

If you still have errors, start inserting `Writeln` statements. Do not hesitate to use many `Writeln` statements to find an elusive error.

The art of program debugging can only be learned by experience. It can be time consuming and frustrating, but if you persist, you should be able to find and eliminate most program errors.

An Example Program with Errors

As an example of the techniques discussed previously, consider a program containing a logical error.

```
PROGRAM EX0404 (Output);
{
   Calculate the cubes of the integers from
   5 down to 1 and write the results on a
   text file named CUBES.TXT.
   This program contains logical errors.
}
```

```
var
  FV: text;
  Count, Number: integer;

BEGIN
  Assign (FV, 'CUBES.TXT');
  Rewrite (FV);
  for Count:=5 to 1 do
    begin
    Number:=Count * Count;
    Writeln (FV, Number);
    end;
  Close (FV);
  Writeln ('File CUBES.TXT has been written.');
END.
```

This program produces the output

```
File CUBES.TXT has been written.
```

When the file is examined, however, it appears to be empty and contains no values. A Writeln statement is inserted within the for loop to display on the screen whatever is written on the file. The program then looks like this.

```
PROGRAM EX0405 (Output);
{
  Calculate the cubes of the integers from
  5 down to 1 and write the results on a
  text file named CUBES.TXT.
  This program contains logical errors.
  A temporary Writeln statement has been added.
}
var
  FV: text;
  Count, Number: integer;

BEGIN
  Assign (FV, 'CUBES.TXT');
  Rewrite (FV);
  for Count:=5 to 1 do
    begin
    Number:=Count * Count;
Writeln (Count, '    ', Number);
    Writeln (FV, Number);
    end;
  Close (FV);
  Writeln ('File CUBES.TXT has been written.');
END.
```

Note that the temporary Writeln statement is not indented; so it can be identified easily and deleted when no longer needed.

When Program EX0405 is executed, it produces the same output as Program EX0404. The temporary `Writeln` statement is never executed! Closer examination shows that the `for` statement is not written correctly; the word `to` should be `downto`. After this correction has been made, the program is run again. It produces the following results.

```
5       25
4       16
3        9
2        4
1        1
File CUBES.TXT has been written.
```

When the file itself is examined, it contains the same sequence of numbers that is displayed on the screen. The sequence, however, appears to contain the squares rather than the cubes of integers from 5 down to 1. The expression for calculating `Number`

```
Number:= Count * Count;
```

is wrong and must be changed to

```
Number:= Count * Count * Count;
```

Executing the program again (still containing the temporary `Writeln` statement) produces the output

```
5      125
4       64
3       27
2        8
1        1
File CUBES.TXT has been written.
```

It now appears that the cubes are being calculated correctly and the results written to file `CUBES.TXT`. Examination of the file confirms the latter fact. Here is the final program as corrected, with the temporary `Writeln` statement deleted.

```
PROGRAM EX0406 (Output);
{
  Calculate the cubes of the integers from
  5 down to 1 and write the results on a
  text file named CUBES.TXT.
}
var
  FV: text;
  Count, Number: integer;

BEGIN
  Assign (FV, 'CUBES.TXT');
  Rewrite (FV);
```

```
for Count: = 5 downto 1 do
  begin
    Number: = Count * Count * Count;
    Writeln (FV, Number);
  end;
Close (FV);
Writeln ('File CUBES.TXT has been written.');
END.
```

4.4 USING A PROGRAM DEBUGGER

Program debuggers are available for most implementations of Pascal, usually as a separate program. If they can detect source code errors, they are called *source code debuggers* and are especially useful for debugging programs. Unfortunately, many of the older, separate debuggers are not widely used because they are hard to use. Beginning programmers often find them more trouble than they are worth.

Turbo Pascal Note

One of the significant additions to Turbo Pascal, Version 5, is a simple, built-in source code debugger. This facility allows a user to single step, statement by statement, through a program and watch the values of selected variables. The debugger is part of the Turbo Pascal system, and so is always ready for use.

When Turbo Pascal first starts, the screen displays either one window or two windows. The Zoom key (F5) allows a user to toggle between these two different displays. If two windows are displayed, the upper window is the edit window, while the lower window is usually the watch window. Refer to our discussion in Chapter 1 for further details. We recommend that you use the two-window mode, containing an edit window and a watch window, for debugging short programs.

Some additional information must be generated during compilation if the debugger is to be used. The default values of two compiler directives ($D and $L) cause the compiler to create a table of source code line numbers and a table of local symbol information. If the debugger does not seem to be working properly, add the line

```
{ $D+, $L+}
```

at the beginning of your program.

Single Stepping through a Program

The easiest way to use a debugger with a short program is to *single step* through the program. This method executes all the statements on one program line and then waits until a key is pressed before executing the statements on the next line. In most cases, Pascal programs have only a single statement on each line.

The F7 key is used to step through or trace a program. Pressing the F7 key initially (or selecting the Trace into command from the Run command menu) compiles the program and highlights the first program statement line. Pressing the key again executes the statement in this line, and highlights the next line. You can actually trace, one line at a time, the statements executed by the computer when your program is run. The tracing process stops when the period after the main program END statement is reached.

It is possible to edit your program either before, during, or after tracing the program. If you make changes in the program during the tracing process, the warning message

```
Source modified, rebuild? (Y/N)
```

is displayed in a pop-up window. This message means that the source code has been changed, and these changes may introduce errors into the debugging process. We recommend that you press the Y key in response to the message, and your program will be compiled again.

Watching and Changing Variable Values

The Turbo Pascal debugger not only shows you the order in which program lines are executed, it can also show you, in the watch window, the values of one or more variables. The commands in the command menu of the Break/watch command are used to change variables in the watch window.

Access the Break/watch command menu from the main menu by pressing Alt-B. Figure 4.2 lists the commands in this menu that apply to watch variables.

Add watch	add a new watch variable
Delete watch	delete an existing watch variable
Edit watch	edit an existing watch variable
Remove all watches	delete all exiting watch variables

Figure 4.2   Menu of Break-Watch commands.

The Add watch command can also be invoked directly from the edit window by pressing Ctrl-F7, and this method is recommended. Move the cursor under any character of a variable name that you want to watch and press Ctrl-F7. A pop-up window appears containing that variable name. When the Enter key is pressed, this variable name is displayed in the watch window and the pop-up window disappears. Several variables can be added to the watch window, one after the other.

Notice that the last-added variable name is identified by a bullet (•) in front of the name. This symbol denotes the current watch variable, the one that is deleted or edited when the Delete watch or Edit watch commands are invoked.

As mentioned before, you can move to the watch window by pressing the F6 key. The current watch variable is now marked by a highlight bar. Using the arrow keys, you can select any variable in the watch window as the current variable. You are also able to edit or delete any or all of the watch variables, using the regular edit commands. Most users find this procedure easier than executing the various commands in the Break/watch command menu.

An Example Program

As an exercise, we recommend that you try using the Turbo Pascal debugger with Program EX0404. Be sure that both the edit window and the watch window are displayed on the screen. Use the F7 key to step through the program. Note that the highlight bar jumps directly from the `for` statement to the `close` statement, indicating that the `for` loop is never executed.

Now use Ctrl-F7 to add variables `FV`, `Count`, and `Number` to the watch window. Single step through the program again and note how the variable values change. Note especially the status of the file as shown by the `FV` variable. Correct the `for` statement so it reads

```
for Count:=5 downto 1 do
```

and trace through the program again. Notice how easy it is to detect the logical error in calculating `Number` by watching the values of `Count` and `Number` change.

When you have finished a debugging session, it is a good practice to release any memory allocated to the debugger before starting a new session. Execute the `Program reset` command from the `Run` menu, or press Ctrl-F2. None of the watch variables are reset or changed in any way.

Figure 4.3 is a summary of the short-cut commands we have introduced in this section.

`F6`	switch between the Edit and Watch windows
`F7`	single-step trace through a program, one line at a time
`Ctrl-F7`	add the variable under the cursor to the Watch window
`Ctrl-F2`	terminate tracing and reset the program

Figure 4.3 List of debugging keys.

If you have Version 5 of Turbo Pascal (and if you do not, you should order it immediately), we urge you to start using the debugger now while you are writing short programs. It is a powerful tool, but like any other tool, you have to learn how to use it. We examine other capabilities of the debugger in Chapter 6 and recommend its continued use as you write Turbo Pascal programs.

4.5 PREVENTING PROGRAM ERRORS

Most of our discussion thus far has been about methods for finding and correcting program errors. An equally important topic is how to write programs that have no errors in the first place.

Hints for Writing Correct Programs

When we say that a program is error free, we mean that extensive testing has revealed no errors. There is no way of knowing that every single error has been found and corrected. Unfortunately, some errors are never found until the program has been used by many different people in many different applications.

Throughout the book we stress **logical program design, development of a program in small modules, and use of clear structures for looping and branching.** Keep these points in mind as we discuss some hints for writing better programs.

Understand the Problem.   You cannot write a program to solve a problem until you completely understand the problem. This is an obvious statement, but a lot of people start programming before they understand clearly what the program must do. Keep asking questions or investigate further until you fully understand the problem.

Plan First, Program Later.   A common mistake made by beginning programmers is to start writing their programs too soon. This does not mean to do nothing until just before the programming assignment is due, but it does mean to do a lot of thinking and planning before writing your first program statement. Here are two steps you should take.

First, you must decide how you will solve the problem. The method of solution is called an *algorithm*. You need to find (or develop) an efficient algorithm that will solve the problem accurately and quickly. You learn different algorithms by reading books and articles, by looking at programs written by other programmers, and by discussing methods of solution with experienced programmers.

Second, you must **write an outline of your program**. An outline can be written as one or more descriptive paragraphs or in the more traditional outline form. Try to divide your problem solution into separate tasks and then outline a solution for each task. When you learn about the subprogram capabilities of Pascal in the next chapter, you will be able to organize your program into a collection of program modules. The more detailed your outline, the easier it will be to write the computer program.

We believe that writing an outline is a necessary step in designing a program. We must admit, however, that some of the example programs in this book are so short that a written outline is really unnecessary. You should follow a reasonable, compromise procedure. When you are learning to program, write outlines for several small programs because this is the best way to learn how to write an outline. As you become more experienced, you will find that you need to write outlines only for your longer programs. In our opinion, an outline should be written for almost every program whose source code is longer than a page (about fifty lines).

Only when you have taken these two steps are you ready to start writing the program itself.

Write Simple Programs.   Use all the tools you have available to write a program that is easy to read and understand. Use variable names that are as descriptive as possible. Use indentation to identify the statements in a branch or a loop. Use comments to explain the logical action of the program, not what an individual statement does.

Avoid program structures that are tricky or hard to understand. There is usually no justification for writing programs that are difficult to understand in order to make them more efficient. Remember that computer memory is becoming less expensive and computers are becoming faster. Programs should be written to minimize the time required for maintenance rather than to minimize the amount of memory used or the execution time.

Most importantly, write your program as a series of small modules, as independent from one another as possible. No module should be larger than a single page. We will show you in the next chapter how to write a module as a procedure or function. We recommend that you use this technique.

Thoroughly test each module before adding it to your program. Small modules tend to be easier to write and debug than large programs. If each module is free of errors, the resulting program is likely to be error free.

Test and Debug Carefully. If you are careful in writing your program, it should contain few errors. Test your program for as many conditions as possible that might cause an error. Look carefully at extreme conditions, such as the largest and smallest values of key variables. Ask someone else to run your program and see if they can make it fail.

A common type of error is called the off-by-one bug. This is the error that occurs, for example, when you are counting and the count turns out to be one less or one greater than it should be. Look carefully at your logic and you should be able to find the mistake.

Your ability to write error-free programs will improve quickly if you follow these suggestions. There will be times, however, when in spite of your best efforts, you cannot get a program to work. You should then go back and examine your program outline. If you are not satisfied with it, you may save time by starting over again. It is difficult to write a good program from a bad outline.

IMPORTANT POINTS

- There is no operator defined in Pascal for exponentiation or raising to a power.
- In real number division, the dividend and divisor may be either integers or real numbers, but the result of the operation is always a real value.
- Use lots of temporary Writeln statements to help locate program errors.
- You must understand the problem before writing a program to solve the problem.
- Always write down a program outline before starting to write program statements.
- Develop your program as a series of small, simple modules that have been thoroughly tested.
- Do not use tricky or complicated logic in order to make a program shorter or more efficient.

SELF-STUDY QUESTIONS

1. What is the Pascal arithmetic operator for
   (a) addition;
   (b) multiplication;
   (c) exponentiation?
2. What is the Pascal arithmetic operator for
   (a) integer division;
   (b) real number division?
3. If I is an integer variable and R is a real variable, are the following assignment statements allowed?
   (a) `R := I + 2.0;`
   (b) `I := R + 2;`
4. Are the following arithmetic expressions allowed?
   (a) `7 div 2.0`
   (b) `7 / 2.0`
5. What is meant by the term debugging?
6. What is the method of playing computer?
7. What statement can you insert into a program to display the value of a variable?
8. (a) What is an algorithm?
   (b) Can you develop an algorithm for a problem if you do not understand the problem? Explain your answer.
9. Why is a written program outline preferable to a mental outline?
10. Why is it important to write programs that are clear and easy to understand?

PRACTICE PROGRAMS

1. The power loss in an electrical cable is given by the expression

$$P = RI^2$$

   where P is the power loss in watts, R is the resistance in ohms, and I is the current in amperes.

   Ask a user to enter the resistance of a cable and the current flowing in it. Display the power loss in the following format (underlined numbers mean values that are entered by the user).

   ```
   Resistance in ohms? 0.005
   Current in amperes? 23.2
   Power loss is 2.69 watts.
   ```

   Test your program using $R = 0.005$ ohms and $I = 23.2$ amperes, also $R = 12.0$ ohms and $I = 150$ milliamperes.
2. Use a `for` loop to produce the screen display shown below, listing the integers from 1 through 8 with their calculated squares and cubes. Be sure to include column headings, and format your columns as shown.

Value	Square	Cube
1	1	1
2	4	8
3	9	27
4	16	64
5	25	125
6	36	216
7	49	343
8	64	512

3. Two metal strips, each of length L meters and thickness D meters at temperature T are welded together so that their ends coincide. One strip is made of a metal having a linear coefficient of expansion of α_1 per degree Celsius. The other strip is made of a metal having a linear coefficient of expansion of α_2 per degree Celsius. When the resulting bimetallic strip is heated to a temperature of $(T + \Delta T)$, one strip becomes longer than the other and the bimetallic strip bends into the arc of a circle.

Assume the materials of the two strips are aluminum having a value of α_1 equal to 23.0E−6, and steel having a value of α_2 equal to 11.0E−6. Assume the change in temperature ΔT is 50 degrees Celsius. Calculate the radius of curvature R for the bimetallic strip if each strip has a thickness (D) of one millimeter (1.0E−03 meters). Use the expression

$$R = \frac{D}{|\alpha_1 - \alpha_2| \times \Delta T}$$

Display the radius of curvature with an appropriate label.

4. The total resistance of several resistors in parallel can be calculated using the expression

$$R = \frac{1}{(1/R1) + (1/R2) + \ldots + (1/Rn)}$$

where $R1$, $R2$, and so forth are the individual resistances in ohms, and R is the total resistance.

Calculate the total resistance of ten resistors, each with a value of two megohms (2.0E+06 ohms), that are connected in parallel. Display your result with an appropriate label.

5. The file RESISTOR.DAT contains the values, in ohms, of six resistors. Read the resistance values from the file and calculate the total resistance if all six resistors are connected in series. Also calculate the total resistance if all six resistors are connected in parallel. Display both total values with appropriate labels.

6. You are an engineer asked to design the fire pole in a new fire station. You need to calculate the average vertical force on the pole when a fireman slides down it. After checking the personnel records, you determine that the heaviest fireman weighs 250 pounds or less. From observation, you determine that the maximum average acceleration of a fireman sliding down a pole is 10 feet per second squared.

Using the well-known equation

$$F = ma$$

calculate the average vertical force that a sliding fireman will exert on the pole. Remember that

$$\text{Mass} = \text{Weight}/g$$

where the acceleration of gravity, g, is 32 ft/sec^2. Note: If the fireman is not sliding, the vertical force on the pole is 250 pounds. Consider whether this force increases or decreases when the fireman is sliding.

As a practical engineer, after making the calculation of average vertical force, how would you design the fire pole?

5

SUBPROGRAMS: FUNCTIONS AND PROCEDURES

5.1 INTRODUCTION

Programs written by engineers and scientists often involve numeric calculations; so we first discuss the standard arithmetic functions available in Pascal. We then look at program organization and the use of subprograms. Two kinds of subprograms, procedures and functions, are presented. We also discuss the use of parameters to pass information to subprograms.

5.2 STANDARD FUNCTIONS

When making calculations, an engineer or scientist often needs to use standard functions in addition to the arithmetic operators introduced in Chapter 4. Simple examples are the square root function and the sine function. Figure 5.1 lists some of the standard arithmetic functions available in standard Pascal.

All the functions shown in Figure 5.1 return real values except `Abs(X)` and `Sqr(X)`, which return a real or integer value, depending on the type of X. **Note that trigonometric functions require the angle to be in radians.**

A function has a value associated with its name; that is, the value produced when a function is evaluated is assigned to the function name. Functions can be used in expressions, on the right-hand side of assignment statements and in `Writeln` statements, as shown in the sample statement

```
    Result:= 2 * (Cos(X/2) - Sin(X/2));
```

or

```
    Writeln (Sqrt(Velocity):6:2);
```

FUNCTION	RETURNS
Abs(X)	absolute value of X
Sqr(X)	square of X
Sqrt(X)	square root of X
Sin(X)	sine of angle X, measured in radians
Cos(X)	cosine of angle X, also in radians
ArcTan(X)	angle in radians whose tangent is X
Ln(X)	natural logarithm of X
Exp(X)	exponential function of X

Figure 5.1 Some standard Pascal functions.

Functions can be used in calculations, as shown in the following example program.

```
PROGRAM EX0501 (Input, Output);
{
  Given two sides of a triangle and the angle between
  them, calculate the length of the third side.
}
var
  A, B, C: real;    { The three sides of a triangle  }
  Alpha:   real;    { The angle between sides A and B }

BEGIN
  Write ('Length of first side of triangle? ');
  Readln (A);
  Write ('Length of second side of triangle? ');
  Readln (B);
  Write ('Angle between 1st and 2nd sides,');
  Write (' in degrees? ');
  Readln (Alpha);
  Alpha:= Alpha*Pi/180.0; { Convert angle to radians }
  C:= Sqrt(A*A + B*B - 2*A*B*Cos(Alpha));
  Writeln ('Length of third side is ', C:5:3);
END.
```

This program uses the familiar law of cosines to calculate the third side of a triangle, given two sides and the included angle. Two standard Pascal functions are used in the calculation, the square root (Sqrt) function and the cosine (Cos) function. Note that the angle is entered by the user in degrees but must be converted to radians before being used as a parameter for the Cos function. The standard function Pi, listed in Figure 5.2, is used in making the conversion. Here is a sample of user interaction.

```
Length of first side of triangle? 2.0
Length of second side of triangle? 2.0
Angle between 1st and 2nd sides, in degrees? 60.0
Length of third side is 2.000
```

The availability of exponential and logarithmic functions allows us to calculate easily the value of a number raised to a power. The value of X raised to the Y power is

```
Exp(Y * Ln(X))
```

where X and Y may be either integers or real numbers.

Turbo Pascal Note

Appendix D lists all the standard functions and procedures in Turbo Pascal. A procedure is similar to a function but does not return a value (see Section 5.3). Figure 5.2 lists some of the commonly-used functions and procedures of Turbo Pascal.

FUNCTION	TYPE	RETURNS
Pi	real	value of Pi, 3.14159. . .
Round(X)	integer	real X rounded to nearest integer
Trunc(X)	integer	real X truncated to an integer
Int(X)	real	integer part of real X
Frac(X)	real	fractional part of real X
Chr(N)	char	character with ASCII value N
Ord(C)	integer	ASCII value of character C
UpCase(C)	char	upper case value of character C
*KeyPressed	boolean	true if a key is pressed
*ReadKey	char	character of pressed key (Ver. 4 & 5)
Odd(X)	boolean	true if X is odd
Pred(X)	ordinal	predecessor of X
Succ(X)	ordinal	successor of X
Random	real	random value between zero and one
*WhereX	integer	current column position of cursor
*WhereY	integer	current row position of cursor

PROCEDURE	DESCRIPTION
*ClrScr	clear the screen
*GotoXY (X, Y)	move cursor to column X, row Y
Exit	leave the current subprogram
Halt	stop the program immediately

Figure 5.2   Standard Turbo Pascal functions and procedures.
(* = requires the Crt unit in the program)

All the functions and procedures listed here (except ReadKey, which is in Version 4 and 5 only) are available in all three versions of Turbo Pascal. In Version 4 and 5, subprograms KeyPressed, ReadKey, WhereX, WhereY, ClrScr, and GotoXY require that unit Crt be included in the program (see Section 5.3 and Appendix E).

We encourage you to examine these lists carefully and use any standard function or procedure that helps you solve a problem. We shall discuss many of the standard functions and procedures in more detail as we use them in advanced programs. Refer to Appendices D and E for further information.

5.3 PROGRAM ORGANIZATION WITH SUBPROGRAMS

We have seen in the previous section how standard Pascal functions are needed when performing certain calculations. Because the number of standard functions is limited, the Pascal language allows user-defined functions to be created and included in programs. These functions can be used in calculations just like the standard functions. Before introducing user-defined functions, we need to discuss program organization in more detail.

Expanding on the program outline in Section 2.2, we write a more general program structure as follows:

```
PROGRAM ProgramName (Input, Output);

{ Unit declarations, only in    }
{ Turbo Pascal, Versions 4 and 5. }

{ Global Declaration Block, which }
{ includes variable declarations. }

{ One or more Subprogram Blocks, any of }
{ which may be user-defined functions.  }

BEGIN
  { The Main Program Block }
END.
```

Note that a Pascal program can have only one declaration block for the entire program (which we call the *global declaration block*), and only one main program block. It may have one or more subprogram blocks, each containing its own declaration block.

Turbo Pascal Note

The Uses Statement

Versions 4 and 5 of Turbo Pascal allows the inclusion of *units* (compiled collections of constants, data types, variables, procedures, and functions) in a program. The required statement to include one or more units is

```
uses unit name, unit name, ...;
```

where the unit name can be either a standard unit or a user-written unit. This statement should be placed right after the program statement, before the declaration block.

The standard units supplied with Versions 4 and 5 are named Dos, Crt, Printer, Graph, Turbo3, and Graph3. The contents of the first three units are listed in Appendix E. Each unit is a library of related functions and procedures. We have already mentioned (in Section 4.2) the need to include unit Crt when certain screen-related functions and procedures are used in a program.

Here is an example program, written for Versions 4 and 5, that clears the screen, and then displays a message at the center of the screen. It uses two procedures, ClrScr and GotoXY, from the standard unit Crt.

```
PROGRAM EX0502 (Output);
{
  Display a message at the
  center of the screen.
}
uses    { not needed in }
  Crt; { Version 3      }

BEGIN
  ClrScr;
  GotoXY (32,12);
  Writeln ('Summary of Results');
END.
```

All you need to do to run this program in Version 3 is to remove the uses statement. We do not show the output of the program, but it just displays the message "Summary of Results" starting at column 32, row 12 of the screen.

Section 9.7 describes how to write your own units and should be read carefully if you are using one of the latest versions of Turbo Pascal.

The Declaration Block

We shall examine the declaration block in more detail. All constants and variables defined and declared in the global declaration block are called *global constants* and *variables*. They are given this name because their values are known throughout the entire program. Four kinds of identifiers can be declared in any declaration block.

The Label Declaration. The first kind of identifier is a *label*, which identifies and designates some statement in a Pascal program, usually the target of a goto statement. This section must start with the reserved word label. We do not use labels in our example programs because we do not use goto statements; so labels are not discussed further.

The Const Declaration. The second kind of identifier is a *constant*, whose value does not change during the execution of the program. A constant identifies a mailbox or memory location, very much like a variable, but the mailbox may contain only a single, nonchangeable value. This section of the declaration block must start with the reserved word const; it uses the equal sign (=) to associate each constant identifier with its constant value. Here is an example of a constant declaration section.

```
const
  PI = 3.14159;
  THISYEAR = 1987;
  PROMPT = 'Yes or No?';
  FLAG = false;
```

Note that no type is explicitly declared for each constant, although one can determine from the context that PI must be of type real, FLAG of type boolean, and so forth. Remember that the value of a constant cannot be changed during the execution of a program. Constants make a program more readable; the identifier PI has more meaning than the value 3.14159. We usually write constant names in uppercase characters.

Turbo Pascal Note

The underscore character (_) is an allowed character in Turbo Pascal identifier names. We commonly use it to separate words in a constant name consisting of two or more words. Thus, the constant THISYEAR, shown in the previous example, can be written as THIS_YEAR.

In Turbo Pascal, you can either use the predefined function Pi or declare a global constant PI. The global constant must be declared in most other implementations of Pascal. The function Pi is preferable in Turbo Pascal because it has greater precision, up to 19 digits in Version 5. If you declare a constant PI, it supersedes the predeclared function Pi.

The Type Declaration.   The third kind of identifier in the declaration block is a *type*; that is, a new kind or type of variable, not one of the standard types. This section starts with the reserved word type. We introduce and discuss user-defined types in Chapter 8.

The Var Declaration.   The fourth kind of identifier in the declaration block is a *variable*, which we have already discussed. As you know, this section starts with the reserved word var.

In standard Pascal, the label section must come first in the declaration block, followed by the const section, the type section, and finally the var section. There can be only one of each kind of section.

Turbo Pascal Note

This requirement on the ordered position of each section is not enforced in Turbo Pascal; the sections can be written in any order in a declaration block. Any section can be repeated; that is, there can be two or more const sections, two or more var sections, and so forth. All declaration sections, however, must appear within a declaration block, located outside the main program block or any subprogram statement block.

We recommend that you follow the ordering rules of standard Pascal when writing declaration blocks.

These comments on declaration blocks apply to the global declaration block and to each declaration block in a subprogram.

To demonstrate the use of constants, we present an example program that calculates the speed in miles per hour when a measured distance in feet is traversed in a certain number of seconds. Two constants are used to convert between feet and miles, and between seconds and hours.

```
PROGRAM EX0503 (Input, Output);
{
   Enter the elapsed time to traverse a measured
   distance and calculate the speed in miles per hour.
}
const
   FEET_PER_MILE = 5280;
   SECONDS_PER_HOUR = 3600;
var
   Distance, Time, Speed: real;

BEGIN
   Write ('Measured distance in feet? ');
   Readln (Distance);
   Write ('Elapsed time in seconds? ');
   Readln (Time);
   Distance: = Distance / FEET_PER_MILE;
   Time: = Time / SECONDS_PER_HOUR;
   Speed: = Distance / Time;
   Writeln ('Speed is ', Speed:3:1, ' MPH');
END.
```

The following user interaction is produced:

```
Measured distance in feet? 500
Elapsed time in seconds? 7.46
Speed is 45.7 MPH
```

Subprogram Blocks

Each subprogram is like a miniature program. It has a heading statement, its own local declaration block, and a program block consisting of one or more statements enclosed within begin and end brackets. There are two kinds of subprograms in Pascal, the *function* subprogram and the *procedure* subprogram.

Definition of a Function.   **A function is a subprogram that performs some calculation and returns a value.** The value can then be used in other parts of the program. A function starts with the FUNCTION statement containing the name of the function; it may contain its own declaration block, and begins and ends its block of program statements with begin and end brackets. This subprogram is the user-defined function we mentioned earlier, not a standard function.

Definition of a Procedure.   **A procedure is a subprogram that carries out some task; it does something.** It starts with a PROCEDURE statement containing the name of the procedure; it may contain its own declaration block, and begins and ends its block of program statements with begin and end brackets.

Every subprogram can be used by the main program to calculate a value or carry out a task. The main program *calls* or accesses each subprogram by name whenever it wants to use that particular subprogram.

We explained that each subprogram can have its own declaration block. Constants and variables defined and declared in this block are called *local constants and variables*, and are known only within the subprogram. Constants are usually defined in the global declaration block, but variables are commonly declared in both the global declaration block (making them known everywhere) and in the individual subprogram declaration blocks (where they are local and known only in that subprogram). **A global variable, declared in the main declaration block, may have the same name as a local variable declared in a subprogram declaration block. The program, however, treats these two variables as completely different and distinct identifiers.** Section 9.2 discusses global and local variables in more detail.

Communication with Subprograms

Information is passed to a subprogram from the calling program (usually the main program) through *parameters*. For example, a function to calculate the cube of a number will have to know the value of the number to be cubed. This number is a parameter of the function. The value of the calculation (in this case, the cube of the number) is associated with the function name. We say that the function *returns* this value to the calling program.

Function Subprograms

Here is an example of a function subprogram:

```
FUNCTION Cube (Number: real): real;
begin
  Cube:= Number * Number * Number;
end;
```

The FUNCTION heading statement contains the name of the function (Cube) and the name of the parameter (Number) within parentheses. The type of each parameter and the function itself must be declared; in this case, both Cube and Number are of type real.

The function body in our example consists of a single executable statement, enclosed in begin and end brackets. A value is calculated, in this case the cube of Number, and that value is assigned to the function name or identifier Cube. **Every function subprogram must contain an assignment statement of this kind.**

The end bracket is followed by a semicolon, separating this subprogram from the following subprogram or the main program. Remember that only one end bracket in a Pascal program can be followed by a period, and that is the END bracket at the end of the main program.

We now include this new function in a short example program.

```
PROGRAM EX0504 (Input, Output);
{
   Calculate the volume of gas required to fill
   a balloon of given diameter.
}
const
   PI = 3.14159;
var
   Diameter, Radius, Volume: real;

FUNCTION Cube (Number: real): real;
{
   Calculate the cube of a number.
}
begin
   Cube:= Number * Number * Number;
end;  { Cube }

BEGIN  { Main Program }
   Write ('Diameter of balloon in feet? ');
   Readln (Diameter);
   Radius:= Diameter / 2.0;
   Volume:= (4.0 * PI * Cube(Radius)) / 3.0;
   Writeln ('You need ', Volume:1:0,
            ' cubic feet of gas.');
END.
```

This program starts executing with the first statement in the main program. The user is asked to enter a value for the diameter. Note that the variables Diameter, Radius, and Volume are all global variables, known throughout the entire program. The balloon radius is calculated and then the volume. The latter calculation makes use of the global constant PI and the function Cube. Note that comments are used to identify the end of the function and the start of the main program.

The function Cube is called by the use of its name in an expression. It is called with the parameter Radius, whose value has just been calculated. The value of Radius is passed to the local variable Number in the function subprogram, so that Radius and Number both have the same value. Using this value, the cube of

Number is calculated and the result is passed back to the main program through the function named Cube.

For example, if Diameter is given a value of 4.0, Radius has a value of 2.0, Number also has a value of 2.0, and Cube has a value of 8.0.

The parameter variable Number is often called the *formal parameter* of Cube, while the parameter variable Radius is called the *actual parameter*. This type of parameter is further identified as a *value parameter* because a value is passed from the main program to the function.

Going back to the example program, once the cube of Radius has been calculated, it is a simple task to calculate and display the volume of the balloon. The following user interaction is produced:

```
Diameter of balloon in feet? 25.0
You need 8181 cubic feet of gas.
```

Turbo Pascal Note

In Turbo Pascal, the standard function Pi can be used in the expression for calculating the value of variable Volume, and the declared constant PI is not needed.

Here is another example of an arithmetic function that calculates the result of raising a number to a power.

```
FUNCTION Power (Number, Exponent: real): real;
{
   This function returns the value of the variable Number
   raised to the Exponent power. It is the Pascal
   substitute for an exponentiation operator. Number
   must be a positive number.
}
begin
   Power := Exp(Exponent * Ln(Number));
end;  { Power }
```

If this function is used in a program, Power(4,3) (which is 4 cubed or raised to the power of 3) has a value of 64.0.

The Function Statement

The syntax of the FUNCTION heading statement is

```
FUNCTION Name (Parameter List): Function Type;
```

where Name is the function name, and Parameter List is a list of formal parameter variables and their types. The type of the function is denoted by Function Type. **All parameter variables are local variables.** Here are three more examples of function statements.

```
FUNCTION BoxVol (Height, Length, Width: real): real;

FUNCTION Poisson (Lambda: real; N: integer): real;

FUNCTION Altitude (Time: real; Model: char;
                   CutoffTime: integer): real;
```

Note that parameter variables of the same type are grouped together with their names separated by commas. Lists of parameter variables of the same type are separated from each other by semicolons. There is only one set of parentheses enclosing all formal parameters.

The following example program calls the function BoxVol.

```
PROGRAM EX0505 (Output);
{
   Calculate the weight of a box
   of given dimensions.
}
const
   DENSITY = 13.5;        { lbs/cu ft   }
   IN3_PER_FT3 = 1728;    { cu in/cu ft }
var
   BoxWeight: real;       { lbs }
   L: real;               { in  }

FUNCTION BoxVol (Height, Length, Width: real): real;
{
   Calculate the volume of a box.
}
begin
   BoxVol:= Height * Length * Width;
end; { BoxVol }

BEGIN { Main Program }
   L:= 33.0;                  { inches }
   BoxWeight:= DENSITY / IN3_PER_FT3
               * BoxVol(10.0, L, L/2);
   Writeln ('Weight of box is ', BoxWeight:1:1,
            ' pounds');
END.
```

The actual parameters, as shown, can be either variables, constant values, or expressions. The number, order, and type of the actual parameters must agree with the list of formal parameters. In this example, the constant value 10.0 is assigned to Height, the value of variable L is assigned to variable Length, and the value of expression L/2 is assigned to variable Width. The following output is produced:

```
Weight of box is 42.5 pounds
```

The function type can be any one of the simple types we have already discussed; integer, real, character, or boolean. **It cannot be one of the structured types**, such as array or record, that we will introduce in later chapters.

Turbo Pascal Note

In Turbo Pascal, functions can be declared whose type is string. We discuss string types and string variables in Chapter 8.

These simple example programs contain functions with only a single executable statement. It is common, however, for a function to contain several executable statements, as shown in the next example program. We use such a function to calculate the sum of a mathematical series. Here is an outline of the program

> Set number of terms in series, LIMIT, to 10
> Ask user to enter value of X
> Calculate function Y = f(X)
> Display value of Y

where the function Y is calculated from the following outline:

> Set value of temporary variable to zero
> For index I having a value of 1 through LIMIT
>   Calculate numerator of term
>   Calculate denominator of term
>   Calculate term in series and add to temporary variable
> Assign value of temporary variable to function Y

The example program is as follows:

```
PROGRAM EX0506 (Input, Output);
{
   Ask a user to enter a value for X
   and calculate the value of the function Y.
}
const
   LIMIT = 10;   { no. of terms in series }
var
   X: real;      { independent variable   }

FUNCTION Y (X: real; N: integer): real;
{
   Calculate the sum of the series
```

$$Y = \sum_{i=1}^{N} \frac{x^i}{i+1}$$

```
}
var
   I: integer;
   Numerator, Denominator, Result: real;
```

```
begin
  Result: = 0.0;  { initialize Result }
  for I: = 1 to N do
    begin
    Numerator: = Exp(I * Ln(X));
    Denominator: = I + 1;
    Result: = Result + (Numerator / Denominator);
    end;
  Y: = Result;
end;  { Y }

BEGIN  { Main Program }
  Write ('Value of X? ');
  Readln (X);
  Writeln ('Sum of series is ', Y(X, LIMIT):1:3);
END.
```

The constant LIM IT specifies the number of terms in the series to be summed. Variables Numerator and Denominator are used to store intermediate results. We make use of the expression given earlier in this chapter for raising a number X to the power I. This program produces the following results.

```
Value of X? 1.5
Sum of series is 20.319
```

Note that we use a local variable, Result, in the function to accumulate the sum of the terms. If you try to use the function name, Y, for this purpose, you will get an error. The function name cannot be used in expressions, as can a variable name, but can (and must) appear at least once in the function body, on the left side of an assignment statement where it is assigned a value.

The Procedure Statement

Procedure subprograms are very similar to function subprograms. Information is passed from the main program to the subprogram using actual parameter and formal parameter lists. Procedures start with the PROCED URE heading statement that defines the procedure name. In contrast to functions, there is no value associated with the procedure name and, thus, no type declaration of that name.

A procedure is called by using its name as a program statement. The actual parameters must be listed in parentheses after the procedure name. These actual parameters must match the formal parameters by number, order, and type. Actual parameters can be constants, variables, or expressions, but **formal parameters must be variables.**

The syntax of the PROCEDU RE statement is given by

```
PROCEDURE Name (Parameter List);
```

where Name is the procedure name, and Parameter List is a list of formal parameter variables. All parameter variables are local variables.

Let us consider a simple procedure that displays a line consisting of a number of identical characters. There are two formal parameters, the number of characters and the character itself. Here is the procedure.

```
PROCEDURE DisplayRow (Symbol: char; Number: integer);
{
   Display a row of Number characters.
   The desired character is denoted by Symbol.
}
var
   Count: integer;

begin
  for Count:= 1 to Number do
    Write (Symbol);
  Writeln;
end;  { DisplayRow }
```

The name of the procedure is DisplayRow. Two formal parameters are declared, Symbol and Number, that are both local variables. The local variable Count is also declared in the procedure. Note that the procedure name never appears in the body of the procedure; it cannot have a value assigned to it.

The next example program uses this procedure to display a rectangle of asterisks, twenty characters wide and four characters deep.

```
PROGRAM EX0507 (Output);
{
   Display a rectangle of asterisks, twenty
   characters wide and four characters deep.
}
const
   MAX_COL = 20;
   MAX_ROW = 4;
var
   Row: integer;

PROCEDURE DisplayRow (Symbol: char; Number: integer);
{
   Display a row of Number characters.
   Desired character is denoted by Symbol.
}
var
   Count: integer;
begin
   for Count:= 1 to Number do
     Write (Symbol);
   Writeln;
end;  { DisplayRow }

BEGIN  { Main Program }
   for Row:= 1 to MAX_ROW do
     DisplayRow ('*', MAX_COL);
END.
```

Here are the results of our program:

```
* * * * * * * * * * * * * * * * * * * * *
* * * * * * * * * * * * * * * * * * * * *
* * * * * * * * * * * * * * * * * * * * *
* * * * * * * * * * * * * * * * * * * * *
```

The procedure is called by listing its name as a statement. Note that both of the actual parameters are constants; one a literal constant and the other a named constant. Both formal parameters must be variables. The local variables Symbol, Number, and Count cannot be accessed from the main program.

Note that a subprogram, whether a procedure or function, can be called many times, as shown in the previous program. In fact, one of the advantages of a subprogram is that the statements it contains need to be written only once but can be used many times.

Procedures and Variable Parameters

The value parameters we have used in previous example programs permit a one-way transfer of information from a calling program to a procedure or function. Because information is transferred in only one direction, there is no way that changes to variable values in the subprogram can affect variables in the calling program. These latter variables are protected or isolated from such changes, called *side effects*.

Another type of parameter is the *variable parameter* which allows a two-way exchange of information between a calling program and a procedure or function. In practice, variable parameters are used mainly with procedures.

The syntax of a procedure heading statement with variable parameters is

```
PROCEDURE Name (var Parameter List: type; ...);
```

where there can be many parameter lists of the same or different types. Lists of value parameters and variable parameters can be mixed in a single procedure heading. **The actual parameters associated with var formal parameters must be variables, they cannot be constants or expressions.** For the time being, we will use variable parameters only when we wish to establish two-way communications with a procedure through its parameters. Other aspects of both value and variable parameters are discussed in Chapter 8.

We next show three versions of a program that uses a procedure to read information from a text file. The first version relies entirely on global variables. The second and third versions use local variables consisting of variable parameters, as well as global variables. **A program is more readable, and less subject to error, if information is passed between subprograms and the main program using parameters (possibly with global variables) rather than global variables alone.**

Program EX0508 uses global variables A and B when reading the file. Looking at the first statement, ReadFile, in the main program, there is no indication what values will be read from the file. This style of program design is acceptable for a short program, but makes a long program difficult to read.

```
PROGRAM EX0508 (Output);
{
  Use only global variables to read data from
  a text file.
}
var
  A, B: integer;  { global variables }


PROCEDURE ReadFile;
{
  Open and read the file.
}
var
  InFile: text;
begin
  Assign (InFile, 'ORDERS.DAT');
  Reset (InFile);
  Readln (InFile, A);
  Readln (InFile, B);
end;  { ReadFile }


BEGIN  { Main Program }
  ReadFile;
  Writeln ('Value of A is ', A:1);
  Writeln ('Value of B is ', B:1);
END.
```

Program EX0509 uses variable parameters with the ReadFile procedure. This technique makes the program easier to read. When you look at the main program, you know at once that ReadFile uses the global variables A and B as actual parameters. When you look at the procedure heading, you see that local variables A and B are formal var parameters and are used to return information read from the file to the main program.

```
PROGRAM EX0509 (Output);
{
  Use variable parameters and global variables
  to read data from a text file.
}
var
  A, B: integer;  { global variables }


PROCEDURE ReadFile (var A, B: integer);
{
  Open and read the file.
  Formal parameter variables A and B
  are local variables.
}
```

```
var
  InFile: text;
begin
  Assign (InFile, 'ORDERS.DAT');
  Reset (InFile);
  Readln (InFile, A);
  Readln (InFile, B);
end;  { ReadFile }

BEGIN  { Main Program }
  ReadFile (A, B);
  Writeln ('Value of A is ', A:1);
  Writeln ('Value of B is ', B:1);
END.
```

In the previous program, global variable A and local variable A both refer to the same memory location. Global variable B and local variable B also use the same memory location, different from that used by A.

Program EX0510 includes a procedure ReadFile that might be a library procedure, not written by the programmer. Procedure ReadFile has different formal parameter variable names, X and Y. The program still runs properly, however, with global variable A and local variable X referring to a single memory location and global variable B and local variable Y referring to a single location. Thus, this third version of the program is written with different names for corresponding local and global variables.

```
PROGRAM EX0510 (Output);
{
  Use variable parameters and global variables
  to read data from a text file.
}
var
  A, B: integer;  { global variables }

PROCEDURE ReadFile (var X, Y: integer);
{
  Open and read the file.
  Formal parameter variables X and Y
  are local variables, corresponding
  to global variables A and B.
}
var
  InFile: text;
begin
  Assign (InFile, 'ORDERS.DAT');
  Reset (InFile);
  Readln (InFile, X);
  Readln (InFile, Y);
end;  { ReadFile }
```

```
BEGIN  { Main Program }
  ReadFile (A, B);
  Writeln ('Value of A is ', A:1);
  Writeln ('Value of B is ', B:1);
END.
```

Turbo Pascal Note

In Turbo Pascal, it is possible to place a variable declaration block anywhere outside a subprogram body of statements or the main program body of statements. For example, a variable declaration block could be placed just before the BEGIN bracket of the main program, following all functions and procedures. Any variables declared in this block would not be global variables in the sense we have used the term previously. These variables would be local to the main program and, thus, known and available only in the main program.

Here is the previous program using local variables in both the procedure and the main program.

```
PROGRAM EX0511 (Output);
{
  Use variable parameters and local variables in
  the main program to read data from a text file.
}

PROCEDURE ReadFile (var A, B: integer);
{
  Open and read the file. Formal parameter
  variables A and B are local procedure variables,
  corresponding to local main variables A and B.
}
var
  InFile: text;
begin
  Assign (InFile, 'ORDERS.DAT');
  Reset (InFile);
  Readln (InFile, A);
  Readln (InFile, B);
end;  { ReadFile }

var
  A, B: integer;  { local to main program }
BEGIN  { Main Program }
  ReadFile (A, B);
  Writeln ('Value of A is ', A:1);
  Writeln ('Value of B is ', B:1);
END.
```

The structure of Program EX0511 is restricted to Turbo Pascal and possibly a few other Pascal compilers. We do not, however, consider it good programming practice. We recommend that you follow the structure of standard Pascal when writing declaration blocks. All constant, type, and variable definitions and declarations, other than those within subprograms, should be placed at the beginning of a program. The identifiers so defined and declared are then all global identifiers, known throughout the program.

Each one of this sequence of programs produces the following output:

```
Value of A is 37
Value of B is 140
```

IMPORTANT POINTS

- Trigonometric functions require that angle parameters be in radians.
- A function is a subprogram that performs some calculation and returns a value.
- A procedure is a subprogram that carries out some task; it does something.
- A global variable may have the same name as a local variable, but the program will treat them as two different variables.
- Every function subprogram must contain an assignment statement that assigns a value to the function.
- A Pascal program always starts executing with the first statement in the main program.
- Formal parameters of subprograms must be variables.
- A function cannot have a structured type like array or record. In Turbo Pascal, functions of type string are allowed.
- Value parameters pass information in one direction, from the calling program to the subprogram. Variable parameters pass information in both directions between the calling program and the subprogram.
- All formal parameter variables are local variables.
- The actual parameters associated with formal var parameters must be variables; they cannot be constants or expressions.
- A program is more readable and less subject to error if information is passed between subprograms and the main program using parameters (possibly with global variables) rather than global variables alone.

SELF-STUDY QUESTIONS

1. What is a Pascal expression for X raised to the Y power?
2. (a) In standard Pascal, what is the required order of the various sections that make up the main declaration block?
   (b) What is the required order in Turbo Pascal?

3. What is the difference between a declared constant and a declared variable?

4. What is meant by a global constant?

5. Is a specific type associated with the identifier representing
   (a) a function;
   (b) a procedure?

6. What punctuation mark, if any, follows the final end statement in
   (a) a function or procedure;
   (b) the main program?

7. What is meant by a local variable?

8. If a global variable declared in the main declaration block and a nonparameter local variable declared in a subprogram declaration block have the same name, can they both refer to the same memory location? Explain your answer.

9. If a function named Cube has a type of real, how is a value associated with the identifier Cube?

10. If a program has a procedure named Sign that is called from the main program, can it also have a global variable named Sign? Explain your answer.

11. Can an actual value parameter be
   (a) a constant;
   (b) a variable;
   (c) an expression?

12. Can a formal value parameter be
   (a) a constant;
   (b) a variable;
   (c) an expression?

PRACTICE PROGRAMS

1. A text file named COST.DAT contains information on fuel cost and fuel conversion efficiency for three electrical generating plants. There are two values in the file for each plant; each value is on a separate line. The first value is fuel cost in dollars per megaBTU. The second value, in megaBTUs per megawatt-hour, is a measure of fuel conversion efficiency.
The contents of COST.DAT is as follows:

```
0.85
8.560
2.37
14.075
0.69
10.300
```

Read the information for each plant, calculate the unit cost in cents per kilowatt-hour, and display a two-column table showing the plant number (1, 2, or 3) and unit cost.
   Use a function for calculating the cost and a procedure for displaying the result for each plant. Use variable parameters if appropriate.

2. Engineers measure refrigerator performance by a coefficient of performance (COP), given by the formula

$$\text{COP} = \frac{T_i}{T_r - T_i}$$

where T_i is the temperature inside the refrigerator and T_r is the room temperature. These temperatures must be in degrees Rankin, where degrees Rankin equals 459.7 plus degrees Fahrenheit.

Assume the inside temperature is always maintained at 38 degrees F. Ask a user to enter room temperature in summer and winter, and display the refrigerator COP for each season. Your display should look like the following:

```
Summer room temperature? 85
Winter room temperature? 65

Refrigerator COP in summer is 10.6
Refrigerator COP in winter is 18.4
```

Test your program using summer and winter room temperatures of 85 and 65 and of 75 and 70.

3. While the trigonometric functions of Pascal require angles to be expressed in radians, most engineers measure angles in degrees. Write a function to convert an angle in degrees into radians. Write another function to calculate the tangent of an angle measured in radians, using the standard Pascal functions.

Use your functions in a test program that asks a user to enter an angle in degrees, and then displays the tangent of the angle. An appropriate prompt and label must be included. Test using angles of 45, 180, and 215 degrees.

4. In a classical experiment in physics, standing waves in a cylindrical waveguide cavity were used to measure the velocity of electromagnetic waves (that is, the speed of light). The waveguide wavelength λ_g is given by the expression

$$\lambda_g = \frac{2L}{N}$$

where L is the length of the cavity and N is the number of standing half-waves in the cavity at resonance. The free-space wavelength, λ, is related to the waveguide wavelength by the expression

$$\lambda_g = \frac{\lambda}{\sqrt{1 - \left(\dfrac{\lambda}{KR}\right)^2}}$$

where R is the radius of the cavity and K is a geometric constant, equal to 1.64062 for a waveguide with a circular cross-section.

At resonance, the physicists found eight half-waves in a cavity of radius 3.25876 cm and of length 15.64574 cm. The resonant frequency was measured at 9.4983 gigahertz $(9.4983E + 9$ hertz).

Using these theoretical expressions and experimental data, calculate the speed of light using the relationship

$$\text{Speed} = \text{Frequency} \times \text{Wavelength}$$

5. The velocity of small water waves is given by the formula

$$V = \sqrt{\frac{2\pi T}{Ld} + \frac{gL}{2\pi}}$$

where T is the surface tension of the water in newtons per meter and L is the wavelength of the wave in meters. The constant d is water density and has a value of 1000 kg/m^3. The gravitational constant g has a value of 9.8 m/sec^2.

Ask a user to enter values for surface tension and wavelength, and calculate the wave velocity in meters per second.

Test your program using a surface tension of 0.075 N/m and a wavelength of 0.5 m.

6. Write a function that calculates the volume of a pyramid, using the formula

Volume = (1/3) × Area of base × Altitude

Use this function in a program that calculates the cost of materials for building a pyramid from standard solid cinder blocks (16 inches by 8 inches by 8 inches). Assume a 15% additional number of blocks to allow for waste when surface blocks are sawed and trimmed. Assume 10% of block cost for mortar. These two percentages should be entered in the program as declared constants so that they can be changed easily.

Ask a user to enter the dimensions of a pyramid and the unit cost of cinder blocks. Write a procedure, with the number of blocks and the unit block cost as parameters. It should display a table showing the number of blocks, the cost of blocks, cost of mortar, and total cost.

Test your program for a pyramid whose width and depth is 40 meters and whose height is 30 meters. Cinder blocks cost $1.77 per block.

7. Write a procedure with three parameters that displays two lines of characters. The first parameter specifies the character to be displayed, while the second specifies the number of characters in a line. The third parameter specifies the number of blanks to be displayed before the first printing character is displayed. Use this procedure in a program to create the cross-section diagram of an I beam, as shown.

Assume the space between asterisks represents one inch in a vertical direction and one-half inch in a horizontal direction. Test your program by displaying an I beam that is 16 inches high and 5 inches wide.

6

MODULAR AND TOP-DOWN PROGRAM DESIGN

6.1 INTRODUCTION

We discuss modular programming and top-down program design. We use these techniques to design and write a nontrivial Pascal program. We look at additional features of the Turbo Pascal debugger. We also discuss the importance of thorough program testing after a program has been designed and written.

6.2 PROGRAM DESIGN

A program that is designed and written as a sequence of small, relatively-independent units is called a *modular program*. Such a program is easy to write if each module is kept small and simple. It is usually possible to test each module independently as the program is being written, and if all the modules work properly, the chances are good that the entire program will also work.

As part of the program design process, **a written program outline should be developed that lists the major tasks to be accomplished**. This outline serves as a model for the main Pascal program, while the individual tasks are written as subprograms. Program design that starts in this way from an outline is called *top-down program design*.

98

These two principles, top-down program design and modular program construction, are strongly recommended as principles to follow as you write programs. The time required to produce a program is reduced because when error-free modules are used, there will be few if any errors in the final program. The resulting program will be easy to read and, thus, easy to maintain and modify. By careful selection of subprogram names, the main program serves as a self-documenting outline of the program.

We now illustrate this type of program development by considering a set of program specifications.

Program Specifications

A manufacturer of bowling balls produces two types of balls. The type A ball is 7.5 inches in diameter, while the type B ball is 9.5 inches in diameter. A text file named ORDERS.DAT contains two numbers; the first is the number of type A balls that have been ordered, and the second number is the number of type B balls.

Given a plastic material of a known density, the problem is to find out how much material should be purchased to fill the order for bowling balls. Assume that there will be a ten percent waste of material during manufacturing and that the material is available only in 100-pound bags. The amount of material that must be purchased is written on a text file named MATERIAL.DAT and also displayed on the screen.

Program Outline

Here is an outline of the problem:

> Read the order file.
> Calculate the material needed for type A balls.
> Calculate the material needed for type B balls.
> Calculate how much material to purchase.
> Write the material purchase request on a file.
> Tell the user what has happened.

6.3 PROGRAM FORMAT STYLE

There are many different opinions on how a Pascal program should be formatted. We have our own choice of a format style that is readable, but still compact. We use this style consistently in the example programs.

The reserved words PROGRAM, PROCEDURE, and FUNCTION are written in uppercase letters, as are the BEGIN and END words surrounding the main program. We usually place a comment after BEGIN to identify the beginning of the main program. All other reserved words are written in lowercase letters.

System and user-defined constants are written in uppercase characters, mostly letters, using underscore characters (_) where needed to separate English words. Examples of constant names are DENSITY and DIAM_A. Predefined and user-defined types are written in lowercase characters, again using underscores if needed. Example predefined type names are integer and real. We discuss user-defined types in Chapter 8.

Other system and user-defined identifiers, including names of variables, programs, and subprograms, are written in lowercase characters with the first letter of each word capitalized. An example variable name is Symbol. Example procedure names are Writeln and ReadFile. An example program name is MyFirstProgram.

We use a standard indentation of two spaces. A larger indentation makes a program more readable, but tends to push long program statements off the right edge of the screen or paper. We indent all statements between the primary begin and end brackets of a program or subprogram. We also indent all statements (including the begin and end brackets of compound statements) that are controlled by various looping and branching structures. The best way to learn this style of formatting is to look at the example programs in this and subsequent chapters.

If you are learning Pascal in a class, your instructor may have special requirements on how your programs must be formatted. If not, we recommend the style used in our example programs.

6.4 DEVELOPING THE PROGRAM

We now develop a complete program to solve our problem, written from the preceding outline and using subprogram modules. First look at the main program.

```
PROGRAM EX0601 (Output);
{
  This is an incomplete version of the program,
  containing only the global declaration block and
  the main program. None of the procedures or
  functions are shown.
  ***********************************
  ** THIS PROGRAM WILL NOT COMPILE **
  ***********************************
}
const
  DENSITY = 0.037;   { of ball material, lbs/cu in  }
  DIAM_A = 7.5;      { diameter of type A balls, in }
  DIAM_B = 9.5;      { diameter of type B balls, in }
var
  NumTypeA: integer;  { number of type A balls ordered }
  NumTypeB: integer;  { number of type B balls ordered }
  TotalAmt: real;     { lbs of material for balls }
  OrderAmt: real;     { lbs of material ordered   }
```

```
BEGIN  { Main Program }
  ReadOrderFile (NumTypeA, NumTypeB);
  Writeln ('The order file has been read.');
  TotalAmt: = MaterialNeeded(DIAM_A, NumTypeA)
            + MaterialNeeded(DIAM_B, NumTypeB);
  OrderAmt: = BagLot(TotalAmt);
  WriteMaterialFile (OrderAmt);
  DisplayResults (NumTypeA, NumTypeB,
                  TotalAmt, OrderAmt);
END.
```

Note how closely the main program follows the outline. The first procedure, ReadOrderFile, reads a file for the number of type A and type B
balls that have been ordered. The function MaterialNeeded calculates the total
amount of material needed. The function BagLot converts this total amount to the
amount that should be purchased, allowing for waste and bag size. The procedure
WriteMaterialFile then writes the amount that should be purchased on a file.
Finally, the procedure DisplayResults tells the user what has taken place.

We next look at this example program with the first procedure included and a
modified main program. We have placed comment brackets around those statements
in the main program that call subprograms other than ReadOrderFile. This technique is called *commenting out* unwanted statements during program development.
Note that extra statements have been inserted in the main program so that intermediate results can be displayed.

```
PROGRAM EX0602 (Output);
{
  The first stage in developing this program.
  One procedure and a modified main program
  are included.
}
const
  DENSITY = 0.037;    { of ball material, lbs/cu in  }
  DIAM_A = 7.5;       { diameter of type A balls, in }
  DIAM_B = 9.5;       { diameter of type B balls, in }
var
  NumTypeA: integer;  { number of type A balls ordered }
  NumTypeB: integer;  { number of type B balls ordered }
  TotalAmt: real;     { lbs of material for balls }
  OrderAmt: real;     { lbs of material ordered   }

PROCEDURE ReadOrderFile (var NumTypeA,
                             NumTypeB: integer);
{
  Read the number of balls ordered, of type A and
  type B, from the text file ORDERS.DAT.
}
```

```
var
  InFile: text;
begin
  Assign (InFile, 'ORDERS.DAT');
  Reset (InFile);
  Readln (InFile, NumTypeA);
  Readln (InFile, NumTypeB);
  Close (InFile);
  end;  { ReadOrderFile }

BEGIN  { Main Program }
  ReadOrderFile (NumTypeA, NumTypeB);
  Writeln (NumTypeA);  { temporary }
  Writeln (NumTypeB);  { statements }
  Writeln ('The order file has been read.');
(* COMMENT OUT A BLOCK
  TotalAmt:= MaterialNeeded(DIAM_A, NumTypeA)
              + MaterialNeeded(DIAM_A, NumTypeB);
  OrderAmt:= BagLot(TotalAmt);
  WriteMaterialFile (OrderAmt);
  DisplayResults (NumTypeA, NumTypeB,
                  TotalAmt, OrderAmt);
DOWN TO HERE *)
END.
```

Note the variable parameters NumTypeA and NumTypeB in procedure ReadOrderFile. These parameters are used to return the values read from the file to the main program.

When this program is run, if the file exists and is read correctly, the values of NumTypeA and NumTypeB will be displayed by the two temporary Writeln statements. Once the program in this simplified form is working properly, you can be reasonably certain that procedure ReadOrderFile is correct and will do its proper job in the final program.

The process can be continued, adding subprograms one after another and testing the resulting program after each addition. As before, temporary Writeln statements may be needed to display intermediate results, and the comment brackets must be changed to comment out fewer and fewer subprograms.

Finally, we show a listing of the program in its finished form. Careful choice of subprogram names, plus comments, should provide adequate documentation so any programmer can read and understand the program.

```
PROGRAM EX0603 (Output);
{
  A manufacturer of bowling balls produces two types
  of balls. Type A is 7.5 inches in diameter and
  type B is 9.5 inches in diameter. The total orders
  for each type are stored in file ORDERS.DAT. Using
  material of a given density, this program calculates
```

```
  the weight of material needed and the weight of
  material to purchase, assuming the material is
  shipped in 100-pound bags. The amount of material
  to purchase is written on file MATERIAL.DAT.
}
const
  DENSITY = 0.037;    { of ball material, lbs/cu in  }
  DIAM_A = 7.5;       { diameter of type A balls, in }
  DIAM_B = 9.5;       { diameter of type B balls, in }
var
  NumTypeA: integer;  { number of type A balls ordered }
  NumTypeB: integer;  { number of type B balls ordered }
  TotalAmt: real;     { lbs of material for balls }
  OrderAmt: real;     { lbs of material ordered   }

PROCEDURE ReadOrderFile (var NumTypeA, NumTypeB: integer);
{
  Read the number of balls ordered, of type A and
  type B, from the text file ORDERS.DAT.
}
var
  InFile: text;
begin
  Assign (InFile, 'ORDERS.DAT');
  Reset (InFile);
  Readln (InFile, NumTypeA);
  Readln (InFile, NumTypeB);
  Close (InFile);
end;  { ReadOrderFile }

FUNCTION MaterialNeeded (Diameter: real;
                         Number: real): real;
{
  Calculate the material needed for a given number
  of balls, of given diameter and material density.
}
var
  Radius, Volume: real;
begin
  Radius:= Diameter / 2;
  Volume:= (4.0 * Pi * Radius * Radius * Radius) / 3;
  MaterialNeeded:= Number * DENSITY * Volume;
end;   { MaterialNeeded }

FUNCTION BagLot (Amount: real): real;
{
  Increase amount to allow for waste and
  round to the number of 100-pound bags.
}
```

```
begin
  Amount:=Amount / 0.9;  { allow for 10% waste }
  BagLot:=(Trunc(Amount / 100.0) + 1.0) * 100.0;
end;  { BagLot }

PROCEDURE WriteMaterialFile (Amount: real);
{
  Write the amount of material to be purchased
  on the text file MATERIAL.DAT.
}
var
  OutFile: text;
begin
  Assign (OutFile, 'MATERIAL.DAT');
  Rewrite (OutFile);
  Writeln (OutFile, Amount:1:0);
  Close (OutFile);
end;  { WriteMaterialFile }

PROCEDURE DisplayResults (NumberA, NumberB: integer;
                          TotalAmt, OrderAmt: real);
{
  Display the number of bowling balls ordered
  and the amount of material needed.
}
begin
  Writeln;
  Write ('To make ', NumberA:1);
  Write (' bowling balls of type A and ');
  Writeln (NumberB:1, ' of type B');
  Write ('requires ', TotalAmt:1:0, ' pounds');
  Writeln (' of material. You should order');
  Write (OrderAmt:1:0, ' pounds of material');
  Writeln (' in 100-pound bags.');
  Writeln;
  Write ('The file for purchasing materials');
  Writeln (' has been written.');
end;  { DisplayResults }

BEGIN  { Main Program }
  ReadOrderFile (NumTypeA, NumTypeB);
  Writeln ('The order file has been read.');
  TotalAmt:=MaterialNeeded(DIAM_A, NumTypeA)
            + MaterialNeeded(DIAM_B, NumTypeB);
  OrderAmt:=BagLot(TotalAmt);
  WriteMaterialFile (OrderAmt);
  DisplayResults (NumTypeA, NumTypeB,
                  TotalAmt, OrderAmt);
END.
```

This program produces the following display:

```
The order file has been read.

To make 37 bowling balls of type A and 140 of type B
requires 2628 pounds of material. You should order
3000 pounds of material in 100-pound bags.

The file for purchasing materials has been written.
```

Note the use of named constants in the function `MaterialNeeded`. `DIAM_A` and `DIAM_B` are passed as parameter values to the local variable `Diameter,` because the two calls to the function require different bowling ball diameters. `DENSITY` is used as a global constant because all bowling balls are made of material with the same density.

6.5 MORE ON PROGRAM DEBUGGING

We return here to our discussion of source code debuggers, and examine some of their more advanced capabilities.

Turbo Pascal Note

Now that we have learned more about Pascal programming, and have seen some of the special features of Turbo Pascal, we shall look again at the Turbo Pascal, Version 5, debugger.

Debugging Subprograms

We are now writing programs with subprograms; functions and procedures. In many cases the subprograms have been thoroughly debugged before the whole program is put together. In such cases, we are interested in debugging the main program and skipping over the subprograms.

Pressing the F7 key performs a single-step trace through an entire program, including all subprograms and the initialization statements at the beginning of any included unit. Pressing the F8 key, on the other hand, performs the same trace but skips over all subprogram statements and initialization code.

When debugging short programs, or on the first attempt to debug a longer program, the F7 key is normally used. Once you are convinced, however, that all the subprograms are executing properly, you can save time by using the F8 key for single-step tracing.

Breakpoints

If a program is long and most of its statements contain no errors, it seems a waste of time to single step through many valid statements in order to reach a section of the program where an error is thought to exist. Turbo Pascal solves this problem by allowing one or more *breakpoints* to be set in the source program.

A breakpoint is a designated line where the program stops execution and waits for some action by the user. Most often, a breakpoint is set just before a section of code where an error is suspected, and when the program halts, the F7 or F8 key is used to single step through that section.

The Toggle breakpoint command in the Break/watch command menu sets the line marked by the cursor as a breakpoint. Placing the cursor under any character on the desired line and pressing Ctrl-F8 has the same effect. The program is executed using the normal Run or Ctrl-F9 command, and execution stops when the breakpoint is reached. Pressing the F7 or F8 key at this point starts a single-step trace of the program. Single stepping can be interrupted at any time by pressing Ctrl-F2 or executing the Program reset command in the Run command menu.

Changing Variable Values

We explained in Chapter 4 how selected variables can be placed in the watch window, and changes in the values of these variables observed. It is desirable in some cases, however, for the user to be able to change or modify the value of a variable during the debugging process.

The Evaluate command in the Debug command menu allows this kind of change to be made. The command can be executed at a breakpoint or while single-step tracing through a program. The command can also be invoked by pressing Ctrl-F4 when the cursor is under a character in the name of the selected variable.

A pop-up window shows the variable name, and pressing the Enter key displays its current value. The down arrow key can then be used to move to the bottom box, the New value box, and a different value entered here. When the Enter key is pressed again, this newly-entered value is assigned to the selected variable, and program execution can be resumed (with F7 or F8) or restarted (with Ctrl-F9).

Figure 6.1 is an expanded version of the list of debugging keys shown in Chapter 4.

F6	switch between the edit and watch windows
F7	single-step trace through an entire program, one line at a time
F8	same as F7, but skip over subprograms and unit initialization statements
Ctrl-F7	add the variable under the cursor to the watch window
Ctrl-F8	toggle key to set or release a breakpoint
Ctrl-F4	display the value of a variable, and allow this value to be changed
Ctrl-F2	terminate tracing and reset the program

Figure 6.1 Expanded list of debugging keys.

6.6 PROGRAM TESTING

After a program has been designed and written, and any errors removed so that it compiles successfully, it must be tested. The first test is to see if it produces reasonable results, in the expected format. Further tests are run to determine (1) if the results are accurate, (2) if the program runs without error for a wide range of input data, and (3) if the output format agrees exactly with the design specifications. **Program testing is an important, and necessary, part of program development.**

Testing the Example Program

This particular program should be tested with several different order files. Use a hand calculator to determine if the calculated values are correct. You should make sure that the output file contains the proper information.

As a first test, change the contents of the ORDERS.DAT file from 137 and 40 to 0 and 0. This change is in line with our suggestion that you always test a program using values at the limits of the allowed range. The ORDERS.DAT file is just a simple text file, and so you can change its contents using the Turbo Pascal editor or any other text editor.

The program runs as before, but produces the following output:

```
The order file has been read.

To make 0 bowling balls of type A and 0 of type B
requires 0 pounds of material. You should order
100 pounds of material in 100-pound bags.

The file for purchasing materials has been written.
```

As you can see, this result is somewhat misleading. In the calculation of BagLot, a result of 100 is produced even if the value of Amount is zero. A better program would first check to see if the amount of material needed is zero, and in that case order no material.

In Chapter 7, we introduce the if statement that allows a program to make a decision. Even at this point, however, it is easy to understand the meaning of the statement

```
if Amount = 0 then BagLot:=0;
```

This statement should be written as the last statement in the function BagLot.

Another test might be made where a large number of bowling balls is ordered. For example, assume that 50,000 balls of type A and 50,000 of type B are ordered. The file ORDERS.DAT contains 50,000 and 50,000. If we run the program with this version of the file, we get a run-time error. The variables NumTypeA and NumTypeB are declared as type integer, and the maximum value of an integer in Turbo Pascal is 32767. In order to handle large orders, we must change the type of these variables to longint or real.

Here is the modified version of our program

```
PROGRAM EX0604 (Output);
{
  A manufacturer of bowling balls produces two types
  of balls. Type A is 7.5 inches in diameter and
  type B is 9.5 inches in diameter. The total orders
  for each type are stored in file ORDERS.DAT. Using
  material of a given density, this program calculates
  the weight of material needed and the weight of
  material to purchase, assuming the material is
  shipped in 100-pound bags. The amount of material
  to purchase is written on file MATERIAL.DAT.
  Use only with Version 4 or 5 unless modified.
}
const
  DENSITY = 0.037;   { of ball material, lbs/cu in  }
  DIAM_A = 7.5;      { diameter of type A balls, in }
  DIAM_B = 9.5;      { diameter of type B balls, in }
var
{
  The longint type of Turbo Pascal, Versions 4 and 5,
  is used for the number of bowling balls ordered. If
  a large integer type is not available in your version
  of Pascal, use variables of type real.
}
NumTypeA: longint;   { number of type A balls ordered }
NumTypeB: longint;   { number of type B balls ordered }
TotalAmt: real;      { lbs of material for balls }
OrderAmt: real;      { lbs of material ordered   }


PROCEDURE ReadOrderFile (var NumTypeA,
                             NumTypeB: longint);
{
  Read the number of balls ordered, of type A and
  type B, from the text file ORDERS.DAT.
}
var
  InFile: text;
begin
  Assign (InFile, 'ORDERS.DAT');
  Reset (InFile);
  Readln (InFile, NumTypeA);
  Readln (InFile, NumTypeB);
  Close (InFile);
end;  { ReadOrderFile }
```

```
FUNCTION MaterialNeeded (Diameter: real;
                         Number: real): real;
{
  Calculate the material needed for a given number
  of balls, of given diameter and material density.
}
var
  Radius, Volume: real;
begin
  Radius:= Diameter / 2;
  Volume:= (4.0 * Pi * Radius * Radius * Radius) / 3;
  MaterialNeeded:= Number * DENSITY * Volume;
end;   { MaterialNeeded }


FUNCTION BagLot (Amount: real): real;
{
  Increase amount to allow for waste and
  round to the number of 100-pound bags.
}
begin
  Amount:= Amount / 0.9;   { allow for 10% waste }
  BagLot:= (Trunc(Amount / 100.0) + 1.0) * 100.0;
  if Amount = 0 then BagLot:= 0;
end;   { BagLot }


PROCEDURE WriteMaterialFile (Amount: real);
{
  Write the amount of material to be purchased
  on the text file MATERIAL.DAT.
}
var
  OutFile: text;
begin
  Assign (OutFile, 'MATERIAL.DAT');
  Rewrite (OutFile);
  Writeln (OutFile, Amount:1:0);
  Close (OutFile);
end;   { WriteMaterialFile }


PROCEDURE DisplayResults (NumberA, NumberB: longint;
                          TotalAmt, OrderAmt: real);
{
  Display the number of bowling balls ordered
  and the amount of material needed.
}
```

```
begin
   Writeln;
   Write ('To make ', NumberA:1);
   Write (' bowling balls of type A and ');
   Writeln (NumberB:1, ' of type B');
   Write ('requires ', TotalAmt:1:0, ' pounds');
   Writeln (' of material. You should order');
   Write (OrderAmt:1:0, ' pounds of material');
   Writeln (' in 100-pound bags.');
   Writeln;
   Write ('The file for purchasing materials');
   Writeln (' has been written.');
end;  { DisplayResults }

BEGIN  { Main Program }
   ReadOrderFile (NumTypeA, NumTypeB);
   Writeln ('The order file has been read.');
   TotalAmt:= MaterialNeeded(DIAM_A, NumTypeA)
              + MaterialNeeded(DIAM_B, NumTypeB);
   OrderAmt:= BagLot(TotalAmt);
   WriteMaterialFile (OrderAmt);
   DisplayResults (NumTypeA, NumTypeB,
                   TotalAmt, OrderAmt);
END.
```

When we make the change, the program runs without error and produces the following results.

```
The order file has been read.

To make 50000 bowling balls of type A and 50000 of type B
requires 1239155 pounds of material. You should order
1376900 pounds of material in 100-pound bags.

The file for purchasing materials has been written.
```

Thorough testing of a program may take as long as writing the program. It often helps to have someone else, who was not involved in writing the program, test the program. That person should do everything he or she can do to make the program fail, and if it survives, you can be proud of having designed and written a strong, robust program.

Run-time errors specific to a particular implementation of Pascal can arise from time to time. Here is an example in Turbo Pascal.

Turbo Pascal Note

The M Compiler Directive

Every once in a while, a programmer will receive the cryptic error message "Runtime error 202: Stack overflow error." This error usually occurs when a program has many procedures or functions, or if it uses recursion (see Chapter 13). We discuss the problem now so that you will know how to correct it, even though a full explanation of the error is not possible at this time.

The stack is an area of computer memory that is used to store local variables, intermediate results during evaluation of expressions, and certain information during calls to procedures and functions. An area of memory is set aside in Turbo Pascal for the stack.

In Versions 4 and 5, the default stack size is 16,384 bytes. If stack overflow occurs, the M compiler directive can be used to increase the stack size. This directive is not available in Version 3. The syntax is

```
{$M StackSize, HeapMin, HeapMax}
```

and all three parameters are required. Parameter HeapMin has a default value of zero, while parameter HeapMax has a default value of 655,360. These parameters are discussed in the Turbo Pascal Owner's Handbook, but we do not consider them further here. Always use the default values. Parameter StackSize can have a value between 1,024 and 65,520. The default value is 16,384.

If you encounter a stack overflow error, try increasing the size of the stack with the M compiler directive. Place this directive near the start of your program. Keep increasing the size of the stack (up to 65,520) until the error disappears. As a first step, we suggest trying a stack size of 25,000 using the compiler directive {$M 0, 655360, 25000}.

6.7 USE OF SUBPROGRAMS IN SMALL PROGRAMS

Looking at the program developed in this chapter, you might observe that it would be shorter if all subprograms were removed and the program was written as a single main program. A large main program without subprograms will probably execute more quickly. Furthermore, an example program used for teaching purposes should be kept as short and simple as possible.

On the other hand, the design and development method we have presented is most likely to produce an error-free program. For larger and more complicated programs, the time spent searching for, and correcting, errors can be much longer than the time required to write the program. **The advantage of faster, more accurate program development usually far outweighs the slight loss of execution speed due to many subprograms.**

We urge you to learn to design and write programs in a modular style now when the programs are short and simple. You will reap the benefits later on when your programs become long and complicated.

IMPORTANT POINTS

- A written program outline should be developed that lists the major tasks to be accomplished.

- Program testing is an important, and necessary, part of program development.
- The advantage of faster, more accurate program development, using subprograms, usually far outweighs the slight loss of execution speed due to the subprograms.

SELF-STUDY QUESTIONS

1. What is meant by top-down program design?
2. What is meant by modular program design?
3. What is the first step in developing a new program after the problem is thoroughly understood?
4. What is the second step, especially if the program will be of substantial size?
5. How is the technique of commenting out statements used during program development?
6. If a program produces numerical results, how can you check the accuracy of these results?
7. What is the purpose of the M compiler directive?

PRACTICE PROGRAMS

Thoroughly test each practice program. In addition to the specified tests, develop and apply your own test to determine that each program is robust and free of errors. Document your testing procedure for each program.

1. The operating engineer for a salt water desalination plant keeps operating records in computer text files. Two annual files are maintained. One file, named WATER, has information on how many gallons of fresh water are produced each month. For example, the water production file for 1975 is named WATER.75.

   A second file, named FUEL, has data on how many gallons of fuel are consumed each month and the cost of that fuel in dollars per gallon. Two numeric values, on separate lines, are stored in the file each month, one the amount of fuel used and the other the cost of that fuel. The corresponding fuel consumption file for 1975 is named FUEL.75.

   A computer program is needed to calculate the average cost per gallon of water produced during the year and the average conversion rate (gallons of water per gallon of fuel). The fixed costs of operating the plant are 0.0325 dollars per gallon of water produced. As demonstrated in Program EX0603, your main program should consist primarily of calls to procedures or functions. Display the average cost of producing fresh water and the average conversion rate with appropriate labels.

   Test your program using the text files WATER.75 and FUEL.75.

2. The engineering department of a computer disk manufacturer measures the performance of a fixed-disk drive unit in terms of two quantities. One quantity is disk speed variation from the design speed, measured as a percentage. The other quantity is number and size of defective areas on the disk surface, measured as a percentage of the total surface area. These two quantities for 100 randomly-selected drives, along with the drive serial number, are written on a daily file. For day 251 in year 1988, the file is named DISK251.88.

These three numbers are stored in the sequence

Serial number
Percent speed variation
Percent surface defects

A typical entry for one drive might look like

```
178092
1.05
3.73
```

where the serial number is 178092, the speed variation is 1.05 percent, and the surface defects are 3.73 percent.

Calculate the average speed variation percentage and the average surface defects percentage for a day's production, using the sample data written in the daily file. Display the serial number of the first unit tested, the last unit tested, and the two average percentages, all with appropriate labels.

Test your program using the text file `DISK251.88`.

7

CONTROL STATEMENTS:
BRANCHING AND LOOPING

7.1 INTRODUCTION

There are three kinds of computer program structures: sequential, branching, and looping. Most of the simple programs we have written in previous chapters have a sequential structure.

We first discuss simple boolean expressions and their evaluation. As an example of branching, we introduce the `if` statement. As an example of looping, we introduce the `while` statement. Both of these statements require the use of a boolean expression or variable to control the decision to branch or loop.

We look finally at compound boolean expressions, and discuss the precedence of operators. Sets are introduced and used in boolean expressions with the `in` statement.

7.2 BOOLEAN EXPRESSIONS

We discussed boolean variables briefly in Chapter 2. Variables of this type can only have values of true or false. Now we introduce a similar concept; *boolean expressions*. These expressions also have values of true or false. Relational operators are used in simple boolean expressions to compare the values of two variables, or a variable and a constant.

An example boolean expression is

```
Item = 5
```

where the expression itself has a value of true or false. If the variable Item does indeed have a value of exactly 5, the boolean expression has a value of true. Otherwise, the expression has a value of false. **Note that both boolean variables and boolean expressions can only have values of true or false.**

Simple boolean expressions usually have two variables, or a variable and a constant, connected by a relational operator. In the previous example, the equality operator (=) connects the variable Item and the constant 5.

Relational Operators

There are six relational operators, as shown in Figure 7.1.

=	equal
<>	not equal
<	less than
<=	less than or equal
>	greater than
>=	greater than or equal

Figure 7.1   The relational operators and their meanings.

Here is an example program (really a demonstration program) that shows the values of several boolean expressions.

```
PROGRAM EX0701 (Output);
{
   Assigns values to several variables and then
   displays the values of several boolean expressions.
}
const
  C1 = 7;
var
  A1: char;
  X1, X2: integer;

BEGIN
  A1:='A';
  X1:=7;
  X2:=14;
  Writeln ('The value of A1 is ', A1);
  Writeln ('The value of C1 is ', C1);
  Writeln ('The value of X1 is ', X1:1);
  Writeln ('The value of X2 is ', X2:1);
  Writeln;
  Writeln ('The value of (X1 = X2) is ', X1 = X2);
  Writeln ('The value of (X1 <> X2) is ', X1 <> X2);
  Writeln ('The value of (X1 >= X2) is ', X1 >= X2);
  Writeln ('The value of (A1 < ''B'') is ', A1 < 'B');
  Writeln ('The value of (X1 <= C1) is ', X1 <= C1);
END.
```

Note in the next-to-last statement that the character value (B) has two single quotation marks before it and two after it. As mentioned earlier, using two single quotation marks is the proper way to denote a single quotation mark within a string constant. It is not necessary to enclose simple boolean expressions in parentheses; we do it here only for clarity.

This program produces the following output.

```
The value of A1 is A
The value of C1 is 7
The value of X1 is 7
The value of X2 is 14

The value of (X1 = X2) is FALSE
The value of (X1 <> X2) is TRUE
The value of (X1 >= X2) is FALSE
The value of (A1 < 'B') is TRUE
The value of (X1 <= C1) is TRUE
```

Turbo Pascal Note

Some compilers, like the Turbo Pascal compiler, display the value of a boolean variable or expression in uppercase characters (TRUE, FALSE), whereas other Pascal compilers use lowercase characters. A user can enter boolean values in either uppercase or lowercase characters, or a combination of both.

Use of Boolean Variables

Boolean variables are seldom used in simple boolean expressions. If a variable named Flag is of type boolean and has a value of true, then the expression

```
(Flag = true)
```

is perfectly legal but carries no more information than the variable Flag itself. We normally use boolean variables by themselves, rather than including them in boolean expressions. We give an example in the next section, using the boolean variable Affirmative.

Use of Real Variables in Equalities

Real variables can also be used in boolean expressions, but they must be used with care. Remember that the value of a real variable is only an approximate value, maintained internally in Pascal with the highest precision available for the computer being used. **Apparent program errors can occur when real variables are used in equality expressions.**

As an example, consider the following program. The numeric value 2.00000000001 is stored in a text file named TEST.NUM. You can verify the value by using an editor, or the TYPE command of MS-DOS, to display the contents of TEST.NUM on the screen. The example program is executed in Turbo Pascal on a computer system that stores 12 digits internally for real numbers, but only displays 11 digits.

```
PROGRAM EX0702 (Output);
{
   Testing an equality expression
   using a real variable.
} *
{ $N-}   { for Version 5 }
var
   FV: text;
   Number: real;

BEGIN
   Assign (FV, 'TEST.NUM');
   Reset (FV)'
   Readln (FV, Number);
   Writeln ('The value of Number is ', Number);
   Write ('The value of expression (Number = 2.0) is ');
   Writeln (Number = 2.0);
END.
```

The following output is produced on our computer, although different computer systems may produce different results.

```
The value of Number is  2.0000000000E+00
The value of expression (Number = 2.0) is FALSE
```

The displayed results are obviously misleading, due simply to the fact that a computer can store a real number only as an approximate value. **We normally avoid using real variables in equality (=) or inequality (<>) expressions.**

If a boolean expression with real variables must be used, it should be written with one of the other relational expressions (<, <=, >, >=). Instead of comparing two values for equality, check to see if the absolute value of the difference between the two values is less than some small constant (EPS for epsilon). This constant should be small with respect to the size of the values being compared. Here is the previous example program, rewritten using this new comparison technique.

```
PROGRAM EX0703 (Output);
{
   Another test using an equality
   expression with a real variable.
   A small (EPS) constant is used.
}
{ $N-}   { for Version 5 }
const
   EPS = 1.0E-09;
var
   FV: text;
   Number: real;
```

```
BEGIN
  Assign (FV, 'TEST.NUM');
  Reset (FV);
  Readln (FV, Number);
  Writeln ('The value of Number is ', Number);
  Writeln ('The value of EPS is ', EPS);
  Write ('The value of (Abs(Number - 2.0) < EPS) is ');
  Writeln (Abs(Number - 2.0) < EPS);
END.
```

Because the size of Number is about 2.0, we choose a value of EPS equal to 1.0E-09, a value that is small with respect to 2.0. If EPS is too small, however, the test does not work properly. As a rule of thumb, the number of digits in the expression Int(Number / EPS) should be less than the number of digits stored by the computer for real numbers. The program now produces the display

```
The value of Number is  2.0000000000E+00
The value of EPS is  1.0000000000E-09
The value of (Abs(Number - 2.0) < EPS) is TRUE
```

7.3 SIMPLE PROGRAM BRANCHING: THE IF STATEMENT

The programs we have written so far have been mostly *sequential* programs, with one statement being executed after another in the order they appear in the program. This style of program severely limits the usefulness of a computer. We wish to write programs that can make their own decisions, executing one statement (simple or compound) if some condition is true, and another statement if the condition is false.

This ability of a program to make decisions is called *branching*. There are two branching structures available in Pascal, but in this chapter we introduce only the if statement.

An if statement uses a boolean expression or boolean variable as a test to choose which branch to execute next. The syntax is

```
if boolean expression then
    branch 1
else
    branch 2;
```

Note that the four preceding lines constitute a single statement, written on separate lines for convenience and clarity. Both branch 1 and branch 2 can be simple statements, or compound statements enclosed within begin and end brackets.

As an example, the statement

```
if (Reply = 'Y') then
  Writeln ('Answer is yes.')
else
  Writeln ('Answer is no.');
```

displays the sentence "Answer is yes." if variable `Reply` has a value of `Y`; otherwise it displays the sentence "Answer is no." The parentheses around the boolean expression (`Reply = 'Y'`) are not required, but sometimes help make the statement easier to read. In this example, `Reply` is a variable of type `char`. Because the previous example is all one single statement, it contains no semicolon except the one at the end that separates it from the succeeding statement.

As another example, the statement

```
if X >= 0 then Y:= X else Y:= -X;
```

assigns the absolute value of X to Y. Note in this case that the statement is all on a single line.

We first show the outline of an example program that demonstrates how an `if` statement might be used

Ask user to enter a number.

If number is negative

   Display error message.

Else number is non-negative.

   Display square root of number.

and then show the program itself.

```
PROGRAM EX0704 (Input, Output);
{
   Enter a real number. If it is negative, display
   a warning message; if not, display its square root.
}
var
   Number: real;

BEGIN
   Write ('Enter a number: ');
   Readln (Number);
   if Number < 0 then
     begin
     Write ('You cannot take the square root');
     Writeln (' of a negative number.');
     end
   else
     Writeln ('The square root is ', Sqrt(Number):1:1);
END.
```

This program displays a warning message if the number is negative; otherwise it displays the square root. The warning message is produced by a `Write` statement and a `Writeln` statement. These two simple statements are enclosed within begin and end brackets to form a compound statement.

Note the punctuation, especially the lack of a semicolon after the `end` bracket of the compound statement. The following `else` is also part of the `if` statement, and semicolons are used only at the ends of statements to separate adjacent statements. **A common mistake is to put a semicolon at the end of the line preceding an else**, and this mistake almost always produces a syntax error during compilation.

If the number is not negative, its square root is calculated and displayed. The real value of Sqrt(Number) is displayed with one decimal digit in a field that is at least one digit wide. This field specification ensures that there are no extra spaces before the square root.

Here is a sample of the output display produced by running the program twice. User input is underlined in the book, but not, of course, on the screen.

```
Enter a number: 23.2
The square root is 4.8

Enter a number: -23.2
You cannot take the square root of a negative number.
```

Use of Boolean Variables in If Statements

Another example shows a modified version of an earlier program fragment. A boolean variable is used to indicate whether an answer is yes or no.

```
var
  Affirmative: boolean;
     |
     |
  if Affirmative then
    Writeln ('Answer is yes.')
  else
    Writeln ('Answer is no.');
```

If the boolean variable Affirmative is true, the message "Answer is yes." is displayed; otherwise, the message "Answer is no." appears. The vertical lines (|) represent other program statements that are not shown here.

The Multibranch If Statement

There is no reason why an if statement cannot be included as one of the statements in another if statement. Look at the following program fragment (with exaggerated indentation).

```
if X > 0 then
    Sign := 1
else
    begin
        if X < 0 then
            Sign := -1
        else
            Sign := 0
    end;
```

Sign is assigned a value of 1 if X is greater than zero, a value of −1 if X is less than zero, and a value of 0 otherwise. The latter case occurs only if X equals zero. We have effectively set up a structure with three branches.

Note that we do not really need begin and end brackets after the first else because the following if statement is itself a single statement. We include begin and end brackets and large indentations only to make the program fragment easier to read and understand.

It helps make the statement even more readable if we place the first else and the following if on the same line and change the indentation of the last else. We also remove the pair of unnecessary begin and end brackets. Our program fragment then becomes

```
if X > 0 then
    Sign:=1
else if X < 0 then
    Sign:=-1
else  { X = 0 }
    Sign:=0;
```

where we have added a comment after the last else for additional clarity. We think this form is the best and most readable format for writing a multibranch if statement.

The preceding program fragment can be used to develop a function named Sign that returns 1, 0, or −1 depending on the algebraic sign of its parameter. Here is an example program containing such a function.

```
PROGRAM EX0705 (Input, Output);
{
   Demonstrate the use of a Sign function that
   returns 1, 0, or -1 depending on the algebraic
   sign of its parameter.
}
var
   Number: real;

FUNCTION Sign (X: real): integer;
{
   Returns 1, 0, or -1 depending on
   the algebraic sign of X.
}
begin
   if X > 0 then
     Sign:=1
   else if X < 0 then
     Sign:=-1
   else  { X = 0 }
     Sign:=0;
 end;  { Sign }
```

```
BEGIN  { Main Program }
  Write ('Enter a number: ');
  Readln (Number);
  Writeln ('Value of the Sign function is ',
           Sign(Number):1);
END.
```

If the program is executed twice, the following results might be displayed.

```
Enter a number: 57
Value of the Sign function is 1

Enter a number: - 12.5
Value of the Sign function is -1
```

7.4 SIMPLE PROGRAM LOOPING: THE WHILE STATEMENT

In addition to sequential and branching structures, Pascal also supports several *looping* structures. We have already used the for statement and its loop structure. **We now introduce the while structure which allows a statement (again, either simple or compound) to be executed over and over again as long as a boolean expression remains true.** The syntax is

```
while boolean expression do statement;
```

The statement is usually a compound statement, and may, in fact, be a large section of program statements enclosed in begin and end brackets. This statement is executed repeatedly until the boolean expression becomes false.

Use of a Control Variable

Here is a simple example program that prints the digits from 1 through 5 and their squares.

```
PROGRAM EX0706 (Output);
{
  Display column headings and a table
  of numbers and their squares.
}
const
  MAX_NUM = 5;

PROCEDURE WriteTable (N: integer);
{
  Display the digits from 1 to N
  and their squares.
}
var
  X: integer;
```

```
begin
  X := 1;
  while X <= N do
    begin
    Writeln (' ', X:1, '        ', (X*X):2);
    X := X + 1;
    end; { while loop }
end; { WriteTable }

BEGIN { Main Program }
  Writeln ('NUM', '      ', 'SQR');
  Writeln ('---', '      ', '---');
  WriteTable (MAX_NUM);
END.
```

The first statement in procedure WriteTable initializes the value of X to one. When a variable like X is declared in a program, its value is indeterminate until some value is assigned to it. **You cannot assume any initial value for a newly-declared variable.** When used in this manner, X is called a *control variable*.

The control variable is often a number of type integer, but it can be of any type. A variable of type real must be used if the range of the control variable exceeds the value of MaxInt and an extended integer type is not available.

The while loop continues to operate until the boolean expression (X <= 5) becomes false. This occurs when X has the value of 6, and at that point, the compound statement following do (sometimes called the *body of the loop*) is no longer executed and the program ends.

The body of the loop contains a statement (X := X + 1) that increments (increases) the value of X by one each time the loop is executed. **It is important that the body of the loop contain some statement that changes the value of X, otherwise the boolean expression remains true and the loop executes forever.** We call such a loop an *infinite loop*; it is almost always created by error. The only way to exit an infinite loop is to stop the program, usually by pressing Ctrl-Break (same as Ctrl-C). If this fails to work, reset the computer by pressing Alt-Ctrl-Del, but remember that any program not saved on disk will be lost.

Turbo Pascal Note

The Inc and Dec Statements

Versions 4 and 5 of Turbo Pascal have two statements that can be used for incrementing and decrementing (decreasing) the value of a numeric control variable. The statement

```
Inc (X)
```

is equivalent to the statement X := X + 1, while the statement

```
Dec (X)
```

is equivalent to the statement X := X - 1.

In addition, a second parameter can be added to either statement, specifying the amount that the first parameter is to be incremented or decremented. For example, the statement

```
Inc (X, 3)
```

is equivalent to the statement $X := X + 3$.

Returning to our example program, it produces the following output.

```
NUM     SQR
---     ---
 1       1
 2       4
 3       9
 4      16
 5      25
```

Note we have written a comment after the end bracket at the end of the loop body. This comment is not really needed in such a short program, but is helpful when the loop body is long, especially if the loop extends over several pages or screens.

Three characteristics appear in many loops and you should be aware of the purpose of each one:

- a statement to initialize the control variable
- a boolean expression to check the value of the control variable
- a statement to increment or decrement the value of the control variable

Detecting End of File Using a Sentinel Value

Let us develop a more practical program that reads measured values, representing river depths, from a file. This file of water depths (named DEPTH1.DAT) was produced as part of an engineering study of river pollution. The program is designed to display the number of depth values read and their average value. The file is a text file, and the depth values are real numbers.

In Chapter 3, we read sequences of numbers from a text file where we knew how many numbers had been written on the file. Program EX0309 writes five numeric values on a file, and Program EX0310 reads the file and displays the numbers.

In the general case, however, when reading values from a file, we need some way to determine when the last value has been read. One solution is to include a dummy value, called a *sentinel*, as the last value in the file. **The sentinel value must be a value that can never be mistaken for a valid data value.**

In our case, if only positive numbers are valid depth values, the sentinel can be a negative number, say -1. The boolean expression (Number $>=$ 0) is used to control the while loop. As long as the expression is true, the loop continues. When the expression becomes false, the loop stops. Here is an outline of our program.

Open the data file.

Read values from the file.

Calculate and display the average value.

Counting and Summing Numeric Values

The techniques of counting and summing are used often when manipulating sequences of numeric values. These techniques require the use of two variables; a counting variable to hold the count (or number) of numeric values, and a summing variable to hold the sum of numeric values. Both of these variables must have their initial values set to zero.

As each numeric value is read from the file, we take two actions. We increment the count by one; so we know how many values have been read. We also add the new value to the sum of the previous values. When we have finished reading all values from the file, we can calculate the average value by dividing the sum by the count.

We present two outlines, first outlining the main program.

Open file named DEPTH1.DAT.

Call procedure ReadDepths to read file and return number of depth values and sum of depth values.

Display number of depth values.

Calculate and display the average depth value.

Much of the work is done in the procedure ReadDepths whose outline is as follows.

Initialize variable Count to zero.

Initialize variable Sum to zero.

Read first depth value from the file.

While depth value is nonnegative.
    Increment the variable Count.
    Add the depth value to Sum.
    Read next depth value from the file.
Loop back.

Here is the complete example program.

```
PROGRAM EX0707 (Output);
{
   Read depth values from the file DEPTH1.DAT.
   Display the number of values read and their
   average value.
}
var
   DepthFile: text;
   Count: integer;
   Sum, Average: real;
```

```
PROCEDURE ReadNumberFile (var FV: text; var Sum: real;
                          var Count: integer);
{
   Read a file of numbers until sentinel is encountered.
   Count the numbers and calculate their sum.
}
var
   Number: real;
begin
   Count := 0;
   Sum := 0;
   Readln (FV, Number);
   while Number >= 0 do
     begin
     Count := Count + 1;
     Sum := Sum + Number;
     Readln (FV, Number);
     end;
end;   { ReadNumberFile }

BEGIN   { Main Program }
   Assign (DepthFile, 'DEPTH1.DAT');
   Reset (DepthFile);
   ReadNumberFile (DepthFile, Sum, Count);
   Writeln ('Results from file DEPTH1.DAT:');
   Writeln (Count:1, ' depth values are read');
   Average := Sum / Count;
   Writeln ('The average depth is ', Average:1:2);
END.
```

Note that we read the first value in the file before we enter the loop in procedure ReadNumberFile. This technique initializes the value of Number, thus allowing the loop to be skipped if the only value in the file is the sentinel. Note also that although the sentinel value is read, it does not contribute to the count and its value is not added to the sum. The example program produces this display.

```
Results from file DEPTH1.DAT:
10 depth values are read
The average depth is 29.18
```

Detecting End of File Using the Eof Function

Rather than using a sentinel, we can use a standard boolean function in Pascal that detects the end of a file. If a file variable is named FileVar, the function

```
Eof(FileVar)
```

has a value of true if the file pointer points to the end of the file, otherwise it has a value of false. When we say the file pointer points to the end of the file, we mean that the next value in the file is the end-of-file marker. If you are unfamiliar with the concept of a file pointer, you should reread Section 3.4 and its discussion of the Reset statement.

Of course, if we are at the beginning of an empty file, this is the same as being at the end of the file, and Eof has a value of true.

We want our loop to repeat while the file pointer is not at the end of the file. This means we have to create an expression that is true when not at the end of the file. **It is possible to change the logical sense of a boolean variable, function or expression by preceding it with the operator not.** Thus if the expression

```
(Item = 5)
```

is true, then the expression

```
not (Item = 5)
```

is false. In a similar manner, if the function

```
Eof(FileVar)
```

is false, then the function

```
not Eof(FileVar)
```

is true.

Here is our previous program using the Eof function rather than a sentinel. We must, of course, use a file (named DEPTH2.DAT) that contains only valid depth values and does not contain a sentinel. The only significant change is in the procedure ReadNumberFile, so first we show an outline of that procedure.

> Initialize variable Count to zero.
> Initialize variable Sum to zero.
> While not at the end of the file.
>   Read next depth value from the file.
>   Increment the variable Count.
>   Add the depth value to Sum.
> Loop back.

Note that the first depth value is read inside the loop, rather than outside the loop as in Program EX0707. The end of file is detected by the Eof function. Here is the complete program.

```
PROGRAM EX0708 (Output);
{
  Read depth values from the file DEPTH2.DAT.
  Display the number of values read and their average
  value.
}
var
  DepthFile: text;
  Count: integer;
  Sum, Average: real;
```

```
PROCEDURE ReadNumberFile (var FV: text; var Sum: real;
                          var Count: integer);
{
   Read file until end-of-file is encountered.
}
var
   Number: real;
begin
   Count: = 0;
   Sum: = 0;
   while not Eof(FV) do
      begin
      Readln (FV, Number);
      Count: = Count + 1;
      Sum: = Sum + Number;
      end;
end;   { ReadNumberFile }

BEGIN   { Main Program }
   Assign (DepthFile, 'DEPTH2.DAT');
   Reset (DepthFile);
   ReadNumberFile (DepthFile, Sum, Count);
   Writeln ('Results from file DEPTH2.DAT:');
   Writeln (Count:1, ' depth values are read');
   Average: = Sum / Count;
   Writeln ('The average depth is ', Average:1:2);
END.
```

This program produces the same output display as Program EX0707.

7.5 COMPOUND BOOLEAN EXPRESSIONS

Two or more boolean expressions or variables can be joined together with the relational conjunctions and and or, forming a *compound boolean expression*. The individual expressions must usually be enclosed in parentheses. A sample statement is

```
while (Value >= 0) and (not Eof(FileVar)) do
   begin
   |
   end;
```

The statements between the begin and end brackets are executed only if both simple boolean expressions (Value >= 0) and (not Eof(FileVar)) are true. **Standard Pascal always checks all simple boolean expressions in a compound expression.**

Turbo Pascal Note

The B Compiler Directive

The previous statement is not strictly true for Versions 4 and 5 of Turbo Pascal. The default method of boolean expression evaluation in this version is called *short-circuit evaluation*. Only enough of a boolean expression is evaluated for the result of the expression to become evident.

For example, in the previous example, if either simple boolean expression is false, the compound expression is false. Thus, if the expression (Value >= 0) is false, there is no need to evaluate the expression (not Eof(FileVar)).

Full expression evaluation can be restored by including the compiler directive { $B+} in the Pascal program or by customizing the Turbo Pascal system with the Compiler command from the Options command menu.

Truth Table

The rules for calculating the value of a compound boolean expression are given by a logical table (Figure 7.2) called a *truth table*. X and Y are boolean variables or expressions, while T and F stand for true and false.

X	Y	X AND Y	X OR Y
T	T	T	T
T	F	F	T
F	T	F	T
F	F	F	F

Figure 7.2   Logical truth table.

Precedence of Operators

The boolean operator not has the highest precedence, followed by the operator and, and then the operator or. All three boolean operators have higher precedence than the relational operators. Parts of an expression enclosed in parentheses are always evaluated first, starting with the innermost pairs of parentheses. Figure 7.3 is a complete table of operator precedence.

First:	not
Second:	* / div mod and
Third:	+ − or
Fourth:	= <> < <= > >= in

Figure 7.3   Precedence of operators.

As already noted, not has the highest precedence, and all operators on the same line have the same precedence. A new operator, the in operator, is discussed later in this section.

The following example program displays the values of several compound boolean expressions.

```
PROGRAM EX0709 (Output);
{
  Display the values of several
  compound boolean expressions.
}
type
  string80 = string[80];
var
  Num: integer;
  Ch: char;
  Str: string80;
  Flag: boolean;

BEGIN  { Main Program }
  Num:= 13;
  Ch:= 'Z';
  Str:= 'abc';
  Flag:= true;
  Writeln ('Given: variable Num is ', Num);
  Writeln ('       variable Ch is ', Ch);
  Writeln ('       variable Str is ', Str);
  Writeln ('       variable Flag is ', Flag);
  Writeln;

  Write ('(Num = 13) and (Ch < ''Z'') is ');
  Writeln ((Num = 13) and (Ch < 'Z'));
  Write ('(Num = 11) or (Num = 12) or (Num = 13) is ');
  Writeln ((Num = 11) or (Num = 12) or (Num = 13));
  Write ('(Num = 10) or ((Ch <> ''Z'') and Flag) is ');
  Writeln ((Num = 10) or ((Ch <> 'Z') and Flag));
  Write ('(Str = ''abc'') and (Num < 10) is ');
  Writeln ((Str = 'abc') and (Num < 10));
  Write ('not (Str = ''xyz'') or (Ch = ''A'') is ');
  Writeln (not (Str = 'xyz') or (Ch = 'A'));
  Write ('(Num >= 0) and (Num <= 100) is ');
  Writeln ((Num >= 0) and (Num <= 100));
END.
```

This program produces the display

```
Given: variable Num is 13
       variable Ch is Z
       variable Str is abc
       variable Flag is TRUE

(Num = 13) and (Ch < 'Z') is FALSE
(Num = 11) or (Num = 12) or (Num = 13) is TRUE
(Num = 10) or ((Ch <> 'Z') and Flag) is FALSE
(Str = 'abc') and (Num < 10) is FALSE
not (Str = 'xyz') or (Ch = 'A') is TRUE
(Num >= 0) and (Num <= 100) is TRUE
```

Now we shall examine some of these boolean expressions in detail. **Note that parentheses must be used because of the order of precedence of operations.** If the first expression is written without parentheses as

```
Num = 13 and Ch < 'Z'
```

and evaluated, the compiler tries to evaluate the subexpression

```
13 and Ch
```

because and has a higher precedence than any other operator in the expression. This subexpression makes no sense and an error results. When parentheses are inserted, as shown in the program, the subexpression

```
Num = 13
```

is evaluated first, followed by the subexpression

```
Ch < 'Z'
```

The boolean values of the two subexpressions are then reduced to a single boolean value by the and operator.

The expression

```
(Num = 10) or ((Ch <> 'Z') and Flag)
```

is a little more complicated. The expression following or evaluates to false, even though Flag is true, because the subexpression

```
Ch <> 'Z'
```

is false. The subexpression

```
Num = 10
```

is also false, thus, the entire expression is false.

In the last example, the expression

```
(Num >= 0) and (Num <= 100)
```

checks to see if the value of Num is within the range between 0 and 100, inclusive. Note that the operator must be and, not or.

One example that appears somewhat awkward is the boolean expression

```
(Num = 11) or (Num = 12) or (Num = 13)
```

which might be used in a program fragment such as

```
if (Num = 11) or (Num = 12) or (Num = 13) then
   Writeln ('The number is valid.');
```

The In Statement and Sets

Pascal allows us to designate a collection of ordinal values as a *set* by placing the values within square brackets. Remember that types integer, char, and boolean are ordinal types, whereas types real and string are not ordinal. A continuous range of values is represented by an ellipsis (. .), and individual values or value ranges are separated by commas. Note that Pascal uses two unspaced dots for the ellipsis. The reserved word in can be used to check whether the value of the variable is part of the set. Our previous program fragment can be rewritten as

```
if Num in [11..13] then
   Writeln ('The number is valid.');
```

where 11..13 means the range of values from 11 through 13, inclusive.

If the values 5 and 25 are also valid values of Num, the set can be expanded and the program fragment becomes

```
if Num in [5, 11..13, 25] then
   Writeln ('The number is valid.');
```

Turbo Pascal Note

Sets in Turbo Pascal are limited to 256 values. This limit may be different in other implementations of Pascal.

It is worthwhile to note that it takes more time to execute an if statement containing set notation than it does to execute an equivalent if statement containing a compound boolean expression. If program speed is of the utmost importance, use a compound boolean expression. Set notation, however, usually produces a clearer and easier-to-understand program structure.

IMPORTANT POINTS

- There are three kinds of computer program structures: sequential, branching, and looping.
- Both boolean variables and boolean expressions can have only true or false values.
- Apparent program errors can occur when real variables are used in equality expressions, and this use is not recommended.
- The ability of a program to make decisions is called branching.
- A common error is putting a semicolon at the end of the line preceding the else in an if statement.
- The while structure allows a statement to be executed over and over again as long as a boolean expression remains true.
- You cannot assume any initial value for a newly-declared variable.
- It is important that the body of a loop contain some statement that changes the value of the control variable; otherwise the boolean expression containing the control statement remains true and the loop executes forever.

- The sentinel value in a data file must be a value that can never be mistaken for a valid data value.
- It is possible to change the logical sense of a boolean variable, function, or expression by preceding it with the word not.
- Standard Pascal always checks all simple boolean expressions in a compound expression.
- Simple boolean expressions in a compound expression must be enclosed in parentheses because of the order of precedence of operations.
- Sets in Turbo Pascal are limited to 256 values.

SELF-STUDY QUESTIONS

1. What are the allowed values of a boolean expression?
2. What is the relational operator that means not equal?
3. Why is it unwise to use a real variable in an equality expression?
4. Which program statement can be used to implement a two-way branch structure?
5. Which program statement can be used to implement a general loop structure that continues to loop as long as a boolean expression is true?
6. What, if anything, is wrong with the program fragment

```
if X >= 0 then
   Writeln (X);
else
   Writeln (-X);
```

7. Can a boolean variable be used in place of a boolean expression in an if statement?
8. How can the if statement be used to implement a three-way branch structure? Show an example program fragment.
9. What is the initial value of a newly-declared variable, named Number of type real?
10. What is meant by an infinite loop?
11. What is meant by the sentinel value in a text file containing data?
12. What is the purpose of the boolean modifier not?
13. If the variable Item has a value of 6, what is the value of the expression (not (Item = 5))?
14. How does Pascal try to evaluate the expression

```
(Value >= 0) and (not Flag)
```

if the parentheses are removed?

15. In Question 14, if Value is equal to −5, will the second part of the compound boolean expression be checked? Can you qualify your answer?
16. Can real values be used in a set? Explain your answer.
17. What is the maximum number of values that can be included in a set in Turbo Pascal?

PRACTICE PROGRAMS

1. While not of great practical use, the Fibonacci series is of mathematical interest. In this series, the next term is always equal to the sum of the previous two terms in the series. For example, if the first term is 1 and the second term is 1, then the third term is (1 + 1) or 2, and the fourth term is (1 + 2) or 3.

   Ask a user to enter the number of terms in the series and then display the values of all the terms. Assume a value of one for each of the first two terms.

   Test your program using a Fibonacci series of 2, 5 and 13 terms.

2. An engineer has a file named HEAT.DAT containing a series of coolant temperature readings from a test engine. Due to problems with the measuring equipment, some of the reading are much too low and are considered spurious. A program is needed that deletes all temperature readings below 150 degrees, and then writes the remaining values on a new file named NEWHEAT.DAT.

   Design your program to use three procedures: one for opening the input file, one for opening the output file, and one for reading a value from one file and writing it on the other.

3. Trigonometric functions can be calculated by using a finite number of terms in an infinite series. The series for the sine of an angle is given by

   $$\sin(X) = X - \frac{X^3}{3!} + \frac{X^5}{5!} + \frac{X^7}{7!} + \cdots$$

   where the angle X is in radians.

   Write your own sine function that uses the first ten terms of the series. Use a separate function to evaluate the factorial numbers. Remember that factorial numbers become large very quickly; so you will need to use the real, longint, or comp type to represent them.

   Use this function in a program that asks a user to enter an angle in degrees. Display the sine of the angle, using first your function, and then the standard Pascal function. Test your program using angles of 45, 90, and 225 degrees.

4. Write another sine function, based on the series in Practice Program 3, that terminates when the last term in the series is less than a certain value EPS.

   For Turbo Pascal, use a value of EPS = 1.0E-9. For another version of Pascal, consult the reference manual to find out how many digits are stored for real number values. Make the exponent value of EPS one or two less than this number. For example, if 11 digits are stored, the exponent value might be 9 (as shown previously) or 10. If your program goes into an infinite loop, stop it (using Ctrl-Break on an IBM PC-compatible) and try again with a smaller exponent value.

   Use this function in a program that asks a user to enter an angle in degrees. Display the sine of the angle, first using your function, and then the standard Pascal function. Also display the number of terms used in your calculation. Test your program using angles of 45, 90, and 225 degrees.

5. Many engineering problems require the solution of a second-degree polynomial equation with a single variable. Write a function to calculate the roots of the equation

   $$Ax^2 + Bx + C = 0$$

   using the quadratic formula

   $$x = \frac{-B \pm \sqrt{B^2 - 4AC}}{2A}$$

Design a program that asks a user to enter the three coefficients A, B, and C. Display the roots, being sure to check for the special case when the roots are complex. Test your program using the values

A	B	C
3	2	2
2	3	1
4	4	4

6. The equations of motion of a falling body, without air resistance, are given by

$$Y = Y_0 + V_0 T - (1/2)G T^2$$

$$V = V_0 - GT$$

where Y = vertical position in meters

Y_0 = initial height

V = vertical velocity in meters per second

V_0 = initial velocity

G = gravitational constant (9.8 m/sec^2)

T = time in seconds

Assume a brick is dropped from the top of a tall building. Ask a user to enter the height of the building. Display a table, with appropriate column headings, showing the elapsed time in seconds, the speed, and the distance the brick has fallen, for every second after the time of release. Stop your table at the last time reading before the brick hits the ground.

Test your program using a building height of 400 meters.

8

THE ARRAY STRUCTURE AND STRINGS

8.1 INTRODUCTION

A new and useful data type is the `array`, and in this chapter we introduce one-dimensional arrays or indexed lists. The elements of an array can be either numbers or characters. Arrays of characters are often called strings, and this particular data structure provides a useful method for storing and manipulating information.

Turbo Pascal, as well as many other implementations of Pascal, has a pre-defined `string` data type. We discuss ways of using this data type, and look at typical applications that use string variables. We also introduce several standard Turbo Pascal string functions and procedures.

8.2 SIMPLE ARRAY STRUCTURES

The simple types we have discussed so far can have only a single value at any one time; variables of these types identify mailboxes or memory locations in which only a single value can be stored. It is sometimes convenient to use another kind of variable, one that can store several values, each value being of the same type. A good example is a list, say a list of real numbers, such as river depth values.

One-Dimensional Arrays

We refer to the list by its name, and call it a *one-dimensional array*. Each entry (in our example, a number) in the list is called an *element* of the array. We refer to a particular number in the list by specifying two items of information, the list name and the position or *index* of that number in the list.

The array is an indexed list whose index has a minimum value or *lower bound*, as well as a maximum value or *upper bound*. The number of entries allowed in the list is called the *size* of the array.

Array Types

This type of variable is often called a *structured type* because it is a data structure made up of one or more component data types. In our discussions in this chapter, these component data types are the simple data types we introduced in Chapter 2.

An array type is defined in the `type` section of the declaration block. We can choose our own name for this new type—let's name it `list100`. An equal sign (=) associates the type name with the type description. The type definition is then

```
type
   list100 = array [1..100] of real;
```

where we define the size of the array to be large enough to hold one hundred real numbers. The symbol `[1..100]` means that the lower bound of the array index is 1, the upper bound is 100, and thus the size of the array is 100. The ellipsis (`..`) indicates that the index can have any integer value between 1 and 100, inclusive. We choose a type name to remind us that the size of the array is 100.

Array Variables

The type named `list100` is now available for us to use, just like simple, predefined types such as real and integer. Going back to our example of an array of real numbers, we can declare a variable of type `list100` with the statement

```
var
   DepthList: list100;
```

Note that `DepthList` is a variable name, while `list100` is a type name. Individual elements in the array are denoted by using the variable name `DepthList`, followed by an index in square brackets. For example, the first number in the array is element `DepthList[1]`, while the sixth number is element `DepthList[6]`.

The index can be either a constant or a variable. If it is a variable, it must be a variable of an ordinal type (usually an integer or a character). If `Item` is an integer variable with a value of 7, element `DepthList[Item]` is the seventh number in the array.

Shorthand Array Declaration

As an alternative to defining a new type, we can define an array in the variable declaration section with the statement

```
var
   DepthList: array [1..100] of real;
```

While it appears simpler, **this short-hand method of declaring a structured variable can cause problems in some situations**. In particular, it cannot be used to declare a formal parameter in a subprogram heading. You will get an error if you use the statement

```
(*****************************************)
(** THIS STATEMENT WILL NOT COMPILE **)
(*****************************************)
PROCEDURE ReadDepths (DepthList: array [1..100] of real);
```

Instead, you must use the notation

```
PROCEDURE ReadDepths (DepthList: list100);
```

where the type list100 has been defined previously. We will use the shorthand method infrequently until we have had a chance to examine potential problems in more detail in later chapters.

An Ordinal Index Type

It is important to remember that the index must be a countable or ordinal type. Both integers and characters can be used as indices, although integers are used most of the time. **Real numbers cannot be used as indices** because they are not an ordinal type. Here are some additional examples of array types and variables.

```
type
   vector = array [1..3] of real;
   month_length = array [1..12] of integer;
   complex_number = array [1..2] of real;
   letter_equivalent = array ['A'..'E'] of integer;
   standard_string = array [1..80] of char;
var
   Force, Velocity: vector;
   DaysInMonth: month_length;
   Current, Voltage, Impedance: complex_number;
   Quality: letter_equivalent;
   Description: standard_string;
```

Constant Lower and Upper Bounds

A significant limitation of Pascal is that **both the lower bound and the upper bound in an array declaration statement must be constant values or constant identifiers. Variables cannot be used**. For example, we could have used the following program fragment to declare the array DepthList.

```
const
   LOWER_BOUND = 1;
   UPPER_BOUND = 100;
type
   list100 = array [LOWER_BOUND..UPPER_BOUND] of real;
var
   DepthList: list100;
```

The following program fragment cannot be used

```
(*******************************************)
(** THESE STATEMENTS WILL NOT COMPILE **)
(*******************************************)
var
  Top: integer;
  DepthList: array [1..Top] of real;
```

because the upper bound of the array DepthList cannot be a variable (the integer variable Top).

Separate Type for Each Size of Array

One other point is important to recognize when declaring and using arrays. **If you declare two arrays of different sizes, you must use different type names.** For example, consider the statements

```
type
  list100 = array [1..100] of real;
  list1000 = array [1..1000] of real;
```

As shown, the two different array types are declared with different type names.

The individual elements in an array can be used just like ordinary, nonarray variables. They can be assigned values and used in expressions. For example, to assign a value to the fifth element in the array DepthList, use the statement

```
DepthList[5]:= 13.25;
```

We can assign the values of one array variable to another variable of the same type, as in the following example where First and Second are both of type list.

```
var
  First, Second: list;
      |
      |
Second:= First;
```

We have to be careful, however, not to use two arrays of different types in an assignment statement. Assume that types list and long_list have been defined. The following program fragment is not allowed because First and Second are of different types.

```
var
  First: list;
  Second: long_list;
      |
      |
(**************************************)
(** THIS STATEMENT WILL NOT COMPILE **)
(**************************************)
Second := First;
```

Reading and Writing Arrays

An array cannot be read from the keyboard or written on the screen as a single entity, in a single `ReadLn` or `WriteLn` statement. Instead, an array is read or written as a sequence of array elements, often using a `for` loop to read or write each element.

Assume an engineer runs an experiment in which ten speed values are measured and written on a text file. Here is a simple program that reads the ten speed values from the file, and assigns these values to an array. The program then allows a user to display the value of any speed in the array by specifying its index. The file `SPEED.DAT` contains ten real numeric values. First we show an outline of the main program

Read values from a text file and assign to array elements.

Display selected values using procedure `DisplayValue`.

and then an outline of procedure `DisplayValue`.

Ask user to enter a numeric index value.

While index value is not zero.

Display the element of array `Speed` with this index.

Ask user to enter another index value.

Loop back.

The complete program listing is as follows.

```
PROGRAM EX0801 (Input, Output);
{
   Fill an array from a text file
   and display selected elements.
}
type
   list10 = array [1..10] of real;
var
   Speed: list10;

PROCEDURE ReadFile (var Speed: list10);
{
   Read the file and assign values
   to an array.
}
var
   SpeedFile: text;
   Index: integer;
begin
   Assign (SpeedFile, 'SPEED.DAT');
   Reset (SpeedFile);
   for Index:= 1 to 10 do
      Readln (SpeedFile, Speed[Index]);
end; { ReadFile }
```

```
PROCEDURE DisplayValue (Speed: list10);
{
  Display selected values in the list.
}
var
  Index: integer;
begin
  Writeln ('Enter index of zero to stop:');
  Write ('Index? ');
  Readln (Index);
  while Index <> 0 do
    begin
    Writeln ('The speed for this index is ',
             Speed[Index]:1:1);
    Writeln;
    Write ('Index? ');
    Readln (Index);
    end;
end; { DisplayValue }

BEGIN { Main Program }
  ReadFile (Speed);
  DisplayValue (Speed);
END.
```

This program produces the following output.

```
Enter index of zero to stop:
Index? 5
The speed for this index is 49.8

Index? 7
The speed for this index is 58.0

Index? 0
```

Turbo Pascal Note

Turbo Pascal is designed to produce programs that execute as quickly as possible, and because additional time is needed to check whether an index value is within its allowed range, the compiler is not very careful about range checking. In Program EX0801, the array index is specified to be in a range from 1 to 10. If you are using Version 3 and enter the value of 11, however, the value of Speed[11] is displayed, but it makes no sense. The program reads whatever old information is in the memory location following Speed[10].

```
Index? 11
The speed for this index is 6.6E+301
```

To avoid this situation, the compiler must be told to check the range of the index variable.

The R Compiler Directive

The proper directive to turn on range checking is { $R+}. If strict range checking is invoked, the first few lines of the program become

```
PROGRAM EX0801 (Input, Output);
{
  Fill an array from a text file
  and display selected elements.
}
{ $R+} { turn on range checking }
type
  list10 = array [1..10] of real;
```

If range checking is turned on, the program produces a run-time error rather than a nonsensical result when an illegal element of the array is accessed. **We recommend that you always turn on range checking when developing a program**, especially one containing arrays. After the program has been thoroughly debugged, if you wish you can turn off range checking by removing the { $R+} directive and thus allow the program to execute more quickly.

If you wish to keep range checking active in just a section of your program, place a { $R+} directive at the beginning of that section and a { $R-} directive at the end of the section.

In Versions 4 and 5, the Compiler command from the Options command menu allows compiler options to be customized for your particular installation of Turbo Pascal. We recommend that you use this menu to turn on range checking during program development.

Partially-Filled Arrays

We look next at a variation of Program EX0708, a program designed to support an engineering study of river water pollution. The new program reads data values representing river depths from a file and assigns these values to an array. This technique is often used when the individual data values may need to be used again later in the program.

If we knew there would always be exactly ten data values in the file, we could set the array to that size. A more general method is to make the array size large enough to hold a list of any reasonable length, and then partially fill the array. If we use this method, we need to develop a technique for determining how many values have been assigned to the array. In many cases, we can maintain a counter variable, and count the number of values written into the array.

For our example program, we choose to set the array size to 100, and before using the array, we initialize all elements to zero.

Note one disadvantage of this method: It is possible to define an array that is too large to fit into available memory space. We discuss this problem in detail when we introduce dynamic variables in Chapter 12.

It is also possible to define an array that is too small and cannot hold all the values we wish to assign to it. This is a fundamental limitation in the design of Pascal, as mentioned earlier, where *dynamic arrays* (whose sizes can be changed during program execution) are not supported.

Finding Maximum and Minimum Values

Finding the maximum value and minimum value in a sequence is another technique often used when reading sequences of numeric values. One variable (say MaxValue) is declared to hold the maximum value and another (say MinValue) to hold the minimum value. Each of these variables is assigned an initial value.

If looking for the minimum value, assign the largest possible initial value to MinValue. Each time a value is read, it is compared to the current value of MinValue. If the new value is smaller, it is assigned to MinValue in place of the current value. After all values have been read, the current value of MinValue is the minimum value.

A similar technique is used to find the maximum value. Assign the smallest possible initial value to MaxValue. If only positive numbers are read, this initial value is zero. If both positive and negative numbers are read, this initial value is the largest possible negative value. As before, compare each number as it is read with the current value of MaxValue. If the new value is larger, it is assigned to MaxValue in place of the current value.

Expanding on Program EX0708, we have added a program statement to determine the greatest depth. We initially set a variable MaxDepth to the smallest possible value, which is zero in this case. As each depth value is read from the file, we compare it with MaxDepth. If the value is larger than MaxDepth, then that value is assigned to MaxDepth. This technique results in MaxDepth containing the largest depth value.

In addition, because all depth values are saved in an array, we can easily retrieve and display both the first value and the last value read from the file.

The major change is in procedure ReadFile, so we present an outline of that subprogram.

Set variable Count to zero.

Set variable MaxDepth to zero.

Set variable Sum to zero.

While not at the end of the file.

    Increment variable Count.

    Read depth value from file and assign to array element.

    If depth value is greater than MaxDepth, assign this

      depth value to MaxDepth.

    Add depth value to Sum.

Loop back.

Calculate the average depth value.

Note that MaxDepth is set initially to zero because depth values are always positive numbers. Here is the complete program.

```
PROGRAM EX0802 (Output);
{
  Read depth values from the file DEPTH2.DAT and
  assign them to an array named DepthList.
  Display the number of values read, the first value,
  the last value, the average value, and the maximum
  value.
}
const
  SIZE = 100; { size of the array }
type
  list = array [1..SIZE] of real;
var
  FileVar: text;
  N: integer;
  Average, MaxDepth: real;
  DepthList: list;

PROCEDURE OpenFile (var F: text);
{
  Open the DEPTH2.DAT data file for reading.
}
begin
  Assign (F, 'DEPTH2.DAT');
  Reset (F);
end; { OpenFile }

PROCEDURE Initialize (var DepthList: list);
{
  Initialize elements of array DepthList to zero.
}
var
  I: integer;
begin
  for I:= 1 to SIZE do
    DepthList[I]:= 0.0;
end; { Initialize }

PROCEDURE ReadFile (var FV: text;
                    var DepthList: list;
                    var Average, MaxDepth: real;
                    var Count: integer);
{
  Read values from a text file, calculate
  the average value and the maximum value.
}
```

```
var
  Sum: real;
begin
  Count:= 0;
  MaxDepth:= 0.0;
  Sum:= 0.0;
  while not Eof(FV) do
    begin
    Count:= Count + 1;
    Readln (FV, DepthList[Count]);
    if DepthList[Count] > MaxDepth then
      MaxDepth:= DepthList[Count];
    Sum:= Sum + DepthList[Count];
    end; { while loop }
  Average:= Sum / Count;
end; { ReadFile }

PROCEDURE DisplayResults (DepthList: list;
                          Average, MaxDepth: real;
                          N: integer);
{
  Display the required results.
}

begin
  WriteLn ('Results from file DEPTH2.DAT:');
  WriteLn (N:1, ' depth values are read');
  WriteLn ('The first depth is ', DepthList[1]:1:2);
  WriteLn ('The last depth is ', DepthList[N]:1:2);
  WriteLn ('The average depth is ', Average:1:2);
  WriteLn ('The maximum depth is ', MaxDepth:1:2);
end; { DisplayResults }

BEGIN { Main Program }
  OpenFile (FileVar);
  Initialize (DepthList);
  ReadFile (FileVar, DepthList, Average, MaxDepth, N);
  DisplayResults (DepthList, Average, MaxDepth, N);
END.
```

Let us review our use of parameters in this example program. The procedure OpenFile uses a variable parameter because **a file variable must always be passed as a variable parameter, not as a value parameter**. This is a requirement of Pascal that we discuss further in Chapter 9.

The procedure Initialize uses a variable parameter for the data array because the initialized array must be returned to the main program.

The procedure ReadFile uses all variable parameters. The file variable must be a variable parameter, as discussed previously. The four other parameters must all return values to the main program, and thus have to be variable parameters.

The procedure `DisplayResults` uses value parameters for all variables because information is passed only one way, from the main program to the procedure.

Notice once again the short main program, which is a sign of a well-written, modular Pascal program. When you read the main program, you see an outline of the entire program. The following output is displayed.

```
Results from file DEPTH2.DAT:
10 depth values are read
The first depth is 12.31
The last depth is 25.49
The average depth is 29.18
The maximum depth is 55.70
```

8.3 THE STRING TYPE

In standard Pascal, a string variable can be defined by the user as a one-dimensional array of characters. For example, the declaration block might contain the statements

```
type
    name_string = array [1..30] of char;
var
    Description: name_string;
```

A value can be assigned to the variable `Description` using the following program fragment.

```
Description := 'PRESSURE GAUGE            ';
```

Any string constant assigned to `Description` must contain a total of exactly thirty characters. The trailing blanks are needed to erase any old characters that may have been left over from the last value assigned to the string.

While this type of string structure can be used (and is the only string structure available in standard Pascal), most implementations of Pascal support a predefined `string` type. The details of this type vary from one implementation of Pascal to another.

```
┌──────────────────────────────────────────────────────────────┐
│                        Turbo Pascal Note                       │
└──────────────────────────────────────────────────────────────┘
```

The remainder of Section 8.3 describes the implementation in Turbo Pascal of string types and standard string functions and procedures.

Strings in Turbo Pascal

Turbo Pascal includes a predefined `string` type, where the number of characters in a string may vary dynamically between zero and some maximum value.

A string variable is a structured variable, similar to an array. In Version 3 of Turbo Pascal, the type definition must always contain an integer constant specifying the maximum number of characters that can be stored in the string. This number is called the *defined length* of the string. For example, a type definition for a string might be

```
type
   string255 = string[255];
```

for a type that can hold up to 255 characters.

A variable declaration can then be used to specify the names of one or more string variables.

```
var
   Description, Location: string255;
```

Versions 4 and 5 of Turbo Pascal define the type `string`, without square brackets and a number, to represent a string with a maximum length of 255 characters. The previous declaration can then be written

```
var
   Description, Location: string;
```

Dynamic Length of a String Variable

Different string types can be defined, with maximum or defined lengths from 1 to 255 characters. In addition to the defined length, a string variable value also has a *dynamic length*. This length is equal to the number of characters currently stored in the string variable and can change, of course, with each new assignment. The dynamic length cannot exceed the defined length.

Using our previous declarations, we can assign a value to the string variable `Description` using the statement

```
Description:= 'PRESSURE GAUGE';
```

Note that `Description` is of type `string` (or `string255`) which has a defined length of 255, but after the preceding assignment, `Description` has a dynamic length of 14 (the number of characters in `PRESSURE GAUGE`).

A string with a dynamic length of zero is called a *null string*. It is created using the assignment

```
Description:= ''; {two single quotation marks}
```

Here is an example program where a string variable of type `string20` is defined, and used to allow a user to specify a file name.

```
PROGRAM EX0803 (Input, Output);
{
   Test a procedure that opens
   a file for reading.
}
type
   string20 = string[20];
```

```
var
  FileName: string20;
  FileVar: text;

PROCEDURE OpenInFile (var FileName: string20;
                      var FileVar: text);
{
  Ask user to enter a file name
  and then open that file for reading.
}
begin
  Write ('Name of file? ');
  Readln (FileName);
  Assign (FileVar, FileName);
  Reset (FileVar);
end;

BEGIN { Main Program }
  OpenInFile (FileName, FileVar);
  Writeln ('File ', FileName, ' has been opened.');
END.
```

Sample program interaction might look as follows, with user input underlined.

```
Name of file? DEPTH2.DAT
File DEPTH2.DAT has been opened.
```

String Concatenation

An operation similar to arithmetic addition is available for strings. Two or more string variables or constants can be *concatenated* or joined together. The concatenation operator is the plus sign (+). The individual strings can be of different types; that is, they can have different defined lengths. For example, the following program fragment concatenates two string variables and one string constant

```
var
  First, Last: string[10];
       |
First:= 'Alpha';
Last:= 'Omega';
Writeln (First + ' to ' + Last);
```

producing the output

```
Alpha to Omega
```

We rewrite the previous example program to allow a user to specify both the file name and the disk drive. This version of procedure OpenInFile assumes that the disk contains only a single directory, the root directory.

```
PROGRAM EX0804 (Input, Output);
{
  Test a procedure that opens
  a file for reading.
}
type
  string40 = string[40];
var
  PathName: string40;
  FileVar: text;

PROCEDURE OpenInFile (var PathName: string40;
                      var FileVar: text);
{
  Ask user to enter a file name and a disk drive
  name; then open that file for reading.
  Assume that the only directory is the root
  directory.
}

var
  DiskName, FileName: string40;
begin
  Write ('Name of file? ');
  Readln (FileName);
  Write ('On disk in which disk drive? ');
  Readln (DiskName);
  PathName:=DiskName + ':' + FileName;
  Assign (FileVar, PathName);
  Reset (FileVar);
end; { OpenInFile }

BEGIN { Main Program }
  OpenInFile (PathName, FileVar);
  Write ('File ', PathName, ' has been opened.');
END.
```

Both the file name and the disk drive name are requested, and then concatenated together, with a colon between them, to form the path name. Here is a sample of user interaction with this program.

```
Name of file? DEPTH1.DAT
On disk in which disk drive? B
File B:DEPTH1.DAT has been opened.
```

If the disk in drive B contains more than one directory and the named file is not in the current directory, a run-time error will occur.

Strings as Arrays

Remember that we first described strings as one-dimensional arrays of characters. We can actually reference every character in a string by using the normal array notation. For example, assume we have the following program fragment:

```
var
  Name: string[80];
     |
Name:= 'METER';
WriteLn (Name[1]);
WriteLn (Name[5]);
```

A string value METER is assigned to Name. We refer to the first character in Name by the notation Name[1], the second character by Name[2], and so forth. The last character is denoted by Name[5]. In our example, the first WriteLn statement displays the letter M, while the second displays the letter R.

We can even go a step further and assign a single character from a string variable value to a character variable,

```
var
  Name: string[80];
  Ch: char;
     |
Name:= 'METER';
WriteLn (Name[1]);
WriteLn (Name[5]);
Ch:= Name[3];
WriteLn (Ch);
```

where the third WriteLn statement displays the letter T. This capability of extracting individual characters from string variables complements the process of concatenation, and is often used when working with strings.

Standard Turbo Pascal String Functions

Turbo Pascal contains several standard string functions and procedures that make it easier to manipulate strings. We now introduce three of these functions.

The Length Function.   The Length function returns an integer value that is the dynamic length of a string parameter; that is, the number of characters currently stored in the string. The syntax is

```
Length(Strg)
```

where Strg is a string variable or constant. For example, the program fragment

```
Description:= 'PRESSURE GAUGE';
WriteLn ('Length of string ', Description, ' is ',
        Length(Description):1, ' characters.');
```

produces the display

Length of string PRESSURE GAUGE is 14 characters.

The Pos Function.   The Pos function returns an integer value that is the position in a target string where the first character of a specified pattern string occurs. If the pattern occurs more than once, the value returned is the position of the first occurrence. The first character in a string is in position one. The syntax is

```
Pos(Pattern, Target)
```

where parameters Pattern and Target are string variables or constants. If the pattern is not found, Pos returns a value of zero. For example, the program fragment

```
Description: = 'PRESSURE GAUGE';
X: = Pos(' ', Description); { pattern is a space }
WriteLn ('Second word starts at position ', (X + 1):1);
```

produces the display

```
Second word starts at position 10
```

Note that the variable X is assigned the position of the space between the first and second words, and thus the last word starts at position (X + 1). As illustrated by this example, the pattern is often a single-character string variable or constant. Note that a variable of type char cannot be used as the pattern.

The Copy Function.   The Copy function returns a string value that is a substring of its string parameter, starting at the character position specified by an index (P), and containing a specified number of characters (N). The syntax is

```
Copy (Strg, P, N)
```

where parameter Strg is a string variable or constant, and parameters P and N are integer variables or constants. If P is greater than the length of Strg, an empty or null string is returned. If P plus N exceeds the length of Strg, only the characters within Strg after P are returned.

For example, the program fragment

```
Description: = 'PRESSURE GAUGE';
X: = Pos(' ', Description);
FirstWord: = Copy(Description, 1, X - 1);
SecondWord: = Copy(Description, X + 1,
                 Length(Description) - X);
WriteLn ('The first word is ', FirstWord,
         ' and second word is ', SecondWord);
```

produces the display

```
The first word is PRESSURE and second word is GAUGE
```

The first word starts at position 1 and extends through position X − 1. As noted previously, the second name starts at position X + 1. The number of characters in the second word is given by (Length(Description) − X).

Referring to the preceding syntax statement, another property of the `Copy` function is that if N is so large that (P + N) exceeds the length of `Strg`, only the characters within `Strg` after P are returned. Thus the N parameter can be a large integer (large compared to the length of `Description`) when extracting `SecondWord` from `Description`. The statement

```
SecondWord : = Copy(Description, X + 1,
                    Length(Description) - X);
```

can just as well be written

```
SecondWord : = Copy(Description, X + 1, MaxInt);
```

where `MaxInt` is the predefined value representing the largest integer available in Pascal. This second version of the statement executes more quickly than the first version.

We now put these program fragments together in an example program that reads engineering product names from a file named `PRODUCTS.DAT`, and reverses the word order to make the list easier to sort. Much of the work is done by function `Reverse`, whose outline follows.

Find position in the string of the space between words.

Read first word and assign to a variable.

Read second word and assign to a variable.

Concatenate second word, plus comma and space, plus first word.

Assign new concatenated word to function `Reverse`.

Another procedure opens the file. The main program calls this procedure, displays a heading, and then uses the function `Reverse` to modify each part description in the file.

```
PROGRAM EX0805 (Input, Output);
{
   Read product names from file PRODUCTS.DAT,
   and then display each name in reverse order,
   second word followed by first word.
   No more than two words allowed in product name.
}
type
   string80 = string[80];
var
   Description: string80;
   FV: text;

PROCEDURE OpenInFile (var InFile: text);
{
   Ask user to enter a file name
   and then open that file for reading.
}
```

```
var
  FileName: string[30];
begin
  Write ('Name of file? ');
  Readln (FileName);
  WriteLn;
  Assign (InFile, FileName);
  Reset (InFile);
end;

FUNCTION Reverse (Name: string80): string80;
{
  Reverse the position of first and second words.
  The variable Name must contain only two words.
}
var
  FirstWord, SecondWord: string80;
  X: integer;
begin
  X:= Pos(' ', Name);
  FirstWord:= Copy(Name, 1, X-1);
  SecondWord:= Copy(Name, X+1, MaxInt);
  Reverse:= SecondWord + ', ' + FirstWord;
end; { Reverse }

BEGIN { Main Program }
  OpenInFile (FV);
  WriteLn ('Product Descriptions');
  WriteLn;
  while not Eof(FV) do
    begin
    Readln (FV, Description);
    WriteLn (Reverse(Description));
    end;
END.
```

Here is an example of user interaction:

```
Name of file? products.dat

Product Descriptions

GAUGE, PRESSURE
MONITOR, COLOR
MONITOR, MONOCHROMATIC
OSCILLOSCOPE, PORTABLE
RECORDER, MULTI-CHANNEL
RECORDER, TAPE
RECORDER, VCR
VALVE, SHUTOFF
```

Standard Turbo Pascal String Procedures

Turbo Pascal also has several standard string procedures. We list all these procedures in Appendix D, and describe four of them in Figure 8.1. The procedures Str and Val are particularly useful, so we discuss them in more detail in the following paragraphs.

Delete (Strg, P, N);	delete substring of length N, starting at position P, from string Strg
Insert (Sub, Strg, P);	insert substring Sub into string Strg at position P
Str (Num, Strg);	convert integer or real Num to string Strg
Val (Strg, Num, Code);	convert string Strg to real or integer Num, returning integer Code > 0 if error occurs

Figure 8.1 Standard Turbo Pascal string procedures.

The Str and Val Procedures.   These two procedures permit conversion between string values and numeric values. **Remember that the number 123 and the string 123 are entirely different quantities** and are stored in computer memory or on disk in completely different forms. While they may look the same to us when displayed on the screen or printed on paper, the computer treats them as distinct and different entities.

Procedure Str converts a numeric variable into a string variable with the same sequence of digits, and has the syntax

```
Str (Num, Strg);
```

where Num is a real or integer variable, and Strg is a string variable. Appropriate format instructions (similar to those used with the Write and WriteLn procedures) may be included with Num to specify the format of Strg. For example

- If Num has a value of 13, Str (Num:1, Strg) assigns the value '13' to Strg.
- If Num has a value of 12.5, Str (Num:8:2, Strg) assigns the value ' 12.50' to Strg.
- If Num has a value of 12.5, Str (Num, Strg) assigns the value '1.2500000000000E+001' to Strg.

Procedure Val converts a string variable, consisting of a sequence of digits, into a numeric variable. It has the syntax

```
Val (Strg, Num, Code);
```

where Strg is a string variable, and Num is a real or integer variable. The variable Code is of type integer. It is called the *return code* and is assigned a value of zero if the conversion is successful. If not successful, Code is assigned the position of the first character in Strg that is in error.

Here is an example program that shows one use of the Val procedure. A procedure named ReadNum asks the user to enter a number, assigns the characters that are entered to a string variable, and if all characters are valid, converts the string value to a real value. An advantage of this input technique is that an invalid numeric entry does not cause a program crash. Instead, the user is informed of the error, and given another chance to enter a valid number.

```
PROGRAM EX0806 (Input, Output);
{
Demonstrate use of the ReadNum procedure.
}
var
N: real;

PROCEDURE ReadNum (var Num: real);
{
   Ask user to enter a number, assign characters to a
   string variable, try to convert to a real number.
   If error, display message and ask for entry again.
}
var
   Entry: string[20];
   Code: integer;
begin
   Code := 1; { initialize Code > 0 }
   Write ('Number? ');
   Readln (Entry);
   while Code > 0 do
     begin
     Val (Entry, Num, Code);
     if Code > 0 then
       begin
       WriteLn ('This entry is not a valid number');
       WriteLn ('Error in character at position ',
               Code:1);
       WriteLn;
       Write ('Number? ');
       Readln (Entry);
       end; { if branch }
     end; { while loop }
end; { ReadNum }

BEGIN { Main Program }
   ReadNum (N);
   WriteLn ('The number is', N);
END.
```

We show two sample runs of this program:

```
Number? 12.5e5
The number is 1.2500000000E+06

Number? 11,437.25
This entry is not a valid number
Error in character at position 3

Number? 11437.25
The number is 1.1437250000E+04
```

IMPORTANT POINTS

- The shorthand method of declaring a structured variable can cause problems in some situations and, in general, should be avoided. It cannot be used to declare a formal parameter in a procedure or function heading.
- Real variables cannot be used as index variables for arrays.
- Both the lower bound and the upper bound in an array definition statement must be constant values or constant identifiers; they cannot be variables.
- If you declare an array of a different size, you must use a different type name.
- An array cannot be read from the keyboard or written on the screen as a single entity in a single `Readln` or `WriteLn` statement.
- We recommend that you always turn on range checking when developing a program, especially one containing arrays.
- A file variable must be passed as a variable parameter, not as a value parameter.
- The number 123 and the string 123 are entirely different quantities.

SELF-STUDY QUESTIONS

1. If a type is declared as an `array [0..10] of real`, how many numbers can be stored in a variable of this type?
2. In an array named `Matrix`, an element of the array is denoted by `Matrix[Index]`. Can the variable `Index` be
   (a) of type `real`;
   (b) of type `integer`;
   (c) of type `char`?
3. Can a variable be used to specify
   (a) the lower bound of an array;
   (b) the upper bound of an array?

4. Can you assign a value directly to
(a) an entire array;
(b) an individual element of an array?

5. (a) If an array of integers is declared to be of size 100, can it be used to store 25 integer values?
(b) What information, besides the name of the array variable, do you need to pass to a procedure that is designed to display the values stored in the array?

6. What, if anything, is wrong with the variable declaration statement

```
var
   Name: string;
```

7. Given the program fragment

```
var
   Item: string[30];
   |
Item := 'Oscilloscope';
```

what is
(a) the defined length of Item;
(b) the dynamic length of Item?

8. (a) What is the string concatenation operator?
(b) What is its purpose?

9. Does the Length function return the defined length or the dynamic length of its string parameter?

10. How do you assign a null value to a string variable?

11. What value is returned by the Pos function if the specified string pattern is not found?

12. Is a return code provided
(a) in procedure Str;
(b) in procedure Val?

13. Is number formatting provided
(a) in procedure Str;
(b) in procedure Val?

PRACTICE PROGRAMS

1. A series of new photovoltaic cells are tested, and the results are stored in a file named PVCELL.DAT. Each test produces a single number representing the conversion efficiency of that particular cell.

Design a program that writes the contents of this file to an array, and then calculates the average conversion efficiency. Develop a list of sample values by extracting and displaying every tenth element of the array. Be sure to use appropriate labels and headings to explain the displayed results.

2. An engineer is asked to write an executive summary of not more than one-thousand words, explaining the latest design of a local area network. The engineer decides to develop a computer program that counts the words in a text file.

   Write a function that returns the number of words in a line. Assume each line is of type `string80`. Assume there is a word (no initial blank) at the beginning of each line and a word (no final blank) at the end of each line. Any other sequence of one or more characters surrounded by blanks is defined as a word. Assume only one blank between words.

   Test your function in a program that reads all the lines in the text file `TEST.DOC`.

3. In order to make the executive summary of a technical report easily understandable, the average word length must be kept short. Write another function that returns the average word length in a line. Use the same assumptions that are given in Practice Program 2, and also make use of the function developed in that program.

   Test your function in a program that reads all the lines in the text file `TEST.DOC`.

4. The procedure in Program EX0806 is to be used by a scientist to enter experimental data into a computer program, provided two improvements are made. First, the scientist would like to enter numbers with commas between certain digits and have the procedure accept this entry as valid. Second, the scientist wants to use a user-defined prompt for entering the number and have this prompt passed as a parameter to the procedure.

   Test the modified procedure in a program similar to EX0806.

5. An engineer keeps an information file on articles that appear in a technical society journal that are of special significance. The information on each article is stored as one line in a text file and has the following format:

   volume,issue,title,author name,page

   Author name consists of first name followed by last name, with the two names separated by a space. Upon entering the name of the text file, a table of author last names and titles should display, arranged in the following format:

   last name   title

   The last names and titles should appear on the screen in two columns, properly aligned and with appropriate column headings.

   Test your program using the file `INDEX.TXT`.

6. The need sometimes arises for an engineer to use integers that are larger than the maximum integer size supported by a favorite programming language. Write a procedure that adds two integers containing up to 30 digits. The two digits are passed to the procedure as arrays, and the sum is also an array. Test your procedure in a program that passes the two following sequences of digits to the procedure.

   991239564738100953822764831028
   384560283148539876394857261090

7. Writing a procedure to subtract two 30-digit numbers is more difficult than writing a procedure to add them. Assume that both numbers are positive, and that the number being subtracted (the subtrahend) is smaller than the number from which it is being subtracted (the minuend).

Test your procedure with the same numbers used to test Practice Program 6.

9

MORE ABOUT SUBPROGRAMS AND LIBRARIES

9.1 INTRODUCTION

We introduce the concept of scope of variables, as applied to programs containing subprograms. We further examine value and variable parameters, and compare these two ways of exchanging information with subprograms.

Subprogram libraries and their uses are discussed, as well as a method for including library files in a program. We also introduce the concept of user-defined units, compiled program modules that can be accessed by a program.

9.2 SCOPE OF VARIABLES

We have mentioned that local variables are known only in the subprogram where they are declared, and global variables are known throughout the entire program. This statement is not always completely true for local variables, and we need to examine in detail what we mean by the *scope* of variables.

Short and medium length programs, such as our example programs, typically have a main program and several subprograms that are all called from the main program. It is perfectly possible, however, for one subprogram to contain another subprogram, and for the latter subprogram to contain yet another subprogram. This *nesting* of subprograms occurs more often in large programs and can be extended to any depth.

Returning to the concept of scope of variables, **a variable declared in a subprogram is known in that subprogram and in all subprograms contained or**

nested within that subprogram. We define the scope of a variable as that part of the program in which the variable is known, or in which the variable can represent a value.

Global and Local Variables

Referring to Figure 9.1, we see that variable AV is global and known throughout the entire program. Thus AV is a *global variable*. The variable BV is known only in function B and is a *local variable* in that subprogram.

Variable CV is known in procedure C, as well as in procedure D and function E. Variable DV is known only in procedure D, while variable EV is known only in function E.

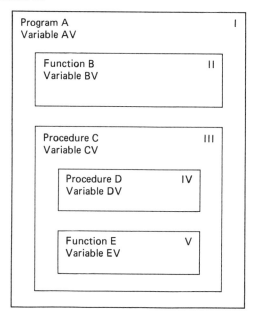

Figure 9.1 Block diagram of Pascal program and subprograms.

Program Blocks

Sometimes it helps to think in terms of *blocks* that contain one or more subprograms (including the main program). Another definition of the scope of a variable is the name of the block that can access that variable. The scope of variable AV, a global variable, is Block I or the entire program. The scope of variable CV is Block III, which contains Blocks IV and V. Figure 9.2 shows the complete list of variables and their scopes.

VARIABLE	SCOPE
AV	Block I
BV	Block II
CV	Block III
DV	Block IV
EV	Block V

Figure 9.2 Scope of variables in program blocks.

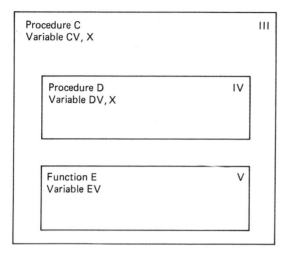

Figure 9.3 Part of a modified block diagram.

We now show part of the previous block diagram again in Figure 9.3, with a variable X declared in both procedure C (Block III) and procedure D (Block IV). There are now two X variables defined in the program. The value in each X variable is not necessarily the same, even though each has the same name.

If we refer to variable X in procedure D, we mean the variable declared in procedure D. If we refer to variable X in function E, we mean the variable declared in procedure C. A locally-declared variable (as in procedure D) always takes precedence over a variable of the same name declared in an outer block.

Turbo Pascal Note

As we discussed in Chapter 5, it is possible in Turbo Pascal to place a variable declaration block anywhere outside a subprogram body of statements or the main program body of statements. Such variables declared after all functions and procedures are local to the main program. This structure is not allowed in standard Pascal, and we do not recommend it.

9.3 SUBPROGRAM PARAMETERS

In Chapter 5, we introduced functions and procedures with value and variable parameters. Now we shall look at these two kinds of parameters in more detail.

Action of Value Parameters

Value parameters transfer a value from the calling program (often the main program) to the subprogram. If the actual parameter is a constant or an expression, the value of this constant or expression is assigned to the formal parameter variable, which is a local variable. Information is thus sent from the calling program to the subprogram.

If the actual parameter is a variable its value is similarly assigned to the formal parameter variable. The actual parameter variable and the formal parameter variable refer to two different mailboxes or memory locations, but each mailbox contains the same value. If the value of the local parameter variable in the subprogram is changed, this action has no effect on the value of the variable in the calling program. This method of transferring information is called *pass-by-value*.

A consequence of this method of passing information is that changes in values of formal parameter variables are isolated from the corresponding actual parameter variables. **Information is passed in one direction only, from the calling program to the subprogram**. Value parameters are also called *one-way parameters*.

Here is an example program containing a procedure with value parameters.

```
PROGRAM EX0901 (Output);
{
   Display variable values in a procedure
   with value parameters.
}
var
   X, Y: real;

PROCEDURE Half (X, Y: real);
{
   Assign half the value of X to Y.
}
begin
   Y: = X / 2.0;
   Writeln ('Value of X in procedure is ', X:1:1);
   Writeln ('Value of Y in procedure is ', Y:1:1);
end; { Half }

BEGIN { Main Program }
   X: = 15.0;
   Y: = 15.0;
   Writeln ('Original value of X in main program is ',
            X:1:1);
   Writeln ('Original value of Y in main program is ',
            Y:1:1);
   Half(X, Y);
   Writeln ('Final value of X in main program is ',
            X:1:1);
   Writeln ('Final value of Y in main program is ',
            Y:1:1);
END.
```

This program produces the following output.

```
Original value of X in main program is 15.0
Original value of Y in main program is 15.0
Value of X in procedure is 15.0
Value of Y in procedure is 7.5
Final value of X in main program is 15.0
Final value of Y in main program is 15.0
```

X and Y both start with values of 15.0. In procedure Half, Y is assigned the value of (X / 2.0) or 7.5. However, Y in the procedure is a different variable from Y in the main program, and so this new value of Y is not passed back to the main program. Thus the final value of Y in the main program is the same as the original value, 15.0. Both the global variable X, and the local variable X, have a value of 15.0, and this value is not changed anywhere in the program.

Action of Variable Parameters

Variable parameters assign the same mailbox to the formal parameter and to the actual parameter. In other words, both a local name and a global name exist for a given mailbox or memory location. Any value stored in this mailbox is known to both the calling program and the subprogram. This method of transferring information is called *pass-by-reference*, because the information that is passed refers to the address or location of the mailbox.

Variable parameters are also called *two-way parameters* because they **permit a two-way exchange of information between the calling program and the subprogram**. As a consequence, there is less isolation between the two entities. **The actual variable parameters must always be variables; they cannot be constants or expressions**.

Both value and variable parameters may be mixed in the same procedure (or function) heading statement, but must be in separate parameter lists. Those parameters in parameter lists starting with the reserved word var are variable parameters, while value parameter lists have no identifying word. For example, a typical subprogram heading might be

```
PROCEDURE Graph (Start, Stop: real; var Source: text;
                 var Data: list; Color: integer);
```

where Start and Stop are value parameters of type real, Source is a variable parameter of type text, Data is a variable parameter of type list, and Color is a value parameter of type integer.

Here is an example program containing a procedure with variable parameters.

```
PROGRAM EX0902 (Output);
{
  Display variable values in a procedure
  with variable parameters.
}
var
  X, Y: real;

PROCEDURE Half (var X, Y: real);
{
  Assign half the value of X to Y.
}
begin
  Y:= X / 2.0;
  Writeln ('Value of X in procedure is ', X:1:1);
  Writeln ('Value of Y in procedure is ', Y:1:1);
end; { Half }
```

```
BEGIN { Main Program }
  X := 15.0;
  Y := 15.0;
  Writeln ('Original value of X in main program is ',
          X:1:1);
  Writeln ('Original value of Y in main program is ',
          Y:1:1);
  Half (X, Y);
  Writeln ('Final value of X in main program is ',
          X:1:1);
  Writeln ('Final value of Y in main program is ',
          Y:1:1);
END.
```

This program produces the following output.

```
Original value of X in main program is 15.0
Original value of Y in main program is 15.0
Value of X in procedure is 15.0
Value of Y in procedure is 7.5
Final value of X in main program is 15.0
Final value of Y in main program is 7.5
```

As before, both X and Y start with values of 15.0. In procedure Half, Y is assigned the value of (X / 2.0) or 7.5. Because Y is a variable parameter, the same memory location is used by Y in the main program and by Y in the procedure. Thus, the final value of Y in the main program becomes 7.5. The value of X remains unchanged at 15.0.

9.4 COMPARING VALUE AND VARIABLE PARAMETERS

Below are listed some of the advantages and disadvantages of the two kinds of parameters.

- Value parameters provide the best isolation between the calling program and the subprogram.
- Variable parameters allow information to be transferred back to the calling program.
- Value parameters require two copies of a variable in two different memory locations; variable parameters require only a single copy.

Remember that isolation between blocks in a program is a technique that often reduces programming errors. Isolation prevents a change in the value of a variable in one block from affecting the value of a variable in another block.

Variable Parameters in Functions

In practice, functions almost always use value parameters. A value is returned through the function name, and maximum isolation is provided between the function and the main program or other subprograms. If more than one value must be returned, a procedure with variable parameters is normally used.

Variable Parameters for Arrays and Files

When a large array is passed as a parameter, it is often passed as a variable parameter to save memory space. Remember that value parameters require two memory locations for each pair of actual and formal parameters, while variable parameters require only one memory location for the pair. **Pascal requires that file variables be passed as variable parameters.**

Variable Parameters in Procedures

Procedures that only carry out some action and do not return values should use value parameters, unless the parameters are files or large arrays. If more than one value must be returned from a subprogram, a procedure with variable parameters should be used.

9.5 PROCEDURES AND FUNCTIONS AS PARAMETERS

Standard Pascal allows procedures and functions to be passed as parameters in subprograms. For example, a procedure heading with a function parameter is shown in the following program fragment.

```
PROCEDURE Display (function Result (X: real): real;
                   X: real);
```

This procedure is designed to display the value of the function `Result` for a particular value of `X`. The calling statement for the procedure might look as follows

```
Display (Sin, PI/4);
```

where `PI` is a user-defined constant.

Note that only the function name, without the function parameter, is included in the calling statement. The sine of X is displayed for $X = \pi/4$.

Turbo Pascal Note

The capability of passing procedures and functions as parameters in other subprograms is not supported in Turbo Pascal, Versions 3 and 4. The lack of this capability is a serious omission for engineering applications.

The `Procedure` Type

In Version 5, however, a `procedure` type can be declared that allows procedures and functions to be treated as objects. These objects can be assigned to variables or passed as subprogram parameters.

The syntax for defining a procedure type is similar to a function or procedure heading statement, but with the function or procedure name omitted. For example, the type definition block

```
type
   trig_func = function (Z: real): real;
   strg_proc = procedure (S1, S2: string; N: integer);
```

defines two procedure types. Type `trig_func` represents any real function that has a single real parameter. Type `strg_proc` represents any procedure with three parameters as shown. **Any function or procedure used as a procedure type cannot be a standard Turbo Pascal function or procedure,** but must be defined in the program. It also cannot be a nested function or procedure.

A further requirement is that the function or procedure must be compiled to produce `far` binary code subprogram calls, a subject beyond the scope of our present discussion. For our purposes, this requirement means that any function or procedure of type `procedure` must be compiled with the {$F+} compiler directive.

Here is an example program that demonstrates the use of a procedure-type variable as a parameter.

```
PROGRAM EX0903 (Output);
{
  Use a procedural variable as a parameter in a procedure
  that displays the value of trigonometric functions.
}
type
  trig_func = function (Z: real): real;

{$F+} { force far subroutine calls }
FUNCTION Sine (X: real): real;
{
  Calculate the sine of an angle.
}
begin
  Sine: = Sin(X);
end; { Sine }

FUNCTION Tangent (X: real): real;
{
  Calculate the tangent of an angle.
}
begin
  Tangent: = Sin(X) / Cos(X);
end; { Tangent }
{$F-} { return to normal subroutine calls }

PROCEDURE Display (Result: trig_func; Angle: real);
{
  Display the trigonometric function of an angle.
}
begin
  Writeln (Result(Angle):1:4);
end; { Display }

BEGIN { Main Program }
  Display (Tangent, Pi/4);
  Display (Sine, Pi/4);
END.
```

The procedure type, trig_func, denotes a real function with a single real variable. We define two functions of this kind, Tangent and Sine. Note that Sine is only a user-defined version of the standard function Sin. Both functions are compiled with the F compiler directive turned on.

In procedure Display, the parameter Result is of type trig_func. This procedure only displays the value parameter function for a given angle. In the main program, procedure Display is called twice with a different function parameter each time.

This program produces the following results.

```
1.0000
0.7071
```

Other applications of the procedure type are discussed in the Version 5 reference material. This new type provides additional important capabilities for Turbo Pascal users, especially engineers and scientists.

9.6 SUBPROGRAM LIBRARIES

Many implementations of Pascal provide a way to save frequently-used functions and procedures in a library, and then include these subprograms in a new program during compilation. In addition to saving time when writing a program, the use of library subprograms reduces errors.

Assuming that the subprograms in a library file have been thoroughly tested, the file can be included in a new program with little chance of introducing errors. A good programmer does not write the same routines over and over again but, having written and debugged a general-purpose function or procedure, saves it in a library file for future use.

The time required to write and debug a new program can be reduced substantially if libraries of subprograms are used. Some thought should be given to organizing library files so that each file contains the same general kind of function and procedure.

Turbo Pascal Note

The Include Compiler Directive

The Include compiler directive consists of the statement

```
{$I pathname }
```

usually placed near the beginning of a program. This directive causes a file of program statements to be included in the program at the position of the compiler directive. We call this kind of file an *include file*. The Include compiler directive is often used to include library functions and procedures in a newly-written program.

The identifier pathname is any valid path name, written in either uppercase or lowercase letters. Leading spaces before the path name are ignored. If the file name has no period and extension, a space must be left between the file name and the closing brace, otherwise the brace is considered part of the file name. Nesting of Include compiler directives is not allowed in Version 3, where a file included in a program cannot use this same compiler directive to call another file. Versions 4 and 5 allow Include compiler directives to be nested up to eight levels deep.

Here is a rewritten version of Program EX0504 that assumes the function Cube (listed in Section 5.3) has been stored in a disk file named CUBE.INC.

```
PROGRAM EX0904 (Input, Output);
{
   Test the Include compiler directive.
   This is a rewritten version of EX0504.
   It includes a function that returns
   the cube of a real number.
}
var
   Diameter, Radius, Volume: real;

{$I CUBE.INC } { Contains function Cube(X) }

BEGIN { Main Program }
   Write ('Diameter of balloon in feet? ');
   Readln (Diameter);
   Radius:=Diameter / 2.0;
   Volume:=(4.0 * Pi * Cube(Radius)) / 3.0;
   Write ('You need ', Volume:1:0);
   Writeln (' cubic feet of gas.');
END.
```

Note that this program uses the standard Turbo Pascal function Pi, rather than a user-defined constant.

Inclusion of File Name Extension

A hard-to-find error can be created by the way Turbo Pascal sometimes handles file names. In the editor, and more importantly, **in the Include compiler directive, the extension PAS is automatically added to a file name without an extension**. Thus the compiler directive

```
{$I MYFILE }
```

looks for the file MYFILE.PAS in the current directory. If you really want a file named MYFILE with no extension, you must use the compiler directive

```
{$I MYFILE. }
```

Both the trailing period after MYFILE, and the space before the closing brace are required.

Library Files

Every programmer should store commonly-used procedures and functions in a Turbo Pascal library file. Here is an example of a short library file for the common trigonometric functions with angles expressed in degrees. If you are writing a program that needs to use any of the functions in this file, include the compiler directive {$I TRIG.INC}.

```
{ Library file TRIG.INC }
{
  Contains the common trigonometric functions
  with angle parameters in degrees.

  Function names: Rad, SinD, CosD, TanD,
}

FUNCTION Rad (Angle: real): real;
{
  Convert angle in degrees to radians.
}
begin
  Rad := (Angle * Pi) / 180.0;
end; { Rad }

FUNCTION SinD (Angle: real): real;
{
  Calculate the sine of an angle
  expressed in degrees.
}
begin
  SinD := Sin(Rad(Angle));
end; { SinD }

FUNCTION CosD (Angle: real): real;
{
  Calculate the cosine of an angle
  expressed in degrees.
}
begin
  CosD := Cos(Rad(Angle));
end; { CosD }

FUNCTION TanD (Angle: real): real;
{
  Calculate the tangent of an angle
  expressed in degrees.
}
begin
  TanD := Sin(Rad(Angle)) / Cos(Rad(Angle));
end; { TanD }

{ End of TRIG.INC }
```

Note that the library file is not a Pascal program, and thus contains no main program or final end statement. It is just a collection of subprograms.

In Versions 4 and 5, it generally is more efficient to store libraries of subprograms in units, rather than include files. Units contain compiled code, and their use reduces the time required to compile your program. We discuss how to write your own units in the next section.

Commercial libraries are also available that can reduce considerably the time and work required to write an application program. A programmer should be aware of these libraries and use them when appropriate. They can save a tremendous amount of programming time when developing a large Turbo Pascal program.

Two of the best library collections for Turbo Pascal are the various toolboxes from Borland International (the developers of Turbo Pascal), and Power Tools Plus, written by Blaise Computing of Berkeley, California.

9.7 COMPILED PROGRAM MODULES

Several implementations of Pascal include provisions for compiling and storing blocks or modules of program code, and then using these modules again, without recompiling the code, in a new Pascal program. This technique is superior to saving and using libraries of source code because time is saved by not compiling the same code over and over again.

Turbo Pascal Note

User-Written Units, Versions 4 and 5

A Turbo Pascal *unit* is a compiled program module that can be used by any Turbo Pascal, Version 4 or 5, program. It almost always contains a group of related procedures and functions. It may contain public constants, types, and variables that become global identifiers of the program. It may even contain initialization statements that are executed when the unit is first accessed by the program.

```
UNIT unit name

INTERFACE
  uses            { optional }
    other units { statements }
  public declarations and definitions
  constants, data types, variables
  procedure and function headers

IMPLEMENTATION
  private declarations and definitions
  code for public procedures and functions
begin                   { optional }
  initialization code  { statements }
END
```

Figure 9.4 Block structure of a unit.

In many ways, units serve as extensions to the Turbo Pascal language. You may remember that we introduced predefined units when we discussed the uses statement in Chapter 5. A unit is made up of several sections. It starts with the reserved word UNIT, followed by the unit name. This unit name must be different from any other global identifier in your program. For example, a unit heading might be

```
UNIT VectorAlgebra
```

where VectorAlgebra is the unit name.

Figure 9.4 shows the general outline of a unit. Note that several parts are optional.

The Interface Section

The first section is the *interface* section, headed by the reserved word INTERFACE. If this unit refers to constants or subprograms from other units, these units must be listed in a uses statement. Remember that the order of listing units is important; **the name of a unit that is called from, or referred to by, another unit must precede the name of the calling unit.** For example, if unit Strg uses a function from unit Crt, the uses statement should be

```
uses
   Crt, Strg;
```

where unit Crt is placed first because it is referred to (one of its functions is used by) unit Strg.

The interface section contains all public declarations and definitions; that is, the names of all identifiers that should be known by a program using the unit. These identifiers include the names of constants, data types, variables, procedures, and functions. Only heading statements are listed for procedures and functions. Here is an example of an interface section.

```
INTERFACE
   uses
      Crt, Strg;
   const
      SIZE = 5;
   type
      list = array [1..SIZE] of real;
   procedure ReadVec (var Vector: list);
   procedure WriteVec (Vector: list);
   procedure VecAdd (VectorA, VectorB: list;
                        var VectorC: list);
```

Note that the constant SIZE is a public constant and is known in any program that uses unit VectorAlgebra. It is possible, however, to define another constant SIZE in the program, and this program definition supercedes the unit definition. Note also that the three procedure headings contain formal parameter lists, but no other procedure code.

The I m ple m entation Section

Following the interface section is the *implementation* section, containing the code
for public procedures and functions, as well as private identifiers. It is headed by
the reserved word IMPLE M ENTATION. For example, an implementation section to
support the previous interface section might look like the following.

```
IMPLEM ENTATION
  PROCEDURE WriteVec;
  var
    I: integer;
  begin
    for I:= 1 to SIZE do
      Writeln (Vector[I]:5:2);
  end; { WriteVec }

PROCEDURE ReadVec;
  { code for this procedure }

PROCEDURE VecAdd;
  { code for this procedure }

END.
```

Note that the subprogram headings in the implementation section contain no parameter lists (these lists are in the interface section).

This particular example does not contain an initialization section. If such a
section is present, however, the statements it contains are executed as soon as the
unit is called. The initialization section can be used, for example, to relax strict
string parameter checking with a {$V−} compiler directive (as discussed in the next
section). This compiler directive is then global to all subprograms in the unit.

After a unit has been written, it should be compiled on disk, using the option
Destination disk from the Compile command menu. The result of this compilation is a TPU file; that is, a binary file having the same file name as the unit
source code file, but with an extension of TPU. Because units are already compiled,
they allow a program to compile much more quickly than if include files are used.
Remember that the uses statement is used to tell a Turbo Pascal program that it
can use one or more precompiled units.

The Turbo Pascal program can occupy up to 64KB of memory, and each unit
can occupy its own 64KB segment of memory. Thus, it is possible with units in
Versions 4 and 5 to write much larger Turbo Pascal programs than it is possible to
write in Version 3.

An Example Unit

We conclude our brief introduction to units with an example of a unit containing
string functions and procedures. First we show outlines for each of the individual
subprograms.

Outline for function `UpCaseStr`

For character position I from 1 through length of string.
  If a string character is in the set 'a' to 'z', change
    the character to uppercase.
Assign modified string to `UpCaseStr`.

Outline for function `LeftTrim Str`

Set index I to 1.
While Ith character is a blank,
  Increment value of I.
Loop back.
If there are any leading blanks (I > 1), delete leading
blanks (characters 1 through I - 1).
Assign modified string to `LeftTrimStr`.

Outline for function `RepeatCh`

Set string to a null string.
For index I from 1 to N (number of characters),
  Concatenate specified character to end of string.
Assign new string to `RepeatCh`.

Outline for procedure `CenterStr`

Subtract length of specified string from width of screen.
Divide result by 2 and assign to N.
Display N blanks, then specified string.

Unit `STRG.PAS`

```
UNIT Strg;
{
  This unit contains a group of string functions and
  procedures.
  Function UpCaseStr converts all lower case characters
  in its parameter to upper case characters.
  Function LeftTrimStr removes all leading blanks from
  its parameter.
  Function RepeatCh creates a string of N characters
  denoted by Ch.
  Procedure CenterStr displays string parameter St
  centered on a screen whose width is given by the
  byte parameter Width.
}
INTERFACE
  function UpCaseStr (St: string): string;
  function LeftTrimStr (St: string): string;
  function RepeatCh (Ch: char; N: byte): string;
  procedure CenterStr (St: string; Width: byte);
```

```
IMPLEMENTATION
  FUNCTION UpCaseStr;
  {
    Convert all lower case characters in St
    to upper case characters.
  }
  var
    I: byte;
  begin
    for I:= 1 to Length(St) do
      if St[I] in ['a'..'z'] then
        St[I]:= UpCase(St[I]);
    UpCaseStr:= St;
  end; { UpCaseStr }

  FUNCTION LeftTrimStr;
  {
    Trim all leading blanks from St.
  }
  var
    I: byte;
  begin
    I:= 1;
    while St[I] = ' ' do
      Inc(I);
    if I > 1 then
      Delete (St, 1, I-1);
    LeftTrimStr:= St;
  end; { LeftTrimStr }

  FUNCTION RepeatCh;
  {
    Create a string containing N values of Ch.
  }
  var
    I: byte;
    St: string;
  begin
    St:= '';
    for I:= 1 to N do
      St:= St + Ch;
    RepeatCh:= St;
  end; { RepeatCh }

  PROCEDURE CenterStr;
  {
    Display St centered on a screen of width Width.
  }
  var
    N: byte;
```

```
begin
  N:=(Width - Length(St)) div 2;
  Writeln (RepeatCh(' ', N), St);
end; { CenterStr }

begin { Initialization section }
{
  Include compiler directive to relax
  strict string type checking. We discuss
  this compiler directive in the next section.
}
{ $V-}

END.
```

This unit, in source code, is stored in directory CH09 of the example program disk, under the name STRG.PAS. A compiled version is stored there under the name STRG.TPU. Here is a short program that uses two of the subprograms in the unit.

```
PROGRAM EX0905 (Input, Output);
{
  Ask the user to enter a title, and then display it
  centered and underlined at the top of the screen,
  in a page width of 60 columns.
  Use only with Version 4 or 5.
}
uses
  Crt, Strg;
var
  Title, Underline: string;

BEGIN
  Write ('Enter title: ');
  Readln (Title);
  ClrScr;
  CenterStr (Title, 60);
  Underline:= RepeatCh('-', Length(Title));
  CenterStr (Underline, 60);
END.
```

This program produces the prompt

```
Enter title: A Table of Measured Adsorptions
```

and after a title is entered, the screen is cleared and the following centered image is displayed:

```
            A Table of Measured Adsorptions
            -------------------------------
```

Remember to keep all programs, units and test files that you are currently using in the current directory of your current disk drive. You can always change the current directory by using the Change dir command from the File command menu of Turbo Pascal, Versions 4 and 5. If you are using a hard disk and several directories, you can tell Turbo Pascal, through the Options and Directories menus, where your units are stored.

9.8 MORE COMPILER DIRECTIVES

In some implementations of Pascal, compiler directives are an important part of the program. They influence directly the manner in which certain statements and subprograms behave. For that reason, we discuss two additional compiler directives available in one implementation of Pascal.

Turbo Pascal Note

The I Compiler Directive and IOResult Variable

The I compiler directive controls I/O (input/output) error checking. **Note that this is a different directive than the Include directive, although both use the symbol $I.** Normally, I/O error checking is on, and if an I/O error occurs, the program stops and an error message is displayed. I/O error checking may be turned off, for example, while opening a file, so that if an error is made when entering the file name, the user can be notified and allowed to enter the name again.

An integer function named IOResult, already predefined in Turbo Pascal, can be checked to find out if a file was successfully opened. If the value of IOResult is zero, the file-opening procedure (Reset, Rewrite or Append) was executed successfully and the file is open. If IOResult returns any other value, the file was not opened successfully or some other I/O error occurred. **Note that the value of IOResult is reset to zero each time it is called.** Thus, instead of checking the value of IOResult, we usually create a boolean expression, such as (IOResult = 0), and check the value of that expression.

Here is an example program containing our previously-written OpenFile procedure, modified to check for a valid file name. We show an outline of this procedure.

> Set flag Opened to false.
> While flag Opened is false.
>> Ask user to enter a file name.
>> Turn off I/O checking.
>> Try to open the file.
>> Turn I/O checking back on.
>> Set Opened to true if file was opened successfully.
>> If Opened is false.
>> Display an error message.
> Loop back.

If the file is not opened successfully, the user should enter the file name again. This error is usually caused by the file name being misspelled. Here is the program.

```
PROGRAM EX0906 (Input, Output);
{
  Test a modified OpenFile procedure that
  checks for a valid file name.
}
var
  FileVar: text;

PROCEDURE OpenFile (var FV: text);
{
  Open a text file for reading.
}
type
  string80 = string[80];
var
  FileName: string80;
  Opened: boolean;
begin
  Opened:= false;
  while not Opened do
    begin
    Write ('Name of file? ');
    Readln (FileName);
    Assign (FV, FileName);
    {$I-} { Turn off I/O checking.}
    Reset (FV);
    {$I+} { Turn I/O checking back on.}
    Opened:= (IOResult = 0);
    if not Opened then
      begin
      Writeln ('Error in file name -',
               ' please try again.');
      Writeln;
      end; { if branch }
    end; { while loop }
end; { OpenFile }

BEGIN { Main Program }
  OpenFile (FileVar);
  Writeln ('File has been successfully opened.');
END.
```

Sample interaction with the program might look like the following:

```
Name of file? REPORT.DAT
Error in file name - please try again.

Name of file? REPORT.TXT
File has been successfully opened.
```

Note that the function IOResult cannot be used in the if and while statements because it will produce erroneous results. Every time IOResult is called, it
is reset to zero. If the if statement

```
if IOResult <> 0 then ...
```

is executed, the value of IOResult is reset to zero. Thus a boolean expression in
the while statement, such as

```
while IOResult <> 0 ...
```

is always false, the loop is not executed, and a new file name is not requested. The
result is that the procedure OpenFile does not operate properly. We solve this problem by introducing a boolean variable named Opened, originally assigning it a value
of false, and then assigning it the value of boolean expression (IOResult = 0).
When IOResult equals zero, Opened is true; otherwise it is false. A new file
name is requested, over and over again, until Opened becomes true.

The V Compiler Directive

The V compiler directive is used to control type checking of string parameter types
and string function types. The default value, {$V+}, provides strict type checking.

If a formal var parameter in a procedure is of type string255 (or type
string in Version 4 or 5) and you try to pass an actual parameter of type
string80, an error message is displayed and the program stops. This error is
caused by a strict type check detecting that the actual and formal parameter are not
both the same type (the same length strings). Similarly, if a function is of type
string255, it cannot return a value of type string80.

By using the {$V-} compiler directive to turn off string type checking (as we
did in the unit Strg), error checking for string type incompatibility is relaxed, and
the program runs without displaying error messages. Here is an example, using a
modified version of Program EX0805.

```
PROGRAM EX0907 (Input, Output);
{
   Ask user to enter a product name containing
   two words and then display the name in reverse
   order, second word followed by first word.
   String parameter type checking relaxed.
   Use only with Version 4 or 5.
}
{$V-} { Turn off string type checking.}
type
   string80 = string[80];
var
   Name: string80;

FUNCTION Reverse (Name: string): string;
{
   Reverse the position of first and second words.
}
```

```
var
  FirstWord, SecondWord: string;
  X: integer;
begin
  X:=Pos(' ', Name);
  FirstWord:=Copy(Name, 1, X-1);
  SecondWord:=Copy(Name, X+1, MaxInt);
  Reverse:=SecondWord + ', ' + FirstWord;
end; { Reverse }

BEGIN { Main Program }
  Write ('Enter a product name: ');
  Readln (Name);
  Writeln ('Reversed name: ', Reverse(Name));
END.
```

A typical display produced by this program is as follows:

```
Enter a product name: MONOCHROMATIC MONITOR
Reversed name: MONITOR, MONOCHROMATIC
```

Note that even though function Reverse is written with a type of string (or string[255] in Version 3), and has a formal parameter of type string, the program runs successfully with an actual parameter of type string80. The {$V-$} compiler directive makes function Reverse more general, and thus more useful as a library function. By the way, this compiler directive must be placed at the beginning of the program, as shown. It cannot, unfortunately, be placed in function Reverse and be made part of an include file.

In Versions 4 and 5, function Reverse should be placed in a unit, not in an include file. The compiler directive {$V-} can then be placed in the initialization section of the unit (see unit Strg in the last section), and does not need to be written at the beginning of the program. As an alternative, you can use the Compiler command from the Options command menu to configure your particular installation of Turbo Pascal for relaxed string type checking.

IMPORTANT POINTS

- A variable declared in a subprogram is known in that subprogram, and in all subprograms contained or nested within that subprogram.
- Value parameters pass information in one direction only, from the calling program to the subprogram.
- Variable parameters permit a two-way exchange of information between the calling program and the subprogram.
- Actual variable parameters must always be variables, they cannot be constants or expressions.

- Pascal requires that file variables be passed as variable parameters.
- Any function or procedure used as a `procedure` type cannot be a standard Turbo Pascal function or procedure.
- In the `Include` compiler directive, the suffix `PAS` is automatically added to a file name without an extension or suffix.
- The system variable `IOResult` is reset each time it is called.
- In a `uses` statement, the name of a unit that is called from, or referred to by, another unit must precede the name of the calling unit.
- The `Include` directive and the `I` directive are different compiler directives, although both use the symbol `$I`.
- A subprogram with formal string parameters of a specific type, like `string255`, must be called with actual parameters of the same type, unless string type checking is relaxed with the `V` compiler directive.

SELF-STUDY QUESTIONS

1. Can an actual variable parameter be
   (a) an expression
   (b) a variable
   (c) a constant?
2. Can a formal variable parameter be
   (a) an expression
   (b) a variable
   (c) a constant?
3. Which kind of parameters are called two-way parameters, value parameters, or variable parameters?
4. If a variable named `Number` in the main program is assigned a value of 10 and is passed to a procedure as a value parameter and assigned a new value of 5, what is the value of `Number` when control returns to the main program?
5. How are variable parameters identified in a parameter list?
6. Which kind of parameter, value or variable, produces two copies of the parameter contents in memory?
7. Which kind of parameter, value or variable, provides the best isolation between main program and subprogram?
8. Which kind of parameter, value or variable, must be used for file variables?
9. Consider the following program fragment.

```
PROCEDURE Outer;
var
  Sum: integer;

  PROCEDURE Inner (Sum: integer);
  begin
    Sum:=5;
  end; { Inner }
```

```
begin { Outer }
  Sum := 10;
  Inner (Sum);
  Writeln (Sum);
end; { Outer }
```

    (a) Do the two variables named Sum refer to the same or different memory locations?

    (b) What value is displayed by the Writeln statement?

10. What compiler directive is used to include another source file in a program?

11. If no extension is specified with a file name, what extension, if any, is added by the Turbo Pascal system?

12. Write a compiler directive to include a file named LINKS, located in the directory TOOLS on the disk in drive B, in a Turbo Pascal program.

13. What is the advantage, if any, of keeping general-purpose procedures and functions in one or more library files?

14. Where is the initialization section of a unit?

15. Are public declarations and definitions placed
    (a) in the interface section or
    (b) in the implementation section of a unit?

16. When a unit is used by a Turbo Pascal program, does it normally contain
    (a) source code or
    (b) object code?

17. Does Turbo Pascal allow procedures and functions to be used as parameters? Explain your answer.

18. What is the value of IOResult after it has been called in a program?

19. The V compiler directive modifies type checking in what kind of variables?

PRACTICE PROGRAMS

1. In many programs using files, a need may arise within a program to copy information from one file to another. Write a procedure that copies information from one text file to another text file. The names of both files are to be passed to the procedure as parameters.

    If the first (input) file does not exist, notify the user and request that the file name be entered again. If the second (output) file exists, erase it or overwrite it. Your program should handle strings up to 255 characters long. Use two separate procedures, called by this procedure, to open the two files.

    Use this procedure in a program for copying text files where the user specifies both file names. Test your program by copying the contents of file REPORT.TXT into a file named REPORT.CPY.

2. An engineer has been told to improve the readability of technical reports by avoiding the use of long words. Write a procedure that receives as parameters a text file variable and an integer representing a maximum word length. The procedure returns an array of strings that are the words found in the text that exceed this maximum length.

    Use this procedure in a program that asks a user to enter a file name and a maximum word length. The program displays a list of words that exceed this maximum length, and the number of times each of these words appears. Use the definition of a word given in Practice Program 2 of Chapter 8.

    Test your program with the file REPORT.TXT and a word length of 7.

3. This problem has nothing to do with engineering or science, but it is a good exercise in writing a program with subprograms, and in manipulating strings.

Ask a user to enter a string and determine if it is a palindrome (spelled the same backward and forward). Include at least three procedures in your program: one to remove all nonalphabetic characters from the string, another to change all letters to uppercase, and the third to reverse the order of characters in the string. Display an appropriate message.

Test your program using the sentences

> Madam, I'm Adam!
>
> A rose is a rose is a rose.
>
> Able was I ere I saw Elba.

4. Expand the library file `TRIG.INC` to include the additional trigonometric functions `SecD`, `CscD`, `CotD` (for secant, cosecant, and cotangent), where all angles are in degrees.

Test your new library file by including it in a program that calculates and displays the secant and cotangent of 45 degrees.

5. A semiconductor chip manufacturer tests each chip produced to determine the highest frequency at which it operates satisfactorily. Chips that operate at or above a threshold frequency are considered good and are sold under the company label. All other chips are considered bad and are destroyed or sold at a low price without warranty. Yield is the ratio of the number of good chips to the total number of chips, expressed as a percentage.

The chips are produced on three assembly lines, five days per week. For each chip produced during the week, three items of information are recorded on a text file:

> assembly line number
> day number (Monday = 1, Friday = 5)
> tested frequency, in MHz.

Each item is written on a separate line.

Ask a user to enter the name of the file containing this information for the week, and the threshold frequency. Calculate the average yield of all chips produced during the week, the average yield of chips produced on each assembly line and the average yield of chips for each day of the week. Display this information with appropriate labels.

Test your program using the text file `YIELD.DAT` and a threshold of 16 Mhz.

6. This problem is designed to give you practice in designing a program with nested subprograms. The problem is to determine the index of refraction of a certain type of glass. A light beam, incident on the glass surface at an angle Θ_1 from the perpendicular, is refracted within the glass to an angle Θ_2 from the perpendicular. Using Fermat's principle, the index of refraction, N, of the glass can be calculated from the equation

$$N = \sin(\Theta_1)/\sin(\Theta_2)$$

Ask a user to enter angles Θ_1 and Θ_2 in degrees and display the index of refraction. Your program should contain a function named `Fermat` that calculates the index of refraction. Within that function is nested another function named `Sine`, the function described in Practice Program 4 of Chapter 7. Within the `Sine` function is nested another function named `Factorial` that calculates the factorial value of a number. Use parameters wherever appropriate to pass information between subprograms.

Test your program using a value of $\Theta_1 = 35.0$ degrees, and a value of $\Theta_2 = 22.5$ degrees.

10

THE CASE AND REPEAT
STATEMENTS

10.1 INTRODUCTION

Here we present the two remaining control structures, case and repeat, and discuss their use in programs.

We then consider two special examples where the Read statement is used to read information from text files. We also introduce several additional standard functions, and examine their use in programs.

10.2 BRANCHING: THE CASE STATEMENT

The if statement is commonly used for two-way branch structures and with the else statement, can be used to construct multibranch structures. For the latter structures, however, the case statement is often a better choice.

The syntax of the case statement is

```
case variable of
   case list 1: statement;
   case list 2: statement;
   case list 3: statement;
end;
```

where the `variable` (called the case variable) must be an ordinal variable or expression (usually of type `integer` or `char`), each `statement` can be either simple or compound, and each `case list` is a list of case constants or ordinal values of the same type as the case variable. Standard Pascal gives an error if the case variable value does not appear in one of the case lists.

Note that the word `end` is part of the case statement syntax and there is no matching `begin`.

Turbo Pascal Note

The case statement syntax is somewhat different in Turbo Pascal. The case structure is

```
case variable of
   case list 1: statement;
   case list 2: statement;
   case list 3: statement;
   else statement;
end;
```

where the statement after `else` is executed if the value of the case variable or expression does not appear in any of the case lists. In other versions of Pascal, the keyword `else` may be replaced by the keyword `otherwise`.

If there is no `else` statement and the case variable value does not appear in one of the case lists, Turbo Pascal just goes on to the first statement after the end of the `case` statement.

Case Lists

Constants or individual values in a case list are separated by commas. For example, the case list

```
'+', '-'
```

means the characters plus (+) and minus (−).

Turbo Pascal Note

Turbo Pascal also allows a range of constant values to be specified with an ellipsis. For example, the case list

```
1, 3, 5, 7, 9..100
```

means the integers constants 1, 3, 5, and 7, as well as the range from 9 through 100, inclusive. A maximum of 256 case constants can be specified in any `case` statement.

In the program fragment

```
var
  Ch: char;
      |
case Ch of
     '+', '-', '0'..'9', 'E': Writeln (Ch);
      |
end; { Case }
```

the character is displayed if it is included in the case list.

Repeated Values in Case Lists

An important point to note is that **the same value cannot appear in more than one case list.** Consider the following invalid program fragment.

```
(******************************************)
(** THIS PROGRAM FRAGMENT IS NOT VALID **)
(******************************************)
var
  Ch: char;
      |
case Ch of
  'C': Writeln ('Average quality');
  'A'..'E': Writeln ('Acceptable quality');
end; { Case }
```

The program fragment contains an error because the character C is included in both the first and second case lists. If you need to write this kind of branching structure, you must use the if statement, as shown in the following program fragment.

```
var
  Ch: char;
      |
if Ch = 'C' then
  Writeln ('Average quality');
if Ch in ['A'..'E'] then
  Writeln ('Acceptable quality');
```

This program fragment takes advantage of the fact that the uppercase letters are part of an ordered set of characters which in Turbo Pascal and most other implementations is the ASCII character set. The ordinal value of each character increases from A to Z, as shown in the ASCII table in Appendix B.

We now show two example programs. The first program is designed to be used by a quality-control engineer to convert a numeric evaluation of the quality of a product to a letter designation, based on conversion equivalents embedded in a case statement. An else clause is used to trap an illegal numeric value.

```
PROGRAM EX1001 (Input, Output);
{
  Ask user to enter a numeric evaluation and
  display the corresponding letter designation.
}
var
  NumericEvaluation: integer;

FUNCTION LetterEquivalent (N: integer): char;
{
  Convert a numeric evaluation to the
  appropriate letter designation.
}
begin
  case N of
    91..100: LetterEquivalent:= 'A';
    81..90: LetterEquivalent:= 'B';
    71..80: LetterEquivalent:= 'C';
    61..70: LetterEquivalent:= 'D';
    51..60: LetterEquivalent:= 'E';
    0..50: LetterEquivalent:= 'F';
  else
    LetterEquivalent:= 'X';
  end; { case branch }
end; { LetterEquivalent }

BEGIN { Main Program }
  Write ('Enter numeric evaluation: ');
  Readln (NumericEvaluation);
  if LetterEquivalent(NumericEvaluation) <> 'X' then
    Writeln ('Letter equivalent is ',
             LetterEquivalent(NumericEvaluation))
  else
    Writeln ('Numeric evaluation must be',
             ' between 0 and 100.');
END.
```

Note that a special character X is assigned to LetterEquivalent if the numeric evaluation is not valid. This character value serves as a flag that can be checked by the following if statement, and used to determine if the letter equivalent or an error message should be displayed.

Note also that the error message is positive, not negative. It is more instructive to tell a user the range of valid entries, rather than to display a message like "Entry is not valid."

It is easy to make the error of writing a numeric range as 100..91 rather than 91..100, because the former notation is often used to specify numeric ranges in noncomputer applications (we must admit that we made this mistake when we first wrote the program). The case statement, like other Pascal statements, requires that **a range of values, denoted by an ellipsis, be given with the smallest value first and the largest value last.**

Here are two sample runs of the program.

```
Enter numeric evaluation: 85
Letter equivalent is B

Enter numeric evaluation: 120
Numeric evaluation must be between 0 and 100.
```

Our second example program uses the same function, but it reads numeric evaluation information from a file and writes a new file containing letter equivalents. Assume we have a text file named EVALS.DAT that contains test codes and numeric evaluations, with each code and evaluation on a separate line. The input file of test codes and evaluations might look like this.

```
A1S7V2132
89
A1S7V2178
93
A1S7V2205
77
A1S7V2259
65
A1S7V2282
82
```

We wish to create and write another text file, named EQUIVS.DAT, that contains the same test codes, but has letter equivalents in place of the numeric ones. We also wish to display a table of test codes and letter equivalents on the screen. An outline of our program might look like this.

Open input file.
Open output file.
Display title line for table.
While not at end of input file
    Read test code and evaluation from input file.
    Convert evaluation to letter equivalent.
    Write code and letter on output file.
    Display code and letter in table.
Loop back.
Close the output file.
Report that new output file has been written.

Here is the example program. It contains our previous function Letter-Equivalent, two procedures to open the input and output files, a procedure named Tab that moves the cursor to a specified column, and a procedure to display the code and letter equivalent table and write the output file.

```
PROGRAM EX1002 (Input, Output);
{
  Read a file of test codes and numeric evaluations.
  Convert evaluations to letter equivalents and write
  a new file of codes and letter equivalents. Also
  display a table of codes and letter equivalents.
}
uses    { Versions 4 and 5 only }
  Crt; { delete for Version 3  }
type
  string80 = string[80];
var
  InFile, OutFile: text;

FUNCTION LetterEquivalent (N: integer): char;
{
  Convert numeric evaluation to letter equivalent.
}
begin
  case N of
    91..100: LetterEquivalent:= 'A';
    81..90:  LetterEquivalent:= 'B';
    71..80:  LetterEquivalent:= 'C';
    61..70:  LetterEquivalent:= 'D';
     0..60:  LetterEquivalent:= 'F';
  else
    LetterEquivalent:= 'X';
  end; { case branch }
end; { LetterEquivalent }

PROCEDURE OpenInFile (var InFile: text);
{
  Open an input file.
}
var
  FileName: string80;
begin
  Write ('Name of input file? ');
  Readln (FileName);
  Assign (InFile, FileName);
  Reset (InFile);
end; { OpenInFile }

PROCEDURE OpenOutFile (var OutFile: text);
{
  Open an output file.
}
var
  FileName: string80;
```

```
begin
  Write ('Name of output file? ');
  Readln (FileName);
  Assign (OutFile, FileName);
  Rewrite (OutFile);
end; { OpenOutFile }

PROCEDURE Tab (N: integer);
{
  Move cursor to column N.
}
begin
  GotoXY (N, WhereY);
end; { Tab }

PROCEDURE DisplayTable (var InFile, OutFile: text);
{
  Display the table of codes and letter equivalents.
  Write the output file.
}
var
  TestCode: string80;
  NumericEvaluation: integer;
  LetterEquiv: char;
begin
  Write ('  CODE'); Tab (35); Writeln ('LETTER');
  Writeln;
  while not Eof(InFile) do
    begin
    Readln (InFile, TestCode);
    Readln (InFile, NumericEvaluation);
    Writeln (OutFile, TestCode);
    LetterEquiv:=LetterEquivalent(NumericEvaluation);
    Writeln (OutFile, LetterEquiv);
    Write (TestCode); Tab (38); Writeln (LetterEquiv);
    end; { while loop }
  Close (OutFile);
end; { DisplayTable }

BEGIN { Main Program }
  OpenInFile (InFile);
  OpenOutFile (OutFile);
  Writeln;
  DisplayTable (InFile, OutFile);
  Writeln;
  Writeln ('The output file has been written.');
END.
```

In the main program, both the input and output files are opened by separate procedures. In the DisplayTable procedure, a loop is established that reads two lines of information from the input file, writes the test code and letter equivalent on the output file, and adds a display line to the table. The loop continues until there is no further data in the input file.

Here is a sample of user interaction with the program.

```
Name of input file? EVALS.DAT
Name of output file? EQUIVS.DAT

    CODE                                            LETTER

A1S7V2132                                              B
A1S7V2178                                              A
A1S7V2205                                              C
A1S7V2259                                              D
A1S7V2282                                              B

The output file has been written.
```

This program pays greater attention to screen display format than do our earlier example programs. A title line is printed and blank lines are inserted to make the display more readable. We use a procedure named Tab to line up the letter equivalents in a vertical column.

Turbo Pascal Note

Other languages have a function or procedure similar to Tab, but it is not a standard procedure in Pascal. We write a Tab procedure that takes advantage of two standard subprograms in Turbo Pascal (see Figure 5.2), the procedure GotoX Y, with integer parameters Xpos and Ypos, and the integer function WhereY. GotoX Y moves the cursor to column Xpos and row Ypos, while WhereY returns the row value of the cursor. Thus the statement

```
GotoX Y (N, WhereY);
```

moves the cursor to column N of the current row, exactly what we want a Tab procedure to do.

Note that the special features of Turbo Pascal, for opening files and moving the cursor, are isolated in small, separate subprograms, rather than being placed in the main program or a more general subprogram. This design structure makes the program easier to modify for a different compiler.

In Version 4, the statement uses Crt must be included in the program if GotoXY and WhereY are to be used.

When writing practical programs, it saves time, and generally produces a more readable program, to use the special features of your particular Pascal implementation. If you isolate these special features in subprograms, it is fairly easy to rewrite the specific subprograms that need to be changed when you change Pascal compilers.

10.3 LOOPING: THE REPEAT STATEMENT

The while loop checks the looping condition at the beginning of the loop. Another loop statement, the repeat statement, checks the looping condition at the end of the loop. The syntax is

```
repeat
  statement
     |
  statement
until boolean expression;
```

One or more statements, enclosed between the repeat and until statements, make up the body of the loop. Note that begin and end brackets are not needed to enclose the body of the loop.

The repeat statement can be used to indicate the end of data when reading a file that has a sentinel value. In the following example program, a flag named Finished is set to true when the sentinel value is read. The file itself is named RAINFALL.90 and contains monthly rainfall totals for the year 1990. A sentinel value of −1 denotes the end of data. The total rainfall for 1990 is calculated.

```
PROGRAM EX1003 (Output);
{
   Read nonnegative rainfall values from text file
   RAINFALL.90, and calculate and display their sum.
   A negative number indicates end of data.
}
var
   FileVar: text;
   Value, Sum: real;
   Finished: boolean;

BEGIN { Main Program }
   Assign (FileVar, 'RAINFALL.90');
   Reset (FileVar);
   Sum := 0.0;
   Finished := false;
   repeat
      Readln (FileVar, Value);
      if Value < 0.0 then
        Finished := true
      else
        Sum := Sum + Value;
   until Finished;
   Writeln ('Total rainfall for 1990 is ',
            Sum:1:1, ' inches.');
END.
```

This program displays the result

```
Total rainfall for 1990 is 310.0 inches.
```

Another example program shows how both the `repeat` and `case` statements can be used when checking an answer. The loop continues to display the prompt until a valid reply is entered. Within the loop, a `case` statement distinguishes between affirmative, negative, and erroneous answers.

```
PROGRAM EX1004 (Input, Output);
{
   Test a procedure that checks the answer
   entered by a user.
}
type
   string80 = string[80];
var
   Answer: string80;

PROCEDURE CheckAnswer (Prompt: string80;
                       var Ans: string80);
{
   Prompt the user for an answer. If it is
   neither Y or N, display an error message
   and prompt again.
}
begin
   repeat
     Write (Prompt);
     Readln (Ans);
     case Ans[1] of
        'Y','y': Ans:= 'Y';
        'N','n': Ans:= 'N';
     else
        begin
        Writeln ('Answer Y or N - please try again');
        Writeln;
        end;
     end; { case }
   until Ans[1] in ['Y','y','N','n'];
end; { CheckAnswer }

BEGIN { Main Program }
   CheckAnswer ('Answer (Y/N)? ', Answer);
   Writeln ('The answer is ', Answer);
END.
```

The string variables `Ans` and `Answer` are made large enough to handle whatever reasonable string of characters may be entered. The variable `Ans[1]` represents the first character of the string `Ans` and is a variable of type `char`. Therefore, it can be used as a case variable in the `case` statement, and in the boolean expression of the until statement.

Here is a typical interactive session produced by this program.

```
Answer (Y/N)? Q
Answer Y or N - please try again

Answer (Y/N)? y
The answer is Y
```

Any loop that is written with the repeat statement can just as well be written with the while statement. There are some situations, however, where the repeat statement is more convenient, as illustrated by the foregoing examples. We encourage you to use whichever loop structure is most suitable for your particular programming need.

10.4 THE READ STATEMENT WITH TEXT FILES

The normal input statement with text files is the Readln statement, reading an entire line at a time. There are some circumstances, however, where the Read statement is required, and we discuss two examples.

Multiple Numbers per Line

Suppose a text file has been written (contrary to our advice) with two or more numeric values per line. A typical small file might contain two lines of text, with spaces used to separate the numbers. The file variable is FV. Here is how the file looks.

```
5.7 8.3 2.35
14.2 3.53 7.8
```

Turbo Pascal Note

Some Pascal compilers allow other separators, such as commas, between numeric values on a line. The only separator allowed in Turbo Pascal is a space.

The program fragment

```
while not Eof(FV) do
   begin
   Readln (FV, Num);
   Writeln (Num:5:2);
   end;
```

produces the display

```
 5.70
14.20
```

After the first numeric value on a line is read, the Readln statement skips past the end of the line, effectively discarding the second and third values on the line.

On the other hand, if a Read statement is used instead of a Readln statement, the program fragment becomes

```
while not Eof(FV) do
  begin
  Read (FV, Num);
  Writeln (Num:5:2);
  end;
```

and produces the display

```
   5.70
   8.30
   2.35
  14.20
   3.53
   7.80
```

Note that the Read statement behaves differently than the Readln statement, reading every value on a line before proceeding to the next line.

Reading Long Strings

We normally use a Readln statement and a string variable when reading character sequences from a text file. If the line or sequence contains more than 255 characters, however, we cannot use a string variable. We must instead read individual characters with a Read statement, assigning the characters to some structure such as an array of characters or displaying them on the screen. This technique may be needed with text files created by certain word processors that treat a paragraph as a long sequence of characters terminated by an end-of-line marker.

Here is the outline of an example program that reads a text file containing long strings, and displays the file contents on the screen.

Set LINE_LENGTH to 70.
Assign and open file REPORT.TXT.
While not at end of text file
   Set counter Count to zero.
   While not at end of a line of text
      Increment counter.
      Read a character from the file.
      Display the character without advancing a line.
      If Count = LINE_LENGTH
         Start a new display line.
         Reset counter back to zero.
      End of if block.
   Loop back to next character in the line.
   Read the end-of-line marker from the file.
   Advance the display one line to start a new paragraph.
End of program.

The program itself follows.

```
PROGRAM EX1005 (Output);
{
  Read characters from text file REPORT.TXT and
  display them on the screen in 70 character lines.
}
const
  LINE_LENGTH = 70; { Length of text lines on screen.}
var
  F1: text;

PROCEDURE ReadWriteLines (var F1: text);
{
  Read individual characters and display the lines.
}
var
  Ch: char;
  Count: integer; { Character counter in a line.}
begin
while not Eof(F1) do
  begin
  Count:=0;
  while not Eoln(F1) do
    begin
    Count:=Count + 1;
    Read (F1, Ch);
    Write (Ch);
    if Count = LINE_LENGTH then
      begin
      Writeln;      { Start new line of text }
      Count:=0;     { and reset counter.     }
      end;
    end; { while not Eoln }
  Readln (F1);  { Gobble up end-of-line mark and }
  Writeln;      { advance to a new paragraph.    }
  end; { while not Eof }
end; { ReadWriteLines }

BEGIN { Main Program }
  Assign (F1, 'REPORT.TXT');
  Reset (F1);
  ReadWriteLines (F1);
END.
```

The function Eoln becomes true whenever the next character in the file
represents an end-of-line or end-of-file condition. The Readln(F1) statement is
needed to advance the file pointer past the end-of-line marker (usually a carriage
return and line feed). The following Writeln statement displays the end-of-line

marker by advancing to the beginning of the next line on the screen, which in this example denotes the start of a new paragraph.

This program breaks each line at the seventieth character, rather than at the preceding space between words. You might try modifying the program so that it always breaks a line at a space between words. We do not show the output produced by this program, but urge you to run it yourself.

10.5 MORE STANDARD FUNCTIONS

Many implementations of Pascal contain predefined functions in addition to those specified in standard Pascal.

Turbo Pascal Note

We look at a group of miscellaneous functions available in Turbo Pascal. Figure 10.1 lists several of these functions with short explanations.

`KeyPressed`	returns a boolean value of true if a key has been pressed, false otherwise.
`ReadKey`	returns a character corresponding to the key that is pressed, but does not echo the character on the screen.
`Random(N)`	returns a random integer (type word in Version 4), greater than or equal to zero and less than the integer `N`.
`Random`	returns a random real number, greater than or equal to zero and less than one.
`Upcase(Ch)`	returns the uppercase equivalent of the value of character `Ch`.

Figure 10.1   More standard Turbo Pascal functions.

The `ReadKey` and `KeyPressed` Functions

If a program is written to read a long text file without stopping, the text scrolls by so fast on the screen that it is impossible to read. A method is needed that stops scrolling when the screen is full, and starts again only when the reader takes some appropriate action.

The next two example programs use the `ReadKey` and `KeyPressed` functions for this purpose. These programs are variations of a program that reads a text file, pausing after displaying each block of text and in one case, asking the user to specify whether more text should be displayed. The `ReadKey` function is available only in Versions 4 and 5, while the `KeyPressed` function is available in all versions. In Versions 4 and 5, both `ReadKey` and `KeyPressed` are in the `Crt` unit.

We show an outline for procedure `DisplayText` in Program EX1006. Global constant `PAGE` is set to twenty-two, the number of lines to be displayed on the screen before pausing.

> Set counter `Count` to zero.
> Set flag `Finished` to false.
> Repeat the following:
>> Read line of text from the input file.
>> Display line of text on the screen.
>> Increment the counter.
>> If counter `Count` = `PAGE`
>>> Sound the bell.
>>> Ask user if more text should be displayed.
>>> Note which key is pressed by the user.
>>> If key is `N, n, Q,` or `q,` set flag `Finished` to true.
>>> Reset counter to zero.
>>> Move display position to beginning of current line.
>> End if block.
> Until `Finished` is true or end of file has been reached.
> If at end of file, display an appropriate message.

We use a previously-developed procedure to open the input file. Here is the complete program.

```
PROGRAM EX1006 (Input, Output);
{
  Read and display a text file, screen by screen.
  Press any key to display the next screen.
  Use only with Version 4 or 5 unless modified.
}
uses
  Crt;
const
  PAGE = 22; { Number of lines to display on screen.}
  BELL = #7; { ASCII code for the bell.}
var
  FileVar: text;

PROCEDURE OpenFile (var FV: text);
{
  Open a text file for reading.
}
var
  FileName: string;
  Opened: boolean;
```

```
begin
  repeat
    Write ('Name of file? ');
    Readln (FileName);
    Assign (FV, FileName);
    {$I-} { Turn off I/O checking.}
    Reset (FV);
    {$I+} { Turn I/O checking back on.}
    Opened:= (IOresult = 0);
    if not Opened then
      begin
      Writeln ('Error in file name -',
               ' please try again.');
      Writeln;
      end;
  until Opened;
end; { OpenFile }

PROCEDURE DisplayText (var FV: text);
{
  Display PAGE lines of text, then pause and
  ask user before displaying the next page.
  Reply of N or Q stops the display process.
}
var
  Count: word;
  Finished: boolean;
  Line: string;
  Reply: char;
begin
  Count:= 0;
  Finished:= false;
  repeat
    Readln (FV, Line);
    Writeln (Line);
    Count:= Count + 1;
    if Count >= PAGE then
      begin
      Write ('More?', BELL);
      Reply:= ReadKey;
      if Reply in ['N','n','Q','q'] then
        Finished:= true;
      Count:= 0;
      GotoXY (1, WhereY);
      end; { if branch }
  until Finished or Eof(FV);
  if Eof(FV) then
    Writeln ('***** End of File *****');
end; { DisplayText }
```

```
BEGIN { Main Program }
  { The following DirectVideo statement may be required }
  { on some non-IBM computers with special displays. }
  DirectVideo:=false;
  OpenFile (FileVar);
  DisplayText (FileVar);
END.
```

Here is sample output from the program, with only the first and last line of each block of text shown. Actually, after the user presses a key other than Q or N in response to the More? prompt, the next line of text over-writes the prompt. Note that no character is displayed when a key is pressed. You should run the program yourself to see the actual results.

```
Name of file? TEXT.DAT
It is customary for first-course computer language books to
  |
  |
the ordinary engineer or scientist was not allowed to
More?
operate. Instead, a computer user prepared his program on
  |
  |
allows a user to use his or her personal computer for most
More?
computing tasks, only accessing another, remote computer
  |
  |
how to design and write computer programs.
***** End of File *****
```

We use the constant PAGE to specify the number of lines to display, and the constant BELL to sound the bell whenever a prompt is displayed.

The DirectVideo Variable.   Notice the first line in the main program that sets the predeclared variable DirectVideo to false. This variable is in the unit Crt, and thus is a global variable of the program. When set to false, it forces the screen to use a slower, but more reliable, method of displaying characters. **This setting is sometimes needed with non-IBM computers and display units**. You may be able to delete this statement when running the program on your own computer, and thus achieve a faster screen display.

In procedure DisplayText, we use the ReadKey function to recognize a key that is pressed, and either display the next block of text or terminate the program. The character set notation ['N','n','Q','q'] specifies those characters that stop the program.

If it is not necessary to know which key is pressed, the empty loop

```
repeat until KeyPressed;
```

can be used to make the program pause until a key is pressed. We use this loop in
Program EX1007_3 in place of the ReadKey function because the latter function is
not available in Version 3.

Here is a somewhat simpler version of the program, written for Version 3, that
does not ask the user if he or she wishes to continue, but does pause at the end of
each page and wait for any key to be pressed.

```pascal
PROGRAM EX1007_3 (Input, Output);
{
  Read and display a text file, screen by screen.
  Press any key to display the next screen.
  Use only with Version 3.
}
const
  PAGE = 22; { Number of lines to display on screen.}
  BELL = #7; { ASCII code for the bell.}
var
  FileVar: text;

PROCEDURE OpenFile (var FV: text);
{
  Open a text file for reading.
}
var
  FileName: string[80];
  Opened: boolean;
begin
  repeat
    Write ('Name of file? ');
    Readln (FileName);
    Assign (FV, FileName);
    {$I-} { Turn off I/O checking.}
    Reset (FV);
    {$I+} { Turn I/O checking back on.}
    Opened: = (IOresult = 0);
    if not Opened then
      begin
      Writeln ('Error in file name -',
               ' please try again.');
      Writeln;
      end;
  until Opened;
end; { OpenFile }

PROCEDURE DisplayText (var FV: text);
{
  Display PAGE lines of text, then pause and
  ask user to press any key before displaying
  the next page.
}
```

```
var
  Count: integer;
  Line: string[255];
begin
  Count:= 0;
  repeat
    Readln (FV, Line);
    Writeln (Line);
    Count:= Count + 1;
    if Count >= PAGE then
      begin
      Write ('Press any key.', BELL);
      repeat until KeyPressed;
      Count:= 0;
      GotoXY (1, WhereY);
      end; { If Branch }
  until Eof(FV);
  Writeln ('***** End of File *****');
end; { DisplayText }

BEGIN { Main Program }
  OpenFile (FileVar);
  DisplayText (FileVar);
END.
```

The output display is similar to that of Program EX1006, except that the prompt at the end of each page is different. As before, the prompt is overwritten by the next page of text. Remember that the Read Key function is not available in Version 3.

The Random Function

It is often convenient to be able to create a file of random numbers or strings, especially for testing a new program. For example, a random file of N real numbers might be needed to test Program EX1003, where the user specifies the value of N. The next program shows how the Random function can be used for this purpose.

```
PROGRAM EX1008 (Input, Output);
{
  Ask the user for a file name, the number of numeric
  values to write on the file, and the minimum and
  maximum value for any number.
}
type
  string80 = string[80];
var
  FileName: string80;
  FV: text;
  N, Count: integer;
  Number: real;
  MaxValue, MinValue, Range: real;
```

```
BEGIN
  Writeln ('Write random real numbers on a file:');
  Write ('Name of file? ');
  Readln (FileName);
  Assign (FV, FileName);
  Rewrite (FV);
  Write ('How many numbers? ');
  Readln (N);
  Write ('Maximum value of any number? ');
  Readln (MaxValue);
  Write ('Minimum value of any number? ');
  Readln (MinValue);
  Range:=MaxValue - MinValue;

  Randomize;
  for Count:=1 to N do
    Writeln (FV, MinValue + (Range * Random));
  Close (FV);
  Writeln;
  Writeln ('File ', FileName, ' has been written.');
END.
```

Note that the function Random returns a real value between 0 and 0.99999999999, inclusive. Thus the expression (5.0 + (10.0 * Random)) returns a random number between 5.0 and 14.999999999.

We have included the standard procedure Randomize in the program before the Random function. This procedure ensures that the random number generator is initialized with a random value or *seed*, thus producing different results each time the program is executed. If the Randomize procedure is not included, the program creates the same sequence of random numbers each time it is run. For testing purposes, it is often preferable to create the same sequence of numbers each time, and if this is the case, the Randomize procedure should be omitted during testing. Here is a sample of user interaction with the program.

```
Write random real numbers on a file:
Name of file? RANDOM.DAT
How many numbers? 12
Maximum value of any number? 25.0
Minimum value of any number? 6.5

File RANDOM.DAT has been written.
```

Note that the Randomize procedure does not always work properly in Version 3, but does work correctly in Version 4. We also show the contents of file RANDOM.DAT produced from a sample run of this program, displayed with one decimal digit.

```
25.0
24.4
9.1
21.3
20.0
12.6
19.1
22.0
18.1
17.1
23.5
16.2
```

The Upcase Function

The last function in our list is the Upcase function. An example program shows how it can be used to write a new function that converts all lowercase characters in a string to uppercase. The new function UpcaseStr is especially useful for converting all string values to uppercase before comparing them in a program.

```
PROGRAM EX1009 (Input, Output);
{
  Test a function for converting lowercase letters
  in a string to uppercase letters.
}
{$V-} { relax string type checking }
type
  string255 = string[255];
var
  Entry: string255;

FUNCTION UpcaseStr (InString: string255): string255;
{
  Examine each character in InString. If lowercase,
  convert to uppercase. Assign all characters to
  OutString.
}
var
  OutString: string255;
  Index: integer;
begin
  OutString:= ''; { null string }
  for Index:= 1 to Length(InString) do
    OutString:= OutString + Upcase(InString[Index]);
  UpcaseStr:= OutString;
end; { UpcaseStr }
```

```
BEGIN { Main Program }
  Write ('Enter string: ');
  Readln (Entry);
  Writeln (UpcaseStr(Entry));
END.
```

There are several features of this program to note. The function `UpcaseStr` works with a string parameter of any declared length, due to relaxation of strict string type checking by the compiler directive `{ $V-}`.

Each character in a string variable is compatible with a character variable, so the predeclared function `Upcase` can be used. `OutString` is set initially to a null string, and then the characters from `InString`, converted if they are lowercase letters, are concatenated to it. The final value of `OutString` is assigned to `UpcaseStr`.

This program produces the following output.

```
Enter string: 123AbcDef
123ABCDEF
```

IMPORTANT POINTS

- The same value cannot appear in more than one case list.
- A range of values, denoted by an ellipsis, must have the smallest value first and the largest value last.
- Special features of a Pascal implementation, like those in Turbo Pascal for opening files and for moving the cursor, should be isolated in small, separate subprograms.
- In Versions 4 and 5, the statement

  `DirectVideo: = false;`

  is sometimes needed with non-IBM computers and display units.
- If the `Randomize` procedure is not included, a program creates the same sequence of random numbers each time it is run.

SELF-STUDY QUESTIONS

1. What is the best structure to use in Pascal for a seven-way branch?
2. Does Turbo Pascal produce an error if the case variable value does not appear in one of the case lists?
3. Is there any restriction on the type of the case variable?
4. Can a case variable value appear in more than one case list?
5. Is the case list `10..5` allowed in Turbo Pascal? Explain your answer.
6. If two or more statements are included in the loop body of a `repeat` loop, must they be enclosed in begin and end brackets?

7. Which statement should be used to read a text file containing two numeric values per line?

8. In your version of Turbo Pascal, what is the type of
   (a) function `KeyPressed`;
   (b) function `ReadKey`?

9. Does the function `Upcase` take a character or a string parameter?

10. What is the purpose of the `DirectVideo` variable in Versions 4 and 5?

11. What is the purpose of the `Randomize` procedure?

PRACTICE PROGRAMS

1. An engineer used an Instron machine to test a batch of 100 metal parts to failure. All of them failed within a tensile stress range of 10,000 to 40,000 psi. The stress required for failure in each case is written in the text file `FAILURE.DAT`, one number per line. Determine the number of parts that failed at a stress between 25,000 and 35,000 psi, inclusive.

2. Another engineer conducted the same tests as the engineer in Practice Program 1. Contrary to company policy, however, the results were entered on a text file named `FAILURE4.DAT`, with four numbers per line. Determine the number of parts that failed at a stress between 30,000 and 39,000 psi, inclusive.

3. An environmental scientist keeps computer records of snowfalls. A text file named `MAXSNOW.DAT` contains values of the maximum recorded snowfall, in inches, for each day in January and the year when that record snowfall occurred. Values of maximum snow fall and the year are written in this file as two numeric values per line, separated by a blank space.

   Another text file named `SNOW1987.DAT` contains 31 numeric values for the snowfall each day in January, 1987. Examine both files before starting the problem.

   Read the information from these files into two or more arrays. Use the file of 1987 snowfalls to update the one or more arrays written from `MAXSNOW.DAT`. Rename file `MAXSNOW.DAT` to `MAXSNOW.BAK` and write a new and updated version of `MAXSNOW.DAT`.

4. An engineer has written a report on a word processor that puts each paragraph into a single string. The file containing the report must be reformatted so that displayed lines end at a blank space between words, with the length of no line exceeding seventy characters. Rewrite Program EX1005 to accomplish this result.

   This problem sounds easy, but requires some thought and planning to solve. If either the seventieth or seventy-first character is a blank, you can break the line after the seventieth character. If not, you must search backwards from the seventieth character to find the first blank, break the line at this point, and keep the right-hand part of the line to use as the beginning of the next line. Unnecessary blanks at the beginning (and possibly the end) of a line can be discarded before the line is displayed.

   Test your program using the text file `REPORT.TXT`.

5. A computer is used on a production line to test the speed (frequency response) of CPU chips. Each chip is inserted into a test socket and the computer screen displays its speed, appropriate model number, and other test information.

Write a program to simulate part of this testing procedure. The user enters an even integer number representing CPU speed. The screen displays the CPU model number corresponding to that speed. The following table relates CPU speed and model number.

SPEED (MHz)	MODEL NUMBER
6	80286-6
8	80286-8
10	80286-10
12	80286-12
14	80286-14

Any other value of speed should result in a display indicating a rejected chip.

Design your program with a loop so that the user can enter a sequence of speed values, one at a time. A negative speed stops the program. Display the model number (or rejected status) with appropriate labels.

Test your program for all valid values of speed, and for at least two invalid values.

6. Practice Program 5 makes the assumption that the measured CPU speed is an even integer value. Modify that program to allow a real value to be entered, using the following table:

SPEED (MHz)	MODEL NUMBER
less than 6.00	reject
6.00 - 7.99	80286-6
8.00 - 9.99	80286-8
10.00 - 11.99	80286-10
12.00 - 13.99	80286-12
14.00 or greater	80286-14

Test your program thoroughly, entering at least one value for each model number and one value for a rejected CPU.

7. Sometimes before comparing string values, it is more convenient to convert these values to lowercase. Write a function that converts all uppercase letters in a string variable to lowercase, but does not affect other, nonalphabetic characters.

Test your function in a short program that asks the user to enter a string of characters from the keyboard.

11

ADVANCED DATA STRUCTURES: RECORDS AND FILES

11.1 INTRODUCTION

In this chapter, we first examine redefined variable types, subrange types, sets, and enumerated types. We also introduce the record type, a special feature of Pascal. This type allows variables of different types to be included in one named data structure. We show how these advanced types are used in Pascal programs to describe more complicated data structures.

We then introduce the concept of a typed file. A typed file differs from a text file in that information is not stored in displayable (ASCII) characters, but in an internal format. The components of a typed file may be of any type, but are often of type `record`.

11.2 ADDITIONAL TYPE DEFINITIONS

So far we have discussed several predefined variable types, and one user-defined type, the `array`. Now we shall look at the definitions and uses of other user-defined types.

Redefined Types

Any predefined type can be defined again with a new type name in the type definition section. For example, if it seems clearer in a program to denote boolean variables as logical variables, the following program fragment can be used.

```
type
  logical = boolean;
var
  Flag: logical;
```

Possibly a better example is a program where several variables represent voltage values. The following program fragment might be used.

```
type
  voltage = real;
var
  InVoltage, OutVoltage: voltage;
  NodeVoltage: array [1..3] of voltage;
```

Type definitions of this kind do make the program a little easier to read and understand. In general, a user can choose his or her own identifiers for any of the predefined variable types.

Subrange Types

Another reason for user-defined types is to limit the range of values of an ordinal variable. A subrange is a *continuous* range of values, denoted by a lower bound and an upper bound separated by an ellipsis (..). The lower bound must be less than or equal to the upper bound.

For example, a subrange of integers can be used to denote the months by number. In this application, only integers from one to twelve have any meaning. The following program fragment defines a new variable type, month_number, that is a subrange of the standard type integer.

```
type
  month_number = 1..12;
var
  TestMonth, CompletionMonth: month_number;
```

If an attempt is made to assign an out-of-range value to a subrange type, the program usually stops with an error.

Turbo Pascal Note

In Versions 4 and 5, an out-of-range value is usually detected during compilation because range checking is on by default. In Version 3, an out-of-range value is detected during execution only if you have turned on range checking, as explained in Chapter 8.

We should mention, however, that a better programming technique is to detect an out-of-range value before an assignment operation is attempted, and thus give the user a chance to correct the value. Rather than use a subrange type, we prefer the following program fragment when asking a user for the value of a variable such as TestMonth.

```
var
  TestMonth: integer;
    |
    |
repeat
  Write ('Number of month? ');
  Readln (TestMonth);
  if not (TestMonth in [1..12]) then
    Writeln ('Month must be designated by ',
             'a number from 1 to 12.');
until TestMonth in [1..12];
```

As we have discussed previously, a separate type definition and variable declaration can be combined into a single variable declaration. Remember that variables declared in this manner cannot be used in certain ways, such as for subprogram parameters. Here is a combined declaration for subrange variables.

```
var
  TestMonth, CompletionMonth: 1..12;
```

In general, we recommend that you use separate type definitions and variable declarations.

The Set Type

A *noncontinuous* range of variable values can be placed in a set type, as explained in Chapter 10, and this set identified by name in a type definition. All elements of the set must be of the same ordinal type.

Turbo Pascal Note

Remember that in Turbo Pascal, the number of elements in a set cannot exceed 256.

Here is a program fragment that defines a set type.

```
type
  special_letter = set of char;
var
  Vowel: special_letter;
begin
  Vowel: = ['a', 'e', 'i', 'o', 'u'];
```

A shorthand declaration can also be used.

```
var
  Vowel: set of char;
begin
  Vowel: = ['a', 'e', 'i', 'o', 'u'];
```

As previously noted, the set may contain a range of elements, denoted by an ellipsis. Note that the list of set members, in this case all the vowels, is enclosed in square brackets. Here is an example program that asks the user to enter a sentence and then counts the number of vowels. Our set has been expanded to include the uppercase vowels.

```
PROGRAM EX1101 (Input, Output);
{
  Ask user to enter a sentence and count
  the number of vowels.
}
type
  special_letter = set of char;
  string80 = string[80];
var
  Vowels: special_letter;
  Sentence: string80;
  I, Count: integer;

BEGIN
  Vowels:=['a', 'e', 'i', 'o', 'u',
           'A', 'E', 'I', 'O', 'U'];
  Writeln ('Enter a sentence on the line below:');
  Readln (Sentence);
  Count:=0;
  for I:=1 to Length(Sentence) do
    begin
    if Sentence[I] in Vowels then
      Count:=Count + 1;
    end; { for loop }
  Write ('Sentence contains ', Count:1, ' vowel');
  if Count = 1 then
    Writeln ('.')
  else
    Writeln ('s.');
END.
```

The following output is produced.

```
Enter a sentence on the line below:
The fuel leakage tests were inconclusive.
Sentence contains 15 vowels.
```

The set type is named `special_letter` and the variable of that type is Vowels. An assignment statement in the program assigns a set of values to Vowels. The begin and end brackets in the for statement are not strictly necessary, but seem to make the program a little easier to read. The last if statement is a program refinement to provide proper grammar in the displayed text.

Enumerated Ordinal Types

It is also possible for a user to define an ordinal type, called an *enumerated ordinal type*, where each constant value in the new ordinal type must be specified. For example, a type denoting the days of the week might be written as

```
type
   days_of_week = (Monday, Tuesday, Wednesday, Thursday,
                   Friday, Saturday, Sunday);
var
   Day: days_of_week;
```

Note that parentheses, not brackets, are used to enclose the constant values of an enumerated ordinal type.

As with any other variable, Day must be assigned a value before it can be used in a program. It can be assigned any one of the seven possible values, such as

```
Day := Wednesday;
```

Note that quotation marks are not used to enclose Wednesday, because it is not a string constant, but rather a value of type days_of_week. Day cannot be assigned a value that is not listed as one of the allowed values of type days_of_week.

The constant values of an enumerated ordinal type cannot be read using a Readln or Read statement, and cannot be written using a Writeln or Write statement. They are restricted to internal program use only. If you need to display the days of the week, you must use a program structure like the following.

```
case Day of
   Monday    : Writeln ('Monday');
   Tuesday   : Writeln ('Tuesday');
   Wednesday : Writeln ('Wednesday');
   Thursday  : Writeln ('Thursday');
   Friday    : Writeln ('Friday');
   Saturday  : Writeln ('Saturday');
   Sunday    : Writeln ('Sunday');
end;
```

An enumerated ordinal type variable can be used in other ways like a standard ordinal type variable. It can be passed as a parameter, and a function can have an enumerated ordinal type. A variable of this type is sometimes used in for statements and in boolean expressions within other looping and branching statements. In general, however, the use of enumerated ordinal types is of limited value in most programs.

For example, an engineer is asked to keep track of hours worked on a specific job, and these hours are assigned to a file named JOB22.HRS. Here is a program that reads numbers from that file and assigns them to an array. The array index is an integer representing the day-of-the-week number.

```
PROGRAM EX1102 (Input, Output);
{
   Read daily hours worked from a text file named
   JOB22.HRS and display selected information on
   the screen. The index variable in the array is
   an integer.
}
```

```
type
  hours = array [1..7] of real;
var
  Time: hours;

PROCEDURE FillArray (var Time: hours);
{
  Read values into array Time from a file.
}
var
  Day: 1..7;
  TimeFile: text;
begin
  Assign (TimeFile, 'JOB22.HRS');
  Reset (TimeFile);
  for Day:=1 to 7 do
    Readln (TimeFile, Time[Day]);
end; { FillArray }

PROCEDURE DisplayRegularHours (Time: hours);
{
  Display regular weekly hours, plus
  hours worked on Monday.
}
var
  Day: 1..7;
  WorkHours: real;
begin
  Writeln ('Monday hours = ', Time[1]:1:1);
  WorkHours:=0.0;
  for Day:=1 to 5 do
    WorkHours:=WorkHours + Time[Day];
  Writeln ('Regular weekly hours = ', WorkHours:1:1);
end; { DisplayRegularHours }

PROCEDURE DisplayOvertimeHours (Time: hours);
{
  Display weekend overtime hours.
}
var
  Day: 1..7;
  Overtime: real;
begin
  Overtime:=0.0;
  if Time[6] > 0.0 then
    Overtime:=Time[6];
  if Time[7] > 0.0 then
    Overtime:=Overtime + Time[7];
  Writeln ('Overtime hours = ', Overtime:1:1);
end; { DisplayOvertimeHours }
```

```
BEGIN { Main Program }
  FillArray (Time);
  DisplayRegularHours (Time);
  DisplayOvertimeHours (Time);
END.
```

In this program, we assume that the first day of the week is Monday and assign the index one to Monday. It is just as common, however, to assume the first day of the week is Sunday, and then day one is Sunday. This possible confusion can be avoided if an enumerated ordinal variable, containing the days of the week as values, is used as an index variable. We show the example program again with a different index variable.

```
PROGRAM EX1103 (Input, Output);
{
  Read daily hours worked from a text file named
  JOB22.HRS and display selected information on
  the screen. The index variable in the array is
  an enumerated ordinal variable.
}
type
  days_of_week = (Monday, Tuesday, Wednesday,Thursday,
                  Friday, Saturday,Sunday);
  hours = array [Monday..Sunday] of real;
var
  Time: hours;

PROCEDURE FillArray (var Time: hours);
{
  Read values into array Time from a file.
}
var
  Day: days_of_week;
  TimeFile: text;
begin
  Assign (TimeFile, 'JOB22.HRS');
  Reset (TimeFile);
  for Day:= Monday to Sunday do
    Readln (TimeFile, Time[Day]);
end; { FillArray }

PROCEDURE DisplayRegularHours (Time: hours);
{
  Display regular weekly hours, plus
  hours worked on Monday.
}
var
  Day: days_of_week;
  WorkHours: real;
```

```
begin
  Writeln ('Monday hours = ', Time[Monday]:1:1);
  WorkHours:=0.0;
  for Day:=Monday to Friday do
    WorkHours:=WorkHours + Time[Day];
  Writeln ('Regular weekly hours = ', WorkHours:1:1);
end; { DisplayRegularHours }

PROCEDURE DisplayOvertimeHours (Time: hours);
{
  Display weekend overtime hours.
}
var
  Day: days_of_week;
  Overtime: real;
begin
  Overtime:=0.0;
  if Time[Saturday] > 0.0 then
    Overtime:=Time[Saturday];
  if Time[Sunday] > 0.0 then
    Overtime:=Overtime + Time[Sunday];
  Writeln ('Overtime hours = ', Overtime:1:1);
end; { DisplayOvertimeHours }

BEGIN { Main Program }
  FillArray (Time);
  DisplayRegularHours (Time);
  DisplayOvertimeHours (Time);
END.
```

Both programs produce the following display.

```
Monday hours = 5.5
Regular weekly hours = 37.0
Overtime hours = 3.0
```

The text file JOB22.HRS contains seven numbers representing the number of hours worked during each day of the week. A for loop reads these numeric values into the array Time. The weekly total of both regular and overtime hours can then be calculated, as well as the time worked on a particular day.

Note the use of values of an enumerated type (days_of_week) as the index values of the user-defined array type (hours). Denoting days of the week by their names, rather than by number, makes the program more readable and understandable, and helps to avoid a possible misunderstanding.

11.3 THE RECORD STRUCTURE

The record type allows a collection of items of different types to be grouped together in a single variable. This is a natural way to organize information. For example, a record might be designed to contain information on an instrument assigned to an engineering research project. This information might consist of an instrument description of type `string`, a cost of type `real`, and a purchase year of type `integer`. A variable, say named `Inventory`, could then be declared to hold all this information.

The syntax of the `record` type is

```
record name = record
  field variable name 1: type;
  field variable name 2: type;
  |
end;
```

where each `field variable name` in the record structure is a *field* of the record.

The list of variables in a record is called its *field list*. These variables may be of any type (standard or user-defined, simple or structured) except they cannot be of a file type. The `end` word is part of the record structure syntax and there is no matching `begin` word.

Returning to the inventory record we discussed earlier, its structure can be written as

```
type
  string80 = string[80];
  inventory_rec = record
    Description: string80;
    Cost       : real;
    PurchYear  : integer;
  end;
```

Note particularly that `inventory_rec` is a type identifier, while `Description`, `Cost` and `PurchYear` are variable identifiers (to be more specific, field variable identifiers).

Once a record type has been defined, one or more record variables can be declared. The usual `var` declaration section is used.

```
var
  Tool, Instrument: inventory_rec;
```

Field variables in a record structure can be used just like any other kinds of variables. They can have values assigned to them, and their values can be displayed on the screen. However, to distinguish them from ordinary variables, they are identified by a special notation. The name of the record variable and the name of the field variable are used together, separated by a period. For example, the statement

```
Tool.Description := 'metric micrometer';
```

assigns the string constant `metric micrometer` to the field variable `Description` in the record variable `Tool`.

Another example is the statement

```
Writeln (Instrument.PurchYear:4);
```

that displays the value of the field variable PurchYear in the record variable Instrument, using a field width of four columns.

The only time a record variable can be read or written as a single entity is when it is read from or written to a file of records, as discussed in the next section.

Note that the record type complements the array type, and both can be combined together into more-extensive data structures. It is possible to have an array element that is a record type. It is possible to have a record field variable of type array. It is even possible to have a record field variable that is itself of type record.

This point is illustrated in another record type definition, used to represent the data produced by several electrical measurements.

```
type
  time_rec = record
    Hour, Minute, Second: integer;
  end;
  node_array = array [1..3] of real;
  electrical_rec = record
    Time         : time_rec;
    InVoltage  : real;
    InCurrent  : real;
    NodeVoltage: node_array;
  end;
```

We first define the type time_rec as a record, and the type node_array as an array. We then use these definitions in the subsequent definition of type electrical_rec. Thus one of the field variables in the record type electrical_rec is a record type, two are real types, and the fourth is an array type.

We emphasize again an important point that is sometimes hard to remember: **The name associated with a record definition is a type name, while the name associated with each field declaration is a variable name**.

There are actually two ways to address a record field value. Assume a variable is declared using the statement

```
Result: electrical_rec
```

and we wish to assign a value to field variable InVoltage. We can use the notation discussed previously,

```
Result.InVoltage:=15.5;
```

or alternatively, the notation

```
with Result do
  InVoltage:=15.5;
```

The latter notation is especially convenient when values are to be assigned to all or many field variables in a record, as in the following example, where a compound statement within begin and end brackets is modified by the with statement.

```
with Result do
  begin
  Time.Hour:=14;
  Time.Minute:=30;
  Time.Second:=0;
  InVoltage:=14.7;
  InCurrent:=12.2E-3;
  NodeVoltage[1]:=-7.5;
  NodeVoltage[2]:=12.6;
  NodeVoltage[3]:=17.7;
  end;
```

The notation assigning a value to the variable Hour is equivalent to the notation

```
Result.Time.Hour:=14;
```

If we wish to assign only time values, we can use the program fragment

```
with Result, Time do
  begin
  Hour:=14;
  Minute:=30;
  Second:=0;
  end;
```

Note that several record variable names, separated by commas, can appear after the reserved word with.

The record data structure provides a useful structure for storing a collection of information whose components are of different types. This structure is especially useful in designing data files, as we shall discuss in the next section.

11.4 THE FILE STRUCTURE

Text Files

We introduced text files in Chapter 3 and discussed how information can be written on and read from these files. You will remember that text files typically contain lines of text. Each line consists of zero or more characters, plus an end-of-line marker that is usually a two-character sequence. Text file characters are stored in their ASCII representation, and so the file contents can be displayed on the screen using, for example, the MS-DOS TYPE command.

Typed Files

Pascal also supports *typed files*. A typed file is a binary file, consisting of a sequence of *components* of the same type (user-defined or standard, simple or structured). Any type is allowed except another file type.

For example, one file might contain only real numbers. Another file might contain only two-dimensional arrays of integers. The length of a file is not fixed; that is, it is not defined when the file is opened. The contents of a typed file (because it is a binary file) cannot be displayed on the screen using a text editor.

The components that make up a typed file are commonly called *file records*. You must watch out for a possible misunderstanding when using the term record. **File records are not necessarily Pascal record structures.**

If the components in a typed file are real numbers, each file record is a number. If the components are two-dimensional arrays of integers, each file record is an array. Only if the components are Pascal structured records is each file record also a Pascal record.

Just like any new type, a typed file must be defined in the declaration block of a program or subprogram. The syntax is

```
file type name = file of component type
```

where `file type name` is any legal identifier, and `component type` is the type of component or file record contained in the file.

For example, the program fragment

```
type
  real_file = file of real;
var
  DepthData: real_file;
```

declares a file named `DepthData` whose type is `real_file` and whose components are real numbers. As before, a shorthand declaration statement can be used, but is not recommended.

```
var
  DepthData: file of real;
```

In the next example, a type named `vector` is defined, and a file is declared whose components are arrays of type `vector`. The file is of type `vector_file`.

```
type
  vector = array [1..5] of real;
  vector_file = file of vector;
var
  OrganicData: vector_file;
```

The third example is more complicated. We define a Pascal record structure which itself contains another Pascal record. The components of file `Card` are records of type `electrical_rec`.

```
type
  time_rec = record
    Hour, Minute, Second: integer;
  end;
  node_array = array [1..3] of real;
  electrical_rec = record
    Time       : time_rec;
    InVoltage  : real;
    InCurrent  : real;
    NodeVoltage : node_array;
  end;
  electrical_file = file of electrical_rec;
var
  Card: electrical_file;
```

The final example is a shorthand version of the previous example. There are no separate definitions of the types `node_array`, `electrical_rec` or `electrical_file`.

```
type
  time_rec = record
    Hour, Minute, Second: integer;
  end;
var
  Card: file of record
          Time        : time_rec;
          InVoltage   : real;
          InCurrent   : real;
          NodeVoltage : array [1..3] of real;
        end;
```

Remember in this last case that the file variable `Card` cannot be passed as a subprogram parameter because it does not have a type name. The structure of the third example would have to be used instead of this shorthand structure. Remember also that file variables of any type can be passed only as `var` parameters.

Examples of Files of Records

One of the common uses of the Pascal record structure is as a component in typed files. Information we wish to store in a file record often consists of field variables of different types. In this case, the file record is indeed a Pascal record structure.

Turbo Pascal Note

Everything we have discussed up until now in this section applies to both standard Pascal and Turbo Pascal. Most implementations of Pascal have their own predefined functions and procedures for operating with typed files. We shall restrict ourselves to discussing how Turbo Pascal handles typed files.

The same `Assign` statement that we used with text files is used with typed files, and it associates the file variable name with the MS-DOS path name or file name. As you will remember, the syntax is

```
Assign (file variable, 'MS-DOS path name');
```

The same `Reset` and `Rewrite` statements are also used, but have slightly different meanings.

`Reset` is used to open an existing file, and produces an error if the file does not exist.

`Rewrite` is used to open a new file. If a file by that name already exists, it is closed and re-opened as a new file, effectively erasing its contents.

A typed file, unlike a text file, can be opened for both reading and writing. The same `Close` statement is used to close a file after use, and is especially important after writing on a file.

The real work of reading or writing is done by a `Read` statement or a `Write` statement. For example, if the file variable `DepthData` represents a file of real numbers and if the variable `Number` is of type `real`, the appropriate `Read` statement is

```
Read (DepthData, Number);
```

and the corresponding `Write` statement is

```
Write (DepthData, Number);
```

Turbo Pascal Note

As long as only a single item variable name appears in the `Read` or `Write` statement, these statements can be used with virtually all implementations of Pascal. Two or more item names, separated by commas, can be used in Turbo Pascal. For example,

```
Write (DepthData, Number1, Number2);
```

As before, we recommend for simplicity that you use only a single item name in `Read` and `Write` statements.

Note that the `Readln` and `Writeln` statements, which we use so extensively with text files, cannot be used with typed files. The concept of a line of characters, terminated by an end-of-line marker, does not apply to typed files because such a line of characters is not a typed component.

It is possible, however, to have a typed file of string components, but each string component must be read with a `Read` statement and written with a `Write` statement. Note that a string does not end with an end-of-line marker. **A typed file of strings is not a text file**.

Here is a simple program, that might be used by a civil engineer studying water pollution, to store measured values of river depths in a typed file. The program asks a user to enter a sequence of numbers, writes these numbers on a typed file, and then reads the file and displays the numbers for verification. In any practical application, the number of entries (denoted by the constant `LIMIT`) would be much larger than five.

```
PROGRAM EX1104 (Input, Output);
{
   Ask a user to enter a sequence of real numbers,
   write these numbers on a file of real, read the
   sequence of numbers from the file, and display
   them on the screen.
}
const
   LIMIT = 5; { Length of number sequence.}
type
   real_file = file of real;
var
   DepthData: real_file;

PROCEDURE WriteFile (var NumFile: real_file);
{
   Write numbers on the file.
}
var
   I: integer;
   Number: real;
```

```
begin
  Rewrite (NumFile); { Open a new file.}
  for I:=1 to LIMIT do
    begin
    Write ('Number ', I:1, '? ');
    Readln (Number);
    Write (NumFile, Number);
    end;
  Close (NumFile);
end; { WriteFile }

PROCEDURE ReadFile (var NumFile: real_file);
{
  Read numbers from the file.
}
var
  Number: real;
begin
  Reset (NumFile); { Open the existing file.}
  while not Eof (NumFile) do
    begin
    Read (NumFile, Number);
    Writeln (Number:1:1);
    end;
  Close (NumFile);
end; { ReadFile }

BEGIN { Main Program }
  Assign (DepthData, 'DEPTH.DAT');
  WriteFile (DepthData);
  Writeln;
  Writeln ('The numbers you entered are:');
  ReadFile (DepthData);
END.
```

Here is the screen display produced by our example program.

```
Number 1? 6.2
Number 2? 7.5
Number 3? 5.7
Number 4? 8.0
Number 5? 5.9

The numbers you entered are:
6.2
7.5
5.7
8.0
5.9
```

A constant named `LIMIT` is used to control the length of the number sequence. We must define a type `real_file` in order to pass the file variable as a parameter. Note also that the parameter must be a `var` parameter.

The `Assign` statement can be in the main program because file opening is done by `Reset` or `Rewrite` statements. The file is closed after we finish using it in each procedure. If you try to display the file `DEPTH.DAT` on the screen using the MS-DOS TYPE command, you just get a random display of odd characters and symbols. This file is a binary file and does not contain ASCII characters.

We could have written these numbers on a text file, and the behavior of the program as far as the user is concerned would have been exactly the same. It would, of course, have been necessary to change a few statements.

One of the disadvantages of using a text file for numeric data is that there is a loss of precision when converting real numbers from their internal form to ASCII code when writing on the file, and back again when reading from the file. This conversion is not necessary when using a typed file.

Direct Access to Typed Files

Many implementations of Pascal allow direct access to the components of a typed file. We discuss only the method used in Turbo Pascal.

Turbo Pascal Note

A major advantage of using a typed file in Turbo Pascal is that any record in the file can be accessed directly, without reading all previous records. We introduce a new statement, the `Seek` statement, that permits direct access to any specified file record or component in a typed file. The syntax is

```
Seek (file variable, file record number);
```

where `file record number` is an integer index specifying the desired component or file record, starting with an index value of zero for the first file record. This statement cannot be used with a text file. **Note that the first record has a record number of zero, not one**.

A predefined function `FileSize` returns the number of records in a file. Given a file variable named `FV`, the statement

```
Seek (FV, FileSize(FV));
```

moves the file pointer to the end of the file because `FileSize(FV)` is one greater than the index number of the last file record. Remember that file record indices start with zero. After this statement has executed, additional records can be appended to the file.

Another example program shows how to access a typed file directly in Turbo Pascal. We first develop an outline of the main program.

Assign file name and open a file of records.

Ask user for number of record to display.

If number is within the allowed range

Move file pointer to beginning of the selected record.

Read this record from the file.

Call procedure Display to display the individual fields in the record.

Else record number is invalid so

Display an error message.

Here is the complete program.

```
PROGRAM EX1105 (Output);
{
   Ask a user to enter a file record number,
   then display the contents of that record.
   The structure of file ELECTRIC.DAT is described
   in the program declaration block.
}
type
   time_rec = record
      Hour, Minute, Second: integer;
   end;
   node_array = array [1..3] of real;
   electrical_rec = record
      Time : time_rec;
      InVoltage : real;
      InCurrent : real;
      NodeVoltage: node_array;
   end;
   electrical_file = file of electrical_rec;
var
   Card: electrical_file;
   Results: electrical_rec;
   RecNum: 1..5;    { record number entered by user }



PROCEDURE Display (Results: electrical_rec);
{
   Display the record values.
}
var
   I: integer;
```

```
begin
  Writeln;
  with Results do
    begin
    Writeln ('Time: ',
             Time.Hour:2, ':',
             Time.Minute:2, ':',
             Time.Second:2);
    Writeln ('Input Voltage: ',
             InVoltage:4:1, ' v');
    Writeln ('Input Current: ',
             InCurrent:4:1, ' ma');
    Writeln ('Node Voltages');
    for I:= 1 to 3 do
      Writeln ('Node ', I:1, ': ',
               NodeVoltage[I]:4:1, ' v');
    end; { With Block }
  end; { Display }

BEGIN { Main Program }
  Assign (Card, 'ELECTRIC.DAT');
  Reset (Card);
  Write ('Record to display (1 - 5)? ');
  Readln (RecNum);
  if RecNum in [1..5] then
    begin
    Seek (Card, RecNum - 1);
    Read (Card, Results);
    Display (Results);
    end
  else
    Writeln ('This record does not exist.');
END.
```

This program produces the following results.

```
Record to display (1 - 5)? 3
Time:  18:45:30
Input Voltage:   7.8 v
Input Current:  40.5 ma
Node Voltages
Node 1:   4.3 v
Node 2:   6.5 v
Node 3:   9.3 v
```

An important point to note is that an entire file record must be read when reading information from a typed file. For example, the statement

```
Read (Card, Results);
```

reads a record from the file and stores that record in the variable `Results`. **An individual field, such as `InVoltage`, cannot be read directly from the file**. Once the file record has been read, it can be divided into fields and the individual fields displayed, as shown in the program. In fact, **the entire record cannot be displayed as one object in a single `Writeln` statement**. Separate `Writeln` statements must be used to display the individual fields.

Human beings usually start counting with the digit one, while computers often start with zero. This difference can introduce errors into a computer program. In our program, the user is reminded by the prompt that a valid record number is between 1 and 5. If the user wants to see the third record, the number 3 should be entered, and this number is then adjusted in the program so that the proper file record, designated record number 2 by the computer, is read.

Remember that our previous discussion applies in specific detail only to Turbo Pascal. The method of opening files varies from one implementation of Pascal to another, and very few implementations are restricted to the limited file-handling capabilities of standard Pascal.

The `Read` and `Write` statements, as shown in our example programs, can be used in virtually all implementations of Pascal, provided only a single file record is read or written by each statement.

IMPORTANT POINTS

- The constant values of an enumerated ordinal type cannot be read using a `Readln` or `Read` statement, and cannot be written using a `Writeln` or `Write` statement.
- The name associated with a record declaration is a type name, while the name associated with each field declaration in the record is a variable name.
- File records are not necessarily Pascal record structures.
- `Readln` and `Writeln` statements, which we use so extensively with text files, cannot be used with typed files.
- A typed file of strings is not a text file.
- Note that the first record in a typed file has a record number of zero, not one.
- An entire file record must be read when reading information from a typed file. Individual record fields cannot be read from the file.
- An entire record cannot be displayed as one object in a single `Writeln` statement.

SELF-STUDY QUESTIONS

1. **(a)** Can the predefined type `integer` be redefined to a type named `whole_number`?
   (b) If so, what statement is used to accomplish this redefinition?
2. If a program contains the program fragment

```
type
   month_number = 1..12;
var
   ArrivalMonth, DepartureMonth: month_number;
```

and later in the program, the assignment statement

```
ArrivalMonth := 13;
```

is written,

(a) will the program compile;

(b) will the program execute? Can you qualify your answer if using Turbo Pascal?

3. Is the type definition statement

```
type
   letter_grade = 'A'..'F';
```

a legal Pascal statement? Explain your answer.

4. Is the type definition statement

```
type
   weekday = 'Monday'..'Friday';
```

a legal Pascal statement? Explain your answer.

5. Is the type definition statement

```
type
   weekday = ['Monday', 'Tuesday', 'Wednesday'
              'Thursday', 'Friday'];
```

a legal Pascal statement? Explain your answer.

6. Is the type definition statement

```
type
   weekday = (Monday, Tuesday, Wednesday,
              Thursday, Friday);
```

a legal Pascal statement? Explain your answer.

7. If Day is a variable of an enumerated type and is assigned the valid value of Wednesday, is the statement

```
Writeln (Day);
```

a valid statement? Explain your answer.

8. What are the restrictions, if any, on what types of field variables are allowed in a record?

9. What, if anything, is wrong with the following program fragment?

```
type
  mail = record
    Name: string80;
    Zip: real;
  end;
var
  Person: mail;

BEGIN
  Mail.Zip := 22901;
END.
```

10. When referring to typed files, what is meant by the term file record?

11. What is the proper variable declaration statement to declare a variable named `Voltage` to be a file of real numbers?

12. Which of the following procedures can be used with a typed file of records:
(a) `Read`;
(b) `Readln`;
(c) `Write`;
(d) `Writeln`?

13. What kind of display is produced when the MS-DOS TYPE command is used to display
(a) a typed file on the screen;
(b) a text file on the screen?

14. Assume a file, with a file variable name of `Info`, consisting of records of the type defined in Question 9. What program fragment is needed to assign a person's name in the third record of the file to a variable named `Recipient`?

PRACTICE PROGRAMS

When writing these programs, use the notation that record 1 is the first record in a typed file, record 2 is the second record, and so forth. Most users are more comfortable with this notation than the record number notation used by Turbo Pascal.

1. Read the contents of file `DEPTH.DAT` produced by Program EX1103. Calculate and display the average river depth.

2. Add three new records to the file `ELECTRIC.DAT` used in Program EX1104. The information contained in these records is to be entered from the keyboard. At the beginning of each new record, the record number (see previous note) is displayed. The user should be prompted, with an appropriate prompt, for each item of information in the record, and then allowed to enter a value.

After all items in a record have been entered and before writing the new record on the file, the user should be asked to verify the correctness of the entered data. If correct, the record is written on the file. If not, the user is asked to enter the record again.

3. Find all records in file `ELECTRIC.DAT` that contain a Node 2 voltage between 6.4 and 6.6 volts, inclusive. Display the record number of each of these records.

4. A sales engineer for a major computer company maintains a list of prospects. This list is a typed file, named PROSPECT.DAT, with components that are records of type person that have the following structure.

```
type
  person = record
  Name    : string[30];
  Address : string[30];
  City    : string[20];
  State   : string[2];
  Zip     : string[5];
end;
```

Add five records to the file from the keyboard and then print out the entire file, with appropriate labels for each record and each field.

5. Read the typed file PROSPECT.DAT whose record structure is given in Practice Program 4 and display the names of all persons whose zip codes lies between two user-specified values.

Test your program for a range of zip codes between 22900 and 23000.

6. Write a procedure that allows a user to change the value of any field in any record of file PROSPECT.DAT. The procedure should show the old value and prompt the user to enter a new value. The user should be allowed to change one or more field values in a record. When all changes have been made, the user should be asked to confirm that the modified record is correct and can be written on the file.

Include this procedure in a program for testing. Change record 5, field 3 to Earlysville and record 5, field 5 to 22936. Display the contents of record 5 before and after the changes.

12

POINTERS, DYNAMIC VARIABLES, AND ARRAYS

12.1 INTRODUCTION

In this chapter, we introduce the concept of a dynamic variable, whose address is the value of a variable of `pointer` type. Dynamic variables are created in memory, when required, and released from memory, when no longer needed. We use a simple stack to illustrate the use of pointers.

We then examine two-dimensional arrays and use dynamic variables to create and manipulate large, multidimensional arrays.

12.2 USE OF MEMORY BY VARIABLES

Static Variables

Most variables in Pascal are *static variables*; that is, at some memory address, memory space is allocated for each variable when the program is compiled. This memory space is called a *memory location*, and the allocation remains unchanged as long as the program is executing. Moreover, the memory location can only be used for storing variable values of the declared type.

Local Subprogram Variables

Local variables declared in the declaration block of a subprogram behave somewhat differently. Memory space is allocated for these variables when the subprogram is called, and released when the subprogram has finished executing. It is for this reason that the value of a local variable is not preserved between successive calls to a subprogram.

Dynamic Variables

We now introduce a new kind of variable called a *dynamic variable*. As the name implies, a dynamic variable is allocated space at some memory address while a program is executing. When one or more of these dynamic variables is no longer needed, the memory space can be released and used by other dynamic variables before execution finishes.

Turbo Pascal Note

In addition to the fact that memory used by a dynamic variable can be released and recovered for further use, dynamic variables have another property in Turbo Pascal that distinguishes them from static variables.

Turbo Pascal limits the size of the *data segment* where static variables are stored to 64 kilobytes (KB). Dynamic variables, on the other hand, are stored in a section of memory called the *heap*. The amount of memory available in the heap varies, but it can be as large as 400KB on a machine with 640KB of memory. In general, space for storing dynamic variables in Turbo Pascal is much larger than space for storing static variables.

For this reason, dynamic variables have an added importance in Turbo Pascal. In this chapter, we discuss the important role of dynamic variables in providing additional space for large, structured variables such as arrays.

12.3 POINTERS TO DYNAMIC VARIABLES

A dynamic variable is referred to by its address. We first declare a static variable of type `pointer` whose value will be the memory address of the dynamic variable. Initially, the pointer variable is undefined and does not contain a valid address. A procedure exists, however, for allocating an address to the pointer, this address being the memory location where the value of the dynamic variable will be stored.

Pointer Variables

Now we look at a specific example. We declare a `pointer` type that will *point to,* or contain the address of, a real dynamic variable. We use the following definition.

```
type
   real_ptr = ^real;
```

where the notation ^real (a caret preceding the type designator) indicates that a variable of type `real_ptr` points to, or contains the address of, a memory location. This location is an area of memory that is of sufficient size to hold a real value. We can declare variables of type `real_ptr` in the usual manner.

```
type
  real_ptr = ^real;
var
  Depth, Width: real_ptr;
```

The New Procedure

At this point, variables `Depth` and `Width` contain whatever old information was left in their mailboxes or memory locations; they have not been initialized. We often use the term *garbage* to describe this useless, leftover information. The standard procedure `New` is used to initialize the pointer variables, allocating the address of a memory location to each variable as its value. The following statements must be executed before `Depth` and `Width` can be used.

```
New (Depth);
New (Width);
```

Note that `Depth` and `Width` now contain addresses of available memory locations. These memory locations, which are the dynamic variable mailboxes, have not yet been initialized, and probably contain garbage themselves.

It is possible, however, to assign real values to these newly-allocated memory locations. We use the syntax

```
Depth^:=1.35;
Width^:=7.22;
```

where the identifiers `Depth^` and `Width^` denote dynamic variables (memory locations that are pointed to by `Depth` and `Width`). We can also, of course, assign values from the keyboard, or from a file, to these dynamic variables. An example program fragment might be

```
Write ('Enter a depth value: ');
Readln (Depth^);
```

Note that a caret prefix (for example, `^real`) before a type name indicates a pointer type, while a caret suffix (for example, `Depth^`) after a pointer variable name indicates a dynamic variable, the memory location pointed to by that pointer variable. It is important to understand the difference between the pointer type (`^real`), the pointer variable (`Depth`), and the associated dynamic variable (`Depth^`).

Here is an outline of the steps we have taken.

1. Define a `pointer` type that can point to the address of a memory space large enough to hold a `real` value.
2. Declare variables of this pointer type.
3. Use `New` to allocate a memory location value to each pointer variable. A pointer variable contains the memory address of a dynamic variable.
4. Assign a `real` value to each of the new dynamic variables.

The NIL Value

Pointer variables are normally given values (that is, address values) by the New procedure. **They cannot be assigned constant values representing addresses, using the assignment operator.** An exception is the value NIL which can be assigned directly to any pointer. NIL is a predefined constant that when assigned to a pointer, signifies that the pointer points to nothing. This assignment is somewhat equivalent to assigning a null value to a string variable.

In standard Pascal, there is a difference between a pointer variable that has not been initialized and one that has been assigned the value NIL. In the latter case, the pointer is considered initialized and its status can be tested in an if statement, as shown in the following program fragment.

```
Depth: = NIL;
    |
if Depth = NIL then
    Writeln ('Pointer has a value of NIL.');
```

Turbo Pascal Note

Turbo Pascal handles pointers that have not been initialized in a nonstandard, but very sensible, manner. If a pointer has not been initialized, it automatically has a value of NIL. Thus, there is no difference in Turbo Pascal between a new pointer that has not been initialized and one that has been assigned the value NIL.

Properties of Pointer Variables

The value of a pointer variable cannot be displayed on the screen, listed on a printer, or written on a file. As mentioned earlier, it is impossible to assign a constant address value (other than NIL) directly to a pointer variable. **The value of a pointer cannot be read from a file or from the keyboard.**

Turbo Pascal Note

The preceding statement is not completely true for Turbo Pascal, where it is possible to obtain the value of a pointer variable.

The technique is to use two predefined functions, Seg and Ofs, that return the segment address and offset address of any variable, either static or dynamic. We discuss memory addresses, including segment and offset, in Chapter 16.

In general, pointer variables are limited to use in boolean expressions. A pointer variable can be compared only for equality or inequality (the = or <> operators) with another pointer variable or the value NIL. The other relational operators (<, >, <=, >=) cannot be used in boolean expressions with pointer variables.

As we have discussed, a pointer points to a dynamic variable. If the pointer value is changed, it is obvious that the pointer no longer points to that particular dynamic variable. **What may not be obvious is that the dynamic variable is now effectively lost, and there is no way to recover its stored value**. Even if we know the previous address, this address (as a constant value) cannot be assigned to the same or another pointer variable. The technique of assigning one pointer to another is used frequently, however, in linked lists which we discuss in the next section. One must always think very carefully before changing the value of a pointer variable.

As an example, the statement

```
Depth := Width
```

is a perfectly valid statement that assigns the value of the pointer Width to the pointer Depth. These two pointers now point to the same dynamic variable, Width^. The original value stored in Depth^ is lost and cannot be recovered.

The Dispose Procedure

Another statement is used to delete a dynamic variable. The statement

```
Dispose (Depth);
```

releases the memory space occupied by Depth^. The pointer Depth is again considered to be not initialized.

Turbo Pascal Note

An Array of Pointers

A common use of pointers in Turbo Pascal is to establish a large array. Remember that static variables must fit within the data segment, whose size is only 64KB., while dynamic variables are placed in the heap which may contain up to 400KB. Thus an array of pointers can be defined in the data segment, where each pointer element points to a dynamic variable in the heap. This is the only way, in Turbo Pascal, to store a very large array in memory.

Here is an example program that defines an array of 1,000 string elements, each string element containing up to 100 characters. This program creates the array, assigns two element values, and then displays these values. It also uses the predefined functions MemAvail and MaxAvail to show how memory is assigned in the heap.

In Versions 4 and 5, functions MemAvail and MaxAvail return values of type longint. MemAvail is the number of bytes of available memory in the heap. MaxAvail is the size of the largest block of contiguous memory, in bytes.

```
PROGRAM EX1201 (Output);
{
   Create and use a large array of string variables to
   demonstrate the effect of Dispose on heap memory.
   Use only with Version 4 or 5.
}
```

```
type
  string100 = string[100];
  string_ptr = ^string100;
  list = array [1..1000] of string_ptr;
var
  Data: list;
  I: integer;

BEGIN { Main Program }
  for I:=1 to 1000 do        { create new dynamic   }
    New (Data[I]);           { variables            }

  Data[1]^:='FIRST';         { assign values to two }
  Data[1000]^:='LAST';       { array elements       }

  Writeln ('First value is ', Data[1]^);
  Writeln ('Last value is ', Data[1000]^);
  Writeln;
  Writeln ('Before dispose:');
  Writeln ('Heap memory available is ',
            MemAvail:1, ' bytes');
  Writeln ('Largest free block is ',
            MaxAvail:1, ' bytes');

  for I:=1 to 900 do         { release the first    }
    Dispose (Data[I]);       { 900 elements of Data  }
  Writeln;
  Writeln ('After dispose:');
  Writeln ('Heap memory available is ',
            MemAvail:1, ' bytes');
  Writeln ('Largest free block is ',
            MaxAvail:1, ' bytes');
END.
```

The number of bytes displayed in the output may vary from one computer to another, even using the same version of Turbo Pascal, depending on how much memory is reserved by the system and other memory-resident programs.

Here is the program output displayed by our example program on our own computer. If a heap overflow error occurs when you try to run the program, reduce the length of the string type in the array or reduce the size of array Data.

```
First value is FIRST
Last value is LAST

Before dispose:
Heap memory available is 38248 bytes
Largest free block is 38248 bytes

After dispose:
Heap memory available is 129140 bytes
Largest free block is 90900 bytes
```

In Version 3, the statement

```
Writeln ('Heap memory available is ',
         MemAvail:1, ' bytes');
```

should be written

```
Writeln ('Heap memory available is ',
         (16.0 * MemAvail):1:0, ' bytes');
```

where the function `MemAvail` is now of type `real` and returns the number of 16-byte paragraphs, rather than the number of bytes. The statements containing `MaxAvail` must be modified in the same manner. Version 3 also produces larger output values because more memory is available in the heap.

Note in this program how the amount of space in the heap changes when part of the array is released. Note also how the array structure is created and how values are assigned to array elements.

12.4 LINKED LISTS

An important data structure that uses pointers is the *linked list*. There are many kinds of linked list structures, including queues, stacks, single-linked lists, and double-linked lists. We discuss only one of these structures, the simple *stack*.

The Stack Structure

A stack is often called a last-in-first-out (LIFO) structure. It gets its name from its similarities in operation to a spring-loaded plate stacker in a cafeteria, where the last plate placed on the stack is the first plate removed. Pascal uses a built-in stack for holding subprogram parameters, and for recursion as discussed in Chapter 13.

The diagram of a typical stack is shown in Figure 12.1. Each *node* or component of the stack is a Pascal record containing two fields. The first field is a string variable named `Value` that holds the information being stored in the stack. The second field is a pointer variable named `Next` that points to the next lower node of the stack. The pointer in the lowest node points to `NIL`.

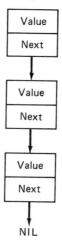

NIL   **Figure 12.1** A typical stack structure.

It is possible, of course, to have much more complicated stack nodes, containing many items of information. Usually, however, the node structure is that of a Pascal record and one field is a pointer to the next lower stack node.

Turbo Pascal Note

We take advantage of the features of Turbo Pascal to write a precompiled unit named Stack that contains functions and procedures for manipulating a stack structure. The purpose of each subprogram is explained in the unit documentation.

```
{ Saved on disk as STACK.PAS }


UNIT Stack;
{
   This unit contains a group of functions and procedures
   for controlling a stack of string values. Other types
   can be used by changing the type of data_type.

   Procedure Push puts a new value on top of the stack.
   Procedure Pop gets the value from the top stack node.
   Procedure Initialize starts a new stack.
   Procedure ListStack lists the contents of the stack.
   Function ShowTop returns the value in the top node.
   Function Empty returns true if the stack is empty,
   otherwise it returns false.
}
INTERFACE
   type
     data_type = string;
     stack_ptr = ^stack_rec;
     stack_rec = record
       Value: data_type;
       Next: stack_ptr;
     end;
   function Empty (Top: stack_ptr): boolean;
   function ShowTop (Top: stack_ptr): data_type;
   procedure Push (var Top: stack_ptr; Item: data_type);
   procedure Pop (var Top: stack_ptr; var Item: data_type);
   procedure CreateStack (var Top: stack_ptr);
   procedure ListStack (Top: stack_ptr);


IMPLEMENTATION
   FUNCTION Empty;
   {
     Returns true if stack is empty, otherwise false.
   }
```

```
begin
  if Top = NIL then
    Empty: = true
  else
    Empty: = false;
end; { Empty }

FUNCTION ShowTop;
{
  Returns value in the top node of the stack. Does not
  remove this value from the stack.
}
begin
  if not Empty(Top) then
    ShowTop: = Top^.Value;
end; { ShowTop }

PROCEDURE Push;
{
  Put a value on the top of the stack.
}
var
  Temp: stack_ptr;
begin
  New (Temp);
  Temp^.Value: = Item;
  Temp^.Next: = Top;
  Top: = Temp;
end; { Push }

PROCEDURE Pop;
{
  Get a value from the top of the stack.
}
var
  Temp: stack_ptr;
begin
  if not Empty(Top) then
    begin
    Item: = Top^.Value;
    Temp: = Top;
    Top: = Top^.Next;
    Dispose (Temp);
    end
  else
    begin
    Writeln ('Error: cannot pop from empty stack');
    Halt;
    end;
end; { Pop }
```

```
PROCEDURE CreateStack;
{
   Create a new stack.
}
begin
   Top := NIL;
end; { CreateStack }


PROCEDURE ListStack;
{
   List the contents of the stack.
}
var
   Temp: stack_ptr;
begin
   Temp := Top;
   if Temp = NIL then
     Writeln ('The stack is empty')
   else
     repeat
       Writeln (Temp^.Value);
       Temp := Temp^.Next;
     until Temp = NIL;
end; { ListStack }

END.
```

Now we shall look at some of these procedures in greater detail. Procedure Push puts a new value on top of the stack. A temporary pointer variable of type stack_ptr is declared, and initialized by the New procedure. Its Value field is assigned the new value. Its Next or pointer field is assigned the address of the previous node on top of the stack. Finally, the address of the temporary pointer variable is assigned to Top, which now points to the top of the modified stack.

Procedure Pop removes the top item from the stack. It displays an error message if the stack is empty. If the stack is not empty, the value in the top node is assigned to variable Item. The address of the top node is assigned to a temporary pointer variable. The address of the next-to-top node is then assigned to Top. Finally, the address in the temporary pointer variable is released.

When the stack is empty, the pointer to the top of the stack, denoted Top, points to NIL. We use this fact in the Create procedure to create a new, empty stack. The Empty function also uses this information to determine if the stack is empty or not. If the stack is not empty, function ShowTop returns the value stored in the top node.

Procedure ListStack lists the contents of the stack. Note that a temporary pointer variable is used so that the address in pointer Top is not changed. Using the pointers in each node, the `repeat` loop descends through the stack, displaying the value stored in every node.

We conclude our discussion of stacks with an example program that demonstrates how the various functions and procedures work. A more practical problem that uses the stack structure is suggested in the practice programs.

```
PROGRAM EX1202 (Input, Output);
{
   Show how to create and use a stack data structure,
   using the Stack unit.
}
uses
   Stack;
var
   Table: stack_ptr;
   Count: integer;
   Item: string;


PROCEDURE PutName (var Table: stack_ptr);
{
   Prompt user for a name and put on the stack.
}
var
   Name: string;
begin
   Write ('Name? ');
   Readln (Name);
   Push (Table, Name);
end; { PutName }


BEGIN { Main Program }
   CreateStack (Table);
   for Count:=1 to 2 do
     PutName (Table); Writeln;
   Writeln ('CONTENTS OF STACK');
   ListStack (Table); Writeln;
   if ShowTop(Table) = 'second' then
     Pop (Table, Item);
   Writeln ('Popped name is ', Item);
   Writeln ('Push new name on stack');
   Push (Table, 'third'); Writeln;
   Writeln ('CONTENTS OF STACK');
   ListStack (Table);
END.
```

This program produces the following output.

```
Name? first
Name? second

CONTENTS OF STACK
second
first

Popped name is second
Push new name on stack

CONTENTS OF STACK
third
first
```

12.5 MULTIDIMENSIONAL ARRAYS

Two-Dimensional Arrays

Two-dimensional arrays can be thought of as arrays of one-dimensional arrays. For example, a table of water quality pollutant concentrations might be represented by a two-dimensional array showing concentrations of various pollutants measured at various depths.

We have used the type definition

```
type
   list = array [1..12] of real;
```

to define a one-dimensional array of real numbers. We can extend this type definition to two dimensions by using the definition

```
type
   table = array [1..8] of array [1..12] of real;
```

A one-dimensional array has one index, while a two-dimensional array has two indices. If we think of the elements in the array forming a two-dimensional table, the row index represents the vertical position of a row of elements, while the column index represents the horizontal position of a column of elements. **Usual convention designates the first index as the row index and the second index as the column index**. Thus in our example, the rows, represented by row index values, run from 1 to 8 while the columns, represented by column index values, run from 1 to 12. In our example, each row represents a different depth and each column represents a different pollutant. Figure 12.2 shows the row and column labels of a two-dimensional array, with the element values denoted by asterisks (one position has an S to identify it for later examples).

```
row                       column index
index  1   2   3   4   5   6   7   8   9   10  11  12
  1    *   *   *   *   *   *   *   *   *   *   *   *
  2    *   *   *   *   *   *   *   *   *   *   *   *
  3    *   *   *   *   *   *   *   *   *   S   *   *
  4    *   *   *   *   *   *   *   *   *   *   *   *
  5    *   *   *   *   *   *   *   *   *   *   *   *
  6    *   *   *   *   *   *   *   *   *   *   *   *
  7    *   *   *   *   *   *   *   *   *   *   *   *
  8    *   *   *   *   *   *   *   *   *   *   *   *
```

Figure 12.2   Row and column index values.

There are other ways to define a two-dimensional array. One of the commonly-used definition statements is

```
type
    table = array [1..8, 1..12] of real;
```

where the lower and upper bounds of both indices are enclosed in a pair of square brackets. The following notation is equivalent.

```
type
    list = array [1..12] of real;
    table = array [1..8] of list;
```

Having defined a two-dimensional array type, we can declare a variable of that type with the usual statement

```
var
    Concentration: table;
```

where Concentration is the identifier for an array with eight rows and twelve columns. We say the *size* of the first dimension is 8 and that of the second dimension is 12. The array Concentration is referred to as an *8-by-12 array*. A specific element in Concentration (denoted by S in Figure 12.2) is identified by the notation

```
Concentration[3,10];
```

meaning the element whose row index is 3 and whose column index is 10. An alternate notation, based on the concept that a two-dimensional array is just an array of one-dimensional arrays, is

```
Concentration[3][10]
```

where each of the rows is thought of as a one-dimensional array.

Remember that the lower and upper bounds of each dimension of an array must be constant values or defined constants; they cannot be variables. It is not necessary that a lower bound have a value of one, although this is often the case. **If any one of the array bounds is changed, then the array must be defined as a different type.**

Nested For Loops

As we have seen previously, a for statement is often used to assign values to the elements of an array, or to display the element values of an array. Two nested for statements are needed for a two-dimensional array, as shown in the following program fragment that reads element values from the keyboard and assigns them to an array.

```
type
  table = array [1..3, 1..10] of real;
var
  Results: table;
  Row, Column: integer;
      |
  for Row:= 1 to 3 do
    for Column:= 1 to 10 do
      Readln (Results[Row, Column]);
```

This program fragment reads element values by row. While the index Row has a value of 1, the index Column runs through its range of values from 1 to 10. This process assigns values to the first row of Results. The index Row then advances to its next value (2) and the second row is read.

A similar program fragment displays a two-dimensional array.

```
for Row:= 1 to 3 do
  begin
  for Column:= 1 to 10 do
    Write (Results[Row, Column]:6:1);
  Writeln; Writeln;
  end;
```

In this example, two Writeln statements are executed after each row is written, one starting the next row on a new line and the other inserting a blank line between the rows of numbers.

As an example, we show a program that reads an array of resistance values from a text file, and displays these values in tabular form on the screen. The array has four rows and six columns, or a total of twenty-four elements. Here is an outline.

Ask user for file name and open the file.

Check for valid file name.

Read file and assign values to a two-dimensional array.

Display the array in matrix format.

Here is the program itself.

```
PROGRAM EX1203 (Input, Output);
{
  Read resistance values from a file into a two-
  dimensional array, and then display the array.
}
  type
    table = array [1..4, 1..6] of real;
```

```
var
  FV: text;
  Matrix: table;

PROCEDURE OpenFile (var FV: text);
{
  Open a text file for reading.
}
var
  FileName: string[80];
  Opened: boolean;
begin
  repeat
    Write ('Name of file? ');
    Readln (FileName);
    Assign (FV, FileName);
    {$I-} { Turn off I/O checking.}
    Reset (FV);
    {$I+} { Turn I/O checking back on.}
    Opened:= (IOresult = 0);
    if not Opened then
      begin
      Writeln ('Error in file name -',
               ' please try again.');
      Writeln;
      end;
  until Opened;
end; { OpenFile }

PROCEDURE ReadFile (var FV: text; var Matrix: table);
{
  Read numbers from a text file and assign to
  a two-dimensional array.
}
var
  Row, Col: integer;
begin
  for Row:= 1 to 4 do
    for Col:= 1 to 6 do
      Readln (FV, Matrix[Row, Col]);
  Close (FV);
end; { ReadFile }

PROCEDURE DisplayArray (Matrix: table);
{
  Display the two-dimensional array named Matrix.
}
var
  Row, Col: integer;
```

```
begin
  Writeln;
  Writeln ('                    RESISTANCE TABLE');
  Writeln;
  for Row:= 1 to 4 do
    begin
    for Col:= 1 to 6 do
      Write (Matrix[Row, Col]:8:1);
    Writeln; Writeln;
    end;
end; { DisplayArray }

BEGIN { Main Program }
  OpenFile (FV);
  ReadFile (FV, Matrix);
  DisplayArray (Matrix);
END.
```

This program produces the following output.

```
Name of file? RESISTOR.TBL

            RESISTANCE TABLE

   100.0   115.7   530.5   201.3   236.5   435.8

   259.3   180.9   286.1   312.8   141.0   337.4

   135.3   520.4   129.9   246.6   558.6   284.0

   487.3   264.0   448.8   522.1   459.1   253.3
```

Turbo Pascal Note

Large Arrays

As previously noted, the data segment of a Turbo Pascal program in MS-DOS is limited in size to 64KB. A 100-by-100 array of real numbers needs almost 80KB of memory space and thus cannot be stored in the data segment. By using pointers, however, we can store an array as a sequence of dynamic variables in the heap, which has much more space available.

The technique is to create a one-dimensional array of pointers, each of which points to a row of the large array. Each row is itself a one-dimensional array of real numbers, and these row arrays are stored as dynamic variables. Thus only the array of pointers is stored in the data segment.

Here is a program fragment used to declare the two-dimensional array named Results.

```
const
  MAX_ROWS = 100;
  MAX_COLS = 100;
type
  row_array = array [1..MAX_COLS] of real;
  row_ptr = ^row_array;
  matrix = array [1..MAX_ROWS] of row_ptr;
var
  Results: matrix;
```

Before the array `Results` can be used, each pointer element of the array must be allocated memory space in the heap. This task can be accomplished with a simple `for` loop.

```
for Index := 1 to MAX_ROWS do
  New (Results[Index]);
```

Finally, any element of the array can be accessed using the notation

```
Results[Row]^[Column];
```

Remember that an individual array element can be identified by the notation `ArrayName[Row,Column]` or the alternate notation `ArrayName[Row][Column]`. The alternate notation is better for our use because the pointer `Results[Row]` points to one of the dynamic row variables, whose identifier is `Results[Row]^`. Thus, an element in the dynamic row variable is denoted by `Results[Row]^[Column]`. The program outline follows.

Create a large array of pointers to arrays.

Fill this two-dimensional array structure from a file.

Ask user to enter row and column values of an element.

While either row or column value is zero

    Display the element.

    Ask user again for row and column values.

Loop back.

Here is the complete program. It initializes a large array from a typed file named `NUMS.DAT` that contains 10,000 real numbers. It asks the user to specify an array element by row and column values, and then displays the value of that element.

```
PROGRAM EX1204 (Input, Output);
{
  Create and use a large two-dimensional array,
  consisting of an array of pointers to arrays.
}
const
  MAX_ROWS = 100;
  MAX_COLS = 100;
type
  row_array = array [1..MAX_COLS] of real;
  row_ptr = ^row_array;
  matrix = array [1..MAX_ROWS] of row_ptr;
  data_file = file of real;
```

```
var
  Results: matrix;
  Row, Col: integer;

PROCEDURE FillMatrix (var Results: matrix);
{
  Fill a large array from a data file named NUMS.DAT.
}
var
  Row, Col: integer;
  List: data_file;
begin
  for Row:= 1 to MAX_ROWS do
    New (Results[Row]);
  Assign (List, 'NUMS.DAT');
  Reset (List);
  for Row:= 1 to MAX_ROWS do
    for Col:= 1 to MAX_COLS do
      Read (List, Results[Row]^[Col]);
  Writeln ('Finished reading the data file.');
  Writeln;
end; { FillMatrix }

PROCEDURE SelectElement (var Row, Col: integer);
{
  Select an array element. Enter zero for
  either row or column value to stop.
}
begin
  repeat
    Write ('Row and column values? ');
    Readln (Row, Col);
    if (Row > 100) or (Col > 100) then
      Writeln ('Row or column value cannot exceed 100.');
  until (Row <= 100) and (Col <= 100);
end; { SelectElement }

PROCEDURE DisplayElement (Row, Col: integer);
{
  Display a specified array element.
}
begin
  Writeln;
  Writeln ('Element value is ', Results[Row]^[Col]:8:4);
  Writeln;
end; { DisplayElement }
```

```
BEGIN { Main Program }
  Writeln ('Starting to read the data file.');
  FillMatrix (Results);
  Writeln ('Enter row and column values of the desired');
  Writeln ('element, separated by a blank. If either');
  Writeln ('value is zero, the program stops.');
  Writeln;
  SelectElement (Row, Col);
  while (Row <> 0) and (Col <> 0) do
    begin
    DisplayElement (Row, Col);
    SelectElement (Row, Col);
    end;
END.
```

Note that Pascal will not accept the notation

```
Results[Row^][Col]; {invalid notation}
```

where the caret is inside the square brackets. The actual pointer name is `Results[Row]`, and the pointer name must be followed by a caret to form the dynamic variable name.

Here is a sample user interaction with the previous program.

```
Starting to read the data file.
Finished reading the data file.

Enter row and column values of the desired
element, separated by a blank. If either
value is zero, the program stops.

Row and column values? 13 78

Element value is 88.8609

Row and column values? 13 105
Row or column value cannot exceed 100.
Row and column values? 13 13

Element value is 56.3237

Row and column values? 0 0
```

If you run this program on a slow computer, it may take a few minutes to fill the array from the file. If your computer contains less than 640KB of memory, you may have to create a smaller typed file of real numbers, and then reduce the size of the constant values `MAX_ROWS` and `MAX_COLS` in the program.

Arrays with Three or More Dimensions

We have used only two-dimensional arrays in our examples, but arrays can have three or more dimensions. Each dimension means another index. It is possible to visualize a three-dimensional array as an indexed stack of tables or two-dimensional arrays. It is difficult to visualize arrays of more than three dimensions, but the methods of declaring and using such arrays are just an extension of the methods discussed in this section. In most applications, arrays of more than two dimensions are not needed.

An array is the ideal data structure for any ordered collection of items that are all of the same type. As we have mentioned before, common examples are lists and tables. **The ordered property of arrays allows any element in the array to be accessed directly if its indices (or single index) are known**.

An array has some limitations as a data structure. **Arrays are of fixed size and this size cannot be changed in a Pascal program**. In fact, **two arrays of different size are considered by Pascal to be of different types**.

IMPORTANT POINTS

- A dynamic variable is referred to by its address.
- Pointer variables cannot be assigned values using the assignment operator. The New procedure must be used instead.
- The value of a pointer variable cannot be displayed or printed, neither can it be read.
- If a pointer value is changed, its associated dynamic variable is lost, and there is no way to recover the value stored in that variable.
- Usual convention designates the first index of a two-dimensional array as the row index, and the second index as the column index.
- If any one of the bounds of an array is changed, the array must be defined as a different type.
- The ordered property of arrays allows any element in the array to be accessed directly if its indices (or single index) are known.
- Arrays defined in a Pascal program are of fixed size, and this size cannot be changed in the program.
- Two arrays of different size are considered by Pascal to be of different type.

SELF-STUDY QUESTIONS

1. What, if anything, is wrong with the following program fragment? Explain your answer.

```
type
  int_ptr = ^integer;
var
  Number: int_ptr;
      |
New (Number);
Number^ := 15.2;
```

2. How would you write the program fragment in Question 1 if you wished to assign the value NIL to the pointer variable Number?

3. What, if anything, is wrong with the following program fragment? Explain your answer.

```
type
  str80 = string[80];
  str_ptr = ^str80;
var
  Name: str_ptr;
    |
Name:= 'John Bishop';
```

4. What statement can be used to release the memory space occupied by the dynamic variable `Result^`?

5. A large array named `Data` is written as a one-dimensional column array of pointers, each of which points to a one-dimensional row array of dynamic variables of type `real`. What statement is used to assign a value of 12.873 to the fifth element in the seventeenth row?

6. Which index in a two-dimensional array is usually called
  (a) the column index;
  (b) the row index?

7. What, if anything, is wrong with the following program fragment?

```
for Row:= 1 to 3 do;
  for Column:= 1 to 10 do;
    Readln (Results[Row, Column]);
```

8. Can you change the size of an array in a Pascal program? Explain your answer.

PRACTICE PROGRAMS

1. Use the text file `LARGE.NUM` to create an array of 1000 real numbers in the heap. Calculate the average value of all elements in this array and the standard deviation. The expression for standard deviation D is given by Equation 12.1

$$D = \sqrt{\frac{1}{N-1} \sum_{i=1}^{N} |S_i - S_{avg}|^2} \qquad 12.1$$

where N is the number of values, S_i is an individual value, and S_{avg} is the average value.

2. Use a stack to determine if the parentheses in a string are balanced; that is, there should be a matching right parenthesis for each left parenthesis. Store each left parenthesis on the stack, and remove it when a right parenthesis is found. If parentheses are balanced, the stack should be empty after you have finished scanning every character in the string. Test your program using the following strings:

```
Writeln (1 + Chr(Random(17)));
while(var("a"),assign("a",minus(var("a"),int(1))))
```

3. A *matrix* is a two-dimensional array of numbers. For example, a 3-by-3 matrix might look like Figure 12.3.

$$\begin{bmatrix} 7 & 1 & 2 \\ 3 & 3 & 5 \\ 4 & 2 & 3 \end{bmatrix}$$

Figure 12.3 A 3-by-3 matrix.

A *square matrix* has the same number of rows and columns. The *trace* of a square matrix is the sum of the elements on the *principal diagonal*, running from the upper left element to the lower right element. The trace of the preceding matrix is $7 + 3 + 3 = 13$.

Read element values into a 20-by-20 matrix from the typed file MATRIX.DAT, a file of integers. Calculate and display the trace of this matrix.

4. The *transpose* of a matrix is the original matrix with its rows and columns interchanged. For example, the transpose of the matrix in Practice Program 3 is shown in Figure 12.4.

$$\begin{bmatrix} 7 & 3 & 4 \\ 1 & 3 & 2 \\ 2 & 5 & 3 \end{bmatrix}$$

Figure 12.4   A transposed matrix.

Read element values into a 20-by-20 matrix from the typed file MATRIX.DAT, a file of integers. Display this matrix on the screen. Prompt the user to press a key, and when a pressed key is detected, display the transpose of the original matrix on the screen.

5. A typed file of real numbers, named QUALITY.84, contains information on air quality measured at various altitudes for the year 1984. All measurements were made once a month at the same location (Washington, D.C.). Five altitudes were selected, from ground level to 40,000 feet in increments of 10,000 feet, and the quantities of five pollutants were measured in parts per million (ppm).

The information for each month is stored in five sequences of six numbers. The first number in each sequence is the altitude, while the other five numbers are pollution concentrations (in ppm) for pollutants P1 through P5. The first sequence for each month is that for ground level measurements. A total of thirty numbers thus comprises the information for one month, and the file contains information for the entire year, January through December.

Write a procedure to read the information from the file and assign it to a three-dimensional array. This array consists of twelve two-dimension arrays, one for each month, with five rows for the different altitudes and six columns for the specific altitude value and the five pollution concentrations.

Ask the user to enter the name of any month and display the pollution concentrations for that month in tabular form, as specified in the previous paragraph.

Test your program by displaying the table for the month of June, 1984.

6. Using file QUALITY.84 and the procedure specified in Practice Program 5, create a three-dimensional array containing air pollution information. Calculate the average level of P2 pollution for the year at an altitude of 20,000 feet. Also calculate the average level of P1 pollution for all altitudes for the year. Display both results on the screen with appropriate labels.

7. Using file QUALITY.84 and the procedure specified in Practice Program 5, create a three-dimensional array containing air pollution information. Calculate the average ratio of P2 pollution level to P4 pollution level for the months of June through September, both at ground level and at an altitude of 40,000 feet. Determine which month in the year has the highest average level of all pollutants at an altitude of 10,000 feet. Display all results on the screen with appropriate labels.

13

SORTING

13.1 INTRODUCTION

Here, we introduce the technique of sorting on computers, an important computer application, and two algorithms for implementing this technique. We first discuss a simple algorithm that is easy to understand, the bubble-sort algorithm.

A more sophisticated, and much faster, algorithm is the quicksort algorithm. In order to understand this algorithm, we must explain recursive subprograms. We also discuss how to measure the sorting times for different sorting algorithms.

13.2 SORTING: THE BUBBLE-SORT ALGORITHM

Sorting lists of names or numbers is a frequent and important application of computers. If the list is large, sorting can take a long time. Many algorithms for sorting have been investigated, and some of these algorithms can sort very rapidly. Unfortunately, many of the efficient and fast algorithms are also difficult to understand.

We introduce first a relatively simple, although not very efficient, sorting algorithm called the *bubble-sort algorithm*. We then use it in a program that sorts a list of real numbers.

A computer program using the bubble-sort algorithm goes through the list of numbers to be sorted, from one end of the list to the other, comparing numbers in pairs. The first pair consists of the first and second numbers, the second pair consists of the second and third numbers, and so forth. We call this process *scanning the list*.

```
First scan    1    7 ⌒ 3    2    5

              1    3    7 ⌒ 2    5

              1    3    2    7 ⌒ 5

              1    3    2    5    7

Second scan   1    3 ⌒ 2    5    7

              1    2    3    5    7

Third scan    1    2    3    5    7
```

Figure 13.1 Sorting a list with bubble-sort.

If a pair is in the wrong numerical order, we swap or interchange the two numbers. If a pair is in the correct numerical order, we move on to the next pair.

We repeat this scanning process until we can scan the list without having to swap any names. We know then that the list is in sorted order.

Figure 13.1 shows the bubble-sort process in detail. Each scan through the list of numbers is labeled, and arrows show the interchange of numbers. Note how large numbers move or "bubble up" to the top (in our case, the right end) of the list.

A third temporary variable must be used when interchanging two numbers. To interchange the numeric values stored in variables A and B, assign the value of A to the variable Temp, next assign the value of B to A, and finally assign the value of Temp to B. The program statements might look like this.

```
Temp := A; { assign value of A to Temp }
A := B;    { assign value of B to A }
B := Temp; { assign value of Temp to B }
```

We use a boolean variable as a flag. Each time we start to scan the list, we set the value of the flag variable to true. If we make an interchange during this scan of the list, the flag value is changed to false. We then examine the flag value at the end of each scan, and if it is true, we know that no interchanges were made during the last scan through the list and that the list is in sorted order.

Our example program consists of three tasks.

Reading numbers from a file and assigning them to an array.

Sorting the array in memory.

Writing the sorted array back out to a file.

This program assumes that we have enough memory to allow the entire file to be placed in an array variable in memory. **It is much easier and quicker to sort a list in memory than it is to sort a list in a disk file**.

The BubbleSort Procedure

Our program uses a procedure for the actual sorting. An array named SortList contains N values. SortList is an array variable of a user-defined type list, a sequence of values that has a length of not more than LIST_LENGTH. Each element in the array is of type list_item. Both types, list and list_item, must be defined in the program. The value of N must be equal to or less than MAX_LIST_LENGTH.

Thus, the procedure BubbleSort is a general procedure, capable of sorting a list of not more than MAX_LIST_LENGTH values of type list_item. As we have discussed previously, **a design limitation in Pascal that requires a different type for an array of a different size limits the generality of a procedure such as BubbleSort that uses an array parameter**.

```
PROCEDURE BubbleSort (var SortList: list; N: integer);
{
  Use the bubble-sort algorithm to sort an array of
  type list = array [1.. LIST_LENGTH] of list_item,
  containing a sequence of N values, where all cons-
  tants and types must be defined in the main program
  or the subprogram calling this procedure.
}
var
  I: integer;
  Sorted: boolean;
  Temp: list_item;
begin
  repeat
    Sorted: = true;
    for I: = 1 to N - 1 do
      if SortList[I] > SortList[I + 1] then
        begin
        Temp: = SortList[I];
        SortList[I]: = SortList[I + 1];
        SortList[I + 1]: = Temp;
        Sorted: = false;
        end;
  until Sorted = true;
end; { BubbleSort }
```

Pairs of list values, denoted by SortList[I] and SortList[I + 1], are compared, and are interchanged if not in sorted order. Note that the for loop only goes up to I = N - 1 because one index in the comparison is I + 1 and the last number in the list is SortList[N]. If the index I were assigned a value of N, the program would try to compare array elements SortList[N] and SortList[N + 1], and would produce unpredictable results because no number has been assigned to SortList[N + 1].

Referring to Figure 13.1, the repeat loop body performs a single scan of the list. The body of the if statement performs a swap of two elements in the list.

This procedure sorts a list of items in ascending order. To sort in descending order, reverse the logical sense of the comparison statement, making it

```
if SortList[I] < SortList[I + 1] then
```

The following program is designed to sort a list of real numbers. It assumes that the numbers are stored in a text file, one number per line. There can be no more than one hundred numbers because the array has a declared size of 100. The program outline is relatively simple.

> Ask user for file name and open input file.
>
> Ask user for file name and open output file.
>
> Read data from input file into an array.
>
> Sort the array.
>
> Write the sorted array to the output file.
>
> Close output file and report results.

Here is the program itself.

```
PROGRAM EX1301 (Input, Output);
{
  Read a list of numbers from a text file,
  use the bubble-sort algorithm to sort this list,
  and write the sorted list to a text file.
}
const
  MAX_LIST_LENGTH = 100;
type
  string80 = string[80];
  list_item = real;
  list = array [1..MAX_LIST_LENGTH] of list_item;
var
  InFile, OutFile: text;
  SortList: list;
  N: integer;

PROCEDURE OpenInFile (var InFile: text);
{
  Open an input file.
}
var
  FileName: string80;
begin
  Write ('Name of input file? ');
  Readln (FileName);
  Assign (InFile, FileName);
  Reset (InFile);
end; { OpenInFile }

PROCEDURE OpenOutFile (var OutFile: Text);
{
  Open an output file.
}
```

```
var
  FileName: string80;
begin
  Write ('Name of output file? ');
  Readln (FileName);
  Assign (OutFile, FileName);
  Rewrite (OutFile);
end; { OpenOutFile }

PROCEDURE FillArray (var InFile: text;
                     var SortList: list;
                     var Count: integer);
{
  Read a list of numeric values from a text file and
  assign to an array. Count the number of values.
}
begin
  Count:= 0;
  while not Eof(InFile) do
    begin
    Count:= Count + 1;
    Readln (InFile, SortList[Count]);
    end;
end; { FillArray }

PROCEDURE BubbleSort (var SortList: list; N: integer);
{
  Use the bubble-sort algorithm to sort an array of
  type list = array [1..MAX_LIST_LENGTH] of list_item,
  containing a sequence of N values, where all constants
  and types must be defined in the main program or the
  subprogram calling this procedure.
}
var
  I: integer;
  Sorted: boolean;
  Temp: list_item;
begin
  repeat
    Sorted:= true;
    for I:= 1 to N - 1 do
      if SortList[I] > SortList[I + 1] then
        begin
        Temp:= SortList[I];
        SortList[I]:= SortList[I + 1];
        SortList[I + 1]:= Temp;
        Sorted:= false;
        end;
  until Sorted = true;
end; { BubbleSort }
```

```
PROCEDURE WriteArray (var OutFile: text;
                      SortList: list; N: integer);
{
  Write an array of N numbers to a text file.
}
var
  I: integer;
begin
  for I: = 1 to N do
    Writeln (OutFile, SortList[I]);
end; { WriteArray }

PROCEDURE DisplayArray (SortList: list; N: integer;
                        Title: string80);
{
  Display a short, single-line array
  of N real numbers on the screen,
  with an appropriate title.
}
var
  I: integer;
begin
  Writeln (Title);
  for I: = 1 to N do
    Write (SortList[I]:5:0);
  Writeln;
end; { DisplayArray }

BEGIN { Main Program }
  OpenInFile (InFile);
  OpenOutFile (OutFile);
  FillArray (InFile, SortList, N);
  Writeln;
  DisplayArray (SortList, N, 'Unsorted List');
  BubbleSort (SortList, N);
  Writeln;
  DisplayArray (SortList, N, 'Sorted List');
  WriteArray (OutFile, SortList, N);
  Close (OutFile);
  Writeln;
  Writeln ('Sorted list is in the output file.');
END.
```

The following output is produced by this program.

```
Name of input file? UNSORTED.NUM

Name of output file? SORTED.NUM

Unsorted List
123    65   887      3    45   110      7    -6   1050      0

Sorted List
-6      0      3      7    45     65   110   123    887   1050

Sorted list is in the output file.
```

We have inserted a call to the procedure `DisplayArray` in the program before and after the `BubbleSort` procedure is called. These procedure calls show the result of sorting, but they can be deleted in a production version of the program.

Our program, as written, cannot sort a file containing more than 100 numbers. Even if the program is modified to increase the size of the array, a practical limit is soon reached because small computers do not have enough memory to hold very large arrays in memory. More sophisticated sorting algorithms have been developed that allow large disk files to be sorted quickly and efficiently. It is possible to sort a typed file directly with the bubble-sort algorithm but not a text file.

You may have noticed that after the first scan through the list, the largest number moved to the right end of the list. Each successive scan moves the next larger number towards the right end. This phenomena is discussed in Practice Program 3, where a modified bubble-sort algorithm is suggested that is more efficient than our original algorithm.

13.3 COMPARING TWO STRINGS

In order to sort or search a list of string values, we need to understand how the computer determines if one string is larger than another string. We shall compare two variables, `Name1` and `Name2`, both of type `string80`.

```
                          Turbo Pascal Note
```

In Turbo Pascal, two strings can still be compared even if they are of different types (different defined lengths).

We want to know if the boolean expression

```
Name1 > Name2
```

is true or false. Comparison of two strings is done character by character and is based on the ordinal values of the characters. These characters can be letters, digits, or nonalphabetic characters. In most implementations of Pascal, the ordinal value of a character is the same as its ASCII value, as listed in Appendix B.

The computer compares the ordinal value of the first character of `Name1` with that of the first character of `Name2`. If the character in `Name1` has the greater value, then the boolean expression (`Name1` > `Name2`) is true. Remember that an uppercase letter and the corresponding lowercase letter are different characters and have different ordinal values.

```
'C' is greater than 'B'
'a' is greater than 'A'
```

If the character in `Name1` has the lesser value, the boolean expression is false. If the first characters in `Name1` and `Name2` are identical, the computer automatically compares the ordinal values of the second character in each string.

This process continues until (1) the value of a character in one string is greater than the value of the corresponding character in the other string, (2) the end of one string is reached while the other string contains more characters, or (3) the ends of both strings are reached because they are equal in length and have the same sequence of characters.

If the ordinal value of a character in `Name1` is greater or less than the ordinal value of the corresponding character in `Name2`, the last comparison determines whether the boolean expression is true or false.

```
'ABC' is greater than 'ABB'
```

If `Name1` is longer than `Name2` and the two strings have an identical sequence of characters up to the end of `Name2`, `Name1` is considered the greater and the boolean expression is true.

```
'QED' is greater than 'QE'
```

If `Name1` and `Name2` are of equal length and have the same sequence of characters, the two strings are equal and the boolean expression is false.

```
'xyz' is equal to 'xyz'
```

Using a boolean expression that compares two string variables, the bubble-sort algorithm can be used to alphabetize a list of string values, or arrange the list in ascending alphabetic order. As mentioned previously, changing the sense of the boolean expression sorts the list into descending alphabetic order.

13.4 RECURSIVE SUBPROGRAMS

Our next example of sorting uses the *quicksort algorithm*. This algorithm is usually written with a sorting subprogram that calls itself again and again, known as a *recursive* subprogram. Thus, we interrupt our discussion of sorting to examine the general subject of *recursion*.

Recursive subprograms are usually not as fast, as efficient or as easy to understand as subprograms using an iterative loop; that is, a loop with a control variable that is incremented each time the body of the loop is executed. We include a short discussion of recursion and an example program because there are some applications where recursion is the most natural way to solve a problem.

As an example, consider the problem of calculating the factorial value of a number. The definition of factorial N (written by mathematicians as $N!$) is

$$N! = 1 \times 2 \times 3 \times \ldots \times N$$

The expression 0! is defined as 1. For example, 3! is equal to $1 \times 2 \times 3$ or 6, while 5! is $1 \times 2 \times 3 \times 4 \times 5$ or 120.

An Iterative Solution

Here is a program that calculates factorials using a while statement in an ordinary iterative loop. It is so simple that no outline is required.

```
PROGRAM EX1302 (Input, Output);
{
   Ask user to enter a nonnegative integer
   and calculate the factorial value.
   Uses a function with an iterative loop.
   Use only with Version 4 or 5 unless modified.
}
var
   Number: integer;

FUNCTION Factorial (N: integer): longint;
{
   Calculate the factorial value of N.
   Change function type to real in Version 3.
}
var
   Index: integer;
   TempResult: longint; { type real in Version 3 }
begin
   TempResult:= 1;
   Index:= 2; { because 0! and 1! both equal 1 }
   while Index <= N do
      begin
      TempResult:= Index * TempResult;
      Index:= Index + 1;
      end;
   Factorial:= TempResult;
end; { Factorial }

BEGIN { Main Program }
   Write ('Enter a nonnegative integer: ');
   Readln (Number);
   if Number > 13 then
      Writeln ('Factorial of number is too ',
               'large for longint type.')
   else
      Writeln ('Factorial ', Number:1, ' is ',
               Factorial(Number):1);
END.
```

                              Turbo Pascal Note

Note that this program is written for Versions 4 and 5 of Turbo Pascal and includes a function of type `longint`. If you wish to run the program under Version 3, you must change the type of the function `Factorial` and its local variable `TempResult` from `longint` to `real`. You must also change the last `Writeln` statement to display a real value rather than an integer value.

The function `Factorial` uses a `while` loop with a control variable `Index` that is incremented each time the body of the loop is executed. The initial value of the function is set at 1. The values of 0! and 1! are not calculated in the loop because both have a value of 1, the initial value of the function. The loop starts with an initial value of 2 for `Index`.

Here is the display produced by this program.

```
Enter a nonnegative integer: 5
Factorial 5 is 120
```

A Recursive Solution

The same results can be obtained by writing the function in a recursive form. We show an example program and then discuss the results.

```
PROGRAM EX1303 (Input, Output);
{
   Ask user to enter a nonnegative integer
   and calculate the factorial value.
   Uses a recursive function.
   Use only with Version 4 or 5 unless modified.
}
var
   Number: integer;


FUNCTION Factorial (N: integer): longint;
{
   Calculate the factorial value of N.
   Change function type to real in Version 3.
}
begin
   if N <= 1 then
      Factorial:= 1
   else
      Factorial:= N * Factorial(N - 1);
end; { Factorial }
```

```
BEGIN { Main Program }
  Write ('Enter a nonnegative integer: ');
  Readln (Number);
  if Number > 13 then
     Writeln ('Factorial of number is too ',
               'large for longint type.')
    else
     Writeln ('Factorial ', Number:1, ' is ',
               Factorial(Number):1);
END.
```

In this version of the program, the function is somewhat simpler in format, but probably more difficult to understand. Assuming a user enters a value of 5, the function is called first with N = 5. The else branch of the if statement is selected, requiring calculation of the expression 5*Factorial(4). **This expression cannot be calculated, however, until Factorial(4) has been evaluated**, requiring calculation of the expression 4*Factorial(3), and so forth.

Whenever a program calls a function, it puts the call statement for that function on a temporary stack. We discussed the operation of a stack in Chapter 12. In the case of a recursive program, all function calls except the last one placed on the stack are not evaluated immediately, but rather evaluated later when they are removed from the stack.

In our example program, the expression Factorial(5) is placed first on the stack. After all function calls are placed on the stack, it looks like Figure 13.2, with the last call on top. None of these functions on the stack can be evaluated, however, until the value of Factorial(1) is known.

The last item placed on the stack is Factorial(1). This function can be evaluated immediately using the first if branch to assign its value of 1, and it is then removed from the stack. The program now returns to the stack, calculates the value of the current top function, Factorial(2), as 2 × 1 or 2, and removes it from the stack.

STACK	VALUE
Factorial(1)	1
Factorial(2)	2 × Factorial(1)
Factorial(3)	3 × Factorial(2)
Factorial(4)	4 × Factorial(3)
Factorial(5)	5 × Factorial(4)

Figure 13.2 Diagram of the stack during recursion.

The program returns to the stack, calculates what is now the top function, Factorial(3) as 3 ×2 ×1 or 6, and removes it from the stack. The next function calculated and removed is Factorial(4) whose value is 4 ×3 ×2 ×1 or 24, while the last function calculated and removed is Factorial(5) which has a value of 5 ×4 ×3 ×2 ×1 or 120, the desired result.

The length of a recursive calculation, and thus the size of the stack, depends only on the amount of memory available for the stack. **There must always be one nonrecursive value, in our case, the value of Factorial(1), for recursion to work properly**.

When all is said and done, recursion is not often used in practical programs, but there are some cases (such as the following QuickSort procedure) where a recursive solution is clearly the best solution. Recursive subprograms are often short and elegant, but they tend to be more difficult to understand than common iterative solutions, and execute more slowly. We recommend that you use recursion only if it appears to be the best way to solve a problem.

13.5 SORTING: THE QUICKSORT ALGORITHM

One of the fastest sorting algorithms used on computers is the *quicksort algorithm*. We again consider the problem of sorting an array or list of elements.

The quicksort algorithm works by separating the list into two partitions. One element of the list is selected and called the *pivot element*. It makes little difference which element is chosen, although it is often the first or last element in the list.

The elements in the list are rearranged in a systematic manner into two partitions. Assuming we wish to sort the list into ascending order from left to right, all list elements less than the pivot element are moved into the left partition. All elements greater than or equal to the pivot element are moved into the right partition. The pivot element is then placed between the two partitions. Note that this rearrangement places the pivot element in its proper position in the final, sorted list.

We now apply the same quicksort algorithm, recursively and separately, to the left partition and the right partition of the original list. Each time we call quicksort, we must define a new pivot element. We work first on the left partition and continue to subdivide it, calling quicksort recursively, until the length of each partition is one element. We then do the same thing to the right partition. Our array is now sorted in ascending order.

Figure 13.3 shows how a list, containing six characters forming the word CATTLE, is sorted. The vertical line represents the division between left and right partitions. The underlined letter is the current pivot element. The arrow shows the interchange of elements that places the pivot element between the two partitions.

We might choose the first element (C) as the pivot element. After the first partitioning, the list appears as ACTTLE. The left partition contains one element

Before separation:	C̲	A	T	T	L	E
After test, no swap:	C̲	A|	T	T	L	E
After moving pivot:	A	C̲	T	T	L	E
Before separation:			T̲	T	L	E
After element swap:			T̲	L|	T	E
After element swap:			T̲	L	E|	T
After moving pivot:			E	L	T̲	T
Before separation:			E̲	L		
After moving pivot:			E̲	L		
Final sorted list:	A	C	E	L	T	T

Figure 13.3   Sorting a list with quicksort.

(A), while the right partition contains four elements (TTLE). The pivot element (C) is in its correct position.

In our example, we note that the left partition is only one element long, and so we cannot subdivide it further. The right partition is a new list containing the four characters TTLE. Applying the quicksort algorithm again, we choose the first element (T) as the pivot element and subdivide the list into two partitions. The resulting list becomes ELTT. The first T is the pivot element, while the second T is the right partition. The left partition is EL. We know now that the letters A and C (in positions 1 and 2), and letters T and T (in positions 5 and 6) are all in their correct final positions in the sorted list.

Continuing with our example, we note that the list EL is already in sorted order, and so it is partitioned into two single-element lists. The quicksort algorithm is called recursively for each single-element partition, but of course it makes no change in the position of the single element. Thus our original list, written in sorted order, becomes ACELTT.

The `QuickSort` Procedure

Here is one implementation of the quicksort algorithm using a procedure named QuickSort. The types list and index are user-defined. Type list is often an array of characters or numbers, while type index is usually the same as type integer.

After checking to see if the list is longer than one element, the first statement calls another procedure, named Separate, that partitions the list. Then QuickSort is called again to sort first the left partition, and then the right partition. A procedure named Swap is called when needed to interchange two elements of the list.

```
PROCEDURE QuickSort (var SortList: list;
                     First, Last: index);
{
  Sort the list named SortList, containing items of
  type list_item, from index First to index Last,
  using the quicksort algorithm.
  This is a recursive procedure.
}
var
  Pivot: index;

begin { QuickSort }
  if First < Last then { more than one element in list }
    begin
    Separate (Pivot, First, Last);
    QuickSort (SortList, First, Pivot - 1);
    QuickSort (SortList, Pivot + 1, Last);
    end;
end; { QuickSort }
```

As you can see, most of the work is done by a procedure named Separate, located within the scope of procedure QuickSort. We first list procedure Separate and then discuss how it works.

```
PROCEDURE Separate (var Pivot: index; First, Last: index);
{
  Separate the list into two parts, one containing
  elements less than PivotValue and the other containing
  elements greater than or equal to PivotValue.
}
var
  PivotValue: list_item;
  New: index;
begin
  Pivot := First; { make first element the pivot }
  PivotValue := SortList[First];
  for New := (First + 1) to Last do
    if SortList[New] < PivotValue then
      begin
      Pivot := Pivot + 1;
      if New <> Pivot then
        Swap (SortList[Pivot], SortList[New]);
      end;
  { Move pivot element to point in list that separates }
  { the smaller elements from the larger elements. }
  Swap (SortList[First], SortList[Pivot]);
end; { Separate }
```

The first element in the list is chosen as the pivot element. Starting with the second element, each other element (denoted as element New) in the list is compared, in turn, with the value of the original pivot element, PivotValue. If the element value is less than PivotValue, the index of the pivot element is incremented. Procedure Swap is called to interchange the values of the current pivot element (SortList[Pivot]) and the new element (SortList[New]).

Note the distinction between the original value of the pivot element (PivotValue), which is used for comparisons, and the index of the current pivot element (Pivot). If a new element is found whose value is less than PivotValue, index Pivot is incremented, moving the position of the current pivot element to the right. The values of the new element and the current pivot element (denoted by index Pivot) are then interchanged, placing the new element before or to the left of the current pivot element. No swap is made, of course, if the new element and current pivot element have the same index (they are the same element).

After a complete scan through the list, the location of the current pivot element marks the division between the two partitions. All elements to the left of the division, including the current pivot element, have values less than PivotValue. All elements to the right of the division have values greater than or equal to PivotValue. The remaining task is then to swap SortList[Pivot] and SortList[First], placing the original pivot element in its proper position in the list. Note that this position is also its proper position when the list is in final sorted order.

This procedure is not easy to read. We recommend that you trace through the procedure by hand (play computer) in order to understand exactly what is taking place.

Testing the `QuickSort` Procedure

Our implementation of the quicksort algorithm is shown in an example program that demonstrates how the algorithm works. The procedure QuickSort does the actual sorting. The user is asked to enter a short string of characters, the characters are sorted in ascending order, and the sorted string is displayed. In addition, a table is created and displayed, showing several intermediate steps in the sorting process.

```
PROGRAM EX1304 (Input, Output);
{
  Test an implementation of the quicksort algorithm.
  Ask the user to enter a short string of characters.
  Display intermediate and final results on the screen.
  Use only with Version 4 or 5 unless modified.
}
type
  list_item = char;
  list = array [1..15] of list_item;
  index = integer;
var
  SortList: list;
  I, N: index;
  Entry: string; { specify type in Version 3 }

PROCEDURE Display1 (Title: string; SortList: list;
                    A, B: index);
{
  Display part or all of list.
}
var
  I: index;
begin
  Write (Title);
  for I:= 1 to (A - 1) do { leading blanks }
    Write (' ');
  for I:= A to B do
    Write (SortList[I], ' ');
  Writeln;
end; { Display 1 }

PROCEDURE Display2 (Title: string; SortList: list;
                    A, B, Pivot: index);
{
  Display list during swapping, showing separator
    between low and high element values.
}
```

```
var
  I: index;
begin
  Write (Title);
  for I:= 1 to (A - 1) do { leading blanks }
    Write (' ');
  for I:= A to (Pivot - 1) do
    Write (SortList[I], ' ');
  Write (SortList[Pivot], '| ');
  for I:= (Pivot + 1) to B do
    Write (SortList[I], ' ');
  Writeln;
end; { Display 2 }

PROCEDURE QuickSort (var SortList: list;
                     First, Last: index);
{
  Sort the list named SortList, containing items of
  type list_item, from index First to index Last,
  using the quicksort algorithm.
  This is a recursive procedure.
}
var
  Pivot: index;

  PROCEDURE Swap (var A, B: list_item);
  {
    Interchange two items in the list.
  }
  var
    Temp: list_item;
  begin
    Temp:= A;
    A:= B;
    B:= Temp;
  end; { Swap }

  PROCEDURE Separate (var Pivot: index;
                      First, Last: index);
  {
    Separate the list into two parts, one containing
    elements less than PivotValue and the other containing
    elements greater than or equal to PivotValue.
  }
  var
    PivotValue: list_item;
    New: index;
```

```
begin
  Pivot:=First; { make first element the pivot }
  PivotValue:=SortList[First];
  Display1 ('Before separation: ',
            SortList, First, Last);
  for New:=(First + 1) to Last do
    if SortList[New] < PivotValue then
    begin
    Pivot:=Pivot + 1;
    if New <> Pivot then
      begin
      Swap (SortList[Pivot], SortList[New]);
      Display2 ('After element swap: ',
                SortList, First, Last, Pivot);
      end
    else
      Display2 ('After test, no swap: ',
                SortList, First, Last, Pivot);
    end;
  { Move pivot element to point in list that separates }
  { the smaller elements from the larger elements. }
  Swap (SortList[First], SortList[Pivot]);
  Display1 ('After moving pivot: ',
            SortList, First, Last);
end; { Separate }

begin { QuickSort }
  if First < Last then { more than one element in list }
    begin
    Separate (Pivot, First, Last);
    Writeln;
    QuickSort (SortList, First, Pivot - 1);
    QuickSort (SortList, Pivot + 1, Last);
    end;
end; { QuickSort }

BEGIN { Main Program }
  Write ('Enter a string of up to 15 characters: ');
  Readln (Entry);
  N:=Length (Entry);
  Writeln;
  for I:=1 to N do
    SortList[I]:=Entry[I];
  QuickSort (SortList, 1, N);
  Write ('Final sorted list: ');
  for I:=1 to N do
    Write (SortList[I], ' ');
  Writeln;
END.
```

We show the results produced when a user enters the string of characters
CATTLE.

```
Enter a string of up to 15 characters : CATTLE

Before separation:     C   A   T   T   L   E
After test, no swap:   C   A|  T   T   L   E
After moving pivot:    A   C   T   T   L   E

Before separation:         T   T   L   E
After element swap:        T   L|  T   E
After element swap:        T   L   E|  T
After moving pivot:        E   L   T   T

Before separation:         E   L
After moving pivot:        E   L

Final sorted list:     A   C   E   L   T   T
```

As in Figure 13.3, underlining identifies the original pivot element in each
case, while the vertical line represents the division between the two partitions. Note
how the vertical line moves through the list until the elements have been properly
divided. The last step is to swap the values of the original pivot element and the
current pivot element.

It is interesting to see how the sorting process is effected when one of the
characters in the input string is changed. Here is a second example of output, with
underlining again added.

```
Enter a string of up to 15 characters: WATTLE

Before separation:     W   A   T   T   L   E
After test, no swap:   W   A|  T   T   L   E
After test, no swap:   W   A   T|  T   L   E
After test, no swap:   W   A   T   T|  L   E
After test, no swap:   W   A   T   T   L|  E
After test, no swap:   W   A   T   T   L   E|
After moving pivot:    E   A   T   T   L   W

Before separation:     E   A   T   T   L
After test, no swap:   E   A|  T   T   L
After moving pivot:    A   E   T   T   L

Before separation:         T   T   L
After element swap:        T   L|  T
After moving pivot:        L   T   T

Final sorted list:     A   E   L   T   T   W
```

We now insert procedure QuickSort into Program EX1301 in place of
procedure BubbleSort, producing Program EX1305. We have changed several

variables from type integer to type index to conform with our notation in
procedure QuickSort. In practice, the two types are considered the same. We
have also deleted the calls to display intermediate results that we used in Program
EX1304. The program outline is unchanged.

```
PROGRAM EX1305 (Input, Output);
{
  Read a list of numbers from a text file,
  use the quicksort algorithm to sort this list,
  and write the sorted list to a text file.
}
const
  MAX_LIST_LENGTH = 100;
type
  string80 = string[80];
  list_item = real;
  list = array [1..MAX_LIST_LENGTH] of list_item;
  index = integer;
var
  InFile, OutFile: text;
  SortList: list;
  N: index;

PROCEDURE OpenInFile (var InFile: text);
{
  Open an input file.
}
var
  FileName: string80;
begin
  Write ('Name of input file? ');
  Readln (FileName);
  Assign (InFile, FileName);
  Reset (InFile);
end; { OpenInFile }

PROCEDURE OpenOutFile (var OutFile: Text);
{
  Open an output file.
}
var
  FileName: string80;
begin
  Write ('Name of output file? ');
  Readln (FileName);
  Assign (OutFile, FileName);
  Rewrite (OutFile);
end; { OpenOutFile }
```

```
PROCEDURE FillArray (var InFile: text;
                     var SortList: list;
                     var Count: index);
{
  Read a list of numeric values from a text file and
  assign to an array. Count the number of values.
}
begin
  Count: = 0;
  while not Eof(InFile) do
    begin
    Count: = Count + 1;
    Readln (InFile, SortList[Count]);
    end;
end; { FillArray }

PROCEDURE QuickSort (var SortList: list;
                     First, Last: index);
{
  Sort the list named SortList, containing N items
  of type list_item, using the quicksort algorithm.
  This is a recursive procedure.
}
var
  Pivot: index;

  PROCEDURE Swap (var A, B: list_item);
  {
  Interchange two items in the list.
  }
  var
    Temp: list_item;
  begin
    Temp: = A;
    A: = B;
    B: = Temp;
  end; { Swap }

  PROCEDURE Separate (var Pivot: index;
                      First, Last: index);
  {
    Separate the list into two parts, one containing
    elements less than PivotValue and the other containing
    elements greater than or equal to PivotValue.
  }
  var
    PivotValue: list_item;
    New: index;
```

```
   begin
     Pivot:= First; { make first element the pivot }
     PivotValue:= SortList[First];
     for New:= (First + 1) to Last do
       if SortList[New] < PivotValue then
         begin
         Pivot:= Pivot + 1;
         if New <> Pivot then
           Swap (SortList[Pivot], SortList[New]);
         end;
     { Move pivot element to point in list that separates }
     { the smaller elements from the larger elements. }
     Swap (SortList[First], SortList[Pivot]);
   end; { Separate }

begin { QuickSort }
  if First < Last then { more than one element in list }
  begin
    Separate (Pivot, First, Last);
    QuickSort (SortList, First, Pivot - 1);
    QuickSort (SortList, Pivot + 1, Last);
    end;
end; { QuickSort }

PROCEDURE WriteArray (var OutFile: text;
                      SortList: list; N: index);
{
  Write an array of N numbers to a text file.
}
var
  I: index;
begin
  for I:= 1 to N do
    Writeln (OutFile, SortList[I]);
end; { WriteArray }

PROCEDURE DisplayArray (SortList: list; N: index;
                        Title: string80);
{
  Display a short, single-line array
  of N real numbers on the screen,
  with an appropriate title.
}
var
  I: index;
begin
  Writeln (Title);
  for I:= 1 to N do
    Write (SortList[I]:6:0);
  Writeln;
end; { DisplayArray }
```

```
BEGIN { Main Program }
  OpenInFile (InFile);
  OpenOutFile (OutFile);
  FillArray (InFile, SortList, N);
  Writeln;
  DisplayArray (SortList, N, 'Unsorted List');
  QuickSort (SortList, 1, N);
  Writeln;
  DisplayArray (SortList, N, 'Sorted List');
  WriteArray (OutFile, SortList, N);
  Close (OutFile);
  Writeln;
  Writeln ('Sorted list is in the output file.');
END.
```

Program EX1305 produces the same results as Program EX1301.

13.6 TIMING PROGRAM SEGMENTS

One of the important properties of sorting algorithms is the speed with which they can sort various kinds of lists. If an implementation of Pascal allows the system clock to be accessed, it is usually possible to measure the time taken by any particular sort. We discuss one method of timing the execution of part of a program.

Turbo Pascal Note

Timing in Turbo Pascal

We claim that the quicksort algorithm is a faster sorting technique than the bubble-sort algorithm. In order to substantiate this claim, we need to have a method for measuring the execution time of a sorting routine in a program.

We first write a function for calculating the current elapsed time in seconds since midnight, using the GetTime procedure of Version 4 or 5. **Your program must include the Dos unit**. Here is an example program.

```
PROGRAM EX1306 (Output);
{
  Demonstrate the Time function.
}
uses
  Dos;

FUNCTION Time: real;
{
  Calculate the number of seconds since midnight.
  Use only with Version 4 or 5.
  Requires the Dos unit.
}
```

```
var
  Hour, Minute, Second, Sec100: word;
begin
  GetTime (Hour, Minute, Second, Sec100);
  Time: = 3600.0 * Hour + 60.0 * Minute + Second
          + (Sec100 / 100.0);
end; { Time }

BEGIN { Main Program }
  Writeln ('Number of seconds past midnight is ',
          Time:1:2);
END.
```

We then insert a statement such as

```
StartTime: = Time;
```

at the beginning of the program section to be timed, and a statement such as

```
StopTime: = Time;
```

at the end of the section. The execution time for that section is given by

```
ExecutionTime: = StopTime - StartTime;
```

As an example, we made timing measurements while sorting an array of one thousand random integers, using different sorting methods. The quicksort algorithm takes 0.54 seconds, while the bubble-sort algorithm takes 51.68 seconds. When sorting long lists, there is a time advantage of almost 100 to 1 if the quicksort algorithm is used instead of the bubble-sort algorithm.

If you are still using Version 3, the following version of function Time can be used. It accesses the system clock (if one exists) through an MS-DOS interrupt call. We discuss interrupt calls, and programs using these calls, in Chapter 16.

```
FUNCTION Time: real; { Saved on disk as EX1307_3.PAS }
{
  Calculate the number of seconds since midnight.
  Use only with Version 3.
}
type
  registers = record
    AX, BX, CX, DX, BP, SI, DI, DS, ES, Flags: integer;
  end;
var
  Regs: registers;
  Hour, Minute, Second, Sec100: integer;
```

```
begin
  with Regs do
    begin
    AX:= $2C00;
    MsDos (Regs);
    Hour:= Hi(CX);
    Minute:= Lo(CX);
    Second:= Hi(DX);
    Sec100:= Lo(DX);
    Time:= 3600.0 * Hour + 60.0 * Minute + Second
             + (Sec100 / 100.0);
    end;
  end; { Time }
```

IMPORTANT POINTS

- A third temporary variable must be used when interchanging two numbers.
- It is much easier and quicker to sort a list in memory than it is to sort a list in a disk file.
- A design limitation in Pascal, that requires a different type for an array of a different size, limits the generality of a procedure such as BubbleSort that uses an array parameter.
- In a recursive function, there must always be one nonrecursive value of the function for recursion to work properly.

SELF-STUDY QUESTIONS

1. Is the bubble-sort algorithm considered to be a fast sorting algorithm? Explain your answer.
2. Explain how assignment statements can be used to exchange the values of two variables?
3. What kind of change must be made in the BubbleSort procedure to produce a descending sort rather than an ascending sort?
4. Can a partially-filled array be sorted by
   (a) the bubble-sort algorithm;
   (b) the quicksort algorithm?
5. Is the string ABCEF larger or smaller than the string ABCDF?
6. Name one or more advantages of the quicksort algorithm.
7. Name one or more advantages of the bubble-sort algorithm.
8. (a) Where does a recursive program store its intermediate results?
   (b) What limitation, if any, does this storage requirement place on a recursive program?

PRACTICE PROGRAMS

1. As written in this chapter, the example program for the bubble-sort algorithm sorts a list into ascending order. Rewrite procedure `BubbleSort` so that it sorts in either ascending or descending order. You will need to ask the user which kind of sort to make and pass an appropriate parameter to the procedure. This parameter should have a value of A for an ascending sort or a value of D for a descending sort.

   Test your program by sorting the file `UNSORTED.NUM` into a new file `ASCEND.NUM` for ascending order, and another new file `DESCEND.NUM` for descending order. Hand in listings of the two new files.

2. Modify the `QuickSort` procedure for either ascending or descending sorts, as described in Practice Program 1. Test your modified procedure in the manner prescribed in that program, using the file `UNSORTED.NUM`.

3. The bubble-sort algorithm scans through an entire list, comparing every pair of contiguous elements in the list. The first scan positions the largest element at the right end of the list. This means that the next scan needs to cover only the first (N − 2) pairs of elements, not (N − 1) pairs. Rewrite procedure `BubbleSort` to take advantage of this fact. Your `for` statement might look like

   ```
   for I := 1 to ScanLimit do
   ```

   where `ScanLimit` starts at (N − 1) and is decreased by one after each scan.

   Test your program by sorting the file `UNSORTED.NAM` into the file `SORT.NAM`.

4. Compare the sorting times for the bubble-sort and quicksort algorithms. Use the timing technique discussed in Section 13.6. Use the text file `LARGE.NUM` for your comparison and display the sorting times with appropriate labels. If the times turn out to be excessively long, reduce the length of `LARGE.NUM`. Be sure to write your output to files other than `LARGE.NUM`.

5. The text file `LARGE.NAM` contains about 500 ten-letter strings. Sort this file and create a typed file named `LARGE.DAT`, containing the strings in sorted order.

6. Practice Program 4 in Chapter 11 refers to a typed file named `PROSPECT.DAT`. Sort this file using the sorting algorithm of your choice. First, sort the file in descending order by zip code and display the sorted results. Second, sort the file in ascending order by last name and display the sorted results.

14

SEARCHING

14.1 INTRODUCTION

Another important technique in programming is searching, looking for a particular value in a list or a file. We discuss two algorithms, the sequential search algorithm and the binary search algorithm. We give examples of searching an array and searching a file. The differences between searching an unsorted list and searching a sorted list are examined.

We also introduce indexed files and design an example program that shows how these files can be searched.

14.2 SEQUENTIAL SEARCH OF AN UNSORTED LIST

If a list has been created by adding items to it from time to time, it is usually not in sorted order. Probably the best and simplest way to search such a list is to use the *sequential search algorithm*.

As the name implies, a sequential search goes through the list, examining each item, until the desired item is found or the end of the list is reached. Starting at the beginning of the list, we read each item in sequence and compare it to a target item. If the two items are equal, we report success. If the target item is not equal to any item in the list, we report failure. **A sequential search can take a long time if the list is long and the desired item is near the end**.

Our example program reads a text file containing uppercase names, assigns these names to an array, and then asks the user for a target name. The array is searched sequentially until a match is found, or until the end of the array is reached. Copying the names from a file to an array reduces the time required for multiple searches of the list but not necessarily for the first search.

Here is an outline of the program.

Ask user for file name and open text file.

Read names from file and assign to array.

Ask user for target name.

While target name <> null string

   Search the array.

   Display found or not found message.

Loop back.

Here is the program itself.

```
PROGRAM EX1401 (Input, Output);
{
  Ask the user to enter a target name. Copy the
  contents of a text file to an array and search for
  the target name. Stop when a null string is entered.
}
const
  MAX_LIST_LENGTH = 100;
  NULL_STRING = '';
type
  string80 = string[80];
  list = array [1..MAX_LIST_LENGTH] of string80;
var
  InFile: text;
  NameList: list;
  Target: string80;
  N: integer;

PROCEDURE OpenInFile (var InFile: text);
{
  Open an input file.
}
var
  FileName: string80;
begin
  Write ('Name of input file? ');
  Readln (FileName);
  Assign (InFile, FileName);
  Reset (InFile);
end; { OpenInFile }
```

```
PROCEDURE FillArray (var InFile: text;
                     var NameList: list;
                     var N: integer);
{
  Read a list of names from a text file and
  assign to an array. Count the number of names.
}
var
  Count: integer;
begin
  Count := 0;
  while not Eof(InFile) do
    begin
    Count := Count + 1;
    Readln (InFile, NameList[Count]);
    end;
  N := Count;
end; { FillArray }

PROCEDURE GetName (var Target: string80);
{
  Ask the user for a target name.
}
begin
  Writeln;
  Write ('Enter target name: ');
  Readln (Target);
end; { GetName }

FUNCTION Found (NameList: list; Target: string80;
                N: integer): boolean;
{
  Search an array for a target name.
  Return true if name is found; if not,
  return false.
}
var
  Count: integer;
  Success: boolean;
begin
  Count := 0;
  Success := false;
  repeat
    Count := Count + 1;
    if NameList[Count] = Target then
      Success := true;
  until (Success) or (Count >= N);
  Found := Success;
end; { Found }
```

```
BEGIN { Main Program }
  OpenInFile (InFile);
  Writeln ('Press the ENTER key to stop.');
  FillArray (InFile, NameList, N);
  GetName (Target);
  repeat
    if Found(NameList, Target, N) then
      Writeln (Target, ' is in the list.')
    else
      Writeln (Target, ' is not in the list.');
    GetName (Target);
  until Target = NULL_STRING;
END.
```

Note that we make use of several procedures written for a previous program. In some cases, a previously-used procedure is modified slightly. You should develop your own library or collection of procedures and functions and use those that are appropriate in new programs that you write. This technique not only reduces the time required to write a program, but also reduces debugging time because previously-used library subprograms tend to have fewer errors then newly-written code.

This program produces the following output.

```
Name of input file? unsorted.nam
Press the ENTER key to stop.

Enter target name: JOHN
JOHN is in the list.

Enter target name: BART
BART is in the list.

Enter target name: Bart
Bart is not in the list.

Enter target name:
```

Note that the program, as written, is case-sensitive. If this behavior is not desired, a procedure can be written to convert all entered characters to uppercase. Program EX1402 contains such a procedure.

14.3 BINARY SEARCH OF A SORTED LIST

When the items in a list are in sorted order, we can use another, faster searching technique called the *binary search algorithm*. This method works by repeatedly dividing the list in half and discarding one half, resulting in successively shorter lists to search.

We assume that the list is sorted with the highest-valued item at the bottom of the list. We assume also that a target name has been specified. We compare the target name with the name at the middle of the list.

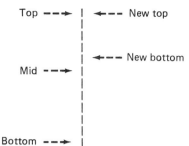

Figure 14.1 Target name is in top half of list.

If the target name is greater than the middle name, we can confine further search to the bottom half of the list. If the target name is less than the middle name, we search only the top half of the list. The process of dividing and comparing is repeated until the desired name is found or the search fails, each comparison effectively cutting the length of the list in half.

Consider a list of names in an array, sorted from top (smallest index) to bottom (largest index). The user enters a name to be found, called the *target name*. If the search is successful, the function returns a value equal to the index of the matching name. If the search is unsuccessful, the function returns a value of zero.

We define a top end point, a midpoint, and a bottom end point. When we start, the top end point is the index of the first name in the list. This index value is usually one. The bottom end point is the index of the last name in the list. The midpoint is approximately half way between the top and bottom end points.

We use the midpoint (an integer value) as an index and designate the name with that index as the *midpoint name*. We compare the target name to the midpoint name. If the target name equals the midpoint name, we have completed a successful search. The function is assigned the index value of the midpoint.

If the target name is less than the midpoint name, we know that any further search can be confined to the top half of the list. We leave the top end point unchanged but designate a new bottom end point equal to the midpoint minus one. In effect, the length of the list to be searched has been cut in half, as shown in Figure 14.1.

Conversely, if the target name is greater than the midpoint name, we know that any further search can be confined to the bottom half of the list. We leave the bottom end point unchanged and designate a new top end point equal to the midpoint plus one. Figure 14.2 shows the result.

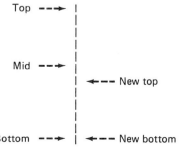

Figure 14.2 Target name is in bottom half of list.

The search is considered unsuccessful when the top and bottom end points cross, that is, when the index of the top end point is greater than the index of the bottom end point. This result (an unsuccessful search) is denoted by assigning a value of zero to the function.

Here is our binary search function.

```
FUNCTION Search (NameList: list;
                 N: integer;
                 Target: string80): integer;
{
  Search an array NameList containing N names,
  using the binary search algorithm.
  Variable Target contains the target name.
}
var
  Top, Mid, Bottom: integer;
  Found: boolean;
begin
  Top := 1;
  Bottom := N;
  Found := false;
  repeat
    Mid := (Top + Bottom) div 2;
    if Target = NameList[Mid] then
      Found := true
    else if Target > NameList[Mid] then
      Top := Mid + 1
    else { Target < NameList[Mid] }
      Bottom := Mid - 1;
  until (Found) or (Bottom < Top);
  if Found then
    Search := Mid
  else
    Search := 0;
end; { Search }
```

We now incorporate this function into an example program, using the following outline.

Ask user for file name and open text file.

Read names from file and write to an array.

Ask user for target name, convert to uppercase.

While target name <> Q or q

Search for target name in array using binary search.

Display results of the search.

Ask user for another target name.

Loop back.

A list of names is read from a text file and assigned to an array. The array is declared large enough to hold one hundred names, although in our example it is only partially filled.

The user is asked to specify a target name. We wish to convert the target name to uppercase because all names in our file are in uppercase. A lowercase letter has an ordinal value that is larger by 32 than the ordinal value of the corresponding uppercase letter. We use this fact to convert all lowercase letters in the target name to uppercase.

The program displays a message showing whether the target name has been found. A new target name is then requested until the user enters the letter Q or q for quit, and the program stops.

```
PROGRAM EX1402 (Input, Output);
{
  Read a list of names from a text file and
  use the binary search algorithm to find
  a target name.
}
const
  MAX_LIST_LENGTH = 100;
type
  string80 = string[80];
  list = array [1..MAX_LIST_LENGTH] of string80;
var
  InFile: text;
  NameList: list;
  N, Result: integer;
  Target: string80;


PROCEDURE OpenInFile (var InFile: text);
{
  Open an input file.
}
var
  FileName: string80;
begin
  Write ('Name of input file? ');
  Readln (FileName);
  Assign (InFile, FileName);
  Reset (InFile);
end; { OpenInFile }
```

```
PROCEDURE FillArray (var InFile: text;
                     var NameList: list;
                     var N: integer);
{
  Read a list of names from a text file and
  assign to an array. Count the number of names.
}
var
  Count: integer;
begin
  Count := 0;
  while not Eof(InFile) do
    begin
    Count := Count + 1;
    Readln (InFile, NameList[Count]);
    end;
  N := Count;
end; { FillArray }

PROCEDURE GetTarget (var Target: string80);
{
  Ask user to specify a target name.
  Convert the entered name to uppercase.
}
var
  I: integer;
begin
  Writeln;
  Write ('Enter the target name: ');
  Readln (Target);
  for I := 1 to Length(Target) do
    if Target[I] in ['a'..'z'] then
      Target[I] := Chr(Ord(Target[I]) - 32);
end; { GetTarget }

FUNCTION Search (NameList: list;
                 N: integer;
                 Target: string80): integer;
{
  Search an array NameList containing N names,
  using the binary search algorithm.
  Variable Target contains the target name.
}
var
  Top, Mid, Bottom: integer;
  Found: boolean;
```

```
begin
  Top := 1;
  Bottom := N;
  Found := false;
  repeat
    Mid := (Top + Bottom) div 2;
    if Target = NameList[Mid] then
      Found := true
    else if Target > NameList[Mid] then
      Top := Mid + 1
    else { Target < NameList[Mid] }
      Bottom := Mid - 1;
  until (Found) or (Bottom < Top);
  if Found then
    Search := Mid
  else
    Search := 0;
end; { Search }

BEGIN { Main Program }
  OpenInFile (InFile);
  FillArray (InFile, NameList, N);
  Writeln ('Enter the letter Q to stop the program.');
  GetTarget (Target);
  while (Target <> 'Q') and (Target <> 'q') do
    begin
    Result := Search(NameList, N, Target);
    if Result > 0 then
      Writeln (Target, ' is in the list.')
    else
      Writeln (Target, ' is not in the list.');
    GetTarget (Target);
    end;
END.
```

The following output is produced by this program.

```
Name of input file? sorted.nam
Enter the letter Q key to stop the program.

Enter target name: JOHN
JOHN is in the list.

Enter target name: BART
BART is in the list.

Enter target name: Bart
Bart is in the list.

Enter target name: q
```

Note two changes from Program EX1401. The letter Q (or q) is used to stop the program instead of just pressing the Enter key. The search process is now insensitive to whether the entered name is written in all uppercase characters, all lowercase characters, or a mixture of both.

Turbo Pascal Note

The function Upcase is available in Turbo Pascal for converting a lowercase character to uppercase. We can use the following program fragment in procedure GetTarget of Program EX1402 as a replacement for the if statement in the for loop.

```
for I := 1 to Length(Target) do
   Target[I] := Upcase(Target[I]);
```

A typed file can be searched directly using the binary search algorithm, provided the components of the file are in sorted order. The method is essentially the same as that used for searching an array, except that the component or file record number is used instead of the array element index. Remember that the first record in a file has a file record number of zero.

A binary search has the advantage of being much faster than a sequential search, especially for a long list. It has the disadvantage of requiring a sorted list. In the problems at the end of the chapter, we suggest that you compare the times required for these two searching methods.

14.4 INDEXED DATA FILES

If a typed data file is long and has large file records, it can take an appreciable amount of time to sort the file each time a record is added or deleted. In addition, the file can be sorted on only one of the fields in the file record. For example, a data file might contain both a part name and a part number in its records. If it was ordered by part name, a binary search could not be used to find a specific part number.

Assume we are working for a marine engineering company that needs an inventory control system for the parts used to build a series of small work boats. The computer program designed to meet this need must access a file of inventory information. The inventory file is a typed file of records, with each record having the following structure.

```
part = record
         PartNumber: string[6];
        Description: string[50];
           Quantity: integer;
          UnitPrice: real;
          BinNumber: string[4]:
       ReorderLevel: integer;
    ReorderQuantity: integer;
         VendorName: string[30];
        VendorPhone: string[12];
end;
```

The part number is used as the primary identifier of a particular part. It is stored in a variable of type string because it is never used in an arithmetic operation. In order to find a specified part, we need to create an index file that shows which record contains the information on a particular part. In this application, the part number field is called the *key field*.

Using an Index File

To understand the concept and use of an index file, remember that one of the fastest ways to search a file is a binary search, but that type of search only works if the file is in sorted order. We could sort our inventory file on any field, say, part number, but each time we added a new part, we would have to sort the file again. This is a slow process if the file is long and the record size is large.

As an alternative, we can create another file, called an *index file*, that has small records containing only the part number and the record number for that part. This file can be sorted more quickly than the inventory file. When we search the index file for a part number, we find the inventory file record number for that particular part. The index file gets its name because it is similar to an index in a book: It tells us which record in the inventory file contains the desired information.

The index file is also a typed file of records, with each record having the following structure.

```
index1 = record
  PartNumber: string[6];
      RecNum: integer;
end;
```

An index record shows the number of the record in the inventory file that contains information on a particular part number. The part numbers are in sorted order, but not the record numbers.

As mentioned previously, **another advantage of this design is that we can have more than one index file**. In addition to an index file that is sorted by part number, we can have another index file containing the part description and record number, sorted by part description. We can search this second index file for a particular part description and find the corresponding record number in the inventory file.

Program Outline

We design our program as a menu-driven program. We have the usual main program unit and several subprogram units. We have only four commands (including a stop command) in our menu, with each command executing from a separate procedure. Other commands can be added and will be discussed in the practice programs at the end of the chapter. Here is an outline of the main program unit.

Open the inventory file.
Open the index file.
Repeat loop
    Display the command menu.
    Select a command: Quit, Edit, List, or Search.
    Branch to appropriate subprogram.
Until selected command is Quit.
Close all files.

The edit command allows a user to change any field (except the part number) in a specified record. If you do not know the record number, you can use the search command to find the record number corresponding to a given part number. A part number cannot be edited because a part number change would require resorting the index file, a procedure we wish to avoid in our simple program (although included as a practice program). Here is an outline of the edit command.

Get record number.
Read record from inventory file.
Repeat loop
    Display old field value.
    Ask if new field value is wanted.
Until all record fields have been displayed.
Write new record to inventory file.
Return to menu.

The list command displays the contents of the inventory file. Each record is read, and displayed on the screen.

While not end of inventory file
  Read record from inventory file.
  Display record number and record fields.
Loop back.
Return to menu.

The search command uses a binary search function to search in the index file for the record number corresponding to a specified part number. If the record exists, it is read and displayed.

Get part number.
Search index file for record number.
If record exists
  Read record from inventory file.
  Display record number and record fields.
Else
  Display failure message.
Return to menu.

The Main Program

We call four procedures from the main program. Two procedures open the inventory file and the index file. Another displays the command menu. The fourth selects a specific command. This fourth procedure calls one of the command procedures.

Error trapping routines are used when opening both files. This program assumes that both files have already been created and loaded with information. If the inventory file or index file does not exist, the user is asked to try again because the entered file name may have been misspelled.

The procedure DisplayMenu is called next and the menu is displayed. The procedure SelectCommand is used to call the selected command procedure. If an invalid command is entered, an error message is printed and the menu is displayed again.

This program is so long that it is more understandable if presented in sections. We now show the main program and the procedures that it calls directly.

```
PROGRAM EX1403 (Input, Output);
{
   Inventory record file with index.
}
uses
  Crt;
const
  INDENT = '                              ';
```

```
type
  string6 = string[6];
  part = record
         PartNumber: string6;
        Description: string[50];
           Quantity: integer;
          UnitPrice: real;
          BinNumber: string[4];
      ReorderLevel: integer;
   ReorderQuantity: integer;
         VendorName: string[30];
        VendorPhone: string[12];
  end;
  index = record
    PartNumber: string6;
     RecNumber: longint;
  end;
  part_file = file of part;
  index_file = file of index;
var
  FV1: part_file;
  FV2: index_file;
  Command: integer;

PROCEDURE OpenDataFile (var FV1: part_file);
{
  Open the inventory file.
}
var
  Opened: boolean;
  FileName: string;
begin
  Opened := false;
  while not Opened do
    begin
    Write ('Name of inventory file? ');
    Readln (FileName);
    Assign (FV1, FileName);
    {$I-} { Turn off I/O checking }
    Reset (FV1);
    {$I+} { Turn I/O checking back on }
    Opened := (IOResult = 0);
    if not Opened then
      begin
      Writeln ('Inventory file does not exist',
               ' - please try again.');
      Writeln;
      end;
    end; { while loop }
end; { OpenDataFile }
```

```
PROCEDURE OpenIndexFile (var FV2: index_file);
{
  Open the index file.
}
var
  Opened: boolean;
  FileName: string;
begin
  Opened := false;
  while not Opened do
    begin
    Write ('Name of index file? ');
    Readln (FileName);
    Assign (FV2, FileName);
    {$I-} { Turn off I/O checking }
    Reset (FV2);
    {$I+} { Turn I/O checking back on }
    Opened := (IOResult = 0);
    if not Opened then
      begin
      Writeln ('Index file does not exist',
               ' - please try again.');
      Writeln;
      end;
    end; { while loop }
end; { OpenIndexFile }

PROCEDURE DisplayMenu (var Command:integer);
{
  Display the command menu.
}
begin
  ClrScr;
  GotoXY (1, 10);
  Writeln (INDENT, ' Command Menu');
  Writeln;
  Writeln (INDENT, '0.....stop the program');
  Writeln (INDENT, '1.....edit a record');
  Writeln (INDENT, '2.....list all records');
  Writeln (INDENT, '3.....search for a part number');
  Writeln;
  Write (INDENT, 'Your selection.....');
  Readln (Command);
end; { DisplayMenu }
```

```
PROCEDURE SelectCommand (Command: integer);
{
   Select the command procedure
   for an entered command.
}
begin
   case Command of
      0: ; { exit command }
      1: Edit (FV1, FV2);
      2: List (FV1, FV2);
      3: Search (FV1, FV2);
   else
      begin
      Writeln;
      Writeln (INDENT, 'Enter a number between ',
                       '0 and 3.');
      Write (INDENT, 'Press any key to continue.');
      repeat until KeyPressed;
      end;
   end;
end; { SelectCommand }

BEGIN { Main Program }
  ClrScr;
  OpenDataFile (FV1);
  OpenIndexFile (FV2);
  repeat
    DisplayMenu (Command);
    SelectCommand (Command);
  until Command = 0;
  Close (FV1);
  Close (FV2);
END.
```

The Edit Command

The user is asked to enter a record number that is checked to make sure it is within the allowed range. The inventory file record is then read and is ready for editing. As stated earlier, the part number field cannot be edited because if this field is changed, the index file must be sorted again.

Each of the other fields in the record is displayed, and the user is asked to either enter a new value or press the Enter key to keep the same value. After the entire record has been edited, it is written back on the inventory file.

Note that all new values are entered as string values. If a particular value is to be assigned to a numeric field variable, the Val function is used to convert the string value to a numeric value.

Here is the Edit procedure.

```
PROCEDURE Edit (var FV1: part_file;
                var FV2: index_file);
{
  Edit a specified record in the inventory file.
}
var
  PartRec: part;
  Size: integer;
  RecNum: longint;
  FieldNum: integer;
  Field: string;
  Reply: char;
  Code: integer;

begin
  ClrScr;
  Size := FileSize(FV2);
  repeat
    Write ('Record Number? ');
    Readln (RecNum);
    if (RecNum < 1) or (RecNum > Size) then
      begin
      Writeln;
      Writeln ('Record numbers are between 1 and ',
               Size:1);
      Writeln;
      end;
  until (RecNum >= 1) and (RecNum <= Size);
  Seek (FV1, RecNum - 1);
  Read (FV1, PartRec);
  Writeln;
  Writeln ('Press Enter to keep current field value.');
  Writeln;
  with PartRec do
    begin
    Writeln ('Part Number: ', PartNumber);
    Writeln ('The part number cannot be changed');
    Writeln ('Description: ', Description);
    Write ('New value? '); Readln (Field);
    if Field <> '' then Description := Field;
    Writeln ('Quantity: ', Quantity:1);
    Write ('New value? '); Readln (Field);
    if Field <> '' then Val (Field, Quantity, Code);
    Writeln ('Unit Price: ', UnitPrice:1:2);
    Write ('New value? '); Readln (Field);
    if Field <> '' then Val (Field, UnitPrice, Code);
```

```
            Writeln ('Bin Number: ', BinNumber);
            Write ('New value? '); Readln (Field);
            if Field <> '' then BinNumber := Field;
            Writeln ('Reorder Level: ', ReorderLevel:1);
            Write ('New value? '); Readln (Field);
            if Field <> '' then
              Val (Field, ReorderLevel, Code);
            Writeln ('Reorder Quantity: ', ReorderQuantity:1);
            Write ('New value? '); Readln (Field);
            if Field <> '' then
              Val (Field, ReorderQuantity, Code);
            Writeln ('Vendor Name: ', VendorName);
            Write ('New value? '); Readln (Field);
            if Field <> '' then VendorName := Field;
            Writeln ('Vendor Phone: ', VendorPhone);
            Write ('New value? '); Readln (Field);
            if Field <> '' then VendorPhone := Field;
            end;
          Seek (FV1, RecNum - 1);
          Write (FV1, PartRec);
          Writeln;
          Write ('Press any key to continue...');
          Reply := ReadKey;
        end; { Edit }
```

The List Command

The list command simply reads each record from the inventory file and displays
the record number and the record fields on the screen. It pauses after displaying
each record and continues when any key is pressed. It calls a procedure named
PrintRec to display a record, showing the name of each field and the field value.

Here are the PrintRec and List procedures.

```
PROCEDURE PrintRec (var FV1: part_file;
                    RecNum: longint);
{
  Display a specified record in the inventory file.
}
var
  PartRec: part;
```

```
begin
  Seek (FV1, RecNum - 1);
  Writeln ('Record Number ', RecNum:1);
  Writeln;
  Read (FV1, PartRec);
  with PartRec do
    begin
    Writeln ('Part Number: ', PartNumber);
    Writeln ('Description: ', Description);
    Writeln ('Quantity: ', Quantity:1);
    Writeln ('Unit Price: ', UnitPrice:1:2);
    Writeln ('Bin Number: ', BinNumber);
    Writeln ('Reorder Level: ', ReorderLevel:1);
    Writeln ('Reorder Quantity: ', ReorderQuantity:1);
    Writeln ('Vendor Name: ', VendorName);
    Writeln ('Vendor Phone: ', VendorPhone);
    end;
  Writeln;
end; { PrintRec }

PROCEDURE List (var FV1: part_file;
                var FV2: index_file);
{
  Display the entire inventory file.
}
var
  IndexRec: index;
  Reply: char;
begin
  ClrScr;
  Reset (FV2);
  while not Eof(FV2) do
    begin
    Read (FV2, IndexRec);
    PrintRec (FV1, IndexRec.RecNumber);
    Write ('Press any key to continue...');
    Reply := ReadKey;
    Writeln; Writeln;
    end;
end; { List }
```

The Search Command

A major purpose of this program is to provide a fast way to search for a specific inventory record. The record is specified by part number, and the index file is used to determine the corresponding record number. A binary search technique is used to search the index file.

The user enters a part number that must contain six digits. The Found function uses the binary search technique to search the index file. If the part number is found, the function returns the record number; otherwise, it returns a value of zero. Once a record has been found, it is displayed with the PrintRec subroutine.

Here are the Found function and the Search subroutine.

```
FUNCTION Found (var FV2: index_file;
                Target: string6): longint;
{
  Search a typed file for a target name.
  Return record number if name is found;
  if not, return zero.
}
var
  Top, Middle, Bottom: longint;
  Success: boolean;
  IndexRec: index;
  RecNum: longint;
begin
  Top := 0;
  Bottom := FileSize(FV2);
  Success := false;
  repeat
    Middle := (Top + Bottom) div 2;
    if Middle >= FileSize(FV2) then
      begin
      Found := 0;
      Exit;
      end;
    Seek (FV2, Middle);
    Read (FV2, IndexRec);
    if Target = IndexRec.PartNumber then
      begin
      Success := true;
      RecNum := IndexRec.RecNumber;
      end
    else if Target > IndexRec.PartNumber then
      Top := Middle + 1
    else { Target < IndexRec.PartNumber }
      Bottom := Middle - 1;
  until (Success) or (Bottom < Top);
  if Success then
    Found := RecNum
  else
    Found := 0;
end; { Found }
```

```
PROCEDURE Search (var FV1: part_file;
                  var FV2: index_file);
{
  Search the inventory file for a record with
  a specified part number, and display the record.
}
var
  Target: string6;
  RecNum: longint;
  Reply: char;
begin
  ClrScr;
  repeat
    Write ('Part number to find? ');
    Readln (Target);
    if Length(Target) <> 6 then
      begin
      Writeln;
      Writeln ('Part number must have six digits.');
      Writeln;
      end;
  until Length(Target) = 6;
  RecNum := Found(FV2, Target);
  if RecNum = 0 then
    begin
    Writeln;
    Writeln ('Part number is not in the file.');
    Writeln;
    end
  else
    begin
    Writeln;
    PrintRec (FV1, RecNum);
    end;
  Write ('Press any key to continue...');
  Reply := ReadKey;
end; { Search }
```

The disk of example programs provided with this book includes both an inventory file and an index file that are designed to be used with this program. The inventory file is named PARTS.DAT and the index file is named XPARTS.DAT. We recommend that you run the program with these files. In several of the practice programs, we suggest ways to expand this example program.

As mentioned previously, this program is listed in sections to make it easier to read. If you wish to see the program in its entirety, however, you can look at it on the example program disk or print out a program listing on paper.

IMPORTANT POINTS

- A sequential search can take a long time if the list is long and the desired name is near the end.
- An advantage of the indexed file structure is that there can be more than one index file, each for a different field.

SELF-STUDY QUESTIONS

1. Describe a method for searching an unsorted list.
2. Describe a method for searching a sorted list.
3. Is it faster to search a text file by
   (a) searching the file directly or
   (b) copying the file to an array and then searching the array? Explain your answer.
4. Two files, one a text file and the other a typed file, contain 100 real numbers. Both files are in numeric order. Each file is to be searched for a particular number.
   Which searching method would you select to search each file and why?
5. Given the two files described in Question 4, is it always true that one file can be searched more quickly than the other? Explain your answer.
6. Can the binary search algorithm be used to search a disk file directly? Explain your answer.
7. What is the advantage of using an index file to find a particular item in a data file?
8. What is the reason for sometimes having more than one index file for a given data file?

PRACTICE PROGRAMS

1. Ten-letter character strings are used as proprietary code names for different versions of a program being developed by a software engineering firm. Ask the user to specify a code name string and then search for that string in the typed file LARGE.DAT. The components of this file are ten-character strings and are in sorted order. Report whether the specified string is found, and if so, its record number.
   Test your program with the strings TEUMSEJSQR and KUICHPWNZX.
2. The text file LARGE.TXT has ten characters on each line and is in sorted order. Compare the time required to search this file with the time required to search the typed file LARGE.DAT, described in Practice Program 1.
   Test your program with the code name strings FLAFNBTKRO and ZSJHYWGVKW. One of these strings is near the beginning of file LARGE.TXT and the other is near the end, so you should get quite different times for your two sequential searches.

   The following practice programs consist of enhancements or modifications to the example database program in this chapter.

3. Write a `Delete` command procedure to delete a record from the inventory file. Write null strings and zero numeric values in the specified inventory record. This empty record in the inventory file will do no harm, although it wastes space.

   Remove the corresponding entry from the index file and adjust that file so there is no empty record. Do you need to sort the index file again?

4. Modify the `Delete` command procedure to allow a specified range of records to be deleted.

5. Write an `Add` command procedure to add additional records to the inventory file. You should prompt the user with the field name for each field. As minimum error checking, make sure that numeric fields are valid numbers, that the part number contains exactly six digits, and that the telephone number contains exactly ten digits.

   Ask the user to confirm the accuracy of a complete record before writing it on the file. Add an appropriate entry to the index file for each new inventory record. After you have finished adding records, be sure to sort the index file.

6. Write a `Create` command procedure to create a new inventory file. After the inventory file and index file have been opened, call the `Add` procedure to start adding new inventory records.

7. Modify the `PrintRec` procedure to allow optional printed reports on an attached printer. Add another parameter to specify whether the report should be displayed or printed. If you use networked printers, send your report to a text file for later printing.

8. Write a command procedure to display or print the records of all parts supplied by a specified vendor.

9. Write a command procedure to display or print all records of parts whose quantity is less than or equal to the reorder level. For each item, include the reorder quantity in a separate column. The resulting report might be used as the basis for ordering new stock.

10. Write a `Purge` command procedure to purge all empty records from the inventory file. You will have to create and sort a new index file.

15

NUMERICAL METHODS

15.1 INTRODUCTION

In this chapter, we introduce several numerical algorithms for solving problems and the programming techniques for implementing these algorithms. The first technique is numerical integration, and we use the trapezoidal algorithm. The second technique is for finding roots, and we use the bisection algorithm. Both of these techniques are examples of numerical methods often used by engineers and scientists.

The third technique is matrix manipulation, using the principles of matrix algebra. We illustrate this technique by developing a program for matrix multiplication. The fourth technique is curve fitting, finding a functional curve that best fits or describes the meaning of a set of measured values. We use the least squares criterion to fit a straight line to a set of measured points denoted by their x and y coordinates.

15.2 NUMERICAL INTEGRATION

When you were introduced to integration in calculus, you learned that the area under a curve representing a function between points A and B is equal to the definite integral of the function between A and B. We use that fact to develop a method for calculating the definite integral of a function of a single variable. Our calculation gives only an approximate value of the integral, although we can increase the accuracy of the calculation up to the precision of our computer.

The Trapezoidal Algorithm

Assume we wish to calculate the integral

$$\int_a^b f(x)\,dx \tag{15.1}$$

where $f(x)$ is a continuous function of x over the range from $x = a$ to $x = b$. A plot of the function is shown in Figure 15.1.

Our approach is to divide the interval from a to b into subintervals. In each subinterval, we define an area in the shape of a trapezoid, whose base is the subinterval length. If the subinterval is small, the sum of all the trapezoidal areas is a close approximation to the area under the curve and an approximate value of the integral. Figure 15.2 shows the approximation when there are only two subintervals, while Figure 15.3 shows the approximation for four subintervals. This method of approximating the area is called the *trapezoidal algorithm*.

In Figure 15.2, the area of the first subinterval is given by

$$1/2\Delta x(f(a) + f(x_1)) \tag{15.2}$$

and the second subinterval by

$$1/2\Delta x(f(x_1 + f(b)) \tag{15.3}$$

where

$$\Delta x = \frac{(b - a)}{2}. \tag{15.4}$$

The total area is given by

$$T = 1/2\Delta x(f(a) + 2f(x_1) + f(b)) \tag{15.5}$$

In Figure 15.3, the area of the first subinterval is given by

$$1/2\Delta x(f(a) + f(x_1)) \tag{15.6}$$

and the other three subintervals by similar expressions, where

$$\Delta x = \frac{(b - a)}{4}. \tag{15.7}$$

The total area is given by

$$T = 1/2\Delta x(f(a) + 2f(x_1) + 2f(x_2) + 2f(x_3) + f(b)). \tag{15.8}$$

An Integration Formula

In general, for N subintervals, the total area is

$$T = 1/2\Delta x(f(a) + 2\sum_{i=1}^{N-1} f(x_i) + f(b)) \tag{15.9}$$

where

$$\Delta x = \frac{(b - a)}{N}. \tag{15.10}$$

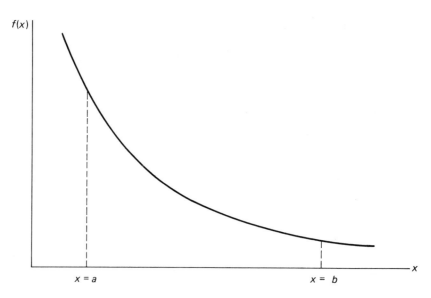

Figure 15.1   Plot of $f(x)$ from $x = a$ to $x = b$.

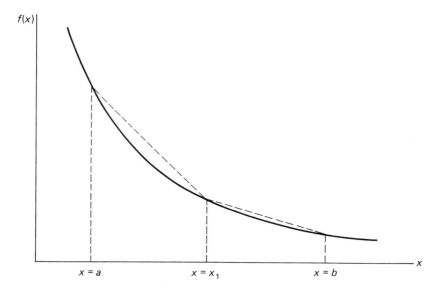

Figure 15.2   Plot of $f(x)$ divided into two intervals.

We now develop a computer program that uses the trapezoidal algorithm to integrate a function. The function itself is included in our program. The user is asked to enter the limits of integration.

Our first calculation of the integral uses a single subinterval. We then double the number of subintervals, and calculate the value of the integral again.

Criterion for Stopping

We continue this process until the difference between the current calculation and the previous calculation is small. We use the criterion

```
Abs(NewValue - OldValue) < EPS * Abs(OldValue)
```

where `NewValue` is the current calculation, and `OldValue` is the previous calculation. We arrived at the value of the constant EPS (which is 1.0E-7) by experimentation on our particular computer system, using a value that gives maximum accuracy with an acceptable calculation time. You may need to change this value for your computer. The previous steps are written in outline form.

Define a function to be integrated.
Ask user to enter the integration limits.
Calculate an approximate value of the integral.
Repeat
    Denote current value of integral as old value.
    Calculate a new value of the integral.
    Calculate difference between new and old values.
Until difference ‹ small number (EPS).
Display final value of the integral.

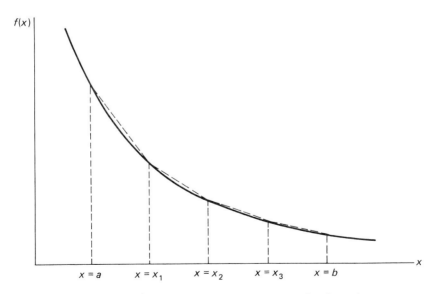

Figure 15.3 Plot of $f(x)$ divided into four intervals.

Here is our example program for numerical integration.

```
PROGRAM EX1501 (Input, Output);
{
  Use the trapezoidal rule to calculate the
  definite integral of a function F(X) between
  the limits A and B.
}
const
  SPACE = '      ';
  EPS = 1.0E-7;
var
  A, B: real;
  Result: real;

FUNCTION F (X: real): real;
{
  The function to integrate.
  Any continuous function of X over
  the range from X = A to X = B.
}
begin
  F := 1.0 / X;
end; { F }

PROCEDURE GetIntegrationLimits (var A, B: real);
{
  Ask user to enter the lower limit
  and upper limit of integration.
}
begin
  Writeln ('Integrate F(X) from X = A to X = B');
  Write ('Value of A? ');
  Readln (A);
  Write ('Value of B? ');
  Readln (B);
end; { GetIntegrationLimits }

PROCEDURE DisplayHeading;
{
  Display headings for table of intermediate results.
}
begin
  Writeln (' Table of Intermediate Results');
  Writeln ('    N        Value of Integral');
  Writeln;
end; { DisplayHeading }
```

```
PROCEDURE Integrate (A, B: real; var Result: real);
{
   Integrate the function F(X) between the limits
   X = A and X = B, using the trapezoidal algorithm.
   This procedure includes code to display intermediate
   results of the integration process.
}
var
   OldValue, NewValue: real;
   DeltaX, Sum: real;
   I, N: integer;
begin
   N := 1;
   NewValue := 0.5 * (B - A) * (F(A) + F(B));
   Writeln (N:5, SPACE, NewValue:1:7); { can be deleted }
   repeat
     OldValue := NewValue;
     N := 2 * N;
     DeltaX := (B - A) / N;
     Sum := 0; I := 1;
     repeat
       Sum := Sum + F(A + (I * DeltaX));
       I := I + 1;
     until I > N - 1;
     NewValue := 0.5 * DeltaX * (F(A) + 2 * Sum + F(B));
     Writeln (N:5, SPACE, NewValue:1:7); { can be deleted }
   until Abs(NewValue - OldValue) < EPS * Abs(OldValue);
   Result := NewValue;
end; { Integrate }

BEGIN { Main Program }
   GetIntegrationLimits (A, B);
   Writeln; { can be deleted }
   DisplayHeading; { can be deleted }
   Integrate (A, B, Result);
   Writeln; { can be deleted }
   Writeln ('The value of the integral is ', Result:1:7);
END.
```

The first approximation of the integral, called NewValue, is calculated outside the repeat loop, using a single subinterval. This calculated value provides the initial value of OldValue, which is used in the until statement at the bottom of the loop. Another repeat loop, inside the outer loop, calculates the heights of the interior subinterval sides (the values F(X1), F(X2), and so forth). The previously-discussed criterion is used to determine if another calculation of the integral is needed. Here is the output produced by this program.

```
Integrate F(X) from X = A to X = B
Value of A? 1.0
Value of B? 2.0

Table of Intermediate Results
   N         Value of Integral

   1         0.7500000
   2         0.7083333
   4         0.6970238
   8         0.6941219
  16         0.6933912
  32         0.6932082
  64         0.6931624
 128         0.6931510
 256         0.6931481
 512         0.6931474
1024         0.6931472
2048         0.6931472

The value of the integral is 0.6931472
```

If the function is integrated analytically, the value of the indefinite integral is $\ln(x)$. The value at the first end point is $\ln(1)$ or zero, so the value of the definite integral, to seven significant digits, is $\ln(2)$ or 0.6931472. Note that our last calculated value, using 2,048 intervals, agrees with this number.

This program is written to display intermediate results of the calculation as well as the final result. We indicate those program statements that can be deleted if the display of intermediate results is not wanted.

An Improved Integration Formula

If you look carefully at Equations 15.8 and 15.9 and at Program EX1501, you will see that only a few new items are added to variable Sum in each new iteration. These items are the heights (values of the function) at the midpoints of the previous intervals. Thus, approximately half of the function evaluations do not need to be recalculated in a new iteration. A modified version of Equation 15.9 is

$$T_{\text{new}} = (T_{\text{old}})/2 + 1/2\Delta x \left(2 \sum_{\substack{i=1 \text{ (odd only)}}}^{N-1} f(x_i)\right) \qquad (15.11)$$

where Δx is the same as before. We divide T_{old} by two, because the subinterval width is halved. Our sum includes only the values of $f(x_i)$ when i is odd.

Here is the modified version of our example program.

```
PROGRAM EX1502 (Input, Output);
{
  Use the trapezoidal rule to calculate the
  definite integral of a function F(X) between
  the limits A and B. Use a modified formula
  to increase the speed of calculation.
}
const
  EPS = 1.0E-7;
var
  A, B: real;
  Result: real;

FUNCTION F (X: real): real;
{
  The function to integrate.
  Any continuous function of X over
  the range from X = A to X = B.
}
begin
  F := 1.0 / X;
end; { F }

PROCEDURE GetIntegrationLimits (var A, B: real);
{
  Ask user to enter the lower limit
  and upper limit of integration.
}
begin
  Writeln ('Integrate F(X) from X = A to X = B');
  Write ('Value of A? ');
  Readln (A);
  Write ('Value of B? ');
  Readln (B);
end; { GetIntegrationLimits }

PROCEDURE Integrate (A, B: real; var Result: real);
{
  Integrate the function F(X) between the limits
  X = A and X = B, using the trapezoidal algorithm.
}
var
  OldValue, NewValue: real;
  DeltaX, Sum: real;
  I, N: integer;
```

```
begin
  N := 1;
  NewValue := 0.5 * (B - A) * (F(A) + F(B));
  repeat
    OldValue := NewValue;
    N := N * 2;
    DeltaX := (B - A) / N;
    Sum := 0; I := 1;
    repeat
      Sum := Sum + F(A + (I * DeltaX));
      I := I + 2;
    until I > N - 1;
    NewValue := (0.5 * OldValue) + (DeltaX * Sum);
  until Abs(NewValue - OldValue) < EPS * Abs(OldValue);
  Result := NewValue;
end; { Integrate }

BEGIN { Main Program }
  GetIntegrationLimits (A, B);
  Integrate (A, B, Result);
  Writeln ('The value of the integral is ', Result:1:7);
END.
```

The index I is incremented by two within the inner repeat loop, thus adding terms to Sum only for odd values of the index. A revised equation for NewValue has been substituted for the original equation. The final calculated result is the same as that of Program EX1501.

15.3 ROOTS OF AN EQUATION

Another numerical technique is finding the roots of an equation. If the equation is expressed as a function equated to zero, this process is equivalent to finding the zeroes of the function. We consider only continuous functions of a single variable. A zero of the function $f(x)$ is a root of the equation $f(x) = 0$.

Expressed in graphical terms, a root of the equation is the value of x where the graph of the function crosses the x-axis. An equation may have one or more roots, depending on the type of function. Except for the special case where the function has a maximum or minimum on the x-axis, **the function changes algebraic sign as the value of x moves through the position of the zero**. Figure 15.4 illustrates this point.

Finding a Range of X Containing a Root

If the function is simple, you may be able to determine by inspection a value of X where the function is positive, and another value of X where the function is negative. At least one root of the equation lies between these two values of X. If the function

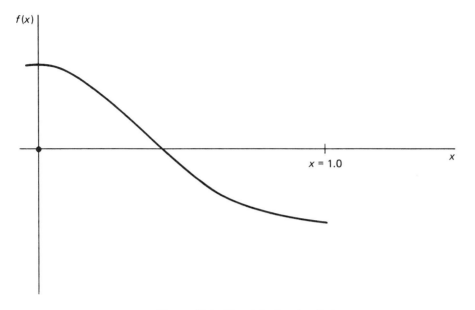

Figure 15.4 Plot of the function $f(x)$.

is more complicated, here is a simple program that will help you find a range of X that contains a root of the equation. First we give an outline.

Define a function F(X).

Ask user to enter lower limit, upper limit, and step.

Assign lower limit to X.

Repeat

  If F(X) > 0 display +

  If F(X) < 0 display −

  If F(X) = 0 display 0

  Increment X by the step.

Until X > upper limit.

Next we show the program.

```
PROGRAM EX1503 (Input, Output);
{
  Examine a function F(X) for a change
  in algebraic sign. This indicates a
  root of the equation F(X) = 0.
}
const
  SPACE = '       ';
var
  MinValue, MaxValue, Step: real;
```

```
FUNCTION F (X: real): real;
{
  Test function.
}
begin
  F := Exp(-X) - Sin(0.5 * Pi * X);
end; { F }

PROCEDURE GetInput (var A, B, S: real);
{
  Get input values.
}
begin
  Write ('Smallest value of X? ');
  Readln (A);
  Write ('Largest value of X? ');
  Readln (B);
  Write ('Step value of X? ');
  Readln (S);
end; { GetInput }

PROCEDURE WriteTable (A, B, S: real);
{
  Write the table of function algebraic signs.
}
var
  X: real;
  Ch: char;
begin
  Writeln (' X', SPACE, 'F(X)');
  Writeln;
  X := A;
  repeat
    if F(X) > 0 then
      Ch := '+'
    else if F(X) < 0 then
      Ch := '-'
    else { F(X) = 0 }
      Ch := '0';
    Writeln (X:6:2, SPACE, Ch);
    X := X + S;
  until X > B;
end; { WriteTable }

BEGIN { Main Program }
  GetInput (MinValue, MaxValue, Step);
  Writeln;
  WriteTable (MinValue, MaxValue, Step);
END.
```

We show two sample runs demonstrating how the approximate value of a root is found.

```
Smallest value of X? −5
Largest value of X? 5
Step value of X? 1

          X          F(X)

        −5.00          +
        −4.00          +
        −3.00          +
        −2.00          +
        −1.00          +
         0.00          +
         1.00          −
         2.00          +
         3.00          +
         4.00          +
         5.00          −
```

This display shows at least one root between X = 0 and X = 1, one between X = 1 and X = 2, and one between X = 4 and X = 5. A second run looks more closely at the value of the first root. It appears that there is one root between X = 0.4 and X = 0.5.

```
Smallest value of X? 0
Largest value of X? 1
Step value of X? 0.1

          X          F(X)

         0.00          +
         0.10          +
         0.20          +
         0.30          +
         0.40          +
         0.50          −
         0.60          −
         0.70          −
         0.80          −
         0.90          −
         1.00          −
```

If we run the program again with the last values of X as end points, and with a smaller step (say 0.001), we see that there is no sign of more than one root in the

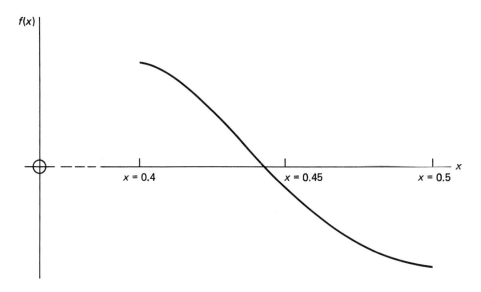

Figure 15.5 Plot of $f(x)$ showing first bisection.

interval. We do not show this last run because the list of values it generates is so long.

The Bisection Algorithm

We can now design a program for finding a more accurate value of the root, using the *bisection algorithm*. Assume we have found two values of X, assigned to variables Left and Right, where the function has different algebraic signs. The function is positive at Left and negative at Right. We can also identify a value of X, assigned to the variable Mid, halfway between Left and Right. Figure 15.5 shows this situation.

If the function is negative at Mid, we know that the root must lie between Mid and Left. We move Right to Mid (assign the value of Mid to Right) and repeat the process. In effect, we have reduced the range of possible values of the root to one-half its original range. Figure 15.6 illustrates this point.

Conversely, if the function is positive at Mid, we assign the value of Mid to Left and restrict further searching to the right half of the original range.

We continue this process until the distance between Left and Right is a small fraction of the value of either Left or Right. Our criterion for stopping is that within the accuracy of our computer, the two points Left and Right have met. The desired value of the root is then the value of either Left or Right.

There is one other possibility we should not overlook. If the value of the function equals zero for any value of Left or Right, we have found the root and

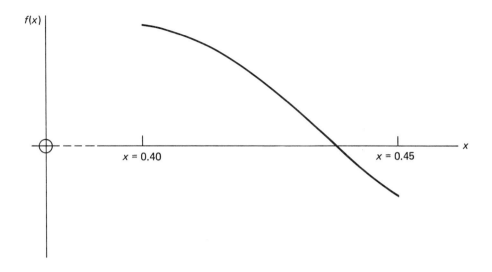

Figure 15.6 Plot of $f(x)$ showing reduced range.

there is no need to search further. We use the boolean variable Found as a flag to tell when a root has been found. This variable is set to false at the beginning of the program. If a root is found, the variable is changed to true. We check the variable at the end of the loop, in the until statement, and if Found is true, we exit the loop. Here is an outline of the process.

Define a function for the equation F(X) = 0.

Ask user to enter left end point and right end point of
the range containing the root.

Repeat

Calculate the midpoint of the range.

If value of F(X) at midpoint is zero then problem is solved, set the flag
Found to true.

If sign of F(X) at midpoint = sign of F(X) at left end point, move left
end point to midpoint.

If sign of F(X) at midpoint = sign of F(X) at right end point, move right
end point to midpoint.

Until flag Found is true or difference between end points is less than a small
number (EPS).

We translate the previous outline into a Pascal program, with the following re-sults.

```pascal
PROGRAM EX1504 (Input, Output);
{
  Find the root of equation F(X) = 0
  within a user-specified range of X.
}
const
  EPS = 1.0E-11;
var
  Left, Right, Root: real;
  Found: boolean;
  Count: integer;

FUNCTION F (X: real): real;
{
  Any function of X that is continuous
  over the specified range.
}
begin
  F := Exp(-X) - Sin(0.5 * Pi * X);
end; { F }

PROCEDURE GetSearchLimits (var Left, Right: real);
{
  Ask the user to enter the lower limit and
  the lower limit of the search range.
}
begin
  Write ('Smallest value of X? ');
  Readln (Left);
  Write ('Largest value of X? ');
  Readln (Right);
end; { GetSearchLimits }

FUNCTION Sgn (X: real): integer;
{
  Returns +1 if X > 0, -1 if X < 0,
  and 0 if X = 0.
}
begin
  if X > 0 then
    Sgn := 1
  else if X < 0 then
    Sgn := -1
  else { X = 0 }
    Sgn := 0;
end; { Sgn }
```

```
PROCEDURE RootSearch (Left, Right: real;
                      var Root: real;
                      var Found: boolean;
                      var Count: integer);
{
  Search for a zero of the function F(X)
  between the limits X = Left and X = Right.
}
var
  Mid, FuncLeft, FuncRight, FuncMid: real;
begin
  Found := false;
  FuncLeft := F(Left);
  FuncRight := F(Right);
  if Sgn(FuncLeft) = Sgn(FuncRight) then
    begin
    Exit; { exits the procedure RootSearch }
    end;
  Count := 0;
  repeat
    Mid := Left + Abs((Right - Left) / 2.0);
    FuncMid := F(Mid);
    if FuncMid = 0 then
      begin
      Root := Mid;
      Found := true;
      end
    else if Sgn(FuncLeft) = Sgn(FuncMid) then
      begin
      Left := Mid;
      FuncLeft := F(Left);
      end
    else
      begin
      Right := Mid;
      FuncRight := F(Right);
      end;
    Count := Count + 1;
  until Found or (Abs(Right - Left) < EPS * Abs(Right));

  if not Found then
    begin
    Root := Right;
    Found := true;
    end;
end; { RootSearch }
```

```
BEGIN { Main Program }
  GetSearchLimits (Left, Right);
  RootSearch (Left, Right, Root, Found, Count);
  Writeln;
  if Found then
    begin
    Writeln ('The root is ', Root:1:10);
    Writeln ('calculated in ', Count:1,
             ' iterations.');
    end
  else
    Writeln ('There is no root between',
             ' these values of X.');
END.
```

There are several special features in this program. Note that we minimize the number of times that the function F must be calculated. We do this by assigning the calculated values to the variables `FuncLeft`, `FuncRight`, and `FuncMid`, rather than using the functions themselves in the boolean expressions of the `if` statements. A function is recalculated only if the value of `Left`, `Right`, or `Mid` changes.

We check in each iteration whether the value of `Mid` is a root of the equation. If it is, we set the boolean variable `Found` to true, and exit the loop.

Criterion for Stopping

Our criterion for stopping the search is almost the same as the criterion used in Program EX1501. The constant EPS, whose value is 1.0E-11, is chosen so that the magnitude of the exponent (11) is about the same as or a little less than the number of significant digits in a real number value. This number of digits varies, of course, from one computer and Pascal system to another.

There is one word of warning. **If the constant in the criterion for stopping is made too small, the criterion is never satisfied, and the program runs in an infinite loop**. If this happens to you, just make EPS larger.

Here is an example run of the program.

```
Smallest value of X? 0.4
Largest value of X? 0.5

The root is 0.4435735341
calculated in 35 iterations.
```

The techniques we have used for integrating and root finding are just examples of a wide variety of numerical analysis algorithms. We chose our examples because they are relatively easy to understand rather than being efficient or fast. In both applications, the function is part of the source program, although separate from other subprograms and the main program. To find the integral or roots of another function, we have to modify the source program and then compile the program again and execute it. **It is difficult to design a program that performs calculations using a function entered by a user from the keyboard**.

15.4 MATRIX ALGEBRA

Mathematicians use the name *matrix* to denote a one-dimensional or two-dimensional array of numbers. A one-dimensional matrix is also called a *vector*. Matrix algebra manipulates matrices and vectors and defines such operations as addition, subtraction, multiplication, and division. Many problems in science and engineering are best solved using matrix algebra, like the problem of solving a system of linear algebraic equations.

Matrix Multiplication

We discuss matrix multiplication as an example of matrix algebra. Consider a case where two matrices, **A** and **B**, are multiplied together and produce a product matrix **C**. The mathematical equation is

$$\mathbf{C} = \mathbf{A} \times \mathbf{B}.$$

This multiplication is defined only if the number of columns in matrix **A** is equal to the number of rows in matrix **B**. For example, if **A** is a 2-by-5 matrix (two rows and five columns) and **B** is a 5-by-3 matrix (five rows and three columns), multiplication is possible. The product matrix **C** will be a 2-by-3 matrix. **Note that the reverse multiplication, $B \times A$, is not defined or allowed, because the number of columns in B (three columns) is not equal to the number of rows in A (two rows).**

Each element in the product matrix **C** is the sum of products between certain individual elements in **A** and **B**. Equation 15.12 is the mathematical equation for calculating an element of the product matrix.

$$C_{ij} = \sum_k A_{ik} B_{kj} \qquad (15.12)$$

In our example, the index k runs through the range of values from 1 to 5. The value of element $C[2,3]$ is calculated by multiplying the elements in the second row of **A**, and the elements in the third column of **B**, as shown below.

$$C(2,3) = A(2,1) \times B(1,3) + A(2,2) \times B(2,3) + A(2,3) \times B(3,3)$$
$$+ A(2,4) \times B(4,3) + A(2,5) \times B(5,3)$$

In Pascal, this calculation is usually accomplished by a for loop, such as

```
C[2,3] := 0;
for K := 1 to 5 do
  C[2,3] := C[2,3] + A[2,K]*B[K,3];
```

Given our example matrices **A** and **B**, the following program fragment calculates the product matrix **C**.

```
for I := 1 to 2 do
  for J := 1 to 3 do
    begin
    C[I,J] := 0;
    for K := 1 to 5 do
      C[I,J] := C[I,J] + A[I,K]*B[K,J];
    end;
```

Calculating the product matrix is the most difficult and complicated part of the program. The values for matrix **A** are entered from the keyboard, while those for matrix **B** are read from a text file. A nested for loop is used to display the product matrix. Here is our example program.

```
PROGRAM EX1505 (Input, Output);
{
  Read two matrices, one from the keyboard
  and the other from a text file.
  Multiply the two matrices together and
  display the product matrix.

  NOTE: This program only works with matrices
  of the sizes shown in the type and var sections.
}
const
  ROW_A = 2; COL_A = 3;
  ROW_B = 3; COL_B = 4;
  ROW_C = 2; COL_C = 4;
type
  mat23 = array [1..ROW_A, 1..COL_A] of real;
  mat34 = array [1..ROW_B, 1..COL_B] of real;
  mat24 = array [1..ROW_C, 1..COL_C] of real;
var
  A: mat23;
  B: mat34;
  C: mat24;

PROCEDURE MatRead23 (var A: mat23);
{
  Enter values into matrix A
  from the keyboard.
}
var
  Row, Col: integer;
begin
  Writeln ('Fill matrix A from the keyboard:');
  Writeln;
  for Row := 1 TO ROW_A do
    begin
    for Col := 1 to COL_A do
      begin
      Write ('A[', Row:1, ',', Col:1, ']? ');
      Readln (A[Row, Col]);
      end; { of a row }
    Writeln;
    end; { of the matrix }
end; { MatRead23 }
```

```
PROCEDURE MatRead34 (var B: mat34);
{
  Enter values into matrix B
  from the text file MATB.DAT.
}
var
  Row, Col: integer;
  FV: text;
begin
  Assign (FV, 'MATB.DAT');
  Reset (FV);
  for Row := 1 to ROW_B do
    for Col := 1 to COL_B do
      Readln (FV, B[Row, Col]);
  Close (FV);
  Writeln ('Matrix B filled from file MATB.DAT.');
  Writeln;
end; { MatRead34 }

PROCEDURE MatMultiply (A: mat23; B: mat34;
                       var C: mat24);
{
  Evaluate the product A * B and assign
  the result to C.
}
var
  Row, Col, Index: integer;
  Sum: real;
begin
  for Row := 1 to ROW_A do
    for Col := 1 to COL_B do
      begin
      Sum := 0.0;
      for Index := 1 to COL_A do
        Sum := Sum + A[Row, Index] * B[Index, Col];
      C[Row, Col] := Sum;
      end;
  Writeln ('Expression [C] = [A] * [B] evaluated.');
  Writeln;
end; { MatMultiply }

PROCEDURE MatWrite24 (C: mat24);
{
  Display matrix C on the screen,
}
var
  Row, Col: integer;
```

```
begin
  Writeln ('Matrix C:');
  Writeln;
  for Row := 1 to ROW_C do
    begin
    for Col := 1 to COL_C do
      Write (C[Row, Col]:1:1, ' ');
    Writeln; Writeln;
    end;
end; { MatWrite24 }

BEGIN { Main Program }
  MatRead23 (A);
  MatRead34 (B);
  MatMultiply (A, B, C);
  MatWrite24 (C);
END.
```

The following output is produced by this program.

```
Fill matrix A from the keyboard:

A[1,1]? 4
A[1,2]? 3
A[1,3]? -1

A[2,1]? 7
A[2,2]? 2
A[2,3]? 5

Matrix B filled from file MATB.DAT.

Expression [C] = [A] x [B] evaluated.

Matrix C:

12.4    23.1    42.4    24.7

34.6    52.6    75.7    65.2
```

The operations of matrix addition and subtraction are relatively easy to understand, while the operation of matrix division (actually, matrix inversion) is difficult. These and other matrix operations are discussed in any textbook on matrix algebra.

15.5 CURVE FITTING

Our final numerical method is the technique of fitting a straight line to a number of measured values. Assume we conduct an experiment and measure a number of points identified by values of two variables, x and y. For example, the variable y might represent the distance a body has fallen, while variable x represents the elapsed time, squared, measured from the time the body was released.

The equation of motion of the falling body is

$$y = A + Bt^2. \tag{15.13}$$

In terms of a variable $x = t^2$, the equation becomes

$$y = A + Bx. \tag{15.14}$$

For each measured value of x (or t^2), denoted by x_i, we have a measured value of y, denoted by y_i, and a calculated value of y, denoted by y_i'. We assume that the relationship between x and y is linear (that is, it can be represented by a straight line). The value of y_i' is calculated from the equation

$$y_i' = A + Bx_i \tag{15.15}$$

where coefficient B is the slope of the straight line and coefficient A is the intercept on the y-axis. We now define a *residual value* for each measured value of x, given by

$$R_i = y_i' - y_i = A + Bx_i - y_i. \tag{15.16}$$

This residual value is an indicator of how closely the measured value y_i coincides with the calculated value y_i' at each measured value x_i.

Least Squares Criterion

Our criterion for best fit between the measured value y_i and the calculated value $y_i' = A + Bx_i$, for each value x_i, is called the least squares criterion. This criterion, denoted LSC, states that the sum of the residuals squared should be a minimum. If we have a total of N measured points, the LSC can be represented by the equation

$$\text{LSC} = \sum_{i=1}^{N} (A + Bx_i - y_i)^2 = \text{ minimum.} \tag{15.17}$$

Recall that we are looking for values of A and B to define a calculated equation that best fits the measured values. In order to make the LSC a minimum, we need to find values of A and B such that the derivatives of LSC with respect to A and B are zero. This requirement is expressed by the equations

$$\frac{\partial \text{LSC}}{\partial A} = 0 \text{ and } \frac{\partial \text{LSC}}{\partial B} = 0. \tag{15.18}$$

Expanding the first of equations 15.18, we get

$$\frac{\partial \Sigma (A + Bx_i - y_i)^2}{\partial A} = 2\Sigma (A + Bx_i - y_i) \tag{15.19}$$

where Σ is $\sum_{i=1}^{N}$. Equation 15.19 can be reduced to the equation

$$AN + B\Sigma x_i = \Sigma y_i. \tag{15.20}$$

In a similar manner, the second of equations 15.18 is evaluated as

$$\frac{\partial \Sigma (A + Bx_i - y_i)^2}{\partial B} = 2\Sigma (A + Bx_i - y_i) = 0 \tag{15.21}$$

and produces the following equation

$$A\Sigma x_i + B\Sigma x_i^2 = \Sigma x_i y_i. \tag{15.22}$$

We now solve the two equations, 15.20 and 15.22, for the adjustable coefficients A and B, producing the expressions:

$$A = \frac{\Sigma x_i^2 \Sigma y_i - \Sigma x_i \Sigma x_i y_i}{N \Sigma x_i^2 - \Sigma x_i \Sigma x_i} \tag{15.23}$$

and

$$B = \frac{N \Sigma x_i y_i - \Sigma x_i \Sigma y_i}{N \Sigma x_i^2 - \Sigma x_i \Sigma x_i} \tag{15.24}$$

Returning to our original problem, we have N measured values of x and y from our experimental results, giving us N points that can be plotted on a graph with x and y coordinates. We also have the two coefficients, A and B, for the linear or straight-line curve that best fits our measured points. Our criterion for best fit is the least squares criterion (LSC), as explained previously. Here is a procedure that calculates coefficients A and B.

```
PROCEDURE LeastSquaresFit (X, Y: list;
                           N:integer;
                           A, B: real);
{
   Calculate coefficients A and B for a straight line
   that best fits the set of (X, Y) points.
}
var
   SumX, SumY, SumXY, SumXX: real;
   Denom, NumerA, NumerB: real;
   A, B: real;
   I: integer;
begin
   SumX := 0; SumY := 0; SumXY := 0; SumXX := 0;
   for I := 1 to N do
     begin
     SumX := SumX + X[I];
     SumY := SumY + Y[I];
     SumXY := SumXY + X[I] * Y[I];
     SumXX := SumXX + X[I] * X[I];
     end;
```

```
    Denom  := (N * SumXX) - (SumX * SumX);
    NumerA := (SumXX * SumY) - (SumX * SumXY);
    NumerB := (N * SumX * SumY) - (SumX * SumY);
    A := NumerA / Denom;
    B := NumerB / Denom;
  end; { LeastSquaresFit }
```

This procedure is just a straightforward calculation of the desired coefficients, using the equations we have developed. If you understand the derivation of the equation, you should have no trouble following the procedure. The array type, list, must be specified in the main program.

Displaying the Results

Our example program displays the position of a falling body as a function of time squared. We plot position against time squared, rather than position against time, so that the curve describing this functional relationship will be a straight line (see Figure 15.7). The least squares procedure we developed can be used only with linear, or straight line, relationships. A text file named MEASURE.DAT contains position values and corresponding time values. We use an asterisk (*) to denote each measured point.

Our program uses procedures from the Turbo Graphix Toolbox to create a window, plot the axes, display the measured points, and draw the calculated straight line. This program should work on any IBM PC-compatible computer, provided the appropriate Graphix Toolbox units have been loaded. All the required procedures and units, configured for an IBM PC-compatible computer using CGA graphics, are on the example program disk.

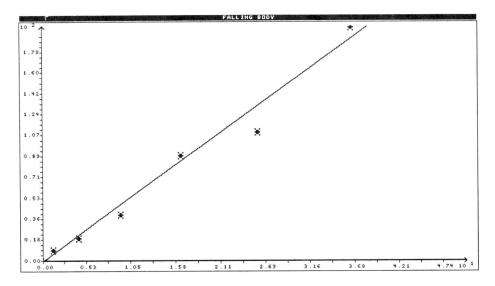

Figure 15.7 Least squares fit of measured data.

```
PROGRAM EX1506 (Output);
{
  Read measured values of Position and Time for a
  falling body from a data file. Calculate the
  coefficients for a curve of Position vs. Sqr(Time)
  that best fits this data. Use the Turbo Pascal
  Graphix Toolbox to plot the measured points and the
  calculated curve.
  Use only with Version 4 or 5.
}
uses
  Dos, Crt, Printer, GDriver,
  GKernel, GWindow, GShell;
const
  MAX_LIST = 100;
type
  list_item = real;
  list = array [1..MAX_LIST] of list_item;
var
  X, Y: list;
  N: integer;
  A, B: real;

PROCEDURE ReadPoints (var X, Y: list;
                      var N: integer);
{
  Read measured values of Position and Time, for a
  falling body, from the text file MEASURE.DAT.
}
var
  FV: text;
  Time, Position: real;
begin
  Assign (FV, 'MEASURE.DAT');
  Reset (FV);
  N := 0;
  while not Eof(FV) do
    begin
    N := N + 1;
    Readln (FV, Time);
    X[N] := Sqr(Time);
    Readln (FV, Position);
    Y[N] := Position;
    end;
  Close (FV);
end; { ReadPoints }
```

```
PROCEDURE LeastSquaresFit (X, Y: list;
                           N: integer;
                           var A, B: real);
{
  Calculate coefficients A and B for a straight line
  that best fits the set of (X, Y) points.
}
var
  SumX, SumY, SumXY, SumXX: real;
  Denom, NumerA, NumerB: real;
  I: integer;
begin
  SumX := 0; SumY := 0; SumXY := 0; SumXX := 0;
  for I := 1 to N do
    begin
    SumX := SumX + X[I];
    SumY := SumY + Y[I];
    SumXY := SumXY + X[I] * Y[I];
    SumXX := SumXX + X[I] * X[I];
    end;
  Denom := (N * SumXX) - (SumX * SumX);
  NumerA := (SumXX * SumY) - (SumX * SumXY);
  NumerB := (N * SumXY) - (SumX * SumY);
  A := NumerA / Denom;
  B := NumerB / Denom;
end; { LeastSquaresFit }

PROCEDURE PlotResults (X, Y: list;
                       N: integer;
                       A, B: real);
{
  Open a graphics window, draw a set of axes, plot a
  number of measured (X,Y) points, and plot a
  calculated straight-line curve.
}
{$I FIXAXIS.INC }
{
  Procedure RedefineAxisWindow in FIXAXIS.INC corrects a
  Turbo Pascal problem. It redefines a window to be within
  the axes and flips the world coordinate system so the
  origin (0,0) is in the lower left corner of the window.
}
var
  I: integer;
  Xbegin, Ybegin, Xend, Yend: real;
```

```
PROCEDURE Axes;
  {
  Draw a set of axes for this particular problem.
  }
  begin
    ClearScreen;
    SetColorWhite;
    SetBackground (0);
    SetBackgroundColor (0);
    DefineHeader (1, 'FALLING BODY');
    SetHeaderOn;
    DefineWorld (1, 0, 0, 50, 200);
    SelectWorld (1);
    SelectWindow (1);
    DrawBorder;
    DrawAxis (8, -6, 0, 0, 0, 0, 0, 0, true);
  end;

begin { PlotResults }
  InitGraphic;
  Axes;
  RedefineAxisWindow;
  for I := 1 to N do
    DrawTextW (X[I], Y[I], 2, '*');
  Xbegin := 0; Ybegin := A;
  Xend := 50; Yend := A + (B * Xend);
  DrawLine (Xbegin, Ybegin, Xend, Yend);
  repeat until KeyPressed;
  LeaveGraphic;
end; { PlotResults }

BEGIN { Main Program }
  ReadPoints (X, Y, N);
  LeastSquaresFit (X, Y, N, A, B);
  PlotResults (X, Y, N, A, B);
END.
```

Much of this program consists of code to produce a graphics display of
the final results. Note that four units from the Turbo Graphix Toolbox are used,
as well as three other built-in units. The procedure PlotResults makes use
of many procedures from these units. It also uses another procedure, named
RedefineAxisWindow, that is loaded from an include file. This latter procedure
can be considered a "black box" that corrects a Turbo Pascal graphics problem, as
described in the program comment.

Most of the procedures in PlotResults have descriptive identifiers and are
easy to understand. Procedure call SetColorWhite sets the color of all lines
and characters to white. Procedure call SetBackground (0) establishes a clear

nonpatterned background. Procedure call `SetBackgroundColor (0)` sets the background color to black. If you have a color monitor, for example, you can set the background color to blue by changing the 0 to 1.

Procedure call `DefineHeader (1, 'FALLING BODY')` has two parameters. The first parameter is the identifying number of the window and is always one in this program. The string constant `'FALLING BODY'` is a label for the display and can, of course, be changed to any other descriptive label. Procedure call `SetHeaderOn` displays this header.

Procedure call `DefineWorld (1, 0, 0, 50, 200)` defines the world coordinate system for window number 1. The modifier world distinguishes this coordinate system from the more common screen coordinate system of pixel locations. The last four parameters (`0, 0, 50, 200`) represent the world coordinate values of `Xmin`, `Ymin`, `Xmax`, and `Ymax` for this particular display. These four values can, and should, be changed for other sets of data.

Procedure call `SelectWorld (1)` selects the world coordinate system described previously, while procedure call `SelectWindow (1)` selects window number 1 for use. Procedure call `DrawBorder` draws a border around the window. The parameters in procedure `DrawAxis` refer to the style of axes, and the axis labels and tick marks. These parameters had best be left unchanged unless you have the opportunity to study a copy of the Turbo Graphix Toolbox manual and learn their significance.

In the body of procedure `PlotResults`, a call to procedure `InitGraphic` initializes the graphics screen. Procedure `DrawTextW` displays text characters using world coordinates. In this case, the displayed characters are asterisks of size 2. Procedure `DrawLine` draws a straight line from one (`X,Y`) point to another. The variables `Xbegin`, `Ybegin`, `Xend`, and `Yend` represent the beginning and ending x and y values. The values of these variables may have to be changed to plot a curve with different beginning and ending points. Finally, procedure call `LeaveGraphic` returns to the normal text screen.

The program as written runs under Versions 4 and 5, not Version 3. For the latter version, replace the `uses` section with the following list of include files.

```
{ Include files from the Graphix Toolbox.}
{ $I TYPEDEF.SYS}
{ $I GRAPHIX.SYS} { use proper version for your system }
{ $I KERNEL.SYS}
{ $I WINDOWS.SYS}
{ $I AXIS.HGH}
```

Be sure that these include files and three other files referenced by the include files (`FLOAT.INC`, `4X6.FON`, and `ERROR.MSG`) are in the same directory as your Pascal program or in a directory that can be found by the program.

Once again, the main program is simply an outline of the actions taken by this program. The measured data points are read from a file, the least square coefficients are calculated, and the results are displayed. Figure 15.7 shows a typical display produced by this program.

We also take the opportunity in this section on curve fitting to show how a library of special routines can be used to help solve a problem. Experienced programmers write as little new code as possible, using previously-developed program libraries whenever they can. The use of the Turbo Graphix Toolbox is a good example of how a relatively difficult program can be written with a minimum of effort.

The material presented in this chapter is only a sample of various numerical methods used in engineering and science. The presentations are not comprehensive and do not cover many of the complexities of the subject. If you are interested in further information on numerical analysis, we suggest a good introductory textbook such as *FORTRAN 77 and Numerical Methods for Engineers* by G. J. Borse of Lehigh University, published by PWS Engineering, 1985.

IMPORTANT POINTS

- A function $f(x)$ changes algebraic sign as the value of x moves through the position of a zero.
- When looking for a root, if the constant in the criterion for stopping is made too small, the criterion is never satisfied and the program runs in an infinite loop.
- It is difficult to design a program that performs calculations using a function entered by the user from the keyboard.
- If a matrix multiplication, $\mathbf{A} \times \mathbf{B}$, is defined, the reverse multiplication, $\mathbf{B} \times \mathbf{A}$, is not necessarily defined.

SELF-STUDY QUESTIONS

1. What is the area of a trapezoid whose base length is 12 and whose two side heights are 4 and 8?

2. Can the trapezoidal algorithm be used to calculate the value of an indefinite integral?

3. Why is Equation 15.11 a better equation to use in a computer program than Equation 15.9?

4. If the value of a function of x is positive at $x = A$ and negative at $x = B$, can there be
   (a) more than one root between A and B;
   (b) two roots between A and B? Explain your answer.

5. Can the bisection algorithm find a root when the value of $f(x)$ is zero at a maximum or minimum of the function?

6. When using the bisection algorithm, what is a criterion for stopping the search?

7. If $\mathbf{A}$ is a 3-by-4 array and $\mathbf{B}$ is a 2-by-3 array,
   (a) is the operation $\mathbf{A} \times \mathbf{B}$ defined;
   (b) is the operation $\mathbf{B} \times \mathbf{A}$ defined?

8. If $H = F(g)$ is a function of the variable g, what is the mathematical requirement for finding the minimum value of H?

9. What value (or values) is minimized by the least squares criterion?

10. What is the equation of a straight line in the (x,y) plane with a slope of S and an intercept of I on the y-axis?

PRACTICE PROGRAMS

1. Use Program EX1502 to calculate the definite integral of

$$f(x) = (x)\sin(x)$$

between the limits of $x = 0$ and $x = \pi/2$.

2. Use a program for numerical integration, developed in this chapter, to integrate two functions between the limits of $x = 0$ and $x = 10$. Compare the number of iterations required to calculate the two integrals.

The functions are

  (a) $f(x) = x/(1 + \exp(x))$

and

  (b) $f(x) = 1/(\exp(x) + \exp(-x))$.

3. Use Programs EX1503 and EX1504 to find the most positive zero of the function

$$f(x) = 2\exp(x) - \cos(1.5x).$$

4. The degree of dissociation, X, of hydrogen sulphide gas is described by the equation

$$(1 - PK^2)X^3 - 3X + 2 = 0$$

where K is the equilibrium constant and P is the total pressure in atmospheres. Assume a temperature of 2,000 degrees Kelvin, giving a value of $K = 0.608$ and a pressure of one atmosphere. The variable X only has meaning over a range from 0 through 1.

Find a value of X that satisfies the equation. Is there more than one possible value in the allowed range?

5. Enter two matrices, **R** and **I**, from the keyboard. **R** is a 2-by-2 matrix of resistances. **I** is a 2-by-1 matrix of currents.

$$\mathbf{R} = \begin{bmatrix} 1.25 & 3.22 \\ -1.04 & 6.53 \end{bmatrix} \qquad \mathbf{I} = \begin{bmatrix} 2.49 \\ 7.22 \end{bmatrix}$$

Calculate and display the product matrix, **R**×**I**, which is a 2-by-1 matrix of voltages.

6. Define the square of matrix **A** as **A**×**A**. Note that this definition is valid only if **A** is a square matrix; that is, a matrix that has an equal number of rows and columns. Write a procedure that calculates the square of a matrix variable passed as a parameter.

Test your procedure in a program that calculates and displays the square of the following matrix.

$$\mathbf{A} = \begin{bmatrix} 4 & 1 & 2 \\ 3 & 2 & 7 \\ 1 & 2 & 1 \end{bmatrix}$$

7. An engineer measures the fluid flow through a valve (Y) as a function of the valve handle dial position (X). Enter values of X and Y, shown in the accompanying table, from the keyboard. Calculate and display the appropriate coefficients for a linear least squares fit of these data. Display the measured data points and the calculated curve.

X	Y
10	80
20	90
30	110
40	130
50	130
60	160
70	160
80	180
90	200
100	190

16

Special Features and Applications of Turbo Pascal

Turbo Pascal Note

Everything discussed in this chapter applies specifically to Turbo Pascal.

16.1 INTRODUCTION

This chapter discusses some of the special features of Turbo Pascal, Version 3, and some of the enhancements introduced in Versions 4 and 5.

At times it is necessary to understand the interaction between Turbo Pascal and the MS-DOS operating system. We see how to address memory in the hexadecimal number system, and write an example program to move blocks of memory information to the screen. We introduce the MsDos procedure, and use it to make direct DOS function calls on the operating system. We discuss how to compile programs on disk, and how to pass information to a program through the command line.

16.2 DIRECT ACCESS TO COMPUTER MEMORY

Programs written in Turbo Pascal have the ability to access memory directly. Certain memory locations have a special meaning for MS-DOS, and we need to be able to access the information stored at these locations.

Addressing Memory

The CPU (an Intel 8088, 8086, 80286, or 80386) used in IBM PC-compatible computers running MS-DOS has a special way of addressing memory. In order to address one million separate memory locations, the maximum amount of memory addressable by MS-DOS, both a 16-bit *segment address* and a 16-bit *offset address* are used.

The size of memory space is normally specified in units of bytes or in units of 1024 bytes, called *kilobytes* and denoted by the symbol KB. Thus 4KB is the same as 4096 bytes.

The segment address is the beginning address of one of 65,536 overlapping 64KB blocks of memory. These blocks can begin every 16 bytes in the CPU address space. The segment address is written in units of 16-byte paragraphs and, is therefore, not an address in bytes. In practice, segment blocks usually begin every 256 paragraphs or 4KB, beginning with location 0 at the start of memory.

The offset address is the relative position of the memory location within a particular segment block. It is written in units of bytes.

Hexadecimal Notation

MS-DOS memory addresses are usually expressed in *hexadecimal* notation (sometimes called *hex* for short), with the segment address first, followed by a colon and the offset address. Hexadecimal notation means base 16 notation and uses sixteen symbols or digits, consisting of the usual decimal digits 0 through 9 and the letters A through F. A hexadecimal memory address in Turbo Pascal is always preceded by the dollar sign character ($).

A segment address of $0100 is an address beginning $0100 paragraphs or $01000 bytes after the start of memory. Note that in hexadecimal notation, you can convert from units of paragraphs to units of bytes by adding a zero to the number. The decimal equivalent of this segment address is 256 paragraphs or 4096 bytes (4KB).

An offset address of $0080 is an address beginning $0080 bytes (decimal 128 bytes) after the start of the segment. Thus, the address $0100:$0080 means a memory location that is 4224 bytes (sum of 4096 and 128) from the start of memory. **Remember that hexadecimal numbers in Turbo Pascal always have leading dollar signs, and numbers without leading dollar signs are assumed to be decimal numbers.**

Figure 16.1 shows some numbers written in both hexadecimal and decimal notation. We use the Turbo Pascal notation for hexadecimal.

$0000	0	$1000	4096
$000F	15	$1E4A	7754
$003F	63	$B000	45056
$0040	64	$FFFF	65535

Figure 16.1 Equivalent hexadecimal and decimal numbers.

The techniques for converting between decimal and hexadecimal notation are discussed in many mathematical texts and in books on assembly language programming. Rather than discussing the techniques here, we show a program that performs this conversion.

The user is asked to enter a value which is read into the string `Entry`. The `Val` function converts this string to a numeric value `Num`. If the first character in `Entry` is a dollar sign ($), function `Val` converts the entered hexadecimal value into a decimal number. This decimal number is displayed.

If the first character is not a dollar sign, a decimal value was entered and is stored in variable `Num`. This value is converted to a hexadecimal value using the procedure `DecToHex`.

Typed Constants

Several new concepts are introduced in this program. The constant `HexDigit` is called a *typed constant* and located in a constant block, although it should more properly be called an *initialized variable*. It can be used anywhere that a regular variable is allowed but not everywhere that a constant is required. In particular, typed constants cannot be used as the lower or upper bounds of an array.

A special advantage of typed constants is that, unlike ordinary variables, they can be initialized when declared. Moreover, in the case of an array type, the syntax for initialization is more compact than a sequence of assignment statements. In the example program, the string variable `HexDigit` is assigned the value `'0123456789ABCDEF'`, the list of all hexadecimal digits.

The `Hi` and `Lo` Functions

The functions `Hi` and `Lo`, of type `byte` in Versions 4 and 5, return the high-order byte and the low-order byte, respectively, of a numeric parameter of type `word`. In Version 3, these functions take a parameter, and return a value, of type `integer`. They are particularly useful for dividing a 16-bit value into its high-order byte and its low-order byte. We also turn on range checking so that numbers larger than 65,535 will not be converted incorrectly.

In our example program, the `div` and `mod` operators are used to find the first and second hexadecimal digits of `Hi(N)`. The appropriate digits are selected from the initialized string `HexDigit`. A similar technique selects the first and second hexadecimal digits from `Lo(N)`. All four digits, with a leading dollar sign, are combined to form the hexadecimal number.

```
PROGRAM EX1601 (Input, Output);
{
  Enter a number of type word in decimal notation
  and display the corresponding hexadecimal number.
  Enter a number of type word in hexadecimal notation
  and display the corresponding decimal number.
  Display error message for invalid entry.
  Use only with Version 4 or 5.
}
{$R+} { turn on range checking }
```

```
var
  Entry: string;
  Num: word;
  Code: integer;


PROCEDURE DecToHex (N: word);
const { initialized variable or typed constant }
  HexDigit: string[16] = '0123456789ABCDEF';
begin
  Writeln ('$' + HexDigit[(Hi(N) div 16) + 1]
              + HexDigit[(Hi(N) mod 16) + 1]
              + HexDigit[(Lo(N) div 16) + 1]
              + HexDigit[(Lo(N) mod 16) + 1]);
end; { DecToHex }


BEGIN { Main Program }
  repeat
    Write ('Value? ');
    Readln (Entry);
    Val (Entry, Num, Code);
    if (Code = 0) then
      if (Entry[1] = '$') then
        Writeln (Num)
      else
        DecToHex (Num)
    else
      begin
      Writeln ('Invalid character at position ', Code:1);
      Writeln ('Please try again.');
      Writeln;
      end;
  until Code = 0;
END.
```

Two examples of program interaction follow.

```
Value? 7,754
Invalid character at position 2
Please try again.

Value? 7754
$1E4A

Value? $1E4A
7754
```

Note that **when a number string is entered in hexadecimal notation, the Val function automatically converts it to a decimal number**. That is the reason we do not need a separate procedure to convert from hexadecimal to decimal.

Another variation of the program is designed for use with Version 3. Variable Num is of type integer, and we must prevent the hexadecimal to decimal conversion process from producing a negative number.

```pascal
PROGRAM EX1602_3 (Input, Output);
{
   Enter a number of type word in decimal notation
   and display the corresponding hexadecimal number.
   Enter a number of type word in hexadecimal notation
   and display the corresponding decimal number.
   Display error message for invalid entry.
   Use only with Version 3.
}
{$R+} { turn on range checking }
var
   Entry: string[20];
   Num: integer;
   Code: integer;


PROCEDURE DecToHex (N: integer);
const
   HexDigit: string[16] = '0123456789ABCDEF';
begin
   Writeln ('$' + HexDigit[(Hi(N) div 16) + 1]
               + HexDigit[(Hi(N) mod 16) + 1]
               + HexDigit[(Lo(N) div 16) + 1]
               + HexDigit[(Lo(N) mod 16) + 1]);
end; { DecToHex }


PROCEDURE HexToDec (N: integer);
var
   Large: real;
begin
   if Num >= 0 then
      Writeln (Num)
   else
      begin
      Large := 65536.0 + Num;
      Writeln (Large:1:0);
      end
end; { HexToDec }
```

```
BEGIN { Main Program }
  repeat
    Write ('Value? ');
    Readln (Entry);
    Val (Entry, Num, Code);
    if (Code = 0) then
      if (Entry[1] = '$') then
        HexToDec (Num)
      else
        DecToHex (Num)
    else
      begin
      Writeln ('Invalid character at position ', Code:1);
      Writeln ('Please try again.');
      Writeln;
      end;
  until Code = 0;
END.
```

This variation of the program does not allow a decimal number greater than 32,767 to be entered. If a hexadecimal number greater than $7FFF is entered, the Val procedure converts it to a negative decimal number. The procedure HexToDec further converts this negative number to the corresponding positive number.

Special Memory Addresses

The range of hexadecimal integers commonly used in Turbo Pascal is from $0000 to $FFFF. Up to four digits are needed, as shown, to write segment and offset addresses, and we follow the practice of including leading zeros so that memory addresses have four digits.

As an example, the IBM monochromatic display unit uses a 4KB text buffer (4,096 bytes) in memory, starting at a segment address of $B000 and an offset address of $0000. For a color monitor (or a black and white monitor that supports graphics), the segment address is $B800, with the same offset. This address is expressed as $B000:$0000 or $B800:$0000. Information about special memory addresses in PC-DOS or MS-DOS is contained in the IBM Technical Reference Manual, or in other reference books such as the *Programmer's Guide to the IBM PC* by Peter Norton (Microsoft Press, 1985).

Determining the Address of a Variable

It is sometimes useful to be able to determine the address of a named variable. A program to make this determination is relatively simple in Versions 4 and 5, and only slightly more complicated in Version 3. Our program displays the beginning address of the data segment (introduced in Chapter 12) where all variables are stored, and then displays the address of a character variable named Test.

The Dseg, Seg, and Ofs Functions

The standard function Dseg returns the beginning address of the data segment. This segment address is in 16-byte paragraphs and must be multiplied by 16 to give an address in bytes. The address is in decimal notation. The standard functions Seg(Test) and Ofs(Test) return the segment and offset addresses, respectively, of the parameter Test. The address of variable Test, in decimal notation, is then calculated. All three functions are of type word in Versions 4 and 5.

```
PROGRAM EX1603 (Output);
{
   Displays the addresses of the data segment
   and of two declared variables.
   Use only with Version 4 or 5.
}
var
   Test: char;
   Address: longint;

BEGIN
   Writeln ('Address of data segment is ',
            (16 * Dseg):1);
   Address := 16 * Seg(Test) + Ofs(Test);
   Writeln ('Address of variable Test is ', Address:1);
   Address := 16 * Seg(Address) + Ofs(Address);
   Writeln ('Address of variable Address is ', Address:1);
END.
```

On our computer using Version 5, this program produces the following output.

```
Address of data segment is 38352
Address of variable Test is 38412
Address of variable Address is 38414
```

Variable Test is the first variable in the program, stored at address 38412. Variable Address is stored right after it at address 38414. The first 60 bytes of the data segment appear to be used for some other purpose.

Here is a similar program written for Version 3 that shows the address of just one variable. The three functions, Dseg, Seg, and Ofs, are now of type integer, and so if one of their values becomes greater than 32,767, a negative number is returned. Special if statements, as shown, ensure that the values of the addresses are always positive.

```
PROGRAM EX1604_3 (Output);
{
   Displays the addresses of the data segment
   and a character variable.
   Use only with Version 3.
}
```

```
var
  Test: char;
  DS, Segment, Offset: real;
  Address: real;

BEGIN
  DS := 16.0 * Dseg;
  if DS < 0 then
    DS := 65536.0 + DS;
  Writeln ('Address of data segment is ', DS:1:0);
  Segment := Seg(Test);
  if Segment < 0 then
    Segment := 65536.0 + Segment;
  Offset := Ofs(Test);
  if Offset < 0 then
    Offset := 65536.0 + Offset;
  Address := 16.0 * Segment + Offset;
  Writeln ('Address of variable Test is ', Address:1:0);
END.
```

This variation of the program may produce quite different results because of the different internal organization of the various versions of Turbo Pascal.

Absolute Variables

Turbo Pascal allows any variable to be placed at a fixed or absolute location in memory if the reserved word `absolute` is included in the variable declaration. For example, to place an array of integers named `Display` at the memory location reserved for the graphics display unit screen buffer, we might use the program fragment

```
type
  buff = array [0..4095] of byte;
var
  Display: buff absolute $B800:$0000;
```

The use of absolute variables can impact the operating system in unexpected ways. **It is the programmer's responsibility to make certain that an absolute variable does not overwrite any important memory locations.**

The Move Procedure

We present an example program that writes two screens of text and stores the contents of each screen in a separate memory buffer. As usual, writing is done with `Write` and `Writeln` statements. Note that it takes several seconds to completely fill the screen with characters.

A standard procedure in Turbo Pascal, the `Move` procedure, is used to store each screen display in memory. This procedure has the syntax

```
Move (InBuff, OutBuff, BuffSize);
```

where `InBuff` is the beginning address of the input buffer, `OutBuff` is the beginning address of the output buffer, and `BuffSize` is the number of bytes to be transferred. **The Move procedure does no checking, and so the programmer must take care not to overwrite important memory locations**.

After both buffers have been filled, a `for` loop alternately displays the contents of each buffer several times. The `Move` procedure is used to produce these displays. Note how quickly the screen is filled using this procedure, in contrast to using `Write` and `Writeln`.

For demonstration purposes, our example program uses two screens containing displays of a single character. A practical application might be a text editor, where one screen is the text being edited, and the other screen is help information.

```
PROGRAM EX1605 (Input, Output);
{
  Write two screens of text and store them in memory
  buffers. Alternately display each stored screen.
  Observe speed of displaying a stored screen, compared
  to the speed of originally writing that screen.
  Use only with Version 4 or 5.

  Note: Change the address of variable Display to
  $B000:$0000 for a monochromatic monitor.
}
uses
  Crt;
const
  BUFF_SIZE = 4096; { screen buffer }
  MAX_BUFF = 4095; { BuffSize - 1 }
  NUMBER_DISPLAYS = 3;
type
  buff = array [0..MAX_BUFF] of byte;
var
  { Location of graphics screen buffer }
  Display: buff absolute $B800:$0000;
  { Start of buffer in unused part of memory }
  Store1: buff absolute $9000:$0000;
  { Second buffer, offset 4KB }
  Store2: buff absolute $9000:$1000;
  I: integer;
  C: char;

PROCEDURE WriteDisplay (ScreenLabel: string;
                        Ch: char);
{
  Write a text screen consisting of a label, 23 lines
  of 79 characters, and a prompt. Pass label and
  character as parameters.
}
```

```
var
  I, J: integer;
begin
  Writeln (ScreenLabel);
  for I := 1 to 23 do
    begin
    for J := 1 to 79 do
      Write (Ch);
    Writeln;
    end;
  Write ('Press any key...');
end; { WriteDisplay }

BEGIN { Main Program }
  { Write and store the first screen.}
  ClrScr;
  WriteDisplay ('First Text Screen', '?');
  Move (Display, Store1, BUFF_SIZE);
  C := ReadKey; { wait for user input }
  { Write and store the second screen.}
  ClrScr;
  WriteDisplay ('Second Text Screen', '*');
  Move (Display, Store2, BUFF_SIZE);
  C := ReadKey; { wait for user input }
  { Now display each screen several times.}
  for I := 1 to NUMBER_DISPLAYS do
    begin
    Move (Store1, Display, BUFF_SIZE);
    C := ReadKey; { wait for user input }
    Move (Store2, Display, BUFF_SIZE);
    C := ReadKey; { wait for user input }
    end;
END.
```

You can only appreciate how this program works by running it yourself. A new screen is displayed each time a key is pressed. Note particularly the differences in time required to fill the screen with characters the first time and each subsequent time. Remember that you may need to set DirectVideo to false when using the ReadKey function with non-IBM computers and display units. This reminder applies, of course, only for Versions 4 and 5 because Version 3 does not have the ReadKey function.

Another variation of this program is written for Version 3. Using the same technique as in Program EX1007_3, we substitute a KeyPressed loop for the ReadKey function. Here is the program.

```
PROGRAM EX1606_3 (Input, Output);
{
  Write two screens of text and store them in memory
  buffers. Alternately display each stored screen.
  Observe speed of displaying a stored screen, compared
  to the speed of originally writing that screen.
  Use only with Version 3.

  Note: Change the address of variable Display to
  $B800:$0000 for a color or graphics monitor.
}
const
  BUFF_SIZE = 4096; { screen buffer }
  MAX_BUFF = 4095; { BuffSize - 1 }
  NUMBER_DISPLAYS = 3;
type
  buff = array [0..MAX_BUFF] of byte;
  string80 = string[80];
var
  { Location of monochromatic screen buffer }
  Display: buff absolute $B000:$0000;
  { Start of buffer in unused part of memory }
  Store1: buff absolute $9000:$0000;
  { Second buffer, offset 4KB }
  Store2: buff absolute $9000:$1000;
  I: integer;
  C: char;

PROCEDURE WriteDisplay (ScreenLabel: string80;
                        Ch: char);
{
  Write a text screen consisting of a label, 23 lines
  of 79 characters, and a prompt. Pass label and
  character as parameters.
}
var
  I, J: integer;
begin
  Writeln (ScreenLabel);
  for I := 1 to 23 do
    begin
    for J := 1 to 79 do
      Write (Ch);
    Writeln;
    end;
  Write ('Press the Enter key...');
end; { WriteDisplay }
```

```
BEGIN { Main Program }
  { Write and store the first screen.}
  ClrScr;
  WriteDisplay ('First Text Screen', '?');
  Move (Display, Store1, BUFF_SIZE);
  repeat until KeyPressed; { wait loop }
  { Write and store the second screen.}
  ClrScr;
  WriteDisplay ('Second Text Screen', '*');
  Move (Display, Store2, BUFF_SIZE);
  repeat until KeyPressed; { wait loop }
  { Now display each screen several times.}
  for I := 1 to NUMBER_DISPLAYS do
    begin
    Readln; { gobble up last char.}
    Move (Store1, Display, BUFF_SIZE);
    repeat until KeyPressed;
    Readln; { again gobble up char.}
    Move (Store2, Display, BUFF_SIZE);
    repeat until KeyPressed;
    end;
END.
```

This program produces the same output as the previous program. Note the use of two Readln statements to remove from the input buffer whatever character is entered to stop the KeyPressed loop. This statement is not needed when writing and storing the second screen because the ClrScr statement performs the same function. It is needed before every display in the for loop where each screen is displayed several times.

16.3 USING THE BUILT-IN ROUTINES OF MS-DOS

The MS-DOS operating system has many built-in routines that it uses itself to execute commands and to manage the disk. In some cases, Turbo Pascal can perform a certain task only if it can access one or more of these routines.

CPU Interrupts

Whenever a hardware device or a program needs the services of the CPU, it sends a signal to the CPU specifying the special task to be performed. This signal is called an *interrupt* because it interrupts the CPU's normal task of processing program instructions.

When the CPU receives the interrupt signal, control is transferred to a location in low memory identified by the interrupt number. There is found a segmented memory address called the *interrupt vector*. This address is the beginning address of the *interrupt handler*, the section of program code that carries out the task requested by the interrupt.

A hardware interrupt can be triggered by a program error, such as an attempt to divide by zero, or by a request for service from a device, such as a key pressed on the keyboard. A software interrupt is triggered by a special program instruction.

CPU Registers

The CPU of an IBM PC-compatible computer has several internal locations, called *registers*, where information is stored temporarily. Some of these registers hold only a single bit and are called *flag registers*. The other registers hold 16 bits, divisible into two 8-bit bytes.

For the purpose of our discussion, we are interested in four of the 16-bit registers. The AX register is called the accumulator and is used for arithmetic operations. The BX, CX, and DX registers have more general uses, although the BX and CX registers do have special properties that will not effect our applications.

Each of these registers can be divided into two 8-bit halves or bytes. For example, the function `Hi(AX)` returns the high-order byte of the AX register, while the function `Lo(AX)` returns the low-order byte.

DOS Function Calls

We are interested in a particular class of software interrupt services associated with interrupt $21 hexadecimal (33 decimal). These services are called *DOS function calls* because they permit a program to use many of the built-in capabilities of the MS-DOS operating system.

Over eighty built-in functions are available through interrupt $21 and are listed in Appendix I. These functions include routines to read a character from the keyboard, to reset the disk, to delete a file, to set the internal clock, and so forth. We examine programs that execute four of these functions.

The `Registers` Type and `MsDos` Procedure

The `MsDos` procedure can be used to access any of the functions associated with interrupt $21 hexadecimal. The parameter of this procedure must be a variable of type `registers`, which is predefined in Versions 4 and 5, but must be defined by the programmer in a Version 3 program. This variable of type `registers` is commonly named `Regs`.

Variable `Regs` is a record containing word or integer fields for each of the CPU registers (see Program EX1608_3). Thus, it is possible, using the `MsDos` procedure, to access any CPU register. The number of the particular DOS function call in interrupt $21 is passed to the `MsDos` procedure through the high-order byte of the AX register. Because hexadecimal notation clearly shows the high-order and low-order bytes, the DOS function call is usually passed as a hexadecimal number.

Example DOS Function Calls

The first example program displays the letter designating the current disk drive. This particular DOS function call is designated by a hexadecimal number of $19 (decimal 25). The drive letter is returned in the low-order byte of the AX register, using the code of 0 = A, 1 = B, 2 = C, and so forth. Here is the program.

```
PROGRAM EX1607 (Output);
{
  Display the output of the Drive function.
  Use only with Version 4 or 5.
}
uses
  Dos;

FUNCTION Drive: char;
{
  Display the current disk drive identifier.
}
var
  Regs: registers;
const { typed constants or initialized variables }
  DriveName: string[26] = 'ABCDEFGHIJKLMNOPQRSTUVWXYZ';
begin
  with Regs do
    begin
    AX := $1900;
    MsDos (Regs);
    Drive := DriveName[Lo(AX) + 1];
    end;
end; { Drive }

BEGIN { Main Program }
  Writeln ('Current disk drive is ', Drive);
END.
```

Note that a typed constant named DriveName is used to convert the drive
number code to a drive letter. Here is an example of program output.

```
Current disk drive is D
```

A similar program is shown next for Version 3. In this case, the type
registers must be defined in the program, and the unit Dos is not needed.

```
PROGRAM EX1608_3 (Output);
{
  Display the output of the Drive function.
  Use only with Version 3.
}

FUNCTION Drive: char;
{
  Display the current disk drive identifier.
}
type
  registers = record
    AX, BX, CX, DX, BP, SI, DI, DS, ES, Flags: integer;
    end;
```

```
var
  Regs: registers;
const { typed constants or initialized variables }
  DriveName: string[26] = 'ABCDEFGHIJKLMNOPQRSTUVWXYZ';
begin
  with Regs do
    begin
    AX := $1900;
    MsDos (Regs);
    Drive := DriveName[Lo(AX) + 1];
    end;
end; { Drive }

BEGIN { Main Program }
  Writeln ('Current disk drive is ', Drive);
END.
```

Two other example programs show how to access the system clock to determine the current date and time. These programs are shown only for use with Version 3 because two procedures, GetDate and GetTime in unit Dos, serve a similar purpose in Versions 4 and 5.

The next program displays a string showing the current date, with both the day of the week and the month of the year spelled out. The DOS function call number is $2A hexadecimal, and date information is returned in the AX, CX, and DX registers. Typed constants are used, as before, to hold the names of days and months.

```
PROGRAM EX1609_3 (Output);
{
  Display output of the Date function.
  Use only with Version 3.
}
{$V-} { relax string type checking }
type
  string80 = string[80];

FUNCTION Date: string80;
{
  Create a date string for the current date.
}
type
  registers = record
    AX, BX, CX, DX, BP, SI, DI, DS, ES, Flags: integer;
  end;
var
  Regs: registers;
  Day: string[2];
  Year: string[4];
```

```
const { typed constants or initialized variables }
  DayName: array [0..6] of string[9] = ('Sunday',
          'Monday','Tuesday','Wednesday','Thursday',
          'Friday','Saturday');
  MonthName: array [1..12] of string[9] = ('January',
             'February','March','April','May','June',
             'July','August','September','October',
             'November','December');
begin
  with Regs do
    begin
    AX := $2A00;
    MsDos (Regs);
    Str (Lo(DX):1, Day);
    Str (CX, Year);
    Date := DayName[Lo(AX)] + ', ' + MonthName[Hi(DX)]
            + ' ' + Day + ', ' + Year;
    end;
end; { Date }

BEGIN { Main Program }
  Writeln ('Current date is ', Date);
END.
```

The function `Date` in this program displays information in a different format than the `GetDate` procedure in Versions 4 and 5. It would be relatively simple to convert the program to run under these versions. An example of program output is

```
Current date is Sunday, April 17, 1988
```

The third program in this section displays the elapsed time since the previous midnight. Function `Time` can be included in other programs and is particularly useful for timing program segments. The DOS function call is $2C hexadecimal, and time information is returned in the CX and DX registers.

```
PROGRAM EX1610_3 (Output);
{
  Display output of the Time function.
  Use only with Version 3.
}

FUNCTION Time: real;
{
  Calculate the number of seconds since midnight.
}
type
  registers = record
    AX, BX, CX, DX, BP, SI, DI, DS, ES, Flags: integer;
  end;
```

```
var
  Regs: registers;
  Hour, Minute, Second, Sec100: integer;
begin
  with Regs do
    begin
    AX := $2C00;
    MsDos (Regs);
    Hour := Hi(CX);
    Minute := Lo(CX);
    Second := Hi(DX);
    Sec100 := Lo(DX);
    Time := 3600.0 * Hour + 60.0 * Minute + Second
            + (Sec100 / 100.0);
    end;
end; { Time }

BEGIN { Main Program }
  Writeln ('Number of seconds since midnight is ',
           Time:1:2);
END.
```

Here is an example of program output.

```
Number of seconds since midnight is 36185.12
```

This same program can be implemented in Versions 4 and 5 by putting the parameter values returned by the GetTime procedure into the following calculation.

```
Time := 3600.0 * Hour + 60.0 * Minute + Second
        + (Sec100 / 100.0);
```

The last program in this series contains a function Ver that returns the MS-DOS version number. The DOS function call number is $30 hexadecimal, and the version number is returned in the AX register. The integer part of the version number is stored in the low-order byte, while the decimal part is stored in the high-order byte.

```
PROGRAM EX1611 (Output);
{
  Display the output of the Ver function.
  Use only with Version 4 or 5.
}
{$V-} { relax string type checking }
uses
  Dos;
type
  string5 = string[5];
```

```
FUNCTION Ver: string5;
{
  Display the current version of MS-DOS.
}
var
  Regs: registers;
  Major, Minor: string[2];
begin
  with Regs do
    begin
    AX := $3000;
    MsDos (Regs);
    Str (Lo(AX):1, Major);
    Str (Hi(AX):1, Minor);
    Ver := Major + '.' + Minor;
    end;
end; { Ver }

BEGIN { Main Program }
  Writeln ('Current version of MS-DOS is ', Ver);
END.
```

This program produces the following output.

```
Current version of MS-DOS is 3.30
```

16.4 COMPILED PROGRAMS

Most of the time after writing a Turbo Pascal program, the Run command is invoked (R in Version 3, Alt-R in Versions 4 and 5), the program is compiled in memory, and it is then executed. A compiled version of the program is not saved on disk.

Compiling Programs on Disk

An alternative procedure, often used with larger programs, is to compile the program on disk. The file created is a COM file in Version 3 and an EXE file in Versions 4 and 5. The program can be executed by entering the executable file name at the MS-DOS prompt.

In order to create an EXE file in Versions 4 and 5, enter the Compile menu, change the option Destination from Memory to Disk, and then invoke the command Compile. An EXE file is created and the program is compiled into that file on disk. Exit the Turbo Pascal system and execute the just-compiled program by typing its name.

In order to create a COM file in Version 3, enter the command O (for Options) to display the optional methods of compilation. The command C is then entered for program compilation into a COM file, and finally the command Q to quit the Options display. Now instead of entering the Run command, enter the C or Compile command. A COM file is created and the program is compiled into that file on disk.

As before, you can exit the Turbo Pascal system and execute the just-compiled program by typing its name.

In general, it is best to debug a program by using the Run command and compiling in memory, and when all errors have been removed, to compile it on disk. Under the MS-DOS operating system, you must leave the Turbo Pascal system to execute an EXE or COM file.

Using the Command Line

Our next example uses a program that is compiled on disk. The program permits information typed on the command line after the EXE or COM file name to be accessed by the program. The *command line* is defined as the string of characters entered in response to the MS-DOS prompt, and it always starts with the EXE or COM file name.

As you may remember, Program EX1002 reads a file containing test codes and numeric evaluations, converts the evaluations to letter equivalents, and writes a file containing codes and letter equivalents. File names are entered in response to prompts. A modified version of this program performs the same function of converting evaluation values, but also allows the names of the input and output files to be included in the command line.

The ParamCount and ParamStr Functions

Two standard functions in Turbo Pascal, ParamCount and ParamStr, are used to obtain information from that part of the command line after the file name, commonly called the *command tail*.

ParamCount returns a value of type word in Versions 4 and 5 or of type integer in Version 3. This value specifies the number of names or parameters included in the command line when the program is executed from an EXE or COM file. Spaces, tabs, and commas are considered separators between individual names. ParamStr(N), with a parameter of type word in Version 4 and 5 or of type integer in Version 3, returns a string containing the Nth name. Here is a revised version of the earlier program.

```
PROGRAM EX1612 (Input, Output);
{
   Get file names from the command line or, if not
   available, from input prompts.
   Read a file of test codes and numeric evaluations.
   Convert evaluations to letter equivalents and write
   a new file of codes and letter equivalents. Also
   display a table of codes and letter equivalents.
   Use only with Version 4 or 5.
}
uses
   Crt;
type
   string80 = string[80];
```

```
var
  InFile, OutFile: text;

FUNCTION LetterEquivalent (N: integer): char;
{
  Convert numeric evaluation to letter equivalent.
}
begin
  case N of
    91..100: LetterEquivalent := 'A';
    81..90:  LetterEquivalent := 'B';
    71..80:  LetterEquivalent := 'C';
    61..70:  LetterEquivalent := 'D';
     0..60:  LetterEquivalent := 'F';
  else
    LetterEquivalent := 'X';
  end; { case branch }
end; { LetterEquivalent }


PROCEDURE OpenInFile (var InFile: text);
{
  Open an input file.
}
var
  FileName: string80;
begin
  if ParamCount = 0 then
    begin
    Write ('Name of input file? ');
    Readln (FileName);
    end
  else { file name is in command tail }
    FileName := ParamStr(1);
  Assign (InFile, FileName);
  Reset (InFile);
end; { OpenInFile }


PROCEDURE OpenOutFile (var OutFile: text);
{
  Open an output file.
}
var
  FileName: string80;
```

```
begin
  if ParamCount = 0 then
    begin
    Write ('Name of output file? ');
    Readln (FileName);
    end
  else  { file name is in command tail }
    FileName := ParamStr(2);
  Assign (OutFile, FileName);
  Rewrite (OutFile);
end; { OpenOutFile }


PROCEDURE Tab (N: integer);
{
  Move cursor to column N.
}
begin
  GotoXY (N, WhereY);
end; { Tab }


PROCEDURE DisplayTable (var InFile, OutFile: text);
{
  Display the table of codes and letter equivalents.
  Write the output file.
}
var
  TestCode: string80;
  NumericEvaluation: integer;
  LetterEquiv: char;
begin
  Write ('  CODE'); Tab (35); Writeln ('LETTER');
  Writeln;
  while not Eof(InFile) do
    begin
    Readln (InFile, TestCode);
    Readln (InFile, NumericEvaluation);
    Writeln (OutFile, TestCode);
    LetterEquiv := LetterEquivalent(NumericEvaluation);
    Writeln (OutFile, LetterEquiv);
    Write (TestCode); Tab (38); Writeln (LetterEquiv);
    end; { while loop }
  Close (OutFile);
end; { DisplayTable }
```

```
BEGIN { Main Program }
  OpenInFile (InFile);
  OpenOutFile (OutFile);
  Writeln;
  DisplayTable (InFile, OutFile);
  Writeln;
  Writeln ('The output file has been written.');
END.
```

Assume that the program has been compiled, and it resides, along with the data file EVALS.DAT, in the root directory of disk B. The proper command line to invoke the program, writing the output to the file EQUIVS.DAT, is

```
B> EX1612 EVALS.DAT EQUIVS.DAT
```

The following output is produced.

```
         CODE                                    LETTER

    A1S7V2132                                       B
    A1S7V2178                                       A
    A1S7V2205                                       C
    A1S7V2259                                       D
    A1S7V2282                                       B

The output file has been written.
```

We have discussed several language enhancements that are available in Turbo Pascal, with special emphasis on Versions 4 and 5. It is possible through Turbo Pascal programs to interact with the operating system, allowing a user to perform many tasks that would otherwise have to be programmed in assembly language.

Other low-level capabilities and enhancements are available, but not discussed here. For more information, we refer you to the Turbo Pascal manual, and to an excellent book by Jeff Duntemann, entitled *Complete Turbo Pascal* and published by Scott, Foresman and Company in 1986.

IMPORTANT POINTS

- Hexadecimal numbers in Turbo Pascal are always written with leading dollar signs, and numbers without leading dollar signs are assumed to be decimal numbers.

- When a number string is entered in hexadecimal notation, the Val function automatically converts it to a decimal number.

- The range of hexadecimal integers commonly used in Turbo Pascal is from $0000 to $FFFF.

- Turbo Pascal allows any variable to be placed at a fixed or absolute location in memory.
- It is the programmer's responsibility to make certain that an absolute variable does not overwrite any important memory locations.
- A typed constant in Turbo Pascal should more properly be called an initialized variable.
- The Move procedure does no checking; so the programmer must take care not to overwrite important memory locations.
- The MsDos procedure can be used to access any of the DOS functions associated with interrupt $21 hexadecimal (33 decimal).

SELF-STUDY QUESTIONS

1. What is the difference between a segment address and an offset address in MS-DOS?
2. (a) What is the decimal equivalent of the hexadecimal number $1A?
   (b) What is the hexadecimal equivalent of the decimal number $32?
3. If a computer has 4KB of memory, what is the decimal value of the number of memory locations?
4. Can a typed constant be
   (a) assigned to a variable;
   (b) used as the upper bound of an array?
5. Write a variable declaration statement that places the variable Reply of type byte at segment address $B000 and offset address $0006.
6. What checking is done by the Move procedure before writing a block of information in memory?
7. What interrupt number is used by the MsDos procedure?
8. Which CPU register is called the accumulator?
9. (a) What DOS function call number is used to access the CPU date routines?
   (b) How is this number transferred to the CPU?
10. (a) In your version of Turbo Pascal, what commands must be given to compile a source file to disk?
    (b) What kind of file is created?
11. (a) Which functions can be used to access the command tail in MS-DOS?
    (b) What value does each function return?

PRACTICE PROGRAMS

1. Write a function for converting all upper case letters in a string variable to lower case.
2. Display the current date in MM-DD-YY format.
3. Display the current time in HH:MM format.

4. Create a text file that contains one hundred computer-generated words. Each four-character word must start with a consonant, followed by two vowels and another consonant. Both vowels and consonants are to be chosen at random.

   Display your word list in a format of ten words per line.

5. Write a Turbo Pascal function, similar to the `KeyPressed` function, that returns a value of true if a key has been pressed and a value of false otherwise. Use DOS function $0B of interrupt $21. When entering the DOS function, register AH is set to the function number. When returning from the DOS function, register AL has a value of $FF if a key has been pressed, otherwise it has a value of zero.

   Test your function in a program that executes a loop and displays something on the screen every time any key is pressed.

6. Write a Turbo Pascal function that returns the number of free bytes remaining on a disk. Given this information, a user can be warned to change disks before saving a large file.

   Use DOS function $36 of interrupt $21. When entering the DOS function, register AH is set to the function number. Register DL is set according to the following disk drive code.

DL = 0	current drive
DL = 1	drive A
DL = 2	drive B
and so forth	

   When returning from the DOS function, the following information is provided in registers AX through DX.

AX =	sectors per cluster
BX =	available (free) clusters on the disk
CX =	bytes per sector
DX =	total clusters (free and used) on the disk

   Test your function in a program that displays the number of free bytes on the disk in a drive whose letter is specified by the user.

APPENDIX A

PASCAL RESERVED WORDS

Note: These words cannot be used as identifiers (names of types, variables, functions, procedures or units).

absolute *	file	mod	shl *
and	for	nil	shr *
array	forward	not	string *
begin	function	of	then
case	goto	or	type
const	in	overlay ***	to
div	if	packed	unit **
do	implementation **	procedure	until
downto	inline *	program	uses **
else	interface **	record	var
end	interrupt **	repeat	while
external *	label	set	with
			xor *

The asterisks denote words not reserved in standard Pascal.

*	reserved in all versions of Turbo Pascal
**	reserved only in Versions 4 and 5
***	reserved only in Version 3

APPENDIX B

THE ASCII SET OF CHARACTERS

NAME	DEC	HEX	NAME	DEC	HEX
^@(null)	0	0	^P	16	10
^A	1	1	^Q	17	11
^B	2	2	^R	18	12
^C (break)	3	3	^S	19	13
^D	4	4	^T	20	14
^E	5	5	^U	21	15
^F	6	6	^V	22	16
^G (bell)	7	7	^W	23	17
^H (backspace)	8	8	^X	24	18
^I (tab)	9	9	^Y	25	19
^J (line feed)	10	A	^Z (end of file)	26	1A
^K	11	B	^[(escape)	27	1B
^L (form feed)	12	C	^\	28	1C
^M (return)	13	D	^]	29	1D
^N	14	E	^^	30	1E
^O	15	F	^_	31	1F

Note: The Caret prefix (^) means a control character, for example, ^A means control A or Ctrl-A.

NAME	DEC	HEX	NAME	DEC	HEX
sp (space)	32	20	J	74	4A
!	33	21	K	75	4B
"	34	22	L	76	4C
#	35	23	M	77	4D
$	36	24	N	78	4E
%	37	25	O	79	4F
&	38	26	P	80	50
' (acute)	39	27	Q	81	51
(	40	28	R	82	52
)	41	29	S	83	53
*	42	2A	T	84	54
+	43	2B	U	85	55
, (comma)	44	2C	V	86	56
- (minus)	45	2D	W	87	57
.	46	2E	X	88	58
/	47	2F	Y	89	59
0 (zero)	48	30	Z	90	5A
1	49	31	[(bracket)	91	5B
2	50	32	\(rev. slash)	92	5C
3	51	33	] (bracket)	93	5D
4	52	34	^(caret)	94	5E
5	53	35	_ (underline)	95	5F
6	54	36	` (grave)	96	60
7	55	37	a (lowercase)	97	61
8	56	38	b	98	62
9	57	39	c	99	63
:	58	3A	d	100	64
;	59	3B	e	101	65
<	60	3C	f	102	66
=	61	3D	g	103	67
>	62	3E	h	104	68
?	63	3F	i	105	69
@	64	40	j	106	6A
A (uppercase)	65	41	k	107	6B
B	66	42	l	108	6C
C	67	43	m	109	6D
D	68	44	n	110	6E
E	69	45	o	111	6F
F	70	46	p	112	70
G	71	47	q	113	71
H	72	48	r	114	72
I	73	49	s	115	73

NAME	DEC	HEX	NAME	DEC	HEX
t	116	74	z	122	7A
u	117	75	{(brace)	123	7B
v	118	76	|(vert. bar)	124	7C
w	119	77	}(brace)	125	7D
x	120	78	˜(tilde)	126	7E
y	121	79	del	127	7F

APPENDIX C

TURBO PASCAL SYNTAX DIAGRAMS

Pascal reserved words are enclosed in special boxes like this ⬭ and are in bold type. Single and double characters are enclosed in circles like this ○ . All other words are enclosed in rectangular boxes like this ▭ .

C.1 SYMBOLS

Letter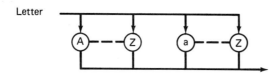

Digit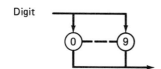

Hex digit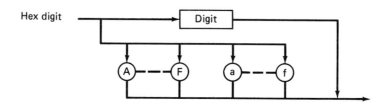

Underscore

C.2 IDENTIFIERS

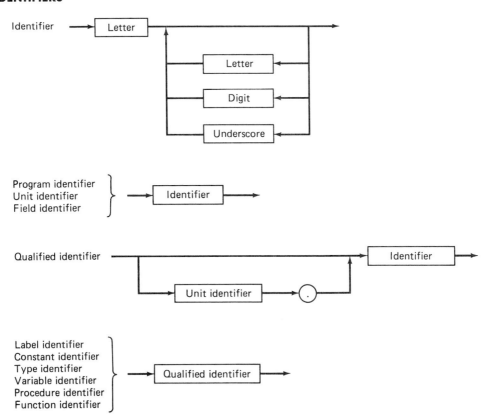

C.3 LABELS

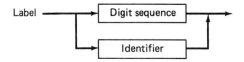

C.4 NUMBERS

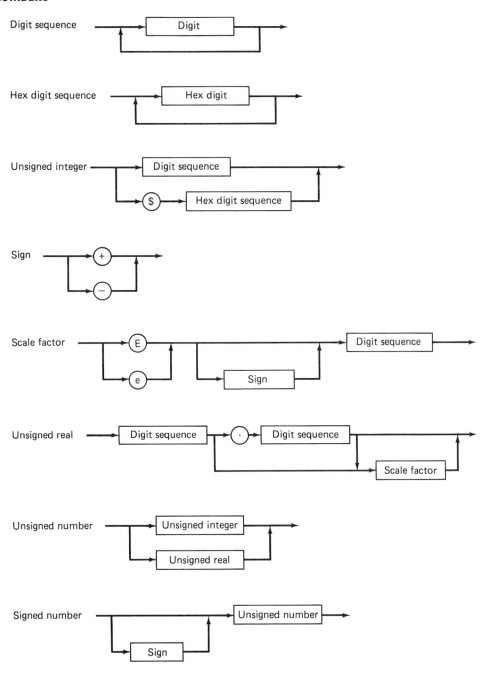

C.5 CHARACTER STRINGS

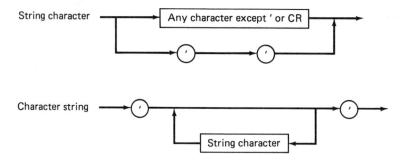

C.6 CONSTANTS

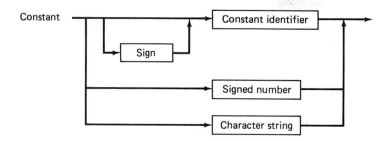

C.7 TYPES

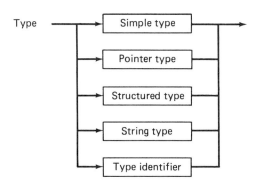

Type
- Simple type
- Pointer type
- Structured type
- String type
- Type identifier

Type declaration ──→ Identifier ──→ (=) ──→ Type ──→ (;) ──→

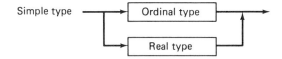

Simple type
- Ordinal type
- Real type

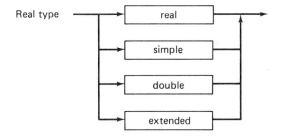

Real type
- real
- simple
- double
- extended

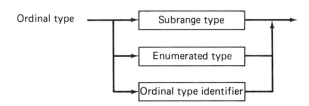

Ordinal type
- Subrange type
- Enumerated type
- Ordinal type identifier

C.7 TYPES (*continued*)

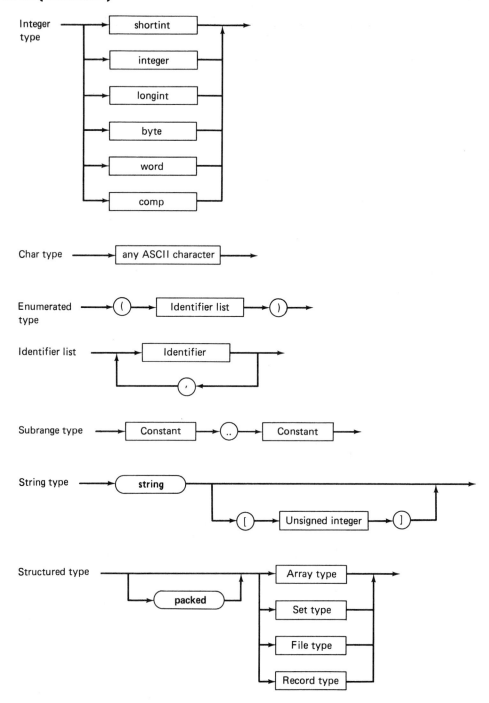

C.7 TYPES (*continued*)

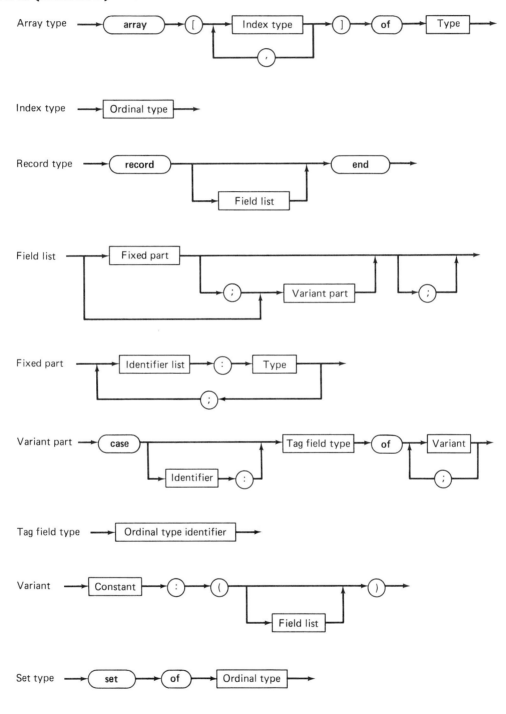

C.7 TYPES (*continued*)

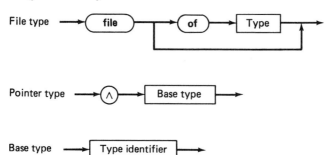

C.8 **VARIABLES**

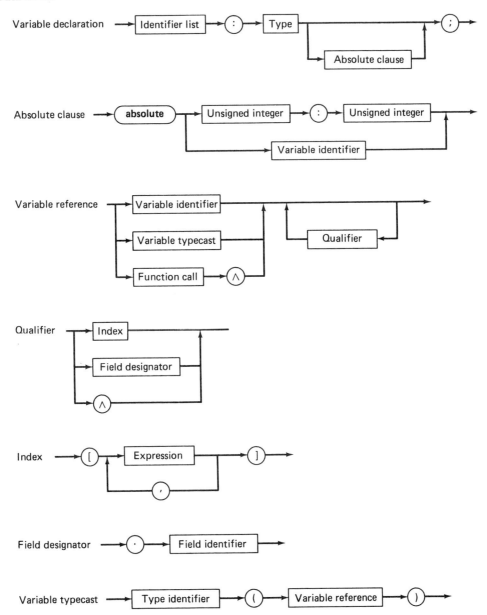

C.9 TYPED CONSTANTS

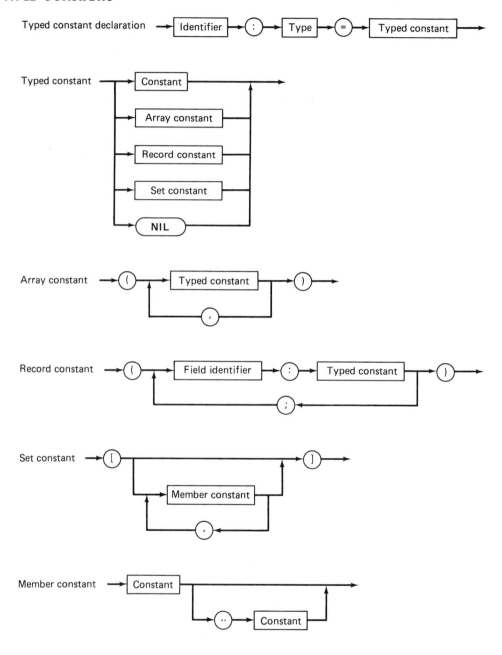

C.10 EXPRESSIONS

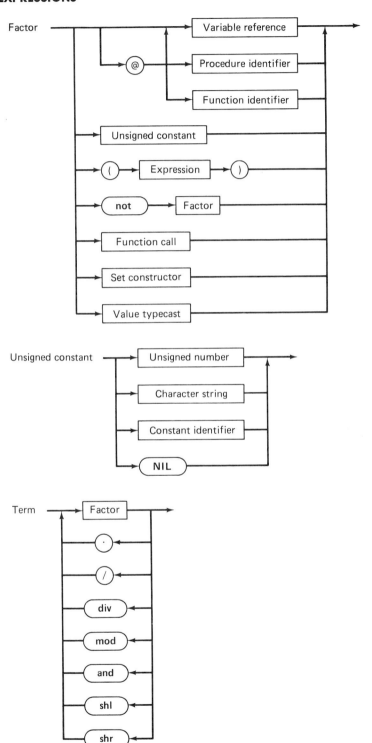

C.10 EXPRESSIONS (*continued*)

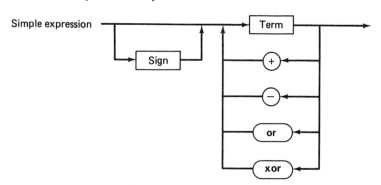

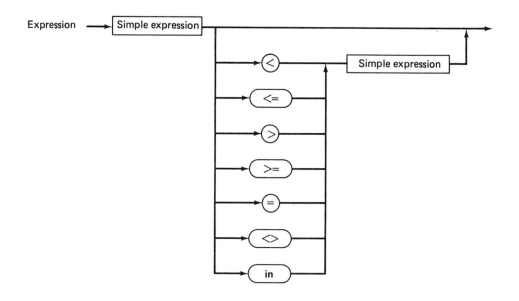

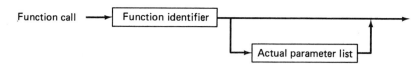

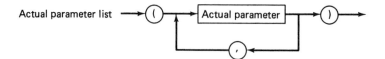

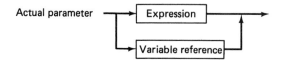

C.10 EXPRESSIONS (*continued*)

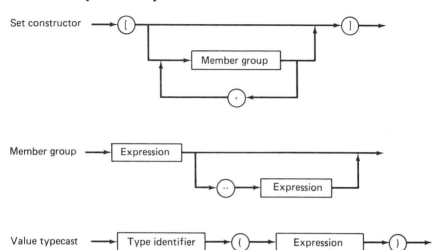

Set constructor

Member group

Value typecast

C.11 STATEMENTS

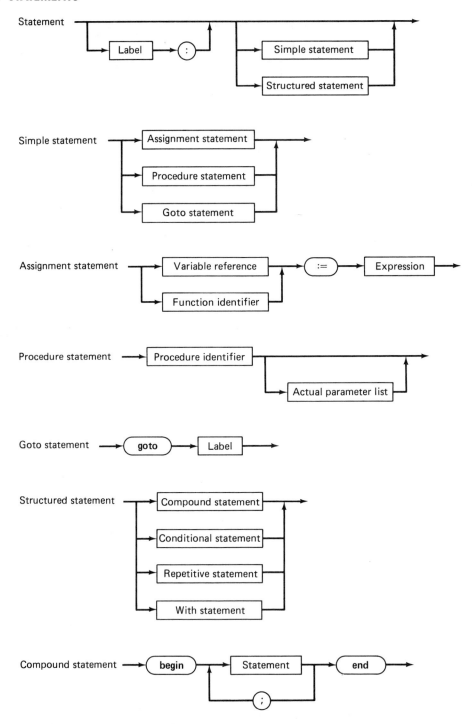

C.11 STATEMENTS (*continued*)

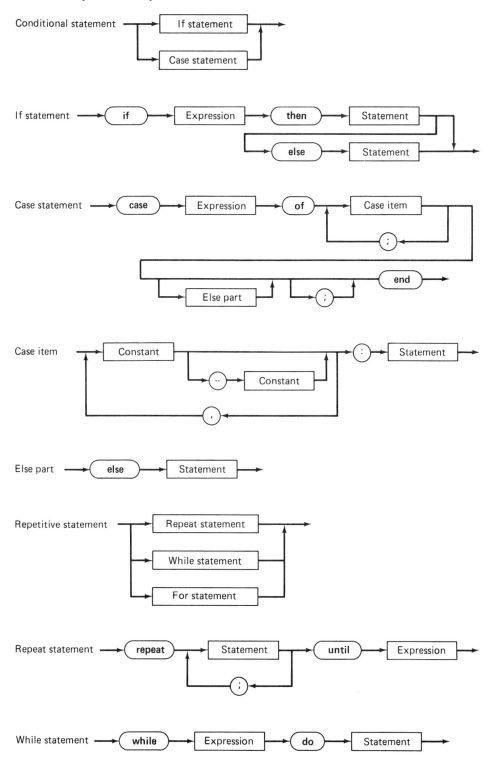

C.11 STATEMENTS (*continued*)

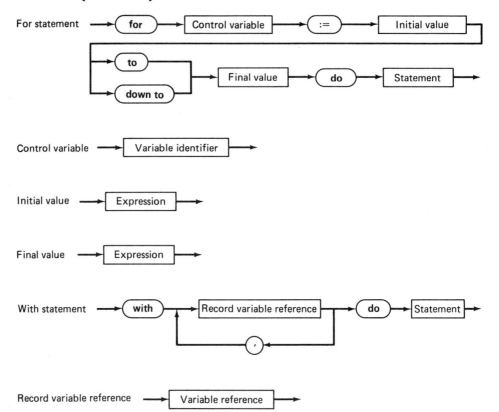

C.12 BLOCKS

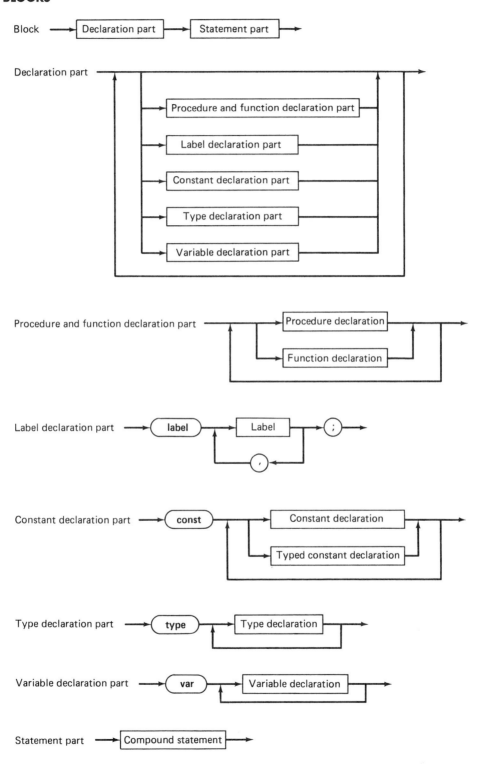

C.13 FUNCTIONS

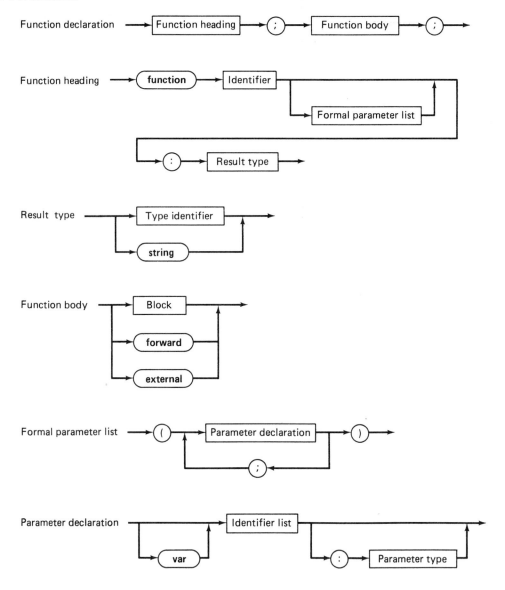

C.14 **PROCEDURES**

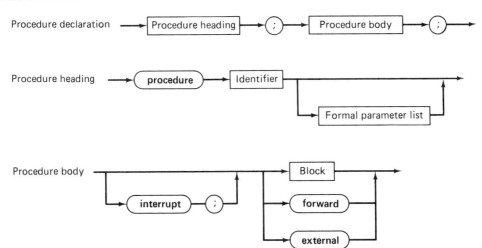

C.15 PROGRAMS

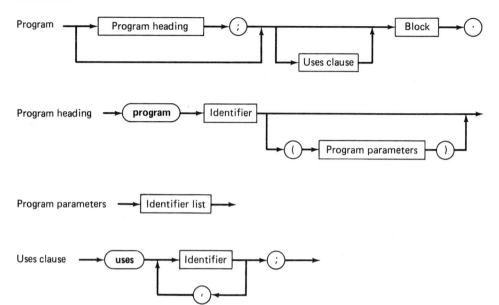

C.16 UNITS

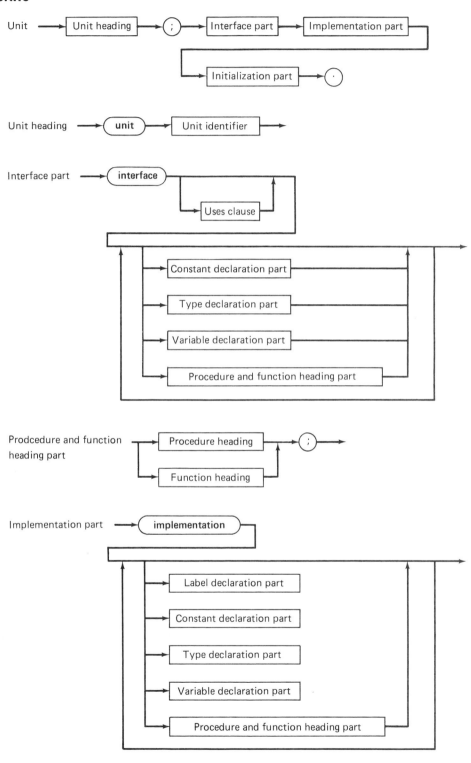

C.16 UNITS (*continued*)

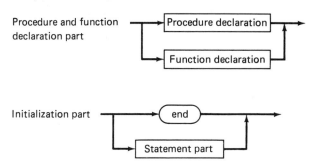

Procedure and function
declaration part

Initialization part

APPENDIX D

STANDARD PROCEDURES AND FUNCTIONS OF TURBO PASCAL

D.1 INPUT/OUTPUT PROCEDURES AND FUNCTIONS, ALL FILES

In the definitions in this section, `FV` is a file variable name of any type, including type text. `Strg` is a string-type constant, variable, or expression.

`Assign (FV, Strg)`
A procedure that assigns an MS-DOS file name or path name, `Strg`, to a Pascal file denoted by `FV`. This statement does not open the file.

`ChDir (Strg)`
A procedure that changes the current MS-DOS directory to the directory whose path name is `Strg`. Parameter `Strg` may include a disk drive letter.

`Close (FV)`
A procedure that closes an open file denoted by `FV`.

`Eof (FV)` `{ standard Pascal }`
A boolean function that returns a value of true if the next character or component in the file denoted by `FV` is the end-of-file marker, otherwise it returns a value of false.

Erase (FV)

A procedure that erases the contents of the file denoted by FV. The file pointer is placed at the beginning of the file. The file must be closed before this procedure is used.

GetDir (Drive, StrgVar)

A procedure that returns the current directory. Drive is an integer constant, variable, or expression. StrgVar must be a string variable. Drive has a value of 0 for the current drive, 1 for drive A, 2 for drive B, and so forth. StrgVar returns the current directory of the specified drive.

IOResult (FV)

An integer function (type word in Versions 4 and 5) that returns a value of zero if the I/O operation on the file denoted by FV was successful. I/O checking must be off { $I-} . IOResult resets to zero each time it is called.

MkDir (Strg)

A procedure that creates a new directory whose path name is Strg. For example:

    MkDir ('D:\ NEW');

creates the subdirectory NEW, in the root directory \, on the disk in drive D.

Rename (FV, Strg)

A procedure that renames a file denoted by FV. Strg is the new file name or path name. The file must be closed before this procedure is used.

Reset (FV)   { standard Pascal }

A procedure that opens an existing file denoted by FV, and positions the file pointer at the beginning of the file.

Rewrite (FV)   { standard Pascal }

A procedure that creates and opens a new file denoted by FV. If the file already exists, its contents are erased.

RmDir (Strg)

A procedure that removes an existing directory whose path name is Strg. The directory must be empty.

D.2 INPUT/OUTPUT PROCEDURES AND FUNCTIONS, TEXT FILES

In the definitions in this section, FV is a file variable name of type text.

Append (FV)

A procedure that opens an existing file denoted by FV, and positions the file pointer at the end of the file.

Eoln (FV)   { standard Pascal }

A boolean function that returns a value of true if the next character in the file denoted by FV is the end-of-line marker (the carriage return, ASCII value 13); otherwise it returns a value of false.

Flush (FV)

A procedure that empties the output file buffer of the file denoted by FV, and transfers all characters in that buffer to the disk.

Read (FV, Var1, Var2,...)   { standard Pascal }

A procedure that reads one or more values from the file denoted by FV, and assigns these values to the variables Var1, Var2, and so forth. This procedure behaves differently in Turbo Pascal than in standard Pascal. It is seldom used with text files. See Chapter 10 and the Turbo Pascal Reference Manual for details.

Readln (FV, Var1)   { standard Pascal }

A procedure that reads all characters in a line of the file denoted by FV, and assigns these characters to the variable Var1. This variable is often of type string. More than one variable parameter can be specified, but this practice is not recommended.

SeekEof (FV)

A boolean function that is similar to Eof. It skips all blanks, tabs, and end-of-line markers before returning the end-of-file status of the file denoted by FV. It is useful when reading numeric values from a text file.

SeekEoln (FV)

A boolean function that is similar to Eoln. It skips all blanks and tabs before returning the end-of-line status of the file denoted by FV.

SetTextBuf (FV, BufVar, [Size])

A procedure that provides a larger file buffer, BufVar, for the text file denoted by FV. The default buffer size is 128 bytes. For example, the program fragment

```
var
  FV: text;
  Buffer: array [1..10240] of char;
    |
SetTextBuf (FV, Buffer);
```

increases the buffer size to 10KB. The parameter Size is optional, but seldom used. See the Turbo Pascal Owner's Handbook for details. This procedure is available only in Versions 4 and 5.

Write (FV, Item1, Item2,...)   { standard Pascal }

A procedure that writes one or more items on the file denoted by FV. Each Item can be a constant, variable, or expression. It does not write an end-of-line marker on the file after writing the items.

Writeln (FV)   { standard Pascal }

A procedure that writes a blank line (an end-of-line marker) on the file denoted by FV.

Writeln (FV, Item1, Item2,...)   { standard Pascal }

A procedure that writes one or more items on the file denoted by FV, and then writes an end-of-line marker on the file. Each Item can be a constant, variable, or expression.

D.3 INPUT/OUTPUT PROCEDURES AND FUNCTIONS, TYPED FILES

In the definitions in this section, FV is a file variable name of any type except text.

FilePos (FV)

An integer function (type longint in Versions 4 and 5) that returns the current position of the file pointer in the file denoted by FV. The file pointer points to the current component of the file. The first component in a typed file has an index value of zero.

FileSize (FV)

An integer function (type longint in Versions 4 and 5) that returns the current size of the file denoted by FV. File size is expressed as the number of components in the file.

Read (FV, Var1)

A procedure that reads the current component value from the file denoted by FV, and assigns this value to the variable Var1. An entire component or file record must be read. More than one variable parameter can be specified, but this practice is not recommended.

Seek (FV, Nmbr)

A procedure that moves the file pointer of the file denoted by FV to the beginning of the component or file record whose index number is Nmbr.

Truncate (FV)

A procedure that truncates the file denoted by FV at the current file pointer position. All file components after the current component are deleted.

Write (FV, Item)

A procedure that writes the value of parameter Item on the current file record or component of the file denoted by FV. Item is usually a variable, but it can be a constant or expression. It must be of the same type as the file components because only an entire component or file record can be written. More than one item can be specified, but this practice is not recommended.

D.4 ARITHMETIC FUNCTIONS

In the definitions in this and following sections, X is a numeric parameter. Real-type means `real` in Version 3, `single`, `double`, `extended` or `real` in Versions 4 and 5. Integer-type means `integer` or `byte` in Version 3, `byte`, `shortint`, `integer`, `word`, `longint` or `comp` in Versions 4 and 5.

Abs (X)   { standard Pascal }
A real-type or integer-type function that returns the absolute value of the real-type or integer-type parameter X.

ArcTan (X)   { standard Pascal }
A real-type function that returns the arctangent of the real-type parameter X.

Cos (X)   { standard Pascal }
A real-type function that returns the cosine of the real-type parameter X.

Exp (X)   { standard Pascal }
A real-type function that returns the exponential of the real-type parameter X.

Frac (X)
A real-type function that returns the fractional part of the real-type parameter X.

Int (X)
A real-type function that returns the integer part of the real-type parameter X.

Ln (X)   { standard Pascal }
A real-type function that returns the natural logarithm of the real-type parameter X.

Pi
A `real` function that returns the value of pi (3.14159...).

Sin (X)   { standard Pascal }
A real-type function that returns the sine of the real-type parameter X.

Sqr (X)   { standard Pascal }
A real-type or integer-type function that returns the square of the real-type or integer-type parameter X.

Sqrt (X)   { standard Pascal }
A real-type function that returns the square root of the real-type parameter X.

D.5 ORDINAL AND TRANSFER PROCEDURES AND FUNCTIONS

As in the previous section, most of these functions come directly from standard Pascal.

Chr (X)   { standard Pascal }

A char function that returns the character corresponding to the integer-type parameter X.

Ord (C)   { standard Pascal }

An integer function (type longint in Versions 4 and 5) that returns the ordinal value corresponding to the char parameter C.

Dec (X, N)

A procedure that decrements the integer-type parameter X by one. The optional integer parameter N decrements X by the value of N. **This procedure is available only in Versions 4 and 5.**

Inc (X, N)

A procedure that increments the integer-type parameter X by one. The optional integer parameter N increments X by the value of N. **This procedure is available only in Versions 4 and 5.**

Round (X)   { standard Pascal }

An integer function (type longint in Versions 4 and 5) that returns the value of the real parameter X, rounded to the nearest whole number.

Trunc (X)   { standard Pascal }

An integer function (type longint in Versions 4 and 5) that returns the value of the real parameter X with the decimal part deleted (rounded toward zero).

Odd (X)   { standard Pascal }

A boolean function that returns a value of true if the integer parameter X is odd, otherwise it returns a value of false. The parameter is of type longint in Versions 4 and 5.

Pred (X)   { standard Pascal }

An ordinal-type function that returns the predecessor of the ordinal-type parameter X. For example,

```
Pred('B') equals A
```

Succ (X)   { standard Pascal }

An ordinal-type function that returns the successor of the ordinal-type parameter X. For example,

```
Succ('B') equals  C
```

D.6 STRING PROCEDURES AND FUNCTIONS

In the definitions in this section, Strg and Sub are string-type constants or variables. P and N are integer-type constants, variables, or expressions. Num is a real-type or integer-type constant, variable, or expression.

Concat (Strg1, Strg2, Strg3,...)

A string-type function that returns a string consisting of the concatenation of all string-type parameters. The concatenation operator (+) is commonly used instead of this function.

Copy (Strg, P, N)

A string-type function that returns a substring of the parameter Strg. P is the index or position of the first character and N is the number of characters in the substring.

Delete (Strg, P, N)

A procedure that deletes a substring of length N characters, starting at character P, from the parameter Strg.

Insert (Sub, Strg, P)

A procedure that inserts a substring Sub into the parameter Strg, starting at character position P.

Length (Strg)

An integer function (type word in Versions 4 and 5) that returns the dynamic length of the string-type parameter Strg.

Pos (Pattern, Target)

An integer function (type byte in Versions 4 and 5) that returns the index or first character position in the string-type parameter Target where the string-type parameter Pattern occurs. If Pattern is not found, a value of zero is returned. **Note: The order of the two parameters is just the opposite from that used in the equivalent BASIC function**.

Str (Num, Strg)

A procedure that converts a real-type or integer-type parameter Num into its equivalent string-type representation Strg.

Val (Strg, Num, Code)

A procedure that converts a string-type parameter Strg into its equivalent real-type or integer-type representation Num. Integer parameter Code has a value of zero if the conversion is successful, otherwise it returns the index or position of the first invalid character in Strg.

D.7 DYNAMIC ALLOCATION PROCEDURES AND FUNCTIONS

This list of procedures and functions is incomplete, but includes those subprograms that are used most often. See the Turbo Pascal Owner's Handbook for further information.

Dispose (P) { standard Pascal }

A procedure that releases memory in the heap used by a dynamic variable. This variable is pointed to by the parameter P of type `pointer`.

MaxAvail

An `integer` function that returns the size of the largest contiguous free block of memory in the heap. Size is expressed in 16-byte paragraphs. In Versions 4 and 5, the function is of type `longint` and size is expressed in bytes.

MemAvail

An `integer` function that returns the sum of all free blocks of memory in the heap. Size of the sum is expressed in 16-byte paragraphs. In Versions 4 and 5, the function is of type `longint` and size is expressed in bytes.

New (P) { standard Pascal }

A procedure that creates a new dynamic variable by allocating a block of memory in the heap. It sets a `pointer` parameter P to point to the block of memory.

D.8 POINTER AND ADDRESS FUNCTIONS

This list of functions is incomplete, but includes those that are used most often. See the Turbo Pascal Owner's Handbook for further information. Pointer-type means of type `pointer`.

Addr (X)

A pointer-type function that returns the address of the parameter X. The value returned is a 32 bit pointer consisting of a segment address and an offset. The parameter can be any variable, procedure or function identifier.

Cseg

An `integer` function (type `word` in Versions 4 and 5) that returns the current value of the CS register, or the segment address of the current code segment.

Dseg

An `integer` function (type `word` in Versions 4 and 5) that returns the current value of the DS register, or the segment address of the data segment.

`Ofs (X)`

An `integer` function (type `word` in Versions 4 and 5) that returns the offset of the segment of memory occupied by the parameter `X`. The parameter can be any variable, procedure or function identifier.

`Seg (X)`

An `integer` function (type `word` in Versions 4 and 5) that returns the address of the segment of memory occupied by the parameter `X`. The parameter can be any variable, procedure or function identifier.

`Sseg`

An `integer` function (type `word` in Versions 4 and 5) that returns the current value of the SS register, or the segment address of the stack segment.

D.9 MISCELLANEOUS PROCEDURES AND FUNCTIONS

Once again, this list of subprograms is not complete, and you should consult the Turbo Pascal Owner's Handbook for more information.

`Exit`

A procedure that exits immediately from the current block (procedure, function, or the main program).

`FillChar (X, N, Ch)`

A procedure that fills `N` contiguous bytes of memory with the value `Ch`, starting at the first byte occupied by `X`. `N` is of type `byte` (type `word` in Versions 4 and 5), `Ch` is an expression of any ordinal type, and `X` is a variable of any type.

`Halt`

A procedure that stops program execution and returns control to the operating system.

`Hi (X)`

An `integer` function (type `byte` in Versions 4 and 5) that returns the high-order byte of the `integer` expression `X`.

`Lo (X)`

An `integer` function (type `byte` in Versions 4 and 5) that returns the low-order byte of the `integer` expression `X`.

`Move (Source, Dest, N)`

A procedure that copies `N` contiguous bytes from variable `Source` to variable `Dest`. Variables `Source` and `Dest` can be of any type.

ParamCount

An `integer` function (type `word` in Versions 4 and 5) that returns the number of parameters passed to the program on the command line.

ParamStr (I)

A string-type function that returns the command line parameter whose index is `I`. Index `I` is of type `integer` (type `word` in Versions 4 and 5).

Random

A `real` function that returns a random numeric value between zero and one.

Random (N)

An `integer` function (type `word` in Versions 4 and 5) that returns a random numeric value between zero and the `integer` parameter `N`.

Randomize

A procedure that initializes the built-in random number generator with a random seed value.

ReadKey (C)

A `char` function that returns the character corresponding to a pressed key, as soon as that key is pressed. **This function is available only in Versions 4 and 5.**

SizeOf (X)

An `integer` function (type `word` in Versions 4 and 5) that returns the number of bytes occupied by the type identifier or variable `X`.

Swap (X)

A function, of the same type as the `integer` or `word` parameter `X`, that returns the parameter value with the low-order and high-order bytes swapped.

Upcase (Ch)

A `char` function that returns the character parameter `Ch` converted to uppercase.

APPENDIX E

STANDARD UNITS OF TURBO PASCAL, VERSIONS 4 AND 5

E.1 DOS UNIT PROCEDURES

Exec	executes a specified program with a specified command line
FindFirst	searches the specified directory for the first entry matching the specified file name and set of attributes
FindNext	returns the next entry that matches the name and attributes specified in a previous call to FindFirst
GetIntVec	returns the address stored in a specified interrupt vector
SetIntVec	sets a specified interrupt vector to a specified address
GetDate	returns the current date set in the operating system
GetFAttr	returns the attributes of a file
GetFTime	returns the date and time a file was last written
GetTime	returns the current time set in the operating system
Intr	executes a specified software interrupt

Keep	terminates the program and makes it stay in memory (creates a TSR program)
MsDos	executes a DOS function call
PackTime	converts a DateTime record into a four-byte, packed date-and-time identifier of type longint used by SetFTime
SetDate	sets the current date in the operating system
SetFTime	sets the date and time a file was last written
SetTime	sets the current time in the operating system
UnpackTime	converts a four-byte, packed date-and-time identifier of type longint, returned by GetFTime, FindFirst, or FindNext, into an unpacked DateTime record

E.2 DOS UNIT FUNCTIONS

Functions marked with an asterisk (*) are available only in Version 5.

DiskFree	returns the number of free bytes available on a specified disk drive
DiskSize	returns the total size in bytes of a specified disk drive
DosExitCode	returns the exit code of a terminating program
DosVersion *	returns the DOS version number
EnvCount *	returns number of strings in the DOS environment
EnvStr *	returns a specified environment string
FExpand *	returns a fully expanded path name
FSearch *	searches for a file in a list of directories
FSplit *	splits a file name into three components; path, name, and extension
GetCBreak *	returns the state of Ctrl-Break checking in DOS
GetEnv *	returns the value of a specified environment variable

GetVerify *	returns the state of the verify flag in DOS
SetCBreak *	sets the state of Ctrl-Break checking in DOS
SetVerify *	sets the state of the verify flag in DOS
SwapVectors *	swaps interrupt vectors

E.3 CRT UNIT PROCEDURES

AssignCrt	associates a text file with the CRT
ClrEol	clears all characters from the cursor position to the end of the line without moving the cursor
ClrScr	clears the screen and places the cursor in the upper left corner
Delay	delays program execution a specified number of milliseconds
DelLine	deletes the line containing the cursor, and moves up all lines below that line
GotoXY	positions the cursor at column X and row Y
HighVideo	selects high intensity characters
InsLine	inserts an empty line at the cursor position
LowVideo	selects low intensity characters
NormVideo	selects normal intensity characters
NoSound	turns off the internal speaker
RestoreCrt	restores the original video mode detected at startup
Sound	turns on the internal speaker
TextBackground	selects the background color
TextColor	selects the foreground character color
TextMode	selects a specific text mode
Window	defines a text window on the screen

E.4 CRT UNIT FUNCTIONS

| KeyPressed | returns true if a key has been pressed, otherwise returns false |
| ReadKey | returns a character from the keyboard |

WhereX   returns the X-coordinate (column) of
                                the current cursor position, relative
                                to the current window

WhereY   returns the Y-coordinate (row) of the
                                current cursor position, relative to
                                the current window

E.5 PRINTER UNIT

This unit declares a text file named Lst and associates it with the LPT1 device
(usually the printer connected to the parallel port). The following program writes
on the printer rather than on the screen.

```
PROGRAM TestPrinter;
uses Printer;

BEGIN
  Writeln (Lst, 'This is a test string.');
END.
```

E.6 GRAPH UNIT

This unit allows simple graphics screens to be created and manipulated in Turbo
Pascal. Graphics drivers are provided for most of the widely-accepted graphics
adapters, both monochromatic and color.

A complete library of sixty or more procedures and functions is available in
the Graph unit, ranging from high-level calls that draw complete figures to bit-level
routines that change the color of an individual pixel. Many useful constant and type
declarations are also provided.

Our discussion of graphics in this book is limited to one example program
(EX1506) in Chapter 15 that plots a simple curve. If you wish to learn how to
use graphics in your programs, we refer you to the Turbo Pascal Owner's Manual,
Version 4 (or Version 5). We also recommend that you acquire and use the Turbo
Graphix Toolbox from Borland, which contains many additional graphics routines.

E.7 OVERLAY UNIT

This unit is available only in Version 5. It provides functions and procedures that
allow overlay files to be used with Turbo Pascal programs. See the Version 5
manual for more information.

APPENDIX F

REDIRECTING TURBO PASCAL SCREEN OUTPUT TO A FILE

Students writing programs as a homework assignment need the ability to duplicate screen images on an attached printer. They can then turn in a printed listing as an example of keyboard input and screen output produced during the running of their programs.

MS-DOS provides this capability, but it requires the buffering of input received from the keyboard and output sent to the screen. Buffering of input and output is provided by default in Versions 4 and 5 of Turbo Pascal.

Buffering Input and Output (Version 3 only)

Compiler directives allow us to buffer input from the keyboard and output to the display screen. As discussed in Chapter 3, compiler directives are instructions to the Turbo Pascal compiler. These directives are enclosed in braces and denoted by a leading dollar sign ($). They consist of an uppercase letter, and one or more additional characters. Two or more compiler directives can be listed together, separated by commas.

The compiler directive {$G1024,P1024} instructs the compiler to use input and output buffers of 1024 bytes. The size of the buffers is arbitrary; 1024 bytes is large enough to allow the file to be written quickly, and yet not so large as to cause problems with lack of available memory. This directive must be placed near the beginning (before the main declaration block) of any Version 3 program whose screen images are to be duplicated on a printer.

Duplicating Screen Images on a Printer

The key sequence Ctrl-PrtSc (holding down the Ctrl key and pressing the PrtSc key) causes a duplicate of whatever is displayed on the screen to be listed on the printer. It is a toggle command, executed once it starts printing, and executed again it stops printing. This command cannot be executed from within Turbo Pascal.

The procedure to follow is to execute the Ctrl-PrtSc command before entering Turbo Pascal. **Be sure to turn on your printer and make certain it is attached to your computer before pressing Ctrl-PrtSc. If you fail to do so, your computer may lock up and stop working**.

After pressing Ctrl-PrtSc, enter Turbo Pascal (the command `turbo` or its equivalent is printed) and edit the Pascal program as desired. None of this editing activity is printed because Turbo Pascal still ignores the Ctrl-PrtSc command. When the program is run, however, all text displayed on the screen is listed on the printer. The program can be run one or more times. After the last run, return to MS-DOS and again press Ctrl-PrtSc to turn off printer duplication of the screen text image.

Remember once again, **execute the Ctrl-PrtSc command before entering the Turbo Pascal system**.

APPENDIX G

ERROR MESSAGES FOR TURBO PASCAL, VERSION 3

G.1 I/O ERROR MESSAGES

1	File does not exist
2	File not open for input
3	File not open for output
4	File not open
10	Error in numeric format
20	Operation not allowed on a logical device
21	Not allowed in direct mode
22	Assignment to standard files not allowed
90	Record length mismatch
91	Seek beyond end-of-file
99	Unexpected end-of-file
F0	Disk write error
F1	Directory is full
F2	File size overflow
F3	Too many open files
FF	File has disappeared

G.2 RUN-TIME ERROR MESSAGES

1	Floating point overflow
2	Division by zero attempted
3	Sqrt argument error
4	Ln argument error
10	String length error
11	Invalid string index
90	Index out of range
91	Scalar or subrange out of range
92	Outside of integer range
F0	Overlay file not found
FF	Heap-stack collision

APPENDIX H

Run-Time Error Messages for Turbo Pascal, Versions 4 and 5

This is an incomplete list of run-time error messages. See the Turbo Pascal Owner's Manual for more information.

H.1 DOS ERROR MESSAGES

2 File not found.   Reported by `Reset` or `Append` if the file variable does not refer to an existing file.

4 Too many open files.   Reported by `Reset`, `Rewrite`, or `Append` if the program has too many open files (by default, more than three). If you need more than three open files, add the line `FILES=xx` to your `CONFIG.SYS file`, where xx should be between 9 and 20.

H.2 I/O ERROR MESSAGES

100 Disk read error.   Reported by `Read` if you attempt to read past the end of a typed file.

101 Disk write error.   Reported by `Write`, `Writeln`, or `Close` if the disk on which you attempt to write is full (has no more space).

102 File not assigned. Reported by `Reset`, `Rewrite`, or `Append` if the file variable has not been assigned a name in an `Assign` statement.

104 File not open for input. Reported by `Read` or `Readln` (or another procedure that tries to read the file) if a text file has not been opened for input (using `Reset`).

105 File not open for output. Reported by `Write` or `Writeln` if a text file has not been opened for output (using `Rewrite`).

H.3 CRITICAL ERROR MESSAGES

150 - 162. Refer to the MS-DOS programmer's reference manual for information about critical errors. These errors are very unlikely to occur.

H.4 FATAL ERROR MESSAGES

201 Range check error. Reported when a program is compiled with range checking on {$R+}, usually when the index expression of an array is outside the declared range.

202 Stack overflow error. Reported when there is not enough stack space for the local variables of a subprogram. Can be corrected by using the M compiler directive to increase the size of the stack.

203 Heap overflow error. Reported by `New` when there is not enough free heap space to allocate a block of memory of the requested size. Can be corrected (1) by using `Dispose` to release heap space, or (2) by requesting a smaller block of memory.

207 Invalid floating point operation.

1. The `real` value passed to `Trunc` or `Round` cannot be converted to an integer within the range of type `longint`.
2. A negative parameter was passed to the `Sqrt` function.
3. A negative or zero parameter was passed to the `Ln` function.
4. A numeric coprocessor stack overflow occurred.

APPENDIX I

DOS FUNCTION CALLS

All these DOS functions are called through interrupt $21 hexadecimal (33 decimal). The function number is placed in the AH register before procedure MsDos is called from Turbo Pascal. See the IBM Technical Reference Manual for more information.

I.1 FUNCTIONS FOR MS-DOS 1.0 AND UP

$00	terminate or end the program, return to DOS
$01	wait for character input from the keyboard
$02	write a character to the standard output device
$03	read a character from the serial port (COM1)
$04	write a character to the serial port (COM1)
$05	write a character to the parallel port (LPT1) or the standard printer port (PRN)
$06	direct keyboard input and screen output
$07	direct keyboard input without echo
$08	character input from the keyboard without echo
$09	write a character string on the display screen
$0A	buffered keyboard input
$0B	check keyboard input status
$0C	clear keyboard buffer and wait for DOS function
$0D	flush file buffers and reset the disk
$0E	select the current default drive

$0F	open a disk file
$10	close a disk file
$11	search for first file to match a file name
$12	search for next file to match a file name
$13	delete a disk file
$14	read the next sequential record in a file
$15	write a sequential record on a file
$16	find or create a directory entry for a file
$17	rename a disk file
$18	not available–used internally by DOS
$19	report the current disk drive
$1A	set the disk transfer area for file I/O
$1B	get file allocation table (FAT) information for the current drive
$1C	get FAT information for the specified drive
$1D	not available–used internally by DOS
$1E	not available–used internally by DOS
$1F	not available–used internally by DOS
$20	not available–used internally by DOS
$21	read one record from a random location in a file
$22	write one record at a random location in a file
$23	get file size in number of records
$24	set the random record field
$25	set an interrupt vector
$26	create a new program segment for an overlay
$27	read one or more random file records
$28	write one or more random file records
$29	parse a command line for a file name
$2A	get the current date
$2B	set the DOS calendar to the specified date
$2C	get the current time of day
$2D	set the DOS clock to the specified time of day
$2E	turn on verification of disk write operations

I.2 FUNCTIONS FOR MS-DOS 2.0 AND UP

$2F	get the disk transfer area (DTA) address
$30	get the DOS version number
$31	enable a terminate-and-stay-resident (TSR) program
$32	not used
$33	get or set status of Ctrl-Break processing
$34	not used
$35	get the specified interrupt vector
$36	get status of free disk space
$37	not used
$38	get country-dependent information

$39	create a new subdirectory
$3A	remove an existing subdirectory
$3B	change the current directory
$3C	open an existing file or create a new file
$3D	open a file with the specified path name
$3E	close a file with the specified file handle
$3F	read from a file or device with a specified file handle
$40	write to a file or device with a specified file handle
$41	delete the directory entry of a file
$42	change the position of a specified file pointer
$43	get or set the attributes of a file
$44	perform a selected I/O operation for a device
$45	duplicate an open file handle and create a new file handle number
$46	duplicate a file handle using an existing file handle
$47	get the current directory
$48	allocate a block of memory
$49	free an allocated block of memory
$4A	modify the size of an allocated block of memory
$4B	load and execute a program
$4C	end a program and pass back a return code
$4D	get the return code of a terminated subprogram
$4E	search for the first file to match a file specification
$4F	continue the search for a matching file
$50	not used
$51	not used
$52	not used
$53	not used
$54	get the current status of the verify switch
$55	not used
$56	move a file name from one directory to another
$57	get or set the date-and-time stamp of a file
$58	not used

I.3 FUNCTIONS FOR MS-DOS 3.0 AND UP

$59	get the extended error code
$5A	create a temporary file
$5B	create a new file, fail if the file exists
$5C	change the locked status of a file
$5D	not used
$5E	not used
$5F	not used
$60	not used
$61	not used
$62	get the program segment prefix (PSP) address

APPENDIX J

How to Use the Example Program Disk

We suggest you use the DISKCOPY command of MS-DOS to make a working copy of the example program disk.

Instructions for Reading Program Files

Example programs are stored in separate directories on the example program disk. For instance, programs for Chapter 3 are stored in a directory named CH03.

To examine these programs, put the example program disk in drive B and change to that drive with the B: command. At the B> prompt, change directories by entering CD \CH03. The command CD means change directory. If you now enter DIR, the names of all files in directory CH03 will be displayed. For example, the file containing Program EX0302 is named EX0302.PAS.

If you want to examine another directory, say the one containing the example programs from Chapter 4, enter the commands CD \CH04 and then DIR.

Turbo Pascal, Version 3. You can access any example program on the disk by specifying its path name, a combination of the drive name, directory name and file name. To access Program EX0302 in Chapter 3, using Version 3 of Turbo Pascal, type the command \ to log on a new drive, and enter the drive letter B.

When the prompt appears again, type the command A to access a new directory and enter the directory name \CH03. Finally, type the command W to specify a new work file and enter the file name EX0302.PAS. As always in Turbo Pascal, specifying the PAS extension is optional.

406

Turbo Pascal, Versions 4 and 5. We recommend that you start Turbo Pascal from the directory containing the programs and files you wish to use. For example, if you wish to access program EX0302.PAS in directory \CH03 on the disk in drive B, use the appropriate MS-DOS commands to make that your current directory. Assuming that the Turbo Pascal system is on disk A, enter the command A:TURBO to start. You can then select the Load command from the File command menu, and enter the file name EX0302.PAS to load the desired program.

If you must start Turbo Pascal from a different directory, your first step should be to change the current directory. Select the File command menu and execute the Change Directory command. Enter the partial path name B:\CH03. Then select the Load command from the File command menu, and load the desired program file.

Instead of using the Load command, a useful shortcut is to just press the F3 key while in the editor. You will see the general program file name (*.PAS) appear in a selection window. Press the Enter key and the contents of directory CH03 are displayed. Use the arrow keys to move the highlight block over the name of the desired program file and press the Enter key again and the program is displayed on the screen ready for editing.

Instructions for Reading Test Files

The practice programs in this book often use test files and sometimes units. These files are stored on the program disk, in the same directories as the example programs. For instance, the test files for practice programs in Chapter 7 are stored in the directory named CH07.

If you start Turbo Pascal from the directory containing these files, as we recommend, then that is your current directory. If not, you should make it your current directory using the appropriate Turbo Pascal commands, as explained in the preceding sections. For example, if the directory containing the test file DEPTH1.DAT is B:\CH07 and it is your current directory, you can use the statement

```
Assign (FV, 'DEPTH1.DAT');
```

in your program to access this file. This method allows you to specify a test file by a simple file name, instead of the complete path name.

INDEX